DATE D"

Essays on Interest Rates

NATIONAL BUREAU OF ECONOMIC RESEARCH

Number 93, General Series

Essays on Interest Rates

VOLUME II

Edited by

JACK M. GUTTENTAG

New York 1971

NATIONAL BUREAU OF ECONOMIC RESEARCH

Distributed by Columbia University Press   New York & London

HG
1623
US
E8
V.2
1971

National Bureau of Economic Research

Relation of the Directors to the Work and Publications of the National Bureau of Economic Research

1. The object of the National Bureau of Economic Research is to ascertain and to present to the public important economic facts and their interpretation in a scientific and impartial manner. The Board of Directors is charged with the responsibility of ensuring that the work of the National Bureau is carried on in strict conformity with this object.

2. The President of the National Bureau shall submit to the Board of Directors, or to its Executive Committee, for their formal adoption all specific proposals for research to be instituted.

3. No research report shall be published until the President shall have submitted to each member of the Board the manuscript proposed for publication, and such information as will, in his opinion and in the opinion of the author, serve to determine the suitability of the report for publication in accordance with the principles of the National Bureau. Each manuscript shall contain a summary drawing attention to the nature and treatment of the problem studied, the character of the data and their utilization in the report, and the main conclusions reached.

4. For each manuscript so submitted, a special committee of the Board shall be appointed by majority agreement of the President and Vice Presidents (or by the Executive Committee in case of inability to decide on the part of the President and Vice Presidents), consisting of three directors selected as nearly as may be one from each general division of the Board. The names of the special manuscript committee shall be stated to each Director when the manuscript is submitted to him. It shall be the duty of each member of the special manuscript committee to read the manuscript. If each member of the manuscript committee signifies his approval within thirty days of the transmittal of the manuscript, the report may be published. If at the end of that period any member of the manuscript committee withholds his approval, the President shall then notify each member of the Board, requesting approval or disapproval of publication, and thirty days additional shall be granted for this purpose. The manuscript shall then not be published unless at least a majority of the entire Board who shall have voted on the proposal within the time fixed for the receipt of votes shall have approved.

5. No manuscript may be published, though approved by each member of the special manuscript committee, until forty-five days have elapsed from the transmittal of the report in manuscript form. The interval is allowed for the receipt of any memorandum of dissent or reservation, together with a brief statement of his reasons, that any member may wish to express; and such memorandum of dissent or reservation shall be published with the manuscript if he so desires. Publication does not, however, imply that each member of the Board has read the manuscript, or that either members of the Board in general or the special committee have passed on its validity in every detail.

6. Publications of the National Bureau issued for informational purposes concerning the work of the Bureau and its staff, or issued to inform the public of activities of Bureau staff, and volumes issued as a result of various conferences involving the National Bureau shall contain a specific disclaimer noting that such publication has not passed through the normal review procedures required in this resolution. The Executive Committee of the Board is charged with review of all such publications from time to time to ensure that they do not take on the character of formal research reports of the National Bureau, requiring formal Board approval.

7. Unless otherwise determined by the Board or exempted by the terms of paragraph 6, a copy of this resolution shall be printed in each National Bureau publication.

(Resolution adopted October 25, 1926, and revised February 6, 1933, February 24, 1941, and April 20, 1968)

Advisory Committee on the Interest Rate Study

Contents

Tables

Charts

Figures

Acknowledgments

The essays in this volume have benefited from the support of the Life Insurance Association of America, as well as computer time contributed by IBM and the University of Pennsylvania. Support for this project was also supplied by general funds of the National Bureau.

The editors are most appreciative of the assistance of H. Irving Forman in preparing the charts, and of Virginia Meltzer in editing the papers and handling the production arrangements.

They also wish to thank the members of the National Bureau Board Reading Committee: R.A. Gordon, Robert V. Roosa, and Eugene P. Foley.

Introduction and Summary

The essays in this volume, which further extend the National Bureau's work on interest rates,[1] fall broadly into three groups. These are concerned with patterns of interest rate fluctuation on a wide variety of instruments (Cagan and Diller), selected determinants of yield (or "quality") on risk instruments (Frankena, Fredrikson, and Cohan), and determinants of maturity structure on riskless securities (Kessel, Sargent, and Diller).

Much of the Bureau's work on interest rates has focused on changes in rate relationships. We have sought evidence of stability versus change in financial markets and institutions, and insights regarding interactions between real and financial processes. This focus on patterns of change characterizes much of our work on the mortgage market, for example, including earlier studies by Klaman as well as my own paper in Volume I of these essays.[2] The essays by Cagan and Diller in this volume are in this tradition. Cagan's essay (which was first published in 1966) examines changes in the cyclical behavior of interest rates relative to fluctuations in general business over a long period (some of his series extend to 1878). Ignoring atypical periods, including World War I and most of the 1930's and 1940's, he finds that in recent years "financial

[1] Publications to date include *The Behavior of Interest Rates: A Progress Report* by Joseph Conard, 1966; *The Cyclical Behavior of the Term Structure of Interest Rates* by Reuben A. Kessel, 1965; *Changes in the Cyclical Behavior of Interest Rates* by Phillip Cagan, 1966; *Yields on Corporate Debt Directly Placed* by Avery Cohan, 1967; *Essays on Interest Rates*, Vol. 1, edited by Jack M. Guttentag and Phillip Cagan, 1969; and *New Series on Home Mortgage Yields Since 1951* by Jack M. Guttentag and Morris Beck, 1970.

[2] Saul B. Klaman, *The Postwar Residential Mortgage Market*, Princeton, Princeton University Press for NBER, 1961; Jack M. Guttentag, "The Behavior of Residential Mortgage Yields Since 1951," in *Essays on Interest Rates*, Vol. I.

markets react more in unison with each other and closer to changes in business conditions than formerly." The change is particularly pronounced in the case of rates on long-term securities, which used to lag both short-term rates and general business at cyclical turning points, but do so no longer. In addition, "the amplitude of cycles in most interest rates has responded more and more sharply to fluctuations in business activity of a given severity." Cagan presents evidence (not included in this volume) indicating that the change in both cyclical timing and amplitude of interest rates can be explained in part by changes in the cyclical pattern of growth in the money supply, which in turn presumably "reflects greater emphasis by the Federal Reserve on counteracting cycles in output and prices. So long as this policy continues, the generally greater fluctuation of interest rates since World War II compared with earlier periods will, other things being the same, be a permanent feature of the money market." Experience during the years since Cagan first penned those words strikingly confirms the accuracy of his prediction.

While the focus of Cagan's analysis is changes over time in cyclical patterns, he might with perhaps equal justification have emphasized what has not changed. The recent conformity of interest rates to business cycles, for example, as indicated by the extent to which cycles in one can be matched against cycles in the other, is not new. "Call money and commercial paper rates had nearly perfect conformity to the ten reference cycles from 1885 to 1919." Diller's essay on seasonal fluctuations in interest rates provides even more dramatic evidence of stability in change. The significant seasonal pattern in rates that emerged in the early 1950's appears very similar to the pattern Macaulay found for call money rates early in the century. Diller suggests that in view of all the changes in financial practices that have occurred perhaps this is a coincidence; but perhaps it is not.

Diller's analysis indicates that a seasonal rate pattern emerged in the early 1950's, the seasonal amplitude rising during 1951–58 and declining thereafter. By 1965, the seasonal had fallen to very modest proportions, comparable to those of the period before 1951. At peak amplitude the seasonal pattern that emerged was most pronounced for short-term securities, next for high grade bonds, and weakest for low grade bonds. Diller shows that the largest part of the variation in seasonal amplitude of Treasury bills can be explained by changes in the seasonal amplitude of the money supply and of total Treasury bills outstanding. Thus, the rise in the bill rate seasonal through 1958 is largely explained by an increase in the seasonal of outstanding bills in the face of only a small change in the money supply seasonal, while the subsequent decline in the rate seasonal during 1958–65 can be attributed largely to a rise in the money supply seasonal.

The substantial influence of the Treasury on the seasonal is not inconsistent with the proposition that the forces underlying the basic configuration of the seasonal—a lull close to midyear and a high in December—are much the same as in the period before 1913. The configuration of the seasonal reflects demand forces, and Treasury operations may simply be one mechanism through which these forces now operate. This is a nice problem for future research.

The rise and decline in the rate seasonal corresponds in a rough way with "tight money" and "easy money" policies of the Federal Reserve. It is somewhat surprising, in the light of recent discussions of the pervasiveness of the Federal Reserve's "defensive" open market operations, that tight money can leave such a substantial margin of seasonal demands unaccommodated. If the Federal Reserve focused exclusively on the condition of the money market as its short run objective we would expect a complete suppression of the rate seasonal regardless of whether policy was one of tightness or ease. While much remains to be learned regarding the interrelationship between the system's general ("dynamic") policy stance and its short run ("defensive") role in offsetting transient disturbances in the market, Diller's findings are consistent with the view that the Federal Reserve employs bank reserve targets in the short run.

A large part of the Bureau's work on interest rates, including the essays here by Frankena, Fredrikson, and Cohan, has been concerned with problems of yield structure. The general problem can be illustrated with an equation of the following form covering a number of individual instruments of a given type (such as residential mortgages or high grade corporate bonds) at a point in time:

$$\text{Yield} = C + a_1 Q_1 + \ldots + a_n Q_n + b_1 N_1 + \ldots + b_n N_n,$$

where the Q's are variables that bear on the probability of repayment—in the aggregate they describe risk or ex ante "quality"; the N's represent nonrisk factors that may affect yield such as options to repay prior to maturity or coupon rate; and the coefficients indicate the degree of sensitivity of the yield to variability in each yield determinant—in the case of quality variables they reflect the lenders' expectations regarding future economic conditions that may affect the ability of borrowers to repay.

Frankena's essay shows that the coupon rate (and to a lesser extent call deferments) is an important nonquality determinant of yield on corporate bonds. The evidence for this rests in good part on the new time series that he constructed covering yields on seasoned public utility bonds, each series pertaining to a specified coupon rate. He finds, for example, that over the period January 1957 to October 1967 the yield to maturity on 5 per cent bonds averaged 32 per cent more than that on $2\frac{3}{4}$ to $2\frac{7}{8}$ per cent bonds. Frankena views this relationship as reflecting the market's essential rationality. Higher coupon bonds are less attractive to investors because, in the event that market yields decline, they have less potential for price appreciation and they are more likely to be called for redemption, forcing lenders to reinvest at lower yields. He questions the reliability, for some purposes at least, of commonly used series on corporate bonds and yield spreads involving such bonds. Adjustment of series for changing coupon rates is not an easy matter, however, since the effect on yield of a given coupon rate differential (or a given call deferment) can vary markedly over time as a result of changes in yield levels, in expectations regarding future yield levels, and in other factors. The yield differential between 5 and $2\frac{3}{4}$ to $2\frac{7}{8}$ per cent bonds referred to above ranged from .03 per cent during periods of high yields to 1.00 per cent during periods of low yields.

The center-stage variable in Fredrikson's essay is the location of the property in securing a conventional residential mortgage loan. Just as Frankena's essay indicates that yield series on corporate bonds should hold coupon rate constant, Fredrikson's essay indicates that yield series on conventional mortgage loans may have to be adjusted for changes in geographical mix. While previous Bureau studies (by Wickens, Morton, and Grebler, Blank, and Winnick) found evidence of significant regional yield differentials in data covering outstanding loans, in-depth analysis of area differentials awaited the development of data on loan commitments of the type used here by Fredrikson. These data, compiled by the Federal Home Loan Bank Board beginning in 1962, indicate that the pattern of area differentials is extremely complex. First, differentials between metropolitan areas within regions are substantial, in some cases exceeding average regional differentials by large margins. In all probability intraregional differentials would be greater still if adequate data were available for nonmetropolitan areas. Second, area yield differentials are usually larger, sometimes substantially larger when measured in terms of effective rate (contract rate adjusted for fees and charges) than when measured in terms of contract rate alone. Third, area yield differentials vary markedly among various loan subsets when loans are classified by type of lender and purpose of loan.

Whether location of property is a quality or nonquality yield determinant is a moot point. Interregional yield differentials are smallest in loan subsets characterized by relatively low risk—notably loans on new homes and loans by life insurance companies—suggesting that area designation may be in part a proxy for risk. Fredrikson shows, however, that when yields are adjusted for the effect of those risk variables for which information is available (loan-value ratio, maturity and property value) area yield differentials are as likely to increase as to decrease. Loan subsets with small yield differentials furthermore are also those within which interregional flows are relatively large, suggesting that in part area differentials may reflect restrictive local market structures and factors segmenting local markets from outside competition. Fredrikson discusses several of these factors including high information costs, legal constraints on out-of-state lending, and the high costs of acquiring and servicing loans at a distance.

In his previous National Bureau study, Avery Cohan isolated specific quality and nonquality factors influencing the yield on directly placed corporate bonds.[3] He then held these factors constant over time to provide yield series on a homogeneous instrument. Referring to the equation above, Cohan in effect solved for Y in each period using the same Q's and N's throughout. The adjusted series, while homogeneous with respect to objective characteristics, reflect changes in the coefficients of the Q's and N's. Cohan's essay in this volume extends this procedure in the following way. Assume for the moment that the N's in the equation for direct placements can be ignored so that only risk variables affect yield, and that yields on a government bond are riskless. In this case, the yield differential between governments and directly placed corporate bonds of the same maturity measures $a_1Q_1 + \ldots + a_mQ_m$ on the direct placement, i.e., it measures the combined effect of all characteristics of the direct placement that affect risk, plus the lenders' evaluation of each characteristic. If it can be assumed further that the markets for direct placements and government bonds are competitive, and that investors in direct placements are not risk averse, Cohan shows that the ratio $[(1 + G)/(1 + r)]^m$, where G and r are the yields and m the maturity, can be interpreted as the market's judgment of the probability that the realized yield on the direct placement will be equal to the promised yield. Thus interpreted, the ratio is the ideal measure of over-all ex ante quality of direct placements.

The assumptions required to interpret the ratio as a probability, how-

---

[3] *Op. cit.*

ever, are not completely met. In Cohan's view the main nonquality factors that affect the ratio are differences in call protection and risk aversion—the requirement of lenders that yield on a risk security exceed the "expected yield" (expected yield on a risk security is the yield on a riskless security plus a premium just large enough to meet expected losses on the risk security). Cohan argues that, in general, risk aversion is not an important factor in the market (although this may not have been true before World War II), but that it can become important when the volume of lower grade securities becomes abnormally large in a short period, as was the case during 1955–58. Hence, Cohan adjusts his probability series both for changes in call protection and for changes in the volume of lower grade corporate offerings. The adjusted quality series tended to decline very modestly over the 1951–61 period.

Three papers in this volume deal with the term structure of interest rates on riskless (government) securities. The question "Why do securities that are exactly the same in every respect but maturity carry different yields?" has long exercised a fascination for economists.

The centerpiece of all three essays is what has come to be called the expectations theory of term structure. This theory in brief states that term structure at a point in time is determined by the market's expectations prevailing at that time of future short-term rates. The theory implies that at a given point in time the expected yield is independent of term to maturity. The expected yield over, say, the next three years is the same regardless of whether one holds a twenty-year security purchased now and sold after three years, a three-year security purchased now, a two-year security purchased now and a one-year security purchased after one year, or any other combination. While this theory has a long and honored list of advocates, including Fisher, Keynes, Hicks, Lutz, and Macaulay, the recent upsurge in interest traces mainly to Meiselman, who first devised a means of testing the theory that did not require that expectations have some predictive content for the theory to pass. "He showed that expectations, whether or not they are correct, nevertheless affect the term structure of rates. His results constitute striking evidence that the expectations hypothesis has empirical validity."[4]

Kessel accepts the expectations theory, and presents some (admittedly limited) evidence that at least at the short end of the yield curve the expectations implied by the theory do indeed have predictive content. He argues, however, that some empirical characteristics of yield curves

---

[4] Kessel, *op. cit.*, p. 344.

are difficult if not impossible to reconcile with a "pure" expectations model, that is, a model which attempts to explain term structure entirely in terms of expectations. The tendency for curves to be upward sloping more often than not, for example, and the occurrence at times of "humped" curves where yields rise with maturity and then decline are facts difficult to reconcile with a pure expectations theory.

To explain these and other aspects of yield curve behavior Kessel joins the expectations theory to the liquidity preference theory, which states that the market on balance prefers short- to long-term securities because of the smaller risk of capital loss on the former. He shows that a combination of the two theories is consistent with a wider range of evidence including most importantly evidence on changes in the shape of yield curves over the business cycle.[5]

When Kessel's paper was first circulated in the early 1960's my impression was that it was an excellent piece of research (which I still believe today) and that little remained to be done on the subject, which was a mistake in judgment. Benefit of hindsight suggests several reasons for the recent upsurge of interest in the problem of term structure. First, there has been a widespread and well-justified conviction that the validity of the expectations hypothesis required additional testing. Malkiel and Kane note that "scientists are skeptical men who know that error of observation and questionable experimental technique are facts of life. If a law verified by one observer is truly valid, it should operate for anyone. Successful and independent repetition of a critical experiment increases our confidence in its supposed results."[6] Sargent's paper is in this spirit. Returning to an approach that has been abandoned after Meiselman's study, he considers the question of whether the expectations of future rates inherent in the yield curve (according to the theory) do in fact have any forecasting value. A negative finding in an inquiry of this type does not dispose of the theory, but a positive finding, to use Sargent's words, "provides a particularly convincing type of evidence confirming the expectations hypothesis."

Sargent turns to a situation where the market can be presumed to have some knowledge of future rates. Seasonal patterns in interest

---

[5] Some additional evidence is given by Phillip Cagan, "A Study of Liquidity Premiums on Federal and Municipal Government Securities," in *Essays on Interest Rates,* Vol. I.

[6] Burton G. Malkiel and Edward J. Kane, "Expectations and Interest Rates: A Cross-Sectional Test of the Error-Learning Hypothesis," *Journal of Political Economy,* July/August 1969, p. 453.

rates should be anticipated in some degree by speculators and, if there is any validity in the expectations hypothesis, the seasonal in longer maturities should lead the seasonal in shorter maturities. (This test of the expectations theory was first proposed and used by Macaulay who examined the timing seasonal in call rates and time rates during the period 1890–1913.) The reemergence of the seasonal in Treasury bills during the 1950's (see Diller's first paper) provides the materials for this test. Using spectral analysis, Sargent finds, as Macaulay did, that the timing patterns are generally consistent with those predicted by the expectations theory.[7]

A second reason for the recent step-up in work on term structure is the relevance of the problem for monetary policy. In 1961, the Federal Reserve adopted the policy of attempting to raise yields on short-term securities while lowering yields or at least limiting increases on long-term securities. This policy, which came to be known as "operation twist," was an attempt to deal simultaneously with the problem of encouraging expansion in the domestic economy, which required low long-term rates, and the problem of restraining capital outflows abroad, which required high short-term rates. A crucial issue was whether a swap transaction by the Federal Reserve, involving simultaneous purchase of long-term securities and sale of short-term securities, could have an appreciable nontransitory effect on the yield curve.

The various theories of how the yield curve is determined appeared to give opposing answers to this question, thus providing *prima facie* justification for extensive efforts to determine which theory was "correct." For a time it was believed by many that the expectations theory implied that the Federal Reserve could not affect the shape of the yield curve while the so-called "segmentation theory" of term structure carried the opposite implication. (This theory states that borrowers and lenders are constrained by institutional factors to prefer specific maturities, so that the rate at each maturity is determined by the supply and demand at that maturity, which is independent of the supply and demand at any other maturity.) It is now evident, however, that this view was overly simplistic. Wood showed that the expectations theory did not imply the inability of the Federal Reserve to twist the yield curve if expectations of future rates embodied in the yield curve are affected by changes in the current rate levels.[8] By the

---

[7] Kessel also ran a test of this sort (see Chapter 6, p. 370).

[8] John H. Wood, "The Expectations Hypothesis, The Yield Curve, and Monetary Policy," *Quarterly Journal of Economics,* August 1964.

same token, the institutional preference of most investors for a given maturity does not necessarily imply that the Federal Reserve has wide latitude to change the yield curve, since enough investors might be enticed from their preferred maturity by small yield premiums on adjoining maturities to make the yield curve relatively insensitive to Federal Reserve swaps.[9] Much the same point can be made regarding the liquidity preference theory; as Kessel notes, this theory implies that a Federal Reserve swap will affect the yield curve but does not imply that the effect is likely to be quantitatively significant.[10] Thus, no amount of testing of the validity of the individual theories is likely to shed much light on the question of the degree of Federal Reserve influence on the shape of the yield curve; the question remains wide open.

The third and perhaps most important reason for continuing interest in the term structure problem is that it is a fascinating intellectual puzzle—or set of puzzles—that ramifies in many directions. Meiselman's original test of the expectations theory was facilitated by prior work in related fields of economics on the formation and revision of expectations. Future work on the expectations theory will surely reverse the flow and contribute to general knowledge in this important area. Diller's paper on "The Expectations Component of the Term Structure" is a significant step in this direction. Diller focuses on the nature of the forecasts that (according to the expectations theory) are embodied in the term structure. He poses the question, What techniques of forecasting future rates does the market use? He distinguishes an autoregressive or extrapolative component of a forecast, which is dependent on the current and prior values of the variables being forecast and on prior values of forecasts of that variable; and an autonomous component, which is dependent on the current values of other variables. He shows that various theories of forecasting, including the error-learning theory used by Meiselman and the "return to normality" theory that has had numerous advocates, can be viewed as specific variants of a general autoregressive model. "There are, in principal, as many models as there are combinations of weights from an autoregression, although the word 'model' is ordinarily used only when the particular combination of weights is consistent with a plausible behavioral hypothesis." This approach allows Diller to examine various "behavioral theories" of forecasting

[9] See Franco Modigliani and Richard Sutch, "Innovations in Interest Rate Policy," *American Economic Review,* May 1966, p. 184.

[10] See Kessel, *op. cit.,* p. 57.

within a single analytical framework, which has the great advantage that alternative theories can be clarified as well as tested.

Other ramifications of the term structure problem are just beginning to be explored. It should be possible to expand the liquidity preference theory, for example, to take account of default risk. This suggests the possibility of a general theory of yield structure in which maturity would be only one (and perhaps not the most important) dimension. Beyond this is the intriguing possibility of merging term structure theory with portfolio selection theory, which has developed rapidly in recent years. (What are the implications for term structure theory of postulating that investors have a diversification incentive for holding several maturities?) If ultimately the several term structure theories are absorbed by broader theories of financial processes we would have to view it as a triumphant demise.

JACK M. GUTTENTAG

Essays on Interest Rates

1

Changes in the Cyclical Behavior of
Interest Rates   *Phillip Cagan*

INTRODUCTION

Along with growth in size and complexity of the financial system over the past century, changes have occurred in the cyclical behavior of interest rates. This paper describes changes in the behavior of a broad group of rates. The long-term interest rates covered are yields on U.S. bonds and high and low grade corporate bonds for the period since World War I, and yields on high grade corporate, municipal, and railroad bonds for a longer period. The short-term series are rates on Treasury certificates and bills, acceptances, bank loans, and discounts, which cover the period since World War I, and rates on call money and prime commercial paper for a much longer period. These are the main monthly and quarterly data available for an extended period. Annual series are less reliable for examining cyclical behavior, and were not used.

NOTE: This paper was originally printed as NBER Occasional Paper 100, 1966, which was reprinted from the August 1966 issue of *Review of Economics and Statistics*.

I wish to acknowledge the suggestions of the late William H. Brown, Jr., the late Joseph W. Conard, Milton Friedman, Jack M. Guttentag, F. Thomas Juster, Allan H. Meltzer, Geoffrey H. Moore, the late Sophie Sakowitz, and members of the advisory committee for the interest rate project. Thanks are due also to Lester V. Chandler, Joseph H. Willits, and Theodore O. Yntema of the National Bureau Board of Director's reading committee.

I am grateful to Josephine Trubek, who assisted in the statistical computations; to James F. McRee, Jr., for editorial help; and to H. Irving Forman for the charts.

An obvious problem in working with interest rate data is that institutional developments have altered the character of the markets and the financial instruments from which the series are derived, making it difficult to distinguish between changes affecting particular rates and changes of broader significance. No series with long coverage exists for which the financial instrument has not changed substantially in quality or function. For example, no instrument of earlier periods quite compares to the role of Treasury bills in the post-World War II money market. Series are available for a long period on call money and commercial paper, but these instruments do not have the same characteristics they used to.[1] Some series for long-term bonds are fairly comparable over a long period, but they are compiled from a changing list of securities over time (to maintain roughly the same average term to maturity) and are subject to the inaccuracies of a changing composition.[2] It should be kept in mind, therefore, that the changing character and possible inaccuracies of these series affect their cyclical timing and amplitude of fluctuation to some extent, particularly over long periods of time. Yet there is no need for undue pessimism; interest rates are largely free of many difficulties inherent in measuring expenditure and income streams or stocks of wealth. The rates need no adjustment for changes in the value of money or in the unit of measurement, and reporting errors appear comparatively small. For business cycle research, interest rates rank among our more reliable and useful time series and provide a body of evidence on cycles that can hardly be ignored.

The dates of cyclical turning points in the series, seasonally adjusted,[3]

[1] Richard T. Selden, *Trends and Cycles in the Commercial Paper Market,* Occasional Paper 85, New York, NBER, 1963.

[2] See the discussion in F. R. Macaulay, *The Movements of Interest Rates, Bond Yields and Stock Prices in the United States since 1856,* New York, NBER, 1938, Chap. III.

[3] The adjustments for the post-World War II period were done by the late William H. Brown, Jr., as part of the NBER interest rate project.

The dates of some turning points in Appendix Table 1-A for the post-World War II period differ from those presented for the same series by Thomas E. Holland ("Cyclical Movements of Interest Rates, 1948–61," *Journal of Business,* Oct. 1964, pp. 364–369). His seasonal adjustment may differ slightly (the Shiskin-Eisenpress computer program, also used here, allows certain options), but the main differences probably reflect Holland's decision to remove "irregular movements" (by a moving average) before dating the turning points. A moving average can shift the date of turning points and was not used in deriving Appendix Table 1-A.

are listed in Appendix Table 1-A and shown graphically in Chart 1-1. The series referred to as Treasury bills is based on Treasury notes and certificates to 1929 and three-month bills thereafter. The dates of the 1919 trough shown for U.S. bonds and corporate bonds Aaa appear correct but might be too late by a few months, since the series begin in that year and an earlier turn cannot be ruled out for certain. For comparison with peaks and troughs in general business activity, the chart shades periods of business contraction.[4] Cyclical movements in the rates that do not correspond to reference cycles, and reference phases skipped by the rates, are noted on the chart. Many such discrepancies occurred, but on the whole all the rates usually conform well to business activity, as has long been recognized. Many of the discrepancies pertain to the 1930–49 period. Financial disorders produced extra cycles in rates in the early 1930's; then, with depressed business activity and rapid growth in the money stock during the second half of the 1930's, interest rates declined steeply and did not respond in the usual way to the business cycle. During and after World War II the Federal Reserve pegged U.S. bond and bill yields, indirectly affecting all interest rates, which explains skipped cycles during the 1940's. Aside from these episodes, the only other discrepancy from 1919 to 1961 was the 1924–26 reference expansion skipped by most bond yields, reflecting prolonged declines from the high levels attained in 1920. Between 1878 and 1913 there were few discrepancies. Beginning the analysis with 1878 avoids atypical behavior in the 1870's, when most series had extra cycles during the 1873–79 business depression; in that respect the decade resembles the 1930's.

Since 1953 the rates covered by Chart 1-1 have conformed to every reference phase, which some commentators take as indication of a fundamental change in the money market. Important changes have occurred, to be sure, but the conformity does not appear exceptional. Call money and commercial paper rates had nearly perfect conformity to the ten reference cycles from 1885 to 1919. The chief discrepancies are associated with special disturbances in the money market. After all, price and output series, most of which conform closely to general business activity, also undergo unusual movements when subject to special developments such as strikes and wartime controls. Yet there is a clear difference: Interest rates appear to reflect special influences

---

[4] For the dates, see Geoffrey H. Moore (ed.), *Business Cycle Indicators,* Princeton for NBER, 1961, Vol. I, p. 670. The latest reference trough is February 1961.

CHART 1-1. Chronology of Specific Cycles in Interest Rates Compared With Reference Cycles

1878–1920

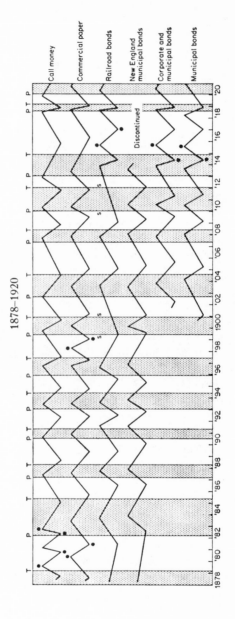

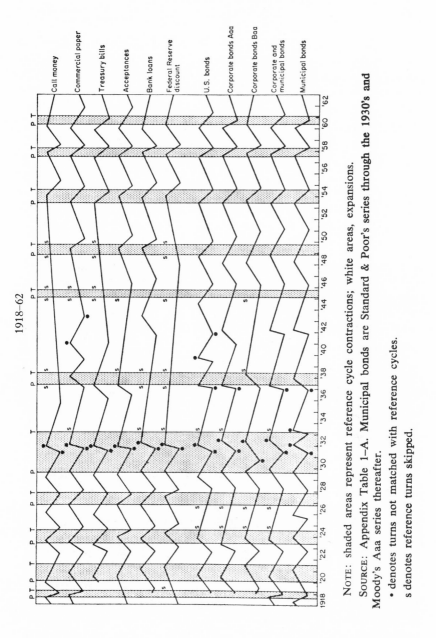

1918–62

NOTE: shaded areas represent reference cycle contractions; white areas, expansions.

SOURCE: Appendix Table 1–A. Municipal bonds are Standard & Poor's series through the 1930's and Moody's Aaa series thereafter.

• denotes turns not matched with reference cycles.

s denotes reference turns skipped.

ber and a trough in July. During the 1957–59 period, it constituted more often than price and output series do, and each time for a longer period. The highly volatile behavior of financial markets is well known and needs no documentation here.

For present purposes it appears more fruitful to confine the analysis to the typical behavior of interest rates. Most of the analysis therefore excludes the 1930's and 1940's, World War I, and the post-Civil War period to 1878. That leaves the period since 1953 to compare with the 1920's, and these two decades to compare with the four and a half decades between 1878 and 1914.

Chart 1-2 shows the cyclical behavior of interest rates on a reference cycle basis. The patterns suggest two tendencies to be examined in detail: a shift toward earlier turning points in relation to reference turns and a greater amplitude of fluctuation in the 1950's than earlier.

TIMING

The generally lagged timing of interest rates at reference turns, evident in Chart 1-1, is summarized by Table 1-1, which gives the median lag of each rate in selected periods. The table covers the 1920's and 1950's (excluding World War I and the period from 1930 to the post-World War II unpegging of long-term rates in 1951), and the period 1879 to 1913 divided at 1900. (The main reason for dividing at 1900 is that two long-term rates are first covered just before that year.) Extra turns in the rates not matching reference cycles are ignored. Also, reference turns which a series skips are excluded. A comparison of median lags for rates that cover a different number or set of turns can be misleading. The medians appear satisfactory, however, for bringing out the changes in timing of each rate over time.

The length of the average lag of long rates has clearly declined at peaks and troughs. Some decline occurred between each period, and by the 1950's the lag had disappeared and in many series gave way to short leads. For short rates the table suggests closer timing to reference peaks in the 1920's than before World War I, but no definite change thereafter, and at troughs apparently no change over all. The lag in timing of long behind short rates, apparent before World War I, has narrowed consistently over the years, so that by the 1950's it was no longer evident.

Timing among the series shows the active open-market rates generally turning first and the rates of thin or negotiated markets turning last. One indication of this pattern is that Treasury bills and U.S. bonds

CHART 1–2. Cyclical Patterns of Interest Rates, Nine Reference Cycle Stages (deviations from cycle averages, basis points)

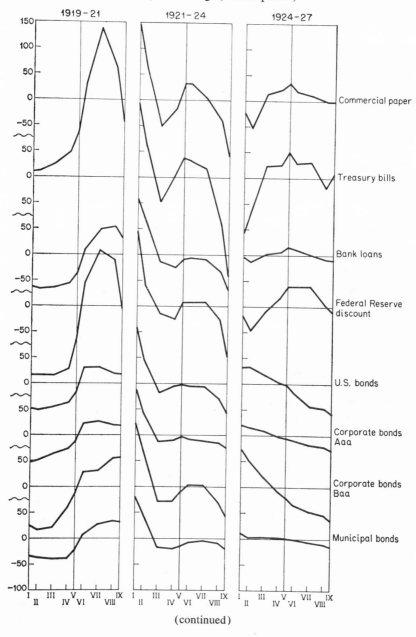

(continued)

CHART 1–2 (concluded)

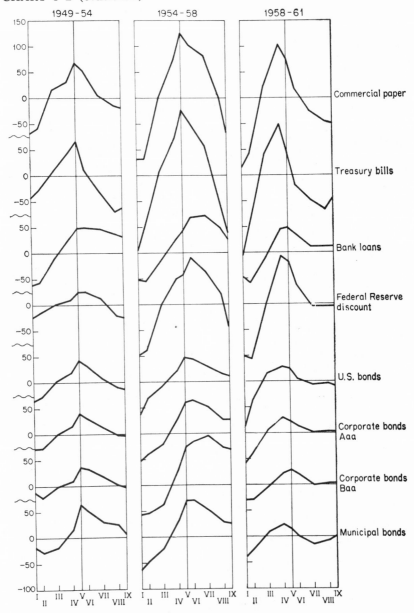

SOURCE: Same as for Appendix Table 1–B. Municipal bonds are Standard & Poor's series for 1919–27 and Moody's Aaa series for 1949–61.

TABLE 1-1. *Median Lead (−) or Lag (+) of Interest Rates at Reference Cycle Turns, Selected Periods (months)*

	Troughs				Peaks			
	Six: 1879–97	Four: 1900–12	Four: 1919–27	Three: 1954–61	Six: 1882–99	Four: 1902–13	Four: 1920–29	Three: 1953–60
Short rates								
Call money	+2	−1	0	+7(1)	+3	+2	−3	+5
Commercial paper	+4	+4	+2	+4	+7	+6	+1	0
Treasury bills	—	—	+1(1)	−2	—	—	−2	−1
Acceptances	—	—	0(1)	+4	—	—	+2	+1
Bank loans	—	—	+3	+4(1)	—	—	+3	+5
Federal Reserve discount	—	—	+12	+5(1)	—	—	+10	+3
Bond yields								
U.S.	—	—	+4(1)	0	—	—	+5(1)	−1
Corporate Aaa	—	—	+5(1)	+1	—	—	+1(1)	−1
Corporate Baa	—	—	+3(1)	+2(1)	—	—	+5(1)	+2
Corporate and municipal	—	+13	+4(1)	+1	—	+9	+4(1)	−1
Municipal	—	+5	+3(1)	0	—	+8	+7(1)	−1
Railroad	+14	+7(2)	+1(1)	—	+8(1)	+11(1)	+4(1)	—
New England municipal	+20	+5	—	—	+10	+8	—	—

NOTE: Numbers in parentheses give the number of reference turns missed or not covered by the series in the period. Calculation of the median sometimes gives numbers with the fraction ½, such as a lag of 2½ or 3½ months; the ½'s have been dropped in the table.

SOURCE: Appendix Table 1-A.

usually have the earliest turns, and bank loans and low grade corporate bonds the latest. The policy-determined Federal Reserve discount rate also turns late. The call money rate used to be consistent with this sequence by generally turning ahead of commercial paper rates, but it became a laggard after World War II. These differences in timing are all well known and, given certain institutional developments, they are to be expected, except perhaps for the discount rate, which could in theory lead all the other rates under certain policies but in fact lagged under the policies pursued.

The varied timing of the short rates points up the difficulty of comparing their behavior before and after World War I. The two short rates for the pre-1914 period differ in function from those available for the later period, and in addition have changed in character over the years. Call money rates are undoubtedly not the sensitive indicator of money market conditions today that they once were. There is some question also about comparing commercial paper rates today with earlier times.[5] A comparison of short rates before and after World War I by means of these data, therefore, may be misleading. For the moment let us disregard this difficulty and summarize the behavior of the open-market short rates (that is, excluding bank loan and discount rates). If we suppress deviant behavior by taking the median lag of rates at each turn, Table 1-2 gives an arithmetic average of these medians for the earlier and later period, excluding the 1930's and 1940's. The lag of short rates at peaks declined significantly, but at troughs it increased (though not significantly). The latter increase appears exceptional, and if we exclude the 1921 depression, from which short rates recovered unusually late, the average lag at troughs for the later period drops to 2.1 months. That figure suggests, more plausibly, that the lag diminished slightly from the earlier period. The table also gives averages for all of the long rates. Their lag declined significantly at both peaks and troughs.

The large ranges of error for troughs in the right-hand column of Table 1-2 reflect large variations in timing between different reference troughs, but not exceptional variability between the rates at each turn. Turning points in the rates actually cluster relatively closer to each other at troughs than at peaks, as demonstrated by a measure of clustering in Table 1-3. The measure compares as a ratio the variation in the average lag of the rates among reference turns with the variation in lags among the rates. The ratio is significantly greater than unity in seven

[5] See Selden, *op. cit.*

TABLE 1-2. *Arithmetic Average of Median Lags in Short and Long Rates at Selected Reference Peaks and Troughs Before and After World War I (months)*

	Period		Later Minus Earlier period
	1879–1913	1919–61	
Short rates			
Troughs	+2.7	+3.7	+1.0 (±5.8)
Peaks	+4.7	+0.1	−4.6 (±2.9)
Bond yields			
Troughs	+11.1	+2.7	−8.4 (±7.7)
Peaks	+9.2	+1.1	−8.1 (±2.7)

NOTE: Parentheses contain range of error at .05 level of significance based on the *t* distribution, which assumes the normal distribution of leads and lags about reference peaks and troughs. Coverage: Turns covered are the same as in Table 1-1 except for the inclusion here of the 1937 peak, and the exclusion of one trough and one peak for bond yields from the beginning of the earlier period (for 1879 and 1882). The excluded turns had very long lags which would make the medians for the earlier period even larger than they are. Rates covered are the same as Table 1-1 except for exclusion here of bank loan and discount rates and of railroad bond yields after World War I. Exact coverage is indicated in Appendix Table 1-A.

SOURCE: Appendix Table 1-A.

of the eight comparisons, indicating substantial clustering. In all cases turns in the rates cluster together more at troughs than at peaks and more in the later than in the earlier period. The two ratios for short rates in the later period would probably be even larger if we excluded the insensitive bank loan rate, not represented in the earlier period.

The one ratio less than unity (absence of clustering) among the eight comparisons—for short rates at peaks in the earlier period— indicates that turning points in call money and commercial paper rates then conformed less closely to each other than to reference turns. The call money market was highly sensitive to business conditions before the 1930's, producing close conformity of the rate to general business activity. The rate was related loosely to commercial paper rates and hardly at all to the long-term rates. In its affinity to business conditions, the call money rate before 1930 resembles the Treasury bill rate in the 1950's. If we link these two series in 1920 (when rates on short-term Treasury securities start) to form a single series representing the most sensitive short-term interest rate over the full period, a definite downtrend in the length of lag has occurred only at peaks (see Table

TABLE 1-3. *Degree of Clustering of Cyclical Turns in Short and Long Rates, as Indicated by Variation in Lags at Selected Reference Peaks and Troughs*

	F Ratios (and levels of significance): Variation Between Reference Cycle Turns as Multiple of Variation Around Each Turn	
	1879–1913	1919–61
Short rates		
Troughs	4.6 (.025)	10.7 (.005)
Peaks	0.27 (.05)	3.8 (.005)
Bond yields		
Troughs	9.4 (.005)	40.0 (.005)
Peaks	4.9 (.005)	7.0 (.005)

NOTE: Coverage is same as Table 1-2 except for the inclusion here of the bank loan rate. Method of computation: If L_{it} is the lag (in months) of ith interest rate at reference turn t, the F ratio is

$$\frac{\overset{T}{\underset{t}{\Sigma}} (\bar{L}_t - \bar{L})^2}{T - 1} \div \frac{\overset{T}{\underset{t}{\Sigma}} \overset{I}{\underset{i}{\Sigma}} (\bar{L}_{it} - \bar{L}_t)^2}{I - T}$$

where $\bar{L}_t$ is the average lag of all rates at turn t and $\bar{L}$ is average lag of all rates at all turns.

1-1). If instead we take commercial paper rates as the best single indicator of short rates over a long time span, that series also suggests that the lag at peaks shortened after World War I but remained substantially the same thereafter, and that the lag at troughs remained largely unchanged over all periods.

Secular trends in the rates can affect timing. A rising trend in rates might be expected to produce longer lags at reference peaks and shorter lags at troughs; and conversely for a falling trend. Table 1-4 tests this expectation for four periods which have fairly definite trends. Bond yields fell secularly from the mid-1870's to around 1900, rose subsequently to World War I, fell again during the 1920's and until after World War II, and then rose thereafter until 1960. The trend since then has been unclear. In Table 1-4 turning points near a change in direction of trend have been omitted. The table covers bond yields only; short-term rates have not displayed well-defined trends.

The relative timing at peaks and troughs is largely the reverse of the expectation. A comparison of periods, summarized in the right-hand

TABLE 1-4. Median Lead (−) or Lag (+) of Bond Yields at Reference Cycle Turns for Periods of Falling and Rising Trend (months)

Bond Yields	FALLING TREND (Expectation: short lags at peaks, long lags at troughs)[a]				RISING TREND (Expectation: long lags at peaks, short lags at troughs)[a]				COMPARISON OF PERIODS Number with Shorter Lag during:			
	1879–97		1919–29		1902–13		1953–60		Falling Trend		Rising Trend	
	Peaks	Troughs	Peaks	Troughs	Peaks	Troughs	Peaks	Troughs	Peaks[a]	Troughs	Peaks	Troughs[a]
U.S.	—	—	+5	+4	—	—	−1	0	—	—	1	1
Corporate Aaa	—	—	+1	+5	—	—	−1	+1	—	—	1	1
Corporate Baa	—	—	+5	+3	—	—	+2	+2	—	—	1	1
Corporate and municipal	—	—	+4	+4	+9	+13	−1	+1	1	1	1	1
Municipal	—	—	+7	+3	+8	+8	−1	0	1	1	1	1
Railroad	+8	+14	+4	+1	+11	+7	—	—	2	1	—	1
New England municipal	+11	+20	—	—	+8	+9	—	—	—	—	1	1
Total									4	3	6	7

NOTE: The fraction ½ has been dropped from the medians, as in Table 1-1.
SOURCE: Appendix Table 1-A.
[a]Expected direction of shift in turning points resulting from trend.

columns, also suggests that trends play no part in the timing changes. While eleven of the twenty comparisons fit the expectation of shorter lags at peaks during falling trends and at troughs during rising trends, this is no more than would occur by chance. By contrast, nineteen of the twenty show a shorter lag in a later period. (Railroad bonds at peaks are the exception.)

The evidence therefore supports the following generalizations: (1) Interest rate fluctuations maintain a sequence, with the active open-market rates usually turning first and the rates of negotiated and inactive markets usually turning last. (2) All long rates used to but no longer lag far behind short rates. (3) The turns within the group of shorts, and within the group of long rates, occur fairly closely together, so that the variability of the lags within each group is much less than the variability of the average lag for the group between cycle turns. (4) Turning points have clustered closer to each other and closer to reference cycle turns over the years, though a shortening of the lag is more evident for longs than shorts, and for shorts more at peaks than at troughs. In recent cycles the vanguard of interest rates turns with, or sometimes even before, business activity as a whole.

So far as turning points are concerned, therefore, financial markets react more in unison with each other and closer to changes in business conditions than formerly. The next section brings out a similar development in amplitude of fluctuation.

AMPLITUDE

The amplitude of expansions and contractions provides, along with timing, a revealing measure of cyclical behavior. The cyclical amplitudes of the interest rate series, listed in Appendix Table 1-A, are summarized in Table 1-5 for the same four periods covered by Table 1-1, except that here the first period begins with 1885 for the shorts also, to omit some early cycles which do not match reference cycles. Unmatched cycles lessen the comparability of data between periods. With the coverage here, the only cyclical movement not matching a reference phase is the contraction in commercial paper rates, 1898–99.

Panel A gives per-month changes in the series from peak-to-trough stages of reference contractions and trough-to-peak stages of expansions, taking the negative of the algebraic change over reference contractions. Hence the measure can be, and sometimes is, negative, reflecting inverted cyclical movements. Panel A amplitudes are generally larger for later periods. As in the timing comparisons, the main exception is the call money rate.

Much of the increase in amplitude appears to reflect the closer conformity in timing. Lags shift the specific cycles out of phase with reference cycles and reduce this measure of amplitude. A measure independent of timing, and therefore a better indicator solely of the amplitude of cyclical fluctuations, is the change for specific cycle phases shown in Panel B. To be comparable with A, Panel B excludes extra specific cycles not matching reference cycles. Also, the B averages incorporate a zero entry when the series skips a reference phase, so as to record the absence of any recognizable cyclical movement.

The specific cycle amplitudes are necessarily always positive and (barring an unusually large number of skipped phases, not a problem here) equal to or greater than the reference cycle amplitudes. Aside from that difference, Panel B does not show a clear difference in amplitude between periods. Among the short rates excepting call money, there is a slight increase from the 1920's to the 1950's; but call money and commercial paper had considerably larger fluctuations before 1900 than in the three periods since, which can be attributed only in part to the pre-1914 cycles with financial panics. Among bond yields, the evidence, though mixed for the later periods, shows a substantial increase from before to after World War I.

A comparison of amplitudes between periods can be influenced, however, by the severity of the reference cycles that each period happens to cover. The 1920's include the 1920–21 contraction, for example, which in severity far exceeds any contraction during the 1950's. To allow for differences in severity, Table 1-6 gives ratios of amplitudes for specific cycle phases in which the amplitudes of the corresponding reference cycle phases are approximately similar as judged by indexes of general business activity.

Well over half the ratios are above unity, indicating that fluctuations in rates, holding the severity of the corresponding reference phases approximately equal, were generally greater in the 1950's. The strongest exceptions are for call money and low grade corporate bonds, and for the short rates in column 4. Also, by these pairings, most rates had a comparatively greater amplitude in the two cycles after 1957 than in previous cycles. The largest increases are shown by commercial paper and Treasury bills and by high grade corporate and municipal bonds (again, the more active rates). The U.S. bond yield is an exception to the behavior of the active rates, perhaps because it already had a comparatively large amplitude in the 1920's (Table 1-5).

TABLE 1-5. *Average Amplitude of Cyclical Phases for Selected Periods (basis points per month)*

	1885–1900: 5 Expansions and 5 Contractions (1)	1900–13: 4 Expansions and 3 Contractions (2)	1919–29: 4 Expansions and 3 Contractions (3)	1953–61: 2 Expansions and 3 Contractions (4)
A. REFERENCE CYCLE PHASES				
Short rates				
Call money	15.5	13.9	15.5	5.7
Commercial paper	3.6	6.8	3.8	11.4
Treasury bills	–	–	6.0[a]	12.4
Acceptances	–	–	5.6	11.3
Bank loans	–	–	0.9	2.7
Federal Reserve discount	–	–	3.0	7.3
Bond yields				
U.S.	–	–	0.8	3.8
Corporate Aaa	–	–	0.2	3.2
Corporate Baa	–	–	0.4	2.4
Corporate and municipal	–	–0.3	0.1	3.5
Municipal	–	–0.1	–0.4	3.4
Railroad	–0.5	0.0	–	–
New England municipal	–1.0	–	–	–
B. MATCHED SPECIFIC CYCLE PHASES				
Short rates				
Call money	31.1	27.9	19.5	7.3[b]
Commercial paper	22.8	11.6	10.7	11.6
Treasury bills	–	–	11.3[c]	14.5
Acceptances	–	–	11.9[c]	12.4
Bank loans	–	–	4.7	5.4[b]
Federal Reserve discount	–	–	8.3	9.4[b]
Bond yields				
U.S.	–	–	3.3	3.8
Corporate Aaa	–	–	2.5	3.9
Corporate Baa	–	–	4.4	3.7[b]
Corporate and municipal	–	1.6	2.2	4.2
Municipal	–	1.5	2.6	4.2
Railroad	1.4	0.9	2.2	–
New England municipal	1.8	1.8	–	–

NOTE: Method of computation: Algebraic change per month from trough-to-peak stages of expansions, plus negative of algebraic change per month from peak-to-trough stages of contractions, divided by number of phases. Inverted conformity to reference

(continued)

Tables 1-5 and 1-6 together give strong evidence of a large though not uniform rise in amplitudes. Bond yields had a doubling or more of amplitude from the 1880's to the 1950's. Increases occurred from before to after World War I as well as later. For short rates, on the other hand, an increase shows up clearly only from the 1920's to the 1950's.

Secular trends in interest rates do not account for these results. Amplitude is measured on a per-month basis, so a steady trend adds the same amount to each expansion and contraction. With contractions treated negatively, the trend cancels out over each cycle. Since the figures cover two expansions and three contractions in the 1950's, however, the upward trend in that decade on net makes our estimates of amplitude slightly too low. Such trend effects in the other periods are insignificant.

The similar behavior of municipal bond yields to the other series appears to deny an explanation based on the high marginal tax rate on corporate and personal income in the 1950's. It has been argued that the tax rate cuts the effectiveness of any given yield to both lenders and corporate borrowers. If corporations take advantage of the tax deductibility of interest costs and individual lenders attempt to avoid the tax on interest income (by seeking capital gains or nontaxable investment income), the level and amplitude of fluctuations in market yields might increase. There is evidence that investors now favor tax exempt municipal bonds and capital gain investments, probably for these reasons. But this cannot explain the increased amplitude of corporate (and taxable U.S.) bond yields from the 1920's to the 1950's, because municipal bond yields display roughly the same increase (Table 1-5).

NOTE TO TABLE 1-5 (concluded)

cycles, therefore, gives a negative amplitude over such cycles. The amplitude for specific cycles, of course, is always positive. If doubled, the figures give the average amplitude of a full cycle in the period.

In Panel B the amplitude is taken as zero when no specific cycle phase matches the reference phase. The only extra specific cycle in the periods covered was the contraction in commercial paper rates, 1898–99; it was suppressed by computing the change per month from one matching specific turn to the next. Skipped and extra cycles for each series are marked on Chart 1-1. Exact coverage is indicated in source.

SOURCE: Appendix Tables 1-A and 1-B.

[a]Five phases only; first two phases not covered.

[b]Four phases only; last contraction not covered.

[c]Six phases only; first expansion not covered.

TABLE 1-6. *Comparison Between Specific Cycle Phase Amplitudes for Which Severity of Corresponding Reference Cycle Phases Is Similar, Ratio of 1950's to 1920's*

	Expansions				Contractions		
	1954–57	1958–60	1958–60	1953–54	1953–54	1957–58	1960–61
	1921–23	1924–26	1927–29	1923–24	1926–27	1923–24	1926–27
	(1)	(2)	(3)	(4)	(5)	(6)	(7)
Short rates							
Call money	.5	.6	.4	.1	.3	.5	—
Commercial paper	.7	3.0	1.5	.6	2.8	1.6	3.1
Treasury bills	.6	1.3	1.3	.9	3.0	1.5	3.8
Acceptances	1.1	2.6	1.4	.2	.8	3.6	1.1
Bank loans	1.4	4.5	1.0	.2	.9	1.7	—
Federal Reserve discount	1.9	3.0	.8	.2	.4	1.0	—
Bond yields							
U.S.	1.6	—	1.0		1.4[a]	1.5	.9
Corporate Aaa	2.0	—	2.8		2.6[a]	3.4	3.2
Corporate Baa	.9	—	.7		.8[a]	1.1	—
Corporate and municipal	2.2	—	2.5		3.2[a]	4.7	2.5
Municipal	2.5	1.1	1.6	2.7	4.2	3.7	5.6

NOTE: Dates are for corresponding reference cycle phases.

SOURCE: Appendix Table 1-A. Paired cycles of similar severity in business activity are based on Geoffrey H. Moore, *Business Cycle Indicators*, Vol. II, pp. 104–5 and unpublished revisions.

[a] Amplitude per month of the unbroken specific cycle contraction from 1923 to 1928 is used for both the 1923–24 and the 1926–27 contractions.

Although the evidence is based on a group of series which are not entirely comparable from period to period, the consensus of the measures is that, along with timing, the amplitude of cycles in most interest rates has responded more and more sharply to fluctuations in business activity of a given severity. The main qualifications involve the timing and amplitude of the two short rates before World War I, which cannot be appropriately compared with the series for the later period. Effects of financial disturbances in the 1930's and of interest rate pegs in the 1940's and early 1950's are wholly excluded from the comparisons. Amplitudes have been larger in the 1950's than the 1940's, of course, because the Federal Reserve pegged interest rates during and after World War II. Amplitudes would not be larger in the 1950's than the 1920's, however, unless monetary policy or other relevant factors differed between the two periods.

SUMMARY OF FINDINGS

Judged by the behavior of interest rates, financial markets have displayed increasing sensitivity to cyclical influences over the years. If the pre-World War I period, the 1920's, and the 1950's are compared, a broad group of rates has responded to moderate cycles in business activity sooner and with greater amplitude. The most dramatic change has occurred in bond yields: before World War I they typically lagged at business cycle peaks and troughs by many months, but they now display practically no lag, and over the same period the amplitude of their cycles appears to have doubled. Although trends in the cyclical behavior of short-term rates are less clear, some decline of the average lag also occurred, though mainly at peaks. These rates once turned long before bond yields, but have not done so in recent cycles.

APPENDIX TABLE 1-A. *Timing and Amplitude of Specific Cycles in Interest Rates, 1878–1961*

Dates of Turning Points		Lead (−) or Lag (+) From Matched Reference Turn (months)		Amplitude of Specific Cycle Phases (change between peak and trough stages in basis points per month)	
Trough	Peak	Trough	Peak	Expansions	Succeeding Contractions
1. CALL MONEY RATE					
Sep. 1878	Aug. 1879	−6	−	38.0[a]	−27.8[a]
Oct. 1880	Feb. 1881	−	−13	133.5[a]	−32.5[a]
May 1882	Sep. 1882	−	−	56.9[a]	−17.7[a]
Jan. 1885	June 1887	−4	+3	20.4	−38.0
Aug. 1888	Aug. 1890	+4	+1	24.4	−28.0
May 1892	June 1893	+12	+5	37.3	−34.3
Nov. 1894	Oct. 1896	+5	+10	23.0	−50.4
July 1897	Oct. 1899	+1	+4	17.7	−37.1
Sep. 1900	Sep. 1902	−3	0	24.4	−31.0
July 1904	Oct. 1907	−1	+5	24.3	−72.8
Nov. 1908	May 1910	+5	+4	13.6	−9.5
Nov. 1911	Dec. 1912	−2	−1	19.5	−8.8[a]
Nov. 1915	Aug. 1918	+11[a]	0[a]	13.3[a]	−28.3[a]
Dec. 1918	Nov. 1919	−3	−2	35.6	−16.0
June 1922	Aug. 1923	+11	+3	9.9	−24.2
Sep. 1924	Feb. 1926	+2	−8	16.1	−5.9
Sep. 1927	Mar. 1929	−2	−5	28.5	−28.0[a]
May 1931	Dec. 1931	−	−	15.6[a]	−5.3[a]
Sep. 1935	Feb. 1954	+30[a]	+7	1.4[a]	−1.6
June 1955	Dec. 1957	+10	+5	5.0	−12.5
Aug. 1958	Apr. 1960	+4	−1	10.0	−
2. COMMERCIAL PAPER RATE					
Aug. 1878	May 1880	−7	−	7.0[a]	−8.0[a]
June 1881	June 1883	−	+15	6.6[a]	−9.7[a]
Sep. 1885	July 1887	+4	+4	12.6	−8.6
May 1889	Dec. 1890	+13	+5	9.0	−14.2
June 1892	July 1893	+13	+6	53.3	−52.2
Oct. 1894	Oct. 1896	+4	+10	16.1	−52.0
Apr. 1897	Apr. 1898	−2	−	12.5[b]	−19.0[b]
Jan. 1899	Mar. 1900	−	+9	11.8[b]	−6.3
Mar. 1901	Aug. 1903	+3	+11	5.9	−12.0
Jan. 1905	Dec. 1907	+5	+7	8.2	−16.0
July 1909	June 1910	+13	+5	17.0	−9.6

(continued)

APPENDIX TABLE 1-A (continued)

Dates of Turning Points		Lead (−) or Lag (+) From Matched Reference Turn (months)		Amplitude of Specific Cycle Phases (change between peak and trough stages in basis points per month)	
Trough	Peak	Trough	Peak	Expansions	Succeeding Contractions
Nov. 1911	June 1913	−2	+5	12.8	−8.7[a]
May 1916	Oct. 1918	+17[a]	+2[a]	10.1[a]	−21.6[a]
Feb. 1919	Oct. 1920	−1	+9	14.4	−18.5
Aug. 1922	May 1923	+13	0	11.7	−12.2
Oct. 1924	Oct. 1926	+3	0	5.3	−2.5
Jan. 1928	Oct. 1929	+2	+2	10.4	−18.4[a]
Sep. 1931	Jan. 1932	−	−	53.0[a]	−5.3[a]
Feb. 1937	Feb. 1938	+47[a]	+9	2.2[a]	−1.8[a]
Aug. 1939	Jan. 1941	+14[a]	−	0.7[a]	−0.4[a]
May 1943	June 1949	−	+7[a]	1.1[a]	−1.9[a]
Apr. 1950	July 1953	+6[a]	0	3.6[a]	−7.1
Dec. 1954	Aug. 1957	+4	+1	8.3	−19.2
July 1958	Jan. 1960	+3	−4	15.7	−7.7
Nov. 1961		+9	−	−	−
		3. TREASURY BILL RATE			
	June 1920	−	+5	−	−11.8
Aug. 1922	Mar. 1923	+13	−2	12.5	−14.1
Aug. 1924	Nov. 1925	+1	−11	12.4	−4.1
Sep. 1927	May 1929	−2	−3	13.0	−21.0[a]
July 1931	Dec. 1931	−	−	43.0[a]	−5.2[a]
Feb. 1936	Apr. 1937	+35[a]	−1	3.9[a]	−1.4[a]
Jan. 1941	June 1953	+31[a]	−1	1.5[a]	−12.5
June 1954	June 1957	−2	−1	7.7	−20.5
June 1958	Dec. 1959	+2	−5	16.3	−15.7
Dec. 1960		−2	−	−	−
		4. BANKERS' ACCEPTANCE RATE			
	June 1920	−	+5	−	−12.6
Aug. 1922	Dec. 1923	+13	+7	7.1	−27.4
July 1924	Oct. 1926	0	0	6.2	−6.8
Sep. 1927	June 1929	−2	−2	11.3	−17.1[a]
Sep. 1931	Nov. 1931	−	−	107.5[a]	−9.3[a]
June 1936	Apr. 1937	+39[a]	−1	4.2[a]	−0.1[a]
Apr. 1946	June 1949	+6[a]	+7[a]	2.0[a]	−1.0[a]

(continued)

APPENDIX TABLE 1-A (continued)

Dates of Turning Points		Lead (−) or Lag (+) From Matched Reference Turn (months)		Amplitude of Specific Cycle Phases (change between peak and trough stages in basis points per month)	
Trough	Peak	Trough	Peak	Expansions	Succeeding Contractions
July 1950	Jan. 1954	+9[a]	+6	2.0[a]	−5.7
Dec. 1954	Aug. 1957	+4	+1	7.8	−24.7
June 1958	Jan. 1960	+2	−4	16.1	−7.5
Nov. 1961		+9	−	−	−
		5. BANK LOAN RATE			
May 1919	Feb. 1921	+2[a]	+13[a]	5.9	−8.9
Sep. 1922	Oct. 1923	+14[a]	+5[a]	2.8	−5.9
Nov. 1924	Oct. 1926	+4[a]	0[a]	1.4	−1.6
Feb. 1928	Oct. 1929	+3[a]	+2[a]	6.3	−6.8[a]
Sep. 1931[c]	Mar. 1932[c]	−	−	−	−
Sep. 1941	June 1943	+39[a]	−20[a]	4.2[a]	−2.1[a]
Sep. 1946	June 1949	+11[a]	+7[a]	2.2[a]	−1.2[a]
Mar. 1950	Dec. 1953	+5[a]	+5[a]	2.5[a]	−1.4
Mar. 1955	Dec. 1957	+7[a]	+5[a]	3.8	−9.9
June 1958	Dec. 1959	+2[a]	−5[a]	6.3	−
		6. FEDERAL RESERVE DISCOUNT RATE			
Nov. 1917	Apr. 1921	+35[a]	+15[a]	7.9[a]	−14.3
Jan. 1923	Apr. 1924	+18[a]	+11[a]	3.3	−16.7
Jan. 1925	July 1927	+6[a]	+9[a]	3.3	−8.3
Jan. 1928	Oct. 1929	+2[a]	+2[a]	11.9	−19.6[a]
Sep. 1931	Jan. 1932	−	−	50.0[a]	−1.3[a]
Dec. 1947	Jan. 1954	+26[a]	+6[a]	1.4[a]	−3.6
Mar. 1955	Oct. 1957	+7[a]	+3[a]	6.4	−17.5
Aug. 1958	May 1960	+4[a]	0[a]	9.9	−
		7. HIGH-GRADE RAILROAD BOND YIELD (Macaulay)			
June 1881	Sep. 1883	+27[a]	+18[a]	0.7[a]	−1.7[a]
July 1886	Oct. 1887	+14	+7	1.2	−1.7
June 1889	Aug. 1891	+14	+13	1.5	−1.9
July 1892	Aug. 1893	+14	+7	2.3	−2.4
Aug. 1895	Aug. 1896	+14	+8	1.7	−1.6
June 1899	Sep. 1903	+24	+12	1.0	−0.7
Feb. 1905	Nov. 1907	+6	+6	1.6	−2.4

(continued)

APPENDIX TABLE 1-A (continued)

Dates of Turning Points		Lead (−) or Lag (+) From Matched Reference Turn (months)		Amplitude of Specific Cycle Phases (change between peak and trough stages in basis points per month)	
Trough	Peak	Trough	Peak	Expansions	Succeeding Contractions
Feb. 1909	Dec. 1913	+8	+11	0.8	−1.5[a]
June 1914	Sep. 1915	−6[a]	−	1.6[a]	−1.8[a]
Jan. 1917	Sep. 1918	−	+1[a]	4.2[a]	−18.4[a]
Nov. 1918	May 1920	−4[a]	+4[a]	5.4	−4.0
Sep. 1922	Oct. 1923	+14[a]	−5[a]	2.6	−1.1
Dec. 1927	Sep. 1929	+1[a]	+1[a]	2.4	−2.5[a]
May 1931	June 1932				
8. NEW ENGLAND MUNICIPAL BOND YIELD (Macaulay)					
Aug. 1882	Nov. 1883	+41[a]	+20[a]	0.5[a]	−0.9[a]
Aug. 1886	Nov. 1887	+15	+8	2.6	−1.5
Feb. 1890	Aug. 1891	+22	+13	1.8	−0.6
Nov. 1892	Nov. 1893	+18	+10	2.6	−2.4
May 1895	Nov. 1896	+11	+11	1.5	−2.0
Aug. 1899	Feb. 1900	+26	+8	2.2	−1.0
Feb. 1901	Aug. 1903	+2	+11	1.3	−0.4
May 1905	Feb. 1908	+9	+9	2.5	−2.8
May 1909	Aug. 1910	+11	+7	1.8	−0.4
Feb. 1912	Aug. 1913	+1	+7	3.2	−
9. HIGH GRADE MUNICIPAL BOND YIELD (S. & P.)					
Feb. 1901	Mar. 1904	+2	+18	1.1	−1.0
Apr. 1905	Jan. 1908	+8	+8	2.2	−2.7
Mar. 1909	July 1910	+9	+6	1.8	−0.5
June 1911	Sep. 1913	−7	+8	1.3	−2.6[a]
June 1914	Aug. 1915	−	−	0.9[a]	−2.1[a]
Jan. 1917	Apr. 1918	+25[a]	−4[a]	4.8[a]	−2.3[a]
Dec. 1918	Feb. 1921	−3	+13	3.1	−5.8
Sep. 1922	Dec. 1923	+14	+7	1.5	−1.4
Aug. 1925	Nov. 1925	+13[a]	−11[a]	3.2	−0.9
Feb. 1928	Sep. 1929	+3	+1	2.2	−2.6[a]
May 1931	Feb. 1932	−	−	12.2[a]	−6.1[a]
Jan. 1933	May 1933	−2[a]	−	20.3[a]	−5.1[a]
Dec. 1936	Dec. 1937	−	+7[a]	2.8[a]	−2.6[a]
Oct. 1941	Mar. 1942	+40[a]	−35[a]	10.1[a]	−2.0[a]

(continued)

APPENDIX TABLE 1-A (continued)

Dates of Turning Points		Lead (−) or Lag (+) From Matched Reference Turn (months)		Amplitude of Specific Cycle Phases (change between peak and trough stages in basis points per month)	
Trough	Peak	Trough	Peak	Expansions	Succeeding Contractions
Feb. 1946	Feb. 1948	+4[a]	−9[a]	4.2[a]	−2.1[a]
Feb. 1951	July 1953	+16[a]	0[a]	3.9[a]	−4.9[a]
Aug. 1954	Aug. 1957	0[a]	+1[a]	4.3[a]	−4.3[a]
June 1958	Jan. 1960	+2[a]	−4[a]	3.6[a]	−

10. YIELDS ON HIGHEST GRADE MUNICIPAL BONDS (Moody's Aaa)

	May 1937	−	0	−	−
Nov. 1941	Mar. 1942	+41[a]	−35[a]	7.6[a]	−1.7[a]
Mar. 1946	Apr. 1948	+5[a]	−7[a]	3.9[a]	−1.6[a]
Feb. 1951	June 1953	+16[a]	−1	3.8[a]	−3.8
Aug. 1954	Aug. 1957	0	+1	3.7	−5.2
May 1958	Jan. 1960	+1	−4	3.5	−5.0
Sep. 1960		−5	−	−	−

11. HIGH GRADE CORPORATE AND MUNICIPAL BOND YIELD (S. & P.)

Apr. 1902	Nov. 1903	+16	+14	1.6	−1.3
Sep. 1905	Nov. 1907	+13	+6	2.8	−2.2
Aug. 1909	Aug. 1910	+14	+7	1.4	−0.8
May 1911	Dec. 1913	−8	+11	0.9	−2.0[a]
June 1914	Sep. 1915	−	−	0.9[a]	−1.3[a]
Jan. 1917	Sep. 1918	+25[a]	+1[a]	4.2[a]	−8.3[a]
Dec. 1918	July 1920	−3	+6	5.3	−5.0
Sep. 1922	Oct. 1923	+14	+5	1.7	−1.2
Mar. 1928	Dec. 1929	+4	+4	1.9	−2.6[a]
June 1931	July 1932	−	−	7.8[a]	−4.2[a]
Dec. 1936	Apr. 1937	−	−1	4.2[a]	−1.3[a]
Nov. 1941	Mar. 1942	+41[a]	−35[a]	4.7[a]	−1.1[a]
Apr. 1946	Nov. 1948	+6[a]	0[a]	1.6[a]	−1.1[a]
Feb. 1951	June 1953	+16[a]	−1	2.9[a]	−3.8
Aug. 1954	Sep. 1957	0	+2	3.7	−5.6
June 1958	Jan. 1960	+2	−4	4.7	−3.0
Mar. 1961		+1	−	−	−

12. LONG-TERM U.S. BOND YIELD

Jan. 1919	Aug. 1920	−2	+7	5.9	−7.4
Aug. 1922	Oct. 1923	+13	+5	2.0	−2.8

(continued)

APPENDIX TABLE 1-A (concluded)

Dates of Turning Points		Lead (−) or Lag (+) From Matched Reference Turn (months)		Amplitude of Specific Cycle Phases (change between peak and trough stages in basis points per month)	
Trough	Peak	Trough	Peak	Expansions	Succeeding Contractions
Mar. 1928	Mar. 1929	+4	−5	5.0	−2.4[a]
June 1931	Jan. 1932	−	−	17.1[a]	−3.4[a]
Feb. 1937	Apr. 1937	−	−1	20.0[a]	−3.0[a]
June 1939	Sep. 1939	+12[a]	−	19.8[a]	−3.5[a]
Nov. 1941	July 1944	−	−7[a]	0.3[a]	−1.8[a]
Apr. 1946	Sep. 1948	+6[a]	−2[a]	1.2[a]	−1.4[a]
Jan. 1950	June 1953	+3[a]	−1	2.0[a]	−4.0
Aug. 1954	July 1957	0	0	3.2	−4.2
Apr. 1958	Jan. 1960	0	−4	4.9	−2.6
May 1961		+3	−	−	−
13. YIELD ON HIGHEST GRADE CORPORATE BONDS (Moody's Aaa)					
Feb. 1919	June 1920	−1	+5	6.0	−5.1
Sep. 1922	Apr. 1923	+14	−1	3.3	−1.2
Apr. 1928	Sep. 1929	+5	+1	1.8	−1.9[a]
July 1931	June 1932	−	−	8.8[a]	−4.1[a]
Jan. 1937	Apr. 1937	−	−1	9.2[a]	−1.4[a]
Dec. 1940	Mar. 1942	+30[a]	−35[a]	0.7[a]	−0.8[a]
Apr. 1946	Feb. 1948	+6[a]	−9[a]	1.7[a]	−0.9[a]
June 1950	June 1953	+8[a]	−1	2.0[a]	−3.1
Sep. 1954	Aug. 1957	+1	+1	3.3	−4.1
June 1958	Jan. 1960	+2	−4	5.0	−3.8
Sep. 1960		−5	−	−	−
14. YIELD ON LOW GRADE CORPORATE BONDS (Moody's Baa)					
June 1919	June 1921	+3	+17	6.1	−11.5
Sep. 1922	Oct. 1923	+14	+5	4.8	−3.9
Mar. 1928	Sep. 1929	+4	+1	4.2	−2.6[a]
Sep. 1930	May 1932	−	−	27.2[a]	−11.9[a]
Jan. 1937	Apr. 1938	+46[a]	+11	11.7[a]	−3.5[a]
Mar. 1946	Mar. 1948	+5	−8[a]	2.4[a]	−1.0[a]
Dec. 1950	Sep. 1953	+14[a]	+2	1.8[a]	−3.0
Oct. 1954	Nov. 1957	+2	+4	4.1	−4.4
July 1958	May 1960	+3	0	3.1	−

SOURCE: See Appendix Table 1-B.

[a]Indicates items not used in Tables 1-1 to 1-6. The municipal bond series used in those tables is No. 9 to 1929 and No. 10 thereafter.

[b]Treated in this study as one expansion with amplitude of 4.1.

[c]Not available because of break in series.

APPENDIX TABLE 1-B. *Amplitude of Movements in Interest Rates Over Reference Cycles, Change Between Peak and Trough Stages (basis points per month)*

Part 1. 1879–1919

Reference Cycles (trough to trough)	Call Money	Comm. Paper	Railroad Bonds	New England Muni. Bonds	Municipal Bonds S&P	High Grade Corp. & Muni. Bonds S&P
Mar. 1879–May 1885						
E[a]	1.2	1.7	-1.7	-1.6		
C[a]	-6.7	-3.5	-0.5	-0.4		
May 1885–Apr. 1888						
E	18.3	6.4	-1.3	-0.4		
C	-22.1	-0.4	0.0	3.3		
Apr. 1888–May 1891						
E	20.0	0.4	-0.3	-1.0		
C	-37.3	2.8	2.0	1.8		
May 1891–June 1894						
E	-1.0	-2.3	-0.7	0.1		
C	-16.2	-12.3	-0.6	0.9		
June 1894–June 1897						
E	11.5	11.6	-0.8	-1.6		
C	-10.0	-9.2	-0.9	-0.3		
June 1897–Dec. 1900						
E	12.6	0.7	-1.0	-1.3		
C	-8.4	0.4	0.5	0.2		
Dec. 1900–Aug. 1904						
E	24.5	5.1	0.6	0.6	0.5	-0.2
C	-29.5	-4.4	0.8	1.0	0.9	0.6

(continued)

APPENDIX TABLE 1-B (continued)

Reference Cycles (trough to trough)	Call Money	Comm. Paper	Railroad Bonds	New England Muni. Bonds	Municipal Bonds S&P	High Grade Corp. & Muni. Bonds S&P
Aug. 1904–June 1908						
E	5.2	6.5	0.7	1.2	1.1	0.6
C	-9.6	-15.0	0.5	1.1	1.3	1.3
June 1908–Jan. 1912						
E	8.6	3.8	-0.2	-0.4	-0.3	-1.1
C	-5.4	-3.0	0.5	0.6	0.5	0.3
Jan. 1912–Dec. 1914						
E	14.8	9.9	0.7		0.8	0.7
C[a]	-3.6	-6.2	1.2		0.2	0.6
Dec. 1914–Mar. 1919						
E[a]	6.3	4.5	1.4		0.8	1.5
C[a]	-9.9	-10.0	-2.4		0.0	-2.0

Part 2. 1919–61
Section a. Short-term Rates

Reference Cycles (trough to trough)	Call Money	Comm. Paper	Treas. Bills	Bankers' Accept.	Bank Loans	Fed. Res. Discount
Mar. 1919–July 1921						
E	36.0	7.8		10.6	2.9	7.3
C	-17.3	1.1		-0.1	4.0	3.2

(continued)

APPENDIX TABLE 1-B (continued)

Reference Cycles (trough to trough)	Call Money	Comm. Paper	Treas. Bills	Bankers' Accept.	Bank Loans	Fed. Res. Discount
July 1921–July 1924						
E	-4.0	-5.2	-4.8	-5.4	-5.3	-6.2
C	-20.1	-10.1	-16.4	-13.7	-4.2	-7.6
July 1924–Nov. 1927						
E	9.4	2.2	5.9	6.1	0.8	2.1
C	-6.8	-2.8	-3.4	-4.8	-2.0	-3.8
Nov. 1927–Mar. 1933						
E	22.8	10.0	9.3	9.0	5.8	9.9
C[a]	-15.5	-8.9	-10.7	-8.9	-2.5	-6.0
Mar. 1933–June 1938						
E[a]	-1.8	-2.5	-1.0	-1.6	-3.5	-3.0
C[a]	0.0	-0.9	-4.6	-0.6	-0.6	-3.8
June 1938–Oct. 1945						
E[a]	0.0	-0.2	0.4	0.0		0.0
C[a]	0.0	0.0	0.0	0.0		0.0
Oct. 1945–Oct. 1949						
E[a]	1.7	2.0	2.1	2.0	1.2	1.4
C[a]	0.0	-1.3	-0.6	-1.2	0.1	0.0
Oct. 1949–Aug. 1954						
E[a]	3.6	3.0	2.4	1.8	2.4	1.1
C	-1.9	-6.7	-9.9	-4.8	-1.2	-3.8
Aug. 1954–Apr. 1958						
E	4.3	6.9	7.8	7.2	2.8	4.4
C	-8.7	-21.0	-26.4	-24.0	-1.8	-11.2

(continued)

APPENDIX TABLE 1-B (continued)

Reference Cycles (trough to trough)	Call Money	Comm. Paper	Treas. Bills	Bankers' Accept.	Bank Loans	Fed. Res. Discount
Apr. 1958–Feb. 1961						
E	6.0	8.4	8.0	8.8	3.8	7.4
C	-7.8	-13.9	-9.8	-11.6	-4.1	-9.8

Part 2. 1919–61
Section b. Long-term Rates

Reference Cycles (trough to trough)	U.S. Bonds	Corporate Bonds, Moody's		High Grade Corp. & Muni. Bonds S&P	Municipal Bonds	
		Aaa	Baa		S&P	Moody's Aaa
Mar. 1919–July 1921						
E	3.1	3.9	6.4	3.7	1.2	
C	2.0	1.8	3.8	2.2	3.0	
July 1921–July 1924						
E	-5.0	-4.2	-6.1	-4.3	-4.3	
C	-3.8	-1.5	-3.3	-1.2	-0.4	
July 1924–Nov. 1927						
E	-1.3	-1.0	-3.5	-0.8	-0.4	
C	-4.2	-1.7	-3.4	-1.3	-1.2	
Nov. 1927–Mar. 1933						
E	2.7	1.4	3.3	1.8	1.9	
Cª	-0.9	-0.3	6.4	0.1	0.9	

(continued)

APPENDIX TABLE 1-B (concluded)

Reference Cycles (trough to trough)	U.S. Bonds	Corporate Bonds, Moody's		High Grade Corp. & Muni. Bonds S&P	Municipal Bonds	
		Aaa	Baa		S&P	Moody's Aaa
Mar. 1933–June 1938						
E[a]	-1.5	-2.6	-7.9	-3.1	-3.1	-1.5
C[a]	-2.5	-0.8	8.5	-1.4	-1.9	1.7
June 1938–Oct. 1945						
E[a]	-1.0	-0.7	-3.2	-0.9	-1.5	
C[a]	-0.7	-0.4	-2.8	0.1	0.2	
Oct. 1945–Oct. 1949						
E[a]	0.2	0.6	0.8	0.8	1.7	1.8
C[a]	-1.9	-1.9	-1.4	-2.1	-1.5	-1.8
Oct. 1949–Aug. 1954						
E[a]	1.8	1.5	1.1	1.6	1.5	1.9
C	-4.2	-3.3	-2.9	-4.0	-4.9	-4.5
Aug. 1954–Apr. 1958						
E	3.2	3.2	3.7	3.6	4.4	3.8
C	-4.2	-3.7	-0.4	-4.5	-4.0	-4.7
Apr. 1958–Feb. 1961						
E	3.7	3.3	2.3	2.9	1.7	2.2
C	-3.7	-2.4	-2.7	-2.7	-5.0	-1.6

NOTE: E denotes expansion; C, contraction.
[a] Indicates phases not used in Table 1-5.

SOURCES FOR TABLES 1-A and 1-B

Call Money Rate: Jan. 1948–Dec. 1961, *Survey of Current Business;* Feb. 1936–Dec. 1947, *Federal Reserve Bulletin;* Jan. 1878–Jan. 1936, Macaulay, *Movements of Interest Rates.*

Commercial Paper Rate: Feb. 1936–Dec. 1961, computed from weekly data in *Commercial and Financial Chronicle;* Jan. 1878–Jan. 1936, Macaulay, *Movements of Interest Rates.*

Treasury Bill Rate: *Federal Reserve Bulletin.* (Treasury notes and certificates to 1929, bills thereafter.)

Bankers' Acceptance Rate: Jan. 1942–Dec. 1961, *Federal Reserve Bulletin;* Aug. 1917–Dec. 1941, *Banking and Monetary Statistics.*

Bank Loan Rate: IQ 1939–IVQ 1961, *Federal Reserve Bulletin;* Jan. 1928–Dec. 1938, unpublished data supplied by Board of Governors of the Federal Reserve System; Jan. 1919–Dec. 1927, *Banking and Monetary Statistics.*

Federal Reserve Bank of New York Discount Rate: Jan. 1922–Dec. 1961, Board of Governors of the Federal Reserve System, *Annual Report,* various years, and *Federal Reserve Bulletin;* Nov. 1914–Dec. 1921, simple averages of weighted rates on commercial, agricultural, and livestock paper from FRB, *Discount Rates of the Federal Reserve Banks,* 1914–21.

High Grade Railroad Bond Yield: Jan. 1878–Dec. 1961, Macaulay, *Movements of Interest Rates.*

New England Municipal Bond Yield: IQ 1878–IVQ 1914, Macaulay, *Movements of Interest Rates.*

High Grade Municipal Bond Yield: Jan. 1900–Dec. 1961, Standard & Poor's Corporation, *Security Price Index Record,* various years.

Yield on Highest Grade Municipal Bonds (Aaa): Moody's Investors Service, *Municipal and Government Manual.*

High Grade Corporate and Municipal Bond Yield: Jan. 1900–Dec. 1961, simple average of municipal, railroad, public utility, and industrial bond yields from Standard & Poor's Corporation, *Security Price Index Record.*

Long-Term U.S. Bond Yield: *Federal Reserve Bulletin.*

Yield on Highest Grade Corporate Bonds (Aaa): Moody's Investors Service, *Industrial Manual.*

Yield on Low Grade Corporate Bonds (Baa): Moody's Investors Service, *Industrial Manual.*

(continued)

SOURCES FOR TABLES 1-A and 1-B (concluded)

Seasonal Adjustment of Series

Call Money Rate: Seasonally adjusted except 1884, 1893, and June 1931–Dec. 1961.

Commercial Paper Rate: Seasonally adjusted except 1927–1952.

Treasury Bill Rate: Seasonally adjusted except 1931–1947.

Bankers' Acceptance Rate: Seasonally adjusted 1955–1961 only.

Bank Loan Rate: Not adjusted.

Federal Reserve Discount Rate: Not adjusted.

High Grade Railroad Bond Yield: Not adjusted.

New England Municipal Bond Yield: Not adjusted.

High Grade Bond Yield (S&P): Seasonally adjusted except 1900–1921.

Yield on Highest Grade Municipal Bonds (Moody's Aaa): Seasonally adjusted.

High Grade Corporate and Municipal Bond Yield (S&P): Not adjusted.

Long-Term U.S. Bond Yield: Seasonally adjusted 1948–1961 only.

Yield on Highest Grade Corporate Bonds (Moody's Aaa): Seasonally adjusted 1948–1961 only.

Yield on Low Grade Corporate Bonds (Moody's Baa): Seasonally adjusted 1948–1961 only.

2

The Seasonal Variation
of Interest Rates   *Stanley Diller*

I. INTRODUCTION

Although variations in interest rates coinciding with the seasons of
the year were virtually nonexistent during the 1930's and World War
II, they reappeared in the late 1940's and grew in amplitude during
the 1950's. The amplitude reached a high point between 1957 and
1959 then diminished substantially in the early 1960's. These gyra-
tions have attracted wide attention among money market analysts.
The seasonal movement in short-term rates reached a peak in December and a trough in July. During the 1957–59 period, it constituted
20 per cent of the average level of the interest rates. For long-term
rates the movement was considerably less.

A study of the seasonal variation of interest rates contributes to our
understanding of the money market and the behavior of interest rates.
Interest rates depend upon the supply and demand for credit; therefore, the seasonal variation of credit conditions is likely to contain an
explanation of seasonal movements in rates. There is a well-known

NOTE: This paper was originally printed as NBER Occasional Paper 108, 1970.

The late William H. Brown, Jr., left a partial manuscript on the present
subject that contributed to this study. In addition I discussed various aspects of
the study with Geoffrey Moore, Phillip Cagan, Jack Guttentag, Anna Schwartz,
Otto Eckstein, Walter D. Fisher, and Walter E. Hoadley, all of whom read at
least one draft of the paper. Although I acted on many of their comments, I
assume full responsibility for the results.

Jae Won Lee assisted me from the beginning both in the considerable data
handling involved, as well as in the development of the ideas.

H. Irving Forman drew the charts, and Gnomi Schrift Gouldin both edited
the manuscript and handled the production arrangements.

and long standing increase in the economy's demand for short-term credit in the fall and early winter and a corresponding decrease in the late spring and summer. There is an equally well known increase in the supply of Federal Reserve credit in the fall and early winter and a withdrawal of credit in the late spring and summer. The seasonal in short-term rates depends upon a combination of the seasonals in the demand and supply for credit. In years of unusually high demand for credit in the fall combined with a smaller increase in supply (and vice versa for late spring and early summer), the seasonal in interest rates will be large. When the seasonal changes in supply and demand are offsetting, no seasonal appears in interest rates. The amount of change in supply required to offset a change in demand is a statistical question considered in Section IV.

The determination and measurement of seasonal movements are hindered by other sources of variation in economic factors, as well as by the volatility of the seasonal component itself. While statistical methods differ in detail, they all attempt to isolate the seasonal component from the other sources of variation and to determine its size and stability. Section II of this study describes some of the methods used to measure seasonal movements, and Section III considers in some detail the application of one of these methods to a variety of interest rate series.

The method used here is the one currently used by the U.S. Bureau of the Census. The nonseasonal variation of the series is captured by a long-term moving average designed to eliminate any seasonal movements. Each term in the time series is then separated into a moving average component and a component consisting of the difference or ratio of the original series to the moving average. If a series has no seasonal component, the ratios will tend to average unity (the differences, zero) for each set of observations relating to a specific month; that is, the mean of all the ratios calculated for July or November (or any other month) will tend to equal unity, and all such means will of necessity tend to be equal. There will, of course, be observable differences in the mean ratios because of erratic movements in the series, but none of these differences will be significantly different from unity. Thus, averages that do differ significantly from unity provide evidence of seasonality.

The remainder of this section describes and analyzes the pattern of seasonal variations in interest rates over the 1948–65 period and discusses some historical developments which are widely thought to have influenced these patterns.

Short-Term Rates

Short-term rates typically decline from a relative high in January through seasonally neutral February, to a trough in June or July, then sharply incline past seasonally neutral August to September, gradually rising to a peak in December. Chart 2-1 plots the seasonal factors for 1951, 1957, and 1965 (the years before, during, and after the period of peak seasonality) for the four short-term rates studied, and Chart 2-2 shows the factors for call money rates in 1915 computed by Macaulay.[1]

Seasonal variation of interest rates is the net result of seasonal variation in both the supply and demand for credit, arising when the effect of a given variable on demand is not offset by a comparable movement in supply, as in the following description of an earlier period:

Before the establishment of the Federal Reserve System, there were four more or less distinct seasonal variations in interest rates. . . . The first movement, from early January until about the middle of February, is characterized by low interest rates, . . . attributable to the fact that the crop movement, with its great demand for money in the West and South, has passed its peak, and has been followed by a heavy flow of cash from the country banks to the primary money market. At the same time, the demand for funds is relatively slack, for business in general is characteristically full during the interval between the holidays and the opening of the spring manufacturing and trading season.

The second period, which is marked by rising interest rates, is largely attributable to the monetary demand of producers and manufacturers. This demand is supplemented, particularly in the latter part of the period, by crop planting requirements.

The third important seasonal variation is that of a weakening money market in April and May, followed by a genuine depression in June and July. This period at its beginning reflects a declining demand for funds by the manufacturing and producing interests of the industrial centers, and in its latter stages the return of funds from the country districts following the completion of the crop planting period.

[1] The 1915 factors are given in Frederick R. Macaulay, *Some Theoretical Problems Suggested by the Movements of Interest Rates, Bond Yields and Stock Prices in the United States since 1856*, New York, NBER, 1938, insert after p. 216. The method used to compute the recent factors is described briefly in Chapter 2. Here it suffices to note that a factor exceeding 100.0 implies a seasonal high. The factors for the postwar period were computed with the Census Bureau's X-11 seasonal adjustment program.

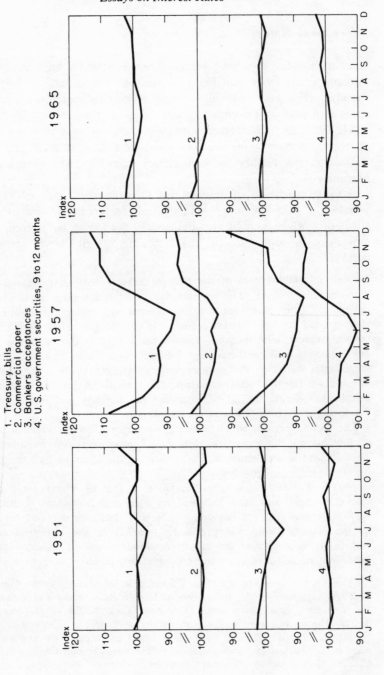

CHART 2–1. Seasonal Factors on Short-Term Securities for Selected Years

1. Treasury bills
2. Commercial paper
3. Bankers acceptances
4. U. S. government securities, 9 to 12 months

CHART 2–2. Seasonal Factors for Yield on Call Money, Macaulay's Series, 1915

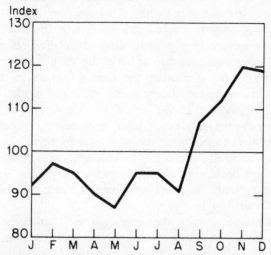

The fourth season is generally referred to as the crop moving period. The demand for funds in the country districts for the paying of farm labor, the storing of grain, and the moving of produce to the primary markets calls for an outflow of funds from the financial centers to the interior. At the same time, the demand from producing and manufacturing enterprises which are making ready for the fall trade becomes very heavy, thus bringing added pressure to bear on the financial markets. This period ordinarily reaches a peak in October, with interest rates commonly remaining high till January.[2]

What, then, are the present sources of seasonal influence on the demand for credit? These sources are likely to be found in wholesale and retail trade; government fiscal activity, particularly short-term borrowing in autumn to close the gap between tax revenues and expenditures; corporate demand for credit to finance tax and dividend payments in the final quarter of the year, which may be regarded as an increased demand for credit or as a diminished supply of funds that at other times are available to finance government and trade debt; and no doubt other factors as well.[3]

[2] Richard N. Owens and Charles O. Hardy, *Interest Rates and Stock Speculation*, Washington, D.C., The Brookings Institution, 1930, pp. 3–5.

[3] One measure of the diminished supply of corporate investment funds in autumn is the increase in government dealer positions, although other forces affect these positions as well. Dealer holdings of government securities increase,

During the fifty years preceding the adoption of the Federal Reserve Act in 1914, seasonal changes in the demand for currency confronted a virtually inelastic currency supply. This situation caused steep movements in both short-term interest rates and, with the fractional reserve system, in the money supply itself. One of the Federal Reserve System's initial objectives was to facilitate the easy transfer of deposits into currency, thereby preventing the sudden declines in the supply of money that had attended the seasonal increases in the demand for currency. Their success in this regard is conspicuous in the contrast between the seasonal amplitudes both in currency outstanding and in short-term interest rates during the periods before and after 1914. The seasonal amplitude of currency outstanding increased substantially in the later period because of the more elastic supply, as well as, given the smaller amplitudes of short-term interest rates, the reduced incentive to economize on its use.[4]

Federal Reserve activity, however, did not entirely eliminate the seasonal variation in short-term interest rates. Seasonal influences persisted, although with much smaller amplitude, throughout the 1920's. In the 1930's, with bank reserves well above legal requirements, seasonal variation in short-term interest rates was barely perceptible despite the absence of the Federal Reserve's seasonal influence. Again in the 1940's, with interest rates pegged within narrow limits, there was little room for seasonal variation. It was only when the authorities removed the peg—gradually in the 1951–53 period—that seasonal variation in short-term rates reappeared. Erratic at first, and with a small amplitude, the seasonal pattern became more systematic in the late 1950's, when its amplitude exceeded 10 per cent on either side of the level of rates. After 1959, however, the seasonal amplitude quickly collasped and became a mere ripple by 1963.[5] The seasonal

on the average, by 33 per cent in December when compared with the preceding June, one study found. See U.S. Congress, Joint Economic Committee, *A Study of the Dealer Market For Federal Securities*, Washington, D.C., 1960, p. 41.

[4] The change in the seasonal amplitude of call money rates is shown graphically in Macaulay, *op. cit.*, p. 217. The change in the seasonal amplitudes of currency outstanding is described in Milton Friedman and Anna Schwartz, *A Monetary History of the United States, 1867–1960*, Princeton for NBER, 1963, p. 293. The smaller the autumn increase in rates the less is the need to rely on money substitutes, such as trade credit, or to increase the velocity of currency.

[5] The evidence for these statements is presented in Section III.

While this study was in final manuscript form, seasonal adjustments through the middle of 1968 became available. These data reveal an apparent resurgence of seasonal variation in both short- and long-term rates. Whereas this study

variation in the period following the Treasury-Federal Reserve accord of 1951 is alike, both in its evolution over the period and its pattern, for the four short-term rates studied: commercial paper, bankers' acceptances, nine- to twelve-month Treasury securities, and 91-day Treasury bills. The variation is similar, moreover, to the pattern Macaulay found for call money rates during the early part of the century; a surprising similarity, in view of the changes in the capital markets resulting from the relatively recent prominence of government fiscal activity.

This study has not attempted a systematic analysis of the factors affecting seasonal variation in the demand for credit. It may be merely coincidental that the changes over time in the incidence and importance of the factors affecting the seasonal variation of demand have not substantially altered the seasonal pattern of interest rates. The timing of crop movements in the earlier period appears to have affected the seasonal demand for credit in approximately the same pattern as the more important fiscal influences do today. There has been, however, some variation in the timing of fiscal activity that appears to have affected the seasonal variation of interest rates. (This variation is considered in Section IV.) Apart from this variation the significant difference between the early and later periods lies not in the variation of demand factors but rather in the conditions of supply. Whereas in the pre-Federal Reserve period the means of accommodating the supply to changes in the demand for credit were limited, these means were virtually unlimited in the later period. Since interest rates vary in response to differences in the rates of change of supply and demand, the ability to vary the supply implies the ability to remove the seasonal factor in interest rates. Of course, the ability to offset changes in demand requires recognition of those changes, the failure of which would result in an unwanted seasonal influence on interest rates.

That the Federal Reserve did not exercise its ability to expunge

calculated a seasonal factor for Treasury bills in December 1965 of 102.6, the more recent data indicate a factor of 104.6 for December 1967. In the case of long-term U.S. government bonds the figures for September, the peak month for this series, are 100.3 and 101.0 for 1965 and 1967, respectively. By the nature of the adjustment process, inclusion of the more recent data will alter the calculated factors for earlier years. The factors for the last three years reported in this study are therefore subject to upward revision just as the most recent figures would be if the seasonal were to change subsequently. (Seasonal factors are measures of seasonal change. The method of computing them is described in Section III.)

the seasonal variation in interest rates does not *imply* an error in judgment. It is arguable, in fact, whether the Federal Reserve should eliminate the seasonality in interest rates—an argument that rests largely on whether removing the symptom of monetary tightness would tend to aggravate the cause of the problem. Just as palliating a sore throat with syrup to increase one's temporary tolerance for cigarettes at the expense of subsequent aggravation, the attempt to ease the cyclical tightness in the money market with infusions of money will stimulate inflationary forces. It is doubtful, however, that a similar response to the more ephemeral seasonal tightness would provoke excessive demand for productive resources—especially in view of the contraction of the money supply some months later that a seasonal monetary policy implies.[6]

In a later section this paper argues that the seasonal pattern, if any, of interest rates is determined by the factors affecting the demand for credit; while the seasonal amplitude is determined by the degree of accommodation of the supply of credit.

Long-Term Rates[7]

While few would contest the occurrence of seasonal shifts in the demand for money or the possibility that the Federal Reserve allows these shifts to affect short-term interest rates, seasonal variation in long-term rates is another matter. There are no obvious reasons for seasonality in long-term rates and some cogent reasons for its absence. To meet seasonal needs for cash, corporations, including banks, seldom sell off long-term securities and thereby raise rates. Firms, moreover, can usually delay their long-term borrowing to take advantage of

[6] For a discussion of whether the Federal Reserve should accommodate short-period fluctuations in the demand for credit see Jack Guttentag, "The Strategy of Open Market Operations," *Quarterly Journal of Economics,* February 1966, pp. 23–25, and the references cited there.

[7] The computation of the monthly bond yields used in this study is described in the *Federal Reserve Bulletin* as follows: *U.S. govt. bonds:* Averages of daily figures for bonds maturing or callable in 10 years or more. *State and local govt. bonds:* General obligations only, based on Thurs. figures. *Corporate bonds:* Averages of daily figures.

"Corporate" bonds comprise industrials, rails, and utilities. Remarks made about monthly movements do not reflect intramonth variation. Evaluation of this variation requires use of weekly or sometimes daily figures, which is beyond the scope of this study.

seasonal (i.e., expected) declines in rates; and in so doing eliminate the seasonal variations. Finally, seasonality of sufficient amplitude would invite arbitrage; that is, investors would buy bonds when rates were high and sell them, say, six months later when rates fell—reducing their incentive in the process. To invite arbitrage the seasonal amplitude must be large enough to cover the significant transaction costs involved in holding long-term securities for limited periods. Rough calculations with respect to the orders of magnitude involved may be found in Section IV.[8]

This study has found significant seasonal movement in all of the long-term securities examined. The evolution of the seasonal pattern over the postwar period resembles that for short-term rates, with a peak in the late fifties, and the pattern, similar for each of the long-term securities, leads that for short-term rates by about three months. Chart 2-3 compares the 1958 seasonal factor for bankers' acceptances

CHART 2–3. Seasonal Factors for Banker's Acceptance Rates and Yields on Municipal Bonds, Highest Rating, 1958

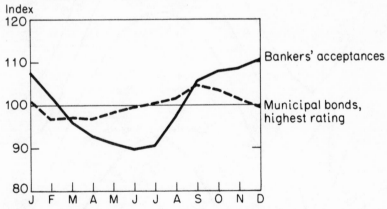

[8] Some additional constraints allow the short-term markets fewer opportunities for arbitrage. Since there is usually six months between the seasonal peak and trough, both for the long- and short-term securities, it is not possible to hold, say, 91-day Treasury bills over the full range of variation—that is, from peak to trough or the reverse. Moreover, while yields on long-term securities differ imperceptibly between, say, a nineteen and one-half and a twenty year maturity, the yield curve for short-term securities has a substantial slope. Therefore, the typically higher yield on six-month compared with three-month securities may nullify the advantage of borrowing for six months at low summer rates instead of for three months at high winter rates. Section IV considers this point in greater detail.

and municipal bonds (highest rating). The seasonal amplitude of long-term rates is much smaller than that of short-term rates, seldom exceeding 3 per cent on either side of the average level during the period of peak seasonality in the late fifties. The common evolution of the longs and shorts together with the inverse relation between seasonal amplitude and term to maturity is shown in Chart 2-4. This

CHART 2–4. Variance of Seasonal Factors of Yields on U.S. Government Securities, 1948–65

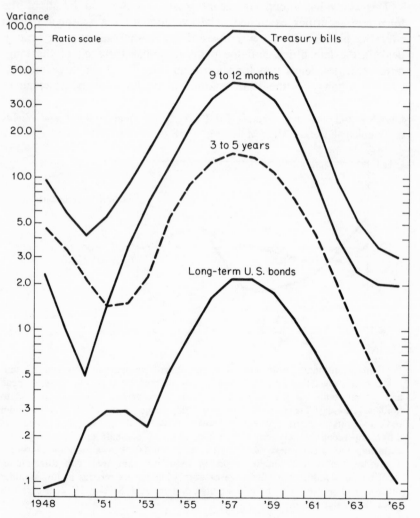

chart, restricted to government securities—ninety-day, nine- to twelve-month, three- to five-year, and long-term Treasury securities—plots the variances, computed separately for each year and each security, of the twelve monthly seasonal factors. Since the variance measures the dispersion of the factors around 100.0, it is a good summary statistic for the seasonal amplitude.[9] These bell-shaped curves neatly sketch the rise and fall in the amplitude of the seasonal components of the four series and order them with respect to seasonal amplitude. The symmetry of the four curves after 1952 is as remarkable as their movements before 1952 are inscrutable. The seasonal amplitude of each of the four series rises steadily from 1952 to its peak in 1957 and then falls off at approximately the same rate at which it rose. After 1952, the evolution of the seasonal factors is virtually identical in all four sets of securities.

This statement, of course, implies nothing about the reliability of the estimates of the seasonal factors, the determination of which is the main objective of this study. Section III concludes, for example, that long-term government bonds evinced no significant seasonality outside the period 1955–60; whereas it finds a significant though small seasonal pattern in the private long-term bonds throughout most of the postwar period. These issues will be considered in greater detail in Section III.

For most of the long-term series considered, 1955 divides the post-war period into two parts with distinctly different seasonal patterns. Typically, the earlier pattern starts with a January low and falls slightly to a trough in March, then rises through May (roughly 100.0) to a plateau extending from June through October, and afterwards returns to the 100.0 level for November and December. Although the general patterns for all the private long-term bonds agree with this picture, there are differences in detail. For most series the plateau actually tilts toward a peak, usually in September but sometimes in June or October. The patterns for all the private long-term bonds are alike with respect to their midyear highs and January lows, the characteristics which distinguish these patterns from those of the same securities in the later period, as well as from the patterns of the short-term rates. Chart 2-5 plots the seasonal factors for 1954 for selected private long-term rates.

Starting in 1955, the seasonal patterns of private long-term bond rates change. The January factors change from lows to highs, the June and July factors from highs to lows. The troughs remain in

---

[9] To conserve space the curves are plotted on four-cycle semi-log paper.

CHART 2–5. Seasonal Factors for Yields on Selected Long-Term Securities, 1954

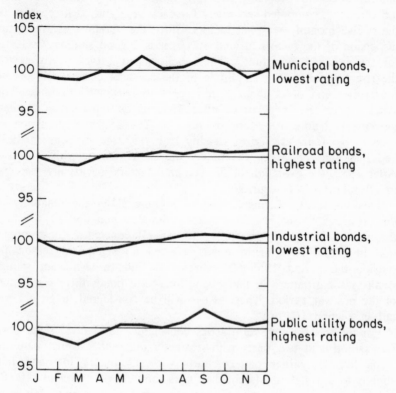

March and April and the peaks in September and October, the amplitude in these months increasing during the late fifties and tapering off afterward.

Chart 2-6 illustrates the differences in both pattern and amplitude between the two periods for two long-term rates. Starting roughly at the 100.0 line in January, the 1957 factor curve drops to a trough in March and gradually rises, crossing the 100.0 line in July to a peak in September, from which it declines to the December position, slightly above the 100.0 line. Unlike the Treasury securities, this pattern persists, though with diminished amplitude, at least through 1963 and, for some series, all the way to 1965.

Unfortunately, analysis of seasonality is not founded on principles that permit the unambiguous determination that a seasonal influence

CHART 2–6. Seasonal Factors for Yields on Corporate and Industrial Bonds, Highest Rating, 1952 and 1957

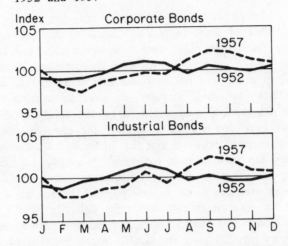

exists at a given time, and whether it is significant or otherwise. Aside from some special cases there are no criteria whose satisfaction provides compelling evidence for or against the existence of seasonality. In many cases, perhaps most cases, this hiatus is academic in the sense that an experienced analyst can profitably rely on his judgment, and forego the statistical accouterments to test for seasonality, although, even here, the problem remains of making the point-estimates of the seasonal factors for the adjustment itself. In borderline cases, however, when the evidence for seasonality is not conclusive, intuitive methods invite disagreement. The dearth of adjusted data for interest rates in the postwar period combined with the widely held belief that a seasonal pattern did exist at least for some of the rates over part of the period is strong evidence that interest rates are a borderline case. Section II reviews the concepts underlying seasonal analysis and some of the methods used for adjustment.[10] Section III then considers the evidence of seasonality in interest rates. Section IV analyzes factors contributing to the extent of seasonal amplitude of both short- and long-term rates and tests a hypothesis relating the seasonal amplitude of short-term rates to that of the money supply. Section V summarizes the report and lists some conclusions.

[10] Those readers already familiar with seasonal analysis can skip this section without loss of continuity.

II. METHODS OF SEASONAL ADJUSTMENT

It is often useful to separate a time series into components that differ in the frequency of their recurrence. Some series, national income, for example, tend to increase over time—to have a positive trend—although any given observation may be smaller than its predecessor because it happens to fall on the down side of a different component, whether cyclical, seasonal, irregular, or some anonymous component. Since each observation is assumed to be the result of the separate influences of each component, to capture the effect on the series of any given component requires that the others be in some way filtered out. Perhaps the main reason for using seasonally adjusted data is to facilitate identification of the cyclical component.[11]

It is sometimes profitable to study the behavior of a particular component for what it reveals about the behavior of the composite series. Investment and interest rates, for example, are sometimes observed to vary together over the course of the business cycle because shifts in the demand for investment goods dwarf the movements along the curve. By abstracting from the cyclical component of either series it may be possible to observe the expected inverse relation, at a given time, between the two series. Ultimately, since the several components of a series are distinct only because they are determined by different factors (by different variables or by different patterns of variation of the same variables), the identification of the components is a step toward the goal of explaining their behavior.[12] In practice, because of the difficulty of specifying those models describing the behavior of each component, the two goals are distinguished and, ordinarily, the second one eschewed.

One way to eliminate from the variation of the combined series that part due to one of the components is to smooth the series with a moving average of which the number of terms equals the period of the recurring variation of that component. Consider, for example, a daily series of retail sales: Every Sunday there is a sharp drop. By replacing each daily value of the series with the value of a centered

---

[11] See Julius Shiskin and Harry Eisenpress, *Seasonal Adjustment by Electronic Computer Methods*, Technical Paper 12, New York, NBER, 1958. Represented in *Business Cycle Indicators*, Vol. 1, Princeton for NBER, 1961.

[12] Horst Mendershausen, "Annual Survey of Statistical Technique: Methods of Computing and Eliminating Changing Seasonal Fluctuations," *Econometrica*, 1937, pp. 234–62.

seven-term moving average—in other words, by replacing, say, the original Wednesday value with the average of the preceding three days, that Wednesday, and the following three days, and similarly for the other days—one obtains a series that is free of the recurring variation. When the moving average is subtracted from or divided into the original series, a new series emerges containing samples of all the components for which the variation has a period of seven or less.

Since seasonal variation is defined as variation that recurs in a period not greater than a year, there is no need to distinguish, for the purpose of seasonal adjustment, among components whose variation recurs in periods exceeding one year. It is enough to smooth the seasonal variation with a twelve-term moving average (assuming monthly data) and use the deviations of the composite series from the moving average as estimates of the components, the period of whose recurring variation does not exceed one year. The moving average is then an estimate of the trend-cycle or low frequency component of the series, and the deviations from it of the seasonal and irregular components. These deviations, usually expressed as ratios of the composite series to the trend-cycle component, are the raw data for the seasonal adjustment. They are called the seasonal-irregular (SI) ratios.[13]

Seasonal-Irregular Ratios

The SI ratios, expressed as percentages, are computed for each month of each year. The twelve SI ratios for each year are adjusted to force their sum to 1,200. This adjustment precludes any discrepancy

[13] When the deviations are expressed as ratios, the adjustment is called multiplicative; when expressed as differences, additive. In the Census Bureau's X-11 seasonal adjustment program, as well as in earlier versions of the program, computation of the SI ratios is a much more complicated procedure than the one described above. First a thirteen-term moving average is computed (half weights at the end points) and divided into the original data. The preliminary SI ratios are adjusted for extreme values and smoothed into moving seasonal factors (to be described below). The preliminary factors are divided into the original series to get a preliminary adjusted series. A Henderson curve, an elastic moving average of varying terms, is fitted to the adjusted series, and a new set of SI ratios computed, adjusted for extremes and smoothed with a moving average into the final seasonal factors. See Shiskin and Eisenpress, *op. cit.*, and U.S. Department of Commerce, Bureau of the Census, *X-11 Variant of the Census Method II Seasonal Adjustment Program*, Technical Paper 15, Washington, D.C., 1965 (hereafter referred to as the X-11 manual).

between the *expected values* of the totals for any consecutive twelve months (as distinct from the observed totals for a given year)[14] of the seasonally adjusted series and the totals of the original series. Year to year changes of the series are therefore unaffected, on average, by seasonal adjustment, while the variation within years is redistributed to eliminate the effect of systematic intrayear variation.

The symmetry thus imposed on the SI ratios reveals an important property of seasonal adjustment; the interrelatedness of the seasonal factors among several months. Consider a series in which the values for the first eleven months of the year are equal (they could even be zero) but for the twelfth month very high.[15] Graphically, the series is shown in Figure 2-1. To maintain the symmetry of the SI ratios the

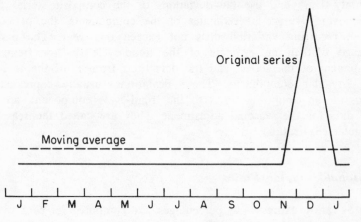

FIGURE 2–1

high point in December must be balanced by a low point elsewhere. Since the datum for the highs and lows is the trend cycle curve, in this case a twelve-term moving average, the symmetry is achieved by raising the datum above the values for the first eleven months of the series thereby imputing seasonal lows to these values. Through its influence on the moving average, the December high in effect creates the January-to-November lows.

There is clearly a certain arbitrariness in imputing significance to the deviations from the moving average. The arbitrariness resides in

[14] Arthur Burns and Wesley C. Mitchell, *Measuring Business Cycles,* New York, NBER, 1946, p. 51.

[15] This hypothetical series is chosen only for simplicity. The principle involved, however, does not depend on the simplicity of the sample.

the connotation of normality attached to the moving average from which the deviations appear, therefore, to be atypical and to invite behavioral explanations. Using a crude method for ascertaining the extent of seasonality in the capital markets, a method that did not abstract from the effects of trend, Kemmerer drew the following conclusion:

The national bank-note circulation curves do not appear to exhibit any considerable seasonal elasticity, i.e., rise and fall according to the seasonal variations in the demands of trade; it is noteworthy, however, that the increase in the circulation, which takes place normally from year to year, takes place largely in the fall and early winter. Apparently banks intending to increase their circulation postpone doing so until the crop-moving season approaches, so that the year's normal increase takes place principally in the latter part of the year. There is no evidence of contraction when the crop-moving demands are over, the national bank-note elasticity being (to use a rather inelegant expression) of the chewing gum variety. Here, however, . . . it is fortunate that the increase which normally does take place each year takes place in the season when it is needed most.[16]

Had the ratio-to-moving-average method of seasonal analysis been available at the time of his study, Kemmerer would probably have affirmed the presence of seasonality in the series because of the effect of the high values in the autumn on the trend-cycle values for the rest of the year. Whether a series declines seasonally in a given month depends not on its average value in the month relative to its average value in the previous month—the averages being taken across years— but on the average of its values relative to what they would have been in the absence of seasonality. A series with positive trend is expècted to increase from, say, April to May; by remaining constant, on the average, it in effect declines relative to the expectation. The arbitrariness resides, therefore, only in the assumed existence of smooth, independent components in fixed relation in the hypothetical population from which the series is drawn.[17]

[16] Edwin W. Kemmerer, *Seasonal Variations in the Demands for Currency and Capital,* National Monetary Commission, Vol. XXII, Washington, D.C., 1911, p. 153.

[17] Using a twelve-month average instead of, say, a six-month or eighteen-month average as the datum for seasonality is also arbitrary unless "the activity represented by a series has a 'natural' business year, with a definite beginning and end, as in movements of products from farms. . . . In the absence of a natural year, there is no basis other than convention for selecting the boundaries of the year; . . . the final seasonal adjustment will then vary

Stable Seasonal Factors

Estimated stable seasonal factors are defined as the mean value of the SI ratios for each month. They are called stable or constant because they are computed once for the entire sample period. Any deviation of the SI ratios computed for a given month from the factor computed for that month is attributed to the irregular component. In other words, the SI ratios consist of a systematic and a random component called, respectively, the seasonal and the irregular components. Since the irregular component, expressed as a fraction of the seasonal component, is defined to vary with equal likelihood above and below the seasonal component, its ratio to the seasonal component is on average equal to 1. (In the additive case the mean of the irregular component is zero.) Therefore, the mean SI ratio, say for January, is equal to the seasonal component, assumed to be a constant, multiplied by 1. In the absence of seasonality the mean SI ratios would not differ significantly from each other or from 1.

A simple test for the presence of stable seasonality is therefore to determine the statistical significance of the differences among the computed mean SI ratios for each month. The test is a one-way analysis of variance of the monthly SI ratios, twelve columns of them for the twelve months, and the number of rows equalling the number of annual observations.[18] The F-statistic, computed for N full years, is equal to

$$\frac{N \text{ times variance of monthly means}}{\text{total variance minus } N \text{ times variance of monthly means}}.$$

Except for the graphic method of fitting smooth curves to SI ratios of a given month over the years most of the earlier methods and many of those used currently result in estimates of stable seasonal factors. For example, the widely used dummy variable technique, whereby the monthly series X is regressed on twelve dummy variables, eleven of which assume the value 1 when the series is measured in a particular month and zero otherwise, the twelfth dummy variable

with the boundaries selected." (Burns and Mitchell, *op. cit.,* p. 49 fn.) In commenting thus, Burns and Mitchell were concerned with a particular method of adjustment, the Kuznets amplitude-ratio method (described later); although the principal is apropos of any method.

[18] The X-11 performs the analysis of variance test on the SI ratios after they have been modified to reduce the effect of extreme observations. See X-11 manual, *op. cit.,* p. 5.

always assumes the value zero, estimates stable seasonal factors.[19] The computation of stable seasonals is justified when there are good reasons for believing that the parameters are stable in the hypothetical population from which the observed series is drawn. This belief is *not* analogous to the assumed constancy of the parameters in the structural relation of, say, consumption and income. A change in the seasonal parameters (as distinct from the estimated factors) of interest rates does not require that the structural relation between, say, interest rates and money supply change but only that the seasonal pattern of money supply change. In fact, by assuming the structural relation fixed, one can, in principle, estimate it by relating the changes in the seasonal pattern of one series to those in the other.[20] Therefore, the assumption of fixed seasonal parameters for a given series implies the assumption of fixed structural relations between this series and others, as well as of fixed seasonal patterns in these related series.

Moving Seasonal Factors

Typically there are changes not so much in the original cause of the seasonal movement but in the economy's adaptation to it. The increased demand for funds in the fall months will result in a seasonal high in interest rates only in the absence of a corresponding increase in the supply of funds. The willingness or ability of the banking system to supply the funds will determine whether the increased demand will result in higher rates. Seasonal increases in the demand, as well as in the supply, of funds have varied in the postwar period, and the seasonal increase in interest rates has varied along with it.

Changes in seasonal patterns are difficult to distinguish from irregular movements—the more difficult, the greater is the variance of the irregular component relative to that of the total series. One identifies with greater confidence very small changes in the seasonal variation of money supply, a series with an almost negligible irregular

[19] Michael C. Lovell, "Seasonal Adjustment of Economic Time Series and Multiple Regression Analysis," *American Statistical Association Journal,* December 1963, p. 993.

[20] The distinction here is between a structural relation between two economic variables, on the one hand, and between an economic variable and time, on the other. Economic models assume constancy in the first case but not the second. The fact that a timing relationship has changed does not imply a change in structural relationship since it may reflect merely the timing change of the variables with which it is structurally related.

component,[21] than changes in the seasonal variation of the highly
irregular Treasury bill rate series. The problem of identifying these
changes is analogous to one of identifying the components themselves:
The method already described for that is predicated on the assumed
smoothness of each of the components within its particular frequency;
a method for dealing with changes in the components is to assume
these changes themselves evolve along a smooth path. This method
involves either fitting by eye a smooth curve to the SI ratios for all
the Januaries, another for the Februaries, and so on, instead of a
straight line at the means of the ratios for each month as in the
stable factors, or computing a moving average, one month at a time,
of the SI ratios adjusted for extreme values. If a simple three-term
moving average were used, for example, the seasonal factor for
January 1953 would equal the average of the SI ratios for January
1952, 1953, and 1954. In practice, such a simple moving average
would be used only for series whose irregular component, being small,
is in little danger of distorting the evolution of the seasonal factors.
A weighted five-term moving average was used to compute the moving seasonal factors of the interest rate series. When the assumption of gradually evolving seasonal factors is not apposite, the use of
this method will impose a spurious similarity on the estimated factors
for adjacent years of a given month. However, by observing graphs
of the SI ratios themselves one may judge the appropriateness of the
method.

There are several alternative methods of calculating moving seasonal
factors. The simplest one merely divides the whole sample period
into subperiods and computes stable seasonal factors for each of the
subperiods. This method is particularly useful for separating the
subperiods with clear evidence of seasonality from those without it.
There is some evidence, for example, that yields on long-term
Treasury securities manifested seasonality during the late fifties but
not before or since. A method based on evolving factors would spread
the estimated period of seasonality past its true period, at the same
time that it dilutes what seasonality there is. The method is also
useful when there is an abrupt change in some institutional factor
affecting the seasonal pattern, as, for example, when the Treasury-
Federal Reserve accord in 1951 removed the peg on U.S. government
bonds. Another method is to compute a set of stable factors for the
whole period and, on the assumption that the true factors for any

---

[21] The variation of the rate of change of the money supply has, of course,
a much larger irregular component.

given year remain in fixed relation, compute factors for each year proportional to the stable factors (that is, with an identical pattern but different amplitude). The proportion used for a given year is the regression coefficient obtained by regressing the SI ratios for that year on the stable factors, one regression for each year.[22] The application of this method to the Treasury bill rates would result in an adjustment not very different, and perhaps a little better, than that obtained with the moving average method. This point is considered in the next section. Finally, some writers recommend tying the moving seasonal factors of one series to the variation of related variables. This method is, of course, limited by the researcher's ability to specify the appropriate relations.[23]

Sometimes the term *moving seasonal* is applied to a different phenomenon than the one described above, where the term referred to changes in the true seasonal component requiring an estimation procedure capable of detecting these changes. If the seasonal component is a function of the trend cycle component of the same series, then an estimation procedure that assumes the components are independent will yield biased estimates of the moving seasonal factors. The seasonal decline in unemployment, for example, is said to be milder when the level of unemployment is low than otherwise because firms are reluctant to temporarily discharge workers at a time when the labor force is fully employed. The appropriate seasonal factor will therefore vary between periods of high and low unemployment. Unlike the other reason for moving seasonals, this one does not involve a change in the relation among the components of the series (sometimes called the structure of the series) but simply a more complicated relation among them.

During the four decades preceding the Federal Reserve Act of 1913, a problem analogous to that alleged for unemployment prevailed on interest rates and the components of the money stock, although with consequences much more severe than the computation of biased estimates of seasonal factors. In his study written for the National Monetary Commission organized in response to the panic of 1907,[24] Kemmerer concluded that the greater incidence of banking

[22] See Simon Kuznets, *Seasonal Variations in Industry and Trade,* New York, NBER, 1933, p. 324.

[23] Mendershausen, *op. cit.,* pp. 254–262.

[24] See also Milton Friedman and Anna Jacobson Schwartz, *A Monetary History of the United States, 1867–1960,* Princeton for NBER, 1963, pp. 171–172.

panics in the fall than at other times of the year was due not to the normal seasonal tightness in the fall money market but to that tightness coming at the same time as a cyclical crisis. The seasonal movement, in effect, played the role of the proverbial straw.[25]

Even if the seasonal component, expressed as a ratio to the moving average, were systematically related to the level of the moving average (or trend-cycle component) the estimated seasonal factors would not reveal this relation. Since the factors are computed from averages of the SI ratios across years, the variation of the SI ratios due to the cyclical variation is canceled out in the averaging process. In the case of an extreme cyclical movement, a related seasonal movement would likely result in an SI ratio that would be regarded as an extreme observation and be eliminated from the computation of the seasonal estimates. However, any relation that exists between the seasonal and cyclical components would present itself in a time series of the SI ratios. Section III considers this point.

Even in the absence of a true relation between the seasonal and cyclical components the inappropriate use of either an additive or multiplicative adjustment, that is, the use of one when the other is required, will result in an apparent relation between the seasonal and cyclical components.

When the level of rates is low the basis point equivalent of a multiplicative adjustment factor is smaller than when the level of rates is high. If the true seasonality were additive, and a multiplicative adjustment method were used, there would result an inverse relation between the SI ratios and the level of rates. Assume, for example, the true seasonal difference for a particular month to be 50 basis points. If in estimating the seasonal variation a multiplicative method were used, the SI ratio computed for this month would be high when the level of rates were, say, 100 basis points (i.e., 150/100) and low when the level were, say, 400 basis points (i.e., 450/400). Application of this test to the computed SI ratios for the Treasury bill rates does not reveal a systematic inverse relation between these ratios and the level of rates.

---

[25] The evidence on this point is mixed. Kemmerer found that "of the eight panics which have occurred since 1873 [as of 1910], four occurred in the fall or early winter (i.e., those of 1873, 1890, 1899, and 1907); three broke out in May (i.e., those of 1884, 1893, and 1901); and one (i.e., that of 1903) extended from March until well along in November." After discussing the "minor panics or 'panicky periods,'" he concludes that "The evidence accordingly points to a tendency for the panics to occur during the seasons normally characterized by a stringent money market." (*Op. cit.,* p. 232.)

However, the opposite procedure designed to test the efficacy of a multiplicative adjustment, assuming the true seasonal were multiplicative and the estimates additive, fails to confirm the appropriateness of a multiplicative adjustment. The question is therefore open and invites deference to convention—which is to use a multiplicative adjustment unless an additive one is clearly indicated.[26]

There is a method that combines elements of both the additive and multiplicative adjustment. Seasonal-irregular ratios are computed for each month and the set for each month regressed on the trend-cycle component for that month; twelve regressions in all. The constant term of each regression is an estimate of the additive component of that month's seasonal factor and the regression coefficient of the multiplicative component. This method, however, assumes stable seasonality in the sense used earlier in this report.[27]

Seasonal Adjustment on Computers

The X-11 program, used in this study, embodies a series of refinements in the original ratio-to-moving-average technique that Macaulay developed in the 1930's. By reducing the cost and virtually eliminating the tedium of the vast number of elementary calculations this method of adjustment requires, the program makes feasible the use of complex weighting schemes in computing moving averages that are both elastic (i.e., remain faithful to the original series) and smooth (i.e., avoid the irregular wiggles). It allows, moreover, the extensive use of iteration to mitigate the obscuring influence of the irregular component on the separation of the seasonal from the trend-cycle components. Its most important advantage is the reduction in the time-cost and skills required in manual adjustments.

[26] See Julius Shiskin and Harry Eisenpress, *Seasonal Adjustment by Electronic Computer Methods,* Technical Paper 12, New York, NBER, 1958, p. 434.

[27] There is clearly room here for variations on a theme. One can adapt the regression method to allow for a moving seasonal by applying the regression method as stated and applying the X-11 method to the residuals of the regressions. In that case one could obtain: an additive component, a component related to the trend cycle, and a moving seasonal component. Since this study uncovered no evidence of a relation between the seasonal and trend-cycle components of the interest rate series there was no reason to experiment with this method. In his exhaustive article, Mendershausen (*op. cit.*) describes many exotic techniques for circumventing this or that problem of conventional methods; virtually all of them are in desuetude either because they introduced other problems or they were too unwieldy.

The program's advantages are particularly obvious through the stage in which the modified seasonal-irregular ratios or differences are computed as, of course, are their mean values, or the stable seasonal factors, when relevant. An experienced draftsman, however, can graphically fit moving seasonals to the SI ratios as well as the program does, and probably better than the program does when the series has a prominent irregular component. Moreover, judgment is often required in determining whether an adjustment for any subperiod should be undertaken at all. Since the analysis of variance is a test of the means of the SI ratios for the whole sample period, there is some danger that the presence of a relatively strong seasonal component in one subperiod will affect the means for the whole period sufficiently to lend an apparent significance to the computed differences among them. (This effect would have to be large enough to overcome the increased within-group variance as a result of the greater heterogeneity of the SI ratios of a given month that a moving seasonal implies.) The program adjusts the whole series regardless of the results of the analysis of variance. The user cannot rely on the F-test alone to decide whether to accept the adjustment in its entirety.

The absence of objective criteria for selecting the period of adjustment, the extent of the adjustment, or the quality of the results[28] precludes an elaborate tabulation of this study's findings replete with standard errors. Nevertheless, from the descriptive statistics, the diagrams, and the verbal entourage, patterns emerge that are worth noting. Section III presents this material for seventeen interest rate series.

III. THE EVIDENCE OF SEASONALITY IN INTEREST RATES

This section evaluates the evidence of seasonality in postwar interest rates and suggests suitable adjustments where appropriate. The evaluation consists of graphically identifying biases in the SI ratios over or under the 100.0 level. While the one-way analysis of variance test for seasonality is a useful method for identifying systematic deviations of the SI ratios from 100.0, its reference to the entire period makes it ineffective as a means of distinguishing the subperiods with evidence of

---

[28] "A statistician who has struggled with seasonal adjustments of numerous time series is not likely to underestimate the part played by 'hunch' and 'judgment' in his operations." (Burns and Mitchell, *op. cit.*, p. 44.)

seasonality from those without it.[29] The consistent deviation of a given month's SI ratio in the same direction from the 100.0 line is strong evidence of seasonality regardless of the variation in the magnitude of these deviations, that is, in the seasonal amplitude. The evidence of seasonality is weak when there are constant reversals of direction or when the relationship among the patterns of SI ratios is generally unstable from year to year. The summary statistics that most computer programs for seasonal adjustment supply (such as the average month-to-month change in the seasonal component by itself or relative to that of the other components) do not help evaluate the evidence of seasonality since, aside from the analysis of variance test, they only summarize what the program has done. They do not provide independent measures of either the evidence of seasonality or the quality of the adjustment. Once the existence of a seasonal pattern is confirmed and the adjustment decided, then the summary statistics provide a useful summary of the results.

In seasonal analysis, as in regression analysis, one places greater confidence in tests for the existence of a relation than in its actual measurement. In addition to the problem of sampling error common to both analyses, the moving seasonal amplitude implies changing parameters and requires the adjustment method, in effect, to shoot at a moving target. Except for a few experiments this study does not originate any methods of adjustment, nor does it even compare the adjustments obtainable with existing methods.[30] Instead, charts of the seasonal factors obtained with the X-11 are superimposed on charts of the corresponding SI ratios to determine the method's success in capturing what appears to be the systematic movement of the SI ratios. There is no question but that one could fit by eye a curve that is more faithful than is the curve of factors to variation of the SI ratios; in the extreme, one could perfectly fit a curve to the SI ratios by simply connecting the points—that is, by simply treating them as the factors. The art of the adjustment is in identifying the *systematic* movement of the SI ratios. When the pattern of SI ratios is stable from year to year there is no problem; nor is there any when the seasonal amplitude changes gradually or the pattern evolves with an apparent method. But during transition periods, in which the series has strong irregular move-

---

[29] One can apply the analysis of variance to separate subperiods, but the problem of choosing the limits of the subperiods remains.

[30] The potential gain from these experiments is not, in this study's view, commensurate with the effort required.

ments, such as 1954, the SI ratios and estimated factors appear to be virtually unrelated. This study recommends ignoring the adjustment when the gap between the two is pervasive.

Short-Term Securities

Summary Statistics

Table 2-1 lists some of the summary statistics that are useful in describing the extent and significance of seasonal influence.[31] Columns 1–3 divide the total variance of the series into the parts due to each of the three components: the trend-cycle, seasonal, and irregular. These figures are analogous to readings from the spectral density function, which decomposes the variance of a time series according to the frequency of the recurring variation.[32] Column 4 lists the average month-to-month percentage changes (without regard to sign) of the seasonal component, and column 5 the ratio of column 4 to the corresponding statistics of the cyclical component. These figures, columns 1 through 5, strike averages for the whole study period, averages not of the true seasonal but of the estimated one, including a spill-over into periods without significant seasonality. Columns 7–10 give the dates and amplitudes of the highest and lowest seasonal factors observed during the study period.

But these figures may be only statistical artifacts; hence, the need exists to ascertain their statistical significance. To partially satisfy this need, column 6 records the F statistics.

The F statistic may be low for any of several reasons, the enumeration of which will help in evaluating the charts that follow. The most

---

[31] The statistics are copied directly from the X-11 printout and are described more fully in the X-11 Manual, *op. cit.*

[32] Some recent studies have applied spectral analysis to the problem of identifying seasonal variation. While the principle is the same as that in the moving average method—to simultaneously or sequentially filter, or separate, different frequencies of variation—spectral analysis is a more sophisticated and more rigorous method of doing so. Some of the mathematical advantage is lost, however, in its application to a limited number of observations. This method, moreover, provides no direct adjustment for the seasonal and resembles, in this respect, analysis of variance instead of regression analysis. In Chapter 7 of this book, Tom Sargent has applied spectral analysis to interest rates, among other financial variables, and has reached conclusions virtually identical to those in the present study with respect to the extent and evolution of the seasonal in interest rates.

TABLE 2-1. *Measures of the Relative Importance of the Seasonal Components of the Four Series of Short-Term Securities, 1948–65*

Series	Percentage of Total Variance of Series Due to Each Component			Average Month-to-Month Percentage Changes Without Regard to Sign of Seasonal Component $\bar{S}$	Ratio of Column 4 to Corresponding Figures for the Cyclical Component $\bar{S}/\bar{C}$	F Test for Stable Seasonality[a]	Date and Factor of Seasonal High and Low for Whole Period[b]			
							High		Low	
	I	C	S				Date	Factor (percentage)	Date	Factor (percentage)
	(1)	(2)	(3)	(4)	(5)	(6)	(7)	(8)	(9)	(10)
Yields on:										
91-day bills	37.72	42.52	19.76	2.54	0.68	9.662	Dec. 1957	113.9	July 1957	87.4
9–12 month securities	35.91	49.77	14.32	1.85	0.54	4.557	Dec. 1956	109.0	June 1957	90.7
Commercial paper[c]	35.38	42.98	21.64	1.81	.71	4.034	Dec. 1958	107.5	May 1959	92.8
Bankers' acceptances	24.57	49.39	26.04	2.07	.72	11.293	Dec. 1957	111.4	July 1956	89.3

[a]All ratios are statistically significant at the 5 per cent level.
[b]A moving seasonal component was estimated for both series. Columns 7 and 9 list the dates when the amplitudes of the seasonal variations were greatest and columns 8 and 10 the values of the estimated seasonal factors for these dates.
[c]The sample period for commercial paper rates ends in June 1965.

important reason, of course, is the absence of any bias in the monthly
SI ratios away from the mean value of 100.0; in other words, no seasonality. But a low F statistic does not imply the absence of seasonality
over the whole sample period. The smaller the subperiod of true seasonality the greater the burden on this period's SI ratios to influence the
means for the whole sample period and thereby enlarge the between
means variance, the numerator of the F ratio. The burden is aggravated
by the fact that a moving seasonal component combines with the irregular component to enlarge the within-group variance, the denominator of the F ratio. When, for example, the F statistic is computed for
long-term Treasury securities over the entire period, its value (1.787)
signifies the absence of seasonality; whereas, when computed over
the period 1955 through 1962 the result (4.726) confirms the presence of seasonality. Similarly, the F statistic in Table 2-1 for nine-
to twelve-month Treasury securities is low because the seasonal pattern before 1955 was at best highly irregular. When the seasonal
pattern changes over the sample period, even when in each subperiod
the pattern is unambiguous, the F statistic suffers as the differences
among the mean monthly SI ratios are reduced. Combine this problem with the fact that seasonal patterns do not change instantaneously
but rather evolve through periods of transition during which a coherent
pattern is virtually nonexistent. In the eighteen-year sample period
the seasonal pattern of commercial paper rates underwent several
changes, and the low F statistic shown in Table 2-1 in part reflects
this fact.[33] Finally, the F statistic may be low not because there is
no seasonality but because of a strong irregular component; the means
of the SI ratios are different from 100.0, but the standard errors of
the means are high. This condition applies to all the interest rate
series and in particular to commercial paper rates and yields on
municipal bonds. Here again the diagrams are essential for determining whether the seasonal pattern has sufficient stability to warrant adjustment.

At its highest the seasonal component pushes the Treasury bill rate
14 per cent (rounded to nearest integer) above its trend-cycle value;
at its lowest, 13 per cent below. For a bill rate in the neighborhood
of 4 per cent (i.e., 400 basis points) these seasonal factors correspond
to about 50 basis points.[34] At 11 per cent on either side of the trend-

---

[33] These changes are described later in the section.

[34] These figures are actually underestimates since they embody the dampening
effects of the lower peak levels of adjacent years. Later in this section an
experiment is described that exemplifies this point.

cycle values, the peak seasonal amplitude for yields on bankers' acceptances is somewhat less. Relative to the total variation of the series, however, the seasonal component of the yields on bankers' acceptances is the most important of the four series, and its *F* statistic is highest. The diagrams, to be discussed presently, support the conclusion that this series evinces the strongest seasonal component. The series for which the summary statistics are least reliable is the series on commercial paper rates, for which, in addition, the *F* statistic is lowest. The diagrams will justify this conclusion as well.

Treasury Bill Rates

Chart 2-7 plots the seasonal factors for Treasury bill rates superimposed on the corresponding SI ratios. From a relative high in January the Treasury bill rate seasonal pattern typically declines past seasonally neutral February, downward through the spring months to its trough in June or July and then turns sharply upward through seasonally neutral August to September, from which it rises gradually to its peak in December.[35] Surprisingly, this pattern is quite apparent, although the amplitude is small, in 1948, when the Federal Reserve pegged the prices of Treasury bills within narrow limits. This curve is shown in the first panel of Chart 2-7 together with the unmodified SI ratios. In subsequent panels of Chart 2-7, the pattern is shown to dissolve until about 1953 and then gradually to emerge again, but with greater amplitude, in the middle fifties, keeping this shape into the sixties as its amplitude virtually disappeared. By 1965 there was little left but a 2 per cent trough in June–July and a 2 per cent peak in December–January.

The factor curves, the broken lines of Chart 2-7, are for the most part dampened versions of the corresponding SI ratios, although at times the factor curve for one year betrays the influence of its predecessor more than that of its contemporary SI ratios. In this regard the factor curves ignore certain abrupt movements of the SI ratios, as in April 1955, the program being designed to sidestep points it regards as extreme.[36]

[35] Before 1957, the movement between September and December was not monotonic.

[36] Briefly, an extreme point is one that falls outside the range of 1.5 standard deviations, the latter computed for the entire set of data several times to eliminate the effect on it of the extreme points. The extremes are weighted

CHART 2–7. SI Ratios and Seasonal Factors for Treasury Bill Rates, 1948–65

——— SI ratios
- - - - Seasonal factors

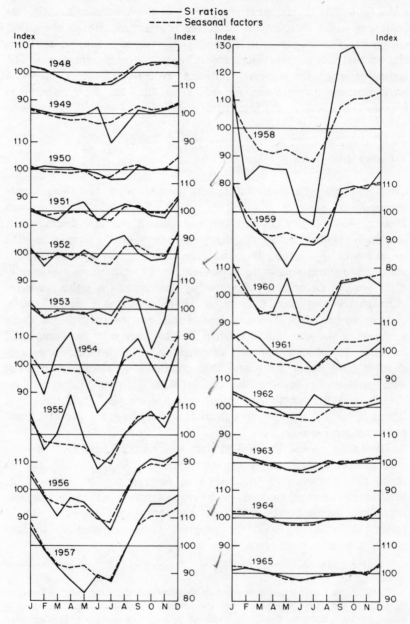

The relative stability of the seasonal pattern is in part a measure of the adjustment's effectiveness since the program does not attempt to directly fit the solid lines in Chart 2-7. Instead it smooths the SI ratios month by month as shown in Chart 2-8. As a given month's

CHART 2–8. Variation of Monthly Factor Curves and SI Ratios of Treasury Bill Rates, 1948–65

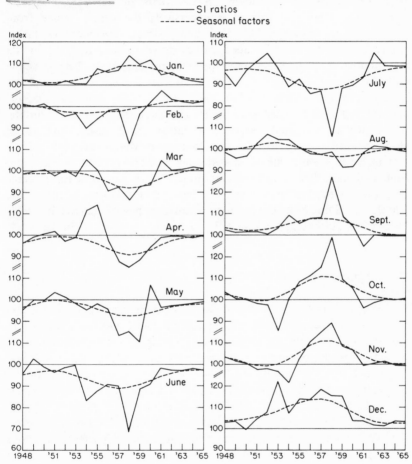

————— SI ratios
------- Seasonal factors

factors evolve through the years, any persistent change in their relation to another month's factors, that is, any change in the ordering

linearly from 1 to 0 as they fall between 1.5 and 2.5 standard deviations. An extreme SI ratio different from 100 by two standard deviations is weighted 0.5. See X-11 Manual, *op. cit.,* pp. 4–5.

of the twelve factors, will change the seasonal patterns given in Chart 2-7. Barring the extremes, the factor curves in Chart 2-8 fit the SI ratios quite closely although severely dampening their movement. One may wish to quarrel with the fit at a few places, but it will soon be shown that any reasonable alterations would have little quantitative importance. The two or three years preceding 1954 and following 1960 appear overly dependent on the years in between; and correspondingly, the peak period is excessively dampened. Aside from the transitional months, February and August, the monthly factor curves trace out the bell-shaped curves noted earlier, inverted in the low months, of course, and most of them remain above 100 or below 100 throughout the period. While most of the curves as of 1965 roughly coincide with the 100.0 line, the curves for July and December are still about 2 per cent under and over the line, denoting the persistence of a small seasonal variation in Treasury bill rates. However, the pattern for the last four years differs somewhat from that in earlier years: the trough appears in June instead of July; the January factors become at least as prominent as the ones for December; and, in the last two years, the November factors dip below the 100.0 line. Similar changes will be shown to have occurred in yields on bankers' acceptances as well.[37]

Other Short-Term Rates

The seasonal patterns of the other short-term rates considered, except for commercial paper rates prior to 1956, are very similar to the one for Treasury bill rates. The similarity is greatest in the peak period, when the patterns for all the series have their greatest stability. Table 2-2 lists the simple correlation coefficients between the twelve seasonal factors for Treasury bill rates and those for the other series over selected years. In 1957 the correlations were all in excess of .95, indicating virtual identity among the four patterns; by 1965, however, the correlations were much less, and could be in part the spurious aftermath of the earlier similarity.

Closest in pattern and evolution to that of Treasury bill rates is the seasonal movement of yields on bankers' acceptances. As in the case of bills, the seasonal pattern for yields on bankers' acceptances

---

[37] The appendix to this section uses alternate adjustment procedures to evaluate the X-11 adjustment of Treasury bill rates.

TABLE 2-2. *Simple Correlation Coefficients Between the Seasonal Factors for Treasury Bill Rates and Those for Other Short-Term Rates for Selected Years*

	1953 (1)	1957 (2)	1963 (3)	1965 (4)
Bankers' acceptances	.6430	.9742	.7926	.5283
Commercial paper	.1380	.9724	.8917	NA
9–12 month Treasury securities	.8447	.9510	.7700	.6492

NOTE: The numbers are all simple correlation coefficients between the seasonal factors of Treasury bill rates and the factors in the corresponding years for the other three series.
NA = not available.

is fairly stable from 1948 through 1950, but, again like bills, the fit is less adequate from 1951 through 1954. In Chart 2-9 the estimated factors are shown to grossly exaggerate the trough in July. Seasonality exists in the period (July, for example, is always below the 100.0 line and December above), but its pattern is less stable than and differs from the patterns of other years. During the peak period its pattern is the familiar high in January, declining past neutral February through the spring lows to a trough in July, then climbing steeply upward to September and, more gradually, to a December peak. Although its peak amplitude, at 12 per cent on either side of the corresponding trend-cycle values, is somewhat less than the peak in the bill rate seasonal pattern, the seasonal amplitude on yields on bankers' acceptances is more prominent in the total variation of the series (columns 3 and 5 of Table 2-1), and the estimated factors are more faithful to the SI ratios (Chart 2-9). Beginning in 1959 the pattern begins to change somewhat, the trough shifts from July to June and the peak from December to January. These changes, as well as the dip in November, are virtually identical to those that occurred somewhat later in Treasury bill rates. Chart 2-9 reveals the low and declining seasonal amplitude in yields on bankers' acceptances in the sixties. Although the last year of the adjustment period is always tricky, the factors for 1965 appear to signal the end of the seasonal component.

Because its pattern is less stable than the patterns of the two short-term series described above, the seasonal variation of commercial paper rates is more difficult to isolate. Chart 2-10 plots the SI ratios and corresponding factors for commercial paper rates. From 1948

CHART 2–9. SI Ratios and Seasonal Factors for Bankers' Acceptance Rates, 1948–65

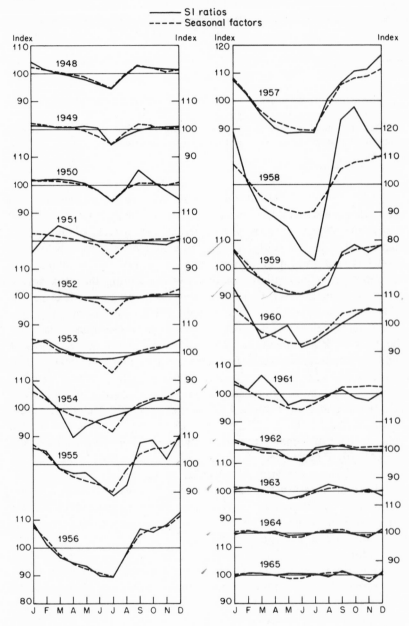

CHART 2–10. SI Ratios and Seasonal Factors for Commercial Paper Rates, 1948–65

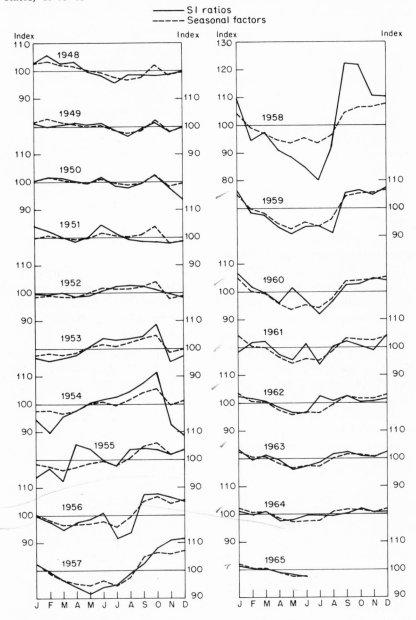

through 1950 the seasonal pattern, except for a high in October, is virtually the mirror image of the pattern in the late fifties—the first half year in the earlier period being above the 100.0 line, the second half below. The pattern evolves through a transition period in 1951 to a pattern that extends through 1955 and is quite similar to the one for long-term rates. Beginning with a low in January the factors drop to a trough in March, turn up through May or June to a peak in October and then sharply down. The pattern in 1955 already blends into the new pattern that is characteristic of the other short-term series: From a high in January the factors turn down through neutral February and the springtime lows to a trough in July then go up through neutral August to a peak in December. This pattern persists throughout the period of peak seasonality in the late fifties, during which, however, the seasonal amplitude never exceeds 8 per cent of the corresponding average values of the series. Beginning in 1962 the pattern appears to drift back towards the earlier one that resembled the pattern of long-term series. Nevertheless, the seasonal amplitude persists through the end of the period.

As in the case of the other short-term series, there is a repetitive ripple in the yields on nine- to twelve-month Treasury securities from 1948 through 1950, but, as Chart 2-11 shows, the factors do not fit the SI ratios as well as in the case of the other short-term series. Several years of erratic movement follow before the final pattern emerges in 1955. Choppy at first, it evolves rapidly into full shape in 1957 and slowly down again but persisting through the end of the period. Indeed, in 1965 the amplitude is greater and the pattern more discernible than in the case of bill rates.

The pattern during the late fifties is very similar to that of the other short-term series except that the trough comes a month earlier (in June) and a fall plateau replaces the December peak. This change in pattern is in the direction of the long-term series.

Summary of Short-Term Series

While the seasonal patterns of short-term rates are not entirely uniform throughout the postwar period, for the most part they have in common springtime lows and a midyear trough, as well as fall highs and a December peak continuing with some diminution through January. This pattern describes all four series in the period of greatest seasonality, 1956 through 1960. Treasury bill rates and yields on

CHART 2–11. SI Ratios and Seasonal Factors for Yields on Nine- to Twelve-Month U.S. Government Securities, 1948–65

——— SI ratios
----- Seasonal factors

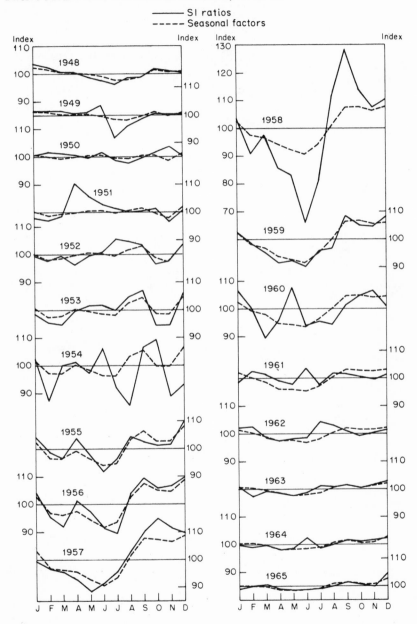

bankers' acceptances sustain this pattern throughout the 1948–65 period, although not with as much stability and amplitude as during the 1956–60 period. The patterns for commercial paper rates prior to 1956 are quite different from those of the other short-term rates and, in fact, resemble those of the long-term rates that are described below. There are actually two distinct patterns for commercial paper rates during 1948–55, a fact making the adjustment for this period of questionable value. While the pattern for nine- to twelve-month Treasury securities prior to 1955 is quite similar to the one for Treasury bills (column 1 of Table 2-2), the factors are not sufficiently faithful to the SI ratios, in this study's view, to warrant an adjustment. In the later period, however, the seasonal influence is unambiguous. Chart 2-12 plots the time series of seasonal factors of the four short-term series considered in this study.

After 1960 the seasonal amplitudes of all the short-term series rapidly decline. While some seasonality persists after 1963, an adjustment will unavoidably introduce some additional error into the series. Whether the elimination of the true seasonal is worth the increased danger of introducing error as a result of adjusting for a spurious seasonal factor is an isssue the user must decide. Table 2-3 lists the periods during which, in this study's view, the seasonal is worth adjusting for.

TABLE 2-3. *Suggested Periods for Adjusting Short-Term Series*

Security	Adjustment Period
Treasury bill rates	1948–65
Bankers' acceptance rates	1948–63
Commercial paper rates	1956–65
9–12 month Treasury security rates	1955–65

Long-Term Securities

Summary Statistics

The seasonal amplitudes of yields on long-term bonds are not high. In only two of the thirteen cases listed in Table 2-4 does the highest estimated factor for a given bond exceed 4 per cent and in only four cases 3 per cent (column 8). Notwithstanding the low amplitudes, the computed F statistics signify stable seasonality in all but two cases and in most cases by a wide margin (column 6). Finally,

CHART 2-12. Seasonal Factors for Short-Term Interest Series, 1948–65

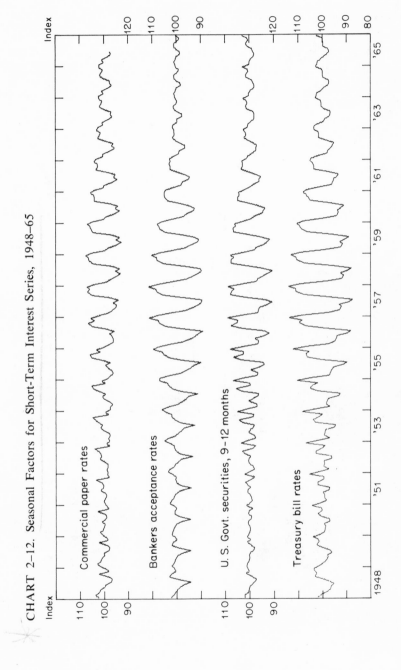

TABLE 2-4. *Measures of the Relative Importance of the Seasonal Components in the Variation of Yields on Long-Term Bonds, 1948–65*

Series	Percentage of Total Variance of Series Due to Each Component			Average Month-to-Month Percentage Changes Without Regard to Sign of Seasonal Component $\bar{S}$	Ratio of Column 4 to Corresponding Figures for the Cyclical Component $\bar{S}/\bar{C}$	F Test for Stable Seasonality	Date and Factor of Seasonal High and Low for Whole Period[a]			
							High		Low	
	I	C	S				Date	Factor (percentage)	Date	Factor (percentage)
	(1)	(2)	(3)	(4)	(5)	(6)	(7)	(8)	(9)	(10)
Municipals[b]										
Highest rating	44.23	34.78	21.00	1.18	0.78	2.855[c]	Sept. 1958	104.7	Feb. 1958	96.6
Lowest rating	45.97	36.30	17.72	0.86	0.70	1.515	Sept. 1958	102.3	Apr. 1960	97.7
High grade (S & P)	55.38	26.74	17.88	1.05	0.82	2.390[c]	Sept. 1958	103.5	Feb. 1955	07.1
Railroads										
Highest rating	34.65	45.46	19.89	0.44	0.66	7.230[c]	Sept. 1957	101.8	Mar. 1957	98.3
Lowest rating	36.92	38.36	24.71	0.59	0.81	7.111[c]	Dec. 1956	101.6	Mar. 1954	97.9

(continued)

TABLE 2-4 (continued)

Series	Percentage of Total Variance of Series Due to Each Component			Average Month-to-Month Percentage Changes Without Regard to Sign of Seasonal Component $\bar{S}$	Ratio of Column 4 to Corresponding Figures for the Cyclical Component $\bar{S}/\bar{C}$	F Test for Stable Seasonality	Date and Factor of Seasonal High and Low for Whole Period[a]			
							High		Low	
	I	C	S				Date	Factor (percentage)	Date	Factor (percentage)
	(1)	(2)	(3)	(4)	(5)	(6)	(7)	(8)	(9)	(10)
Corporates										
Highest rating	37.74	38.63	23.62	.54	.78	5.806[c]	Sept. 1957	102.2	Mar. 1957	97.5
Lowest rating	31.34	45.72	22.94	.43	.72	7.851[c]	Oct. 1957	101.7	Mar. 1955	98.5
Public utilities										
Highest rating	34.60	38.92	26.48	0.61	0.82	7.290[c]	Oct. 1958	103.2	Mar. 1958	97.2
Lowest rating	38.26	41.22	20.52	0.44	0.70	7.078[c]	Oct. 1957	101.7	Mar. 1955	98.5
Industrials										
Highest rating	46.42	29.75	23.83	0.66	0.89	4.130[c]	Sept. 1957	102.3	Mar. 1958	97.6

(continued)

TABLE 24 (concluded)

Series	Percentage of Total Variance of Series Due to Each Component			Average Month-to-Month Percentage Changes Without Regard to Sign of Seasonal Component $\bar{S}$	Ratio of Column 4 to Corresponding Figures for the Cyclical Component $\bar{S}/\bar{C}$	F Test for Stable Seasonality	Date and Factor of Seasonal High and Low for Whole Period[a]			
							High		Low	
	I	C	S				Date	Factor (percent-age)	Date	Factor (percent-age)
	(1)	(2)	(3)	(4)	(5)	(6)	(7)	(8)	(9)	(10)
Industrials Lowest rating	29.12	53.34	17.54	0.36	0.57	6.974[c]	Oct. 1957	101.4	Mar. 1958	98.6
U.S. Treasury Long term	7.51	40.42	2.08	0.50	0.55	1.787	Sept. 1957[b]	102.8	Apr. 1957	98.0
3–5 years	3.73	37.76	8.51	1.45	0.71	3.642[c]	Sept. 1957	105.8	Apr. 1959	95.2

[a] A moving seasonal component was estimated for the four series. Columns 7 and 9 list the dates when the amplitudes of the seasonal component were greatest and columns 8 and 10 the values of the estimated seasonal factors for these dates.

[b] The estimated seasonal factor for September 1958 was also 102.8.

[c] Significant at the 1 per cent level.

again notwithstanding the low peak amplitudes, as well as the seasonal components' relatively low average month-to-month percentage changes without regard to sign (column 4), the estimated percentages of total variation of the series due to the seasonal components (column 3) are roughly comparable and a little higher than the corresponding figure for Treasury bill rates.

These summary statistics are likely to be more reliable than the corresponding statistics for short-term securities because in the long-term bond rates, exclusive of the two Treasury series, the seasonality persisted throughout most of the study period, although with some changes in both pattern and amplitude. The summary statistics for three- to five-year and long-term Treasury securities, however, largely reflect the seasonal flourish in the late fifties. Both its small amplitude and its shifting pattern likely contribute to the persistence of seasonality in long-term bonds (as of 1965 the seasonal influence in most of the series was minute but discernible) since these characteristics in effect obscure the seasonal variation and thereby lessen the likelihood of investors trading them away.[38]

Although there is a general bell-shaped pattern to the seasonal amplitudes of the long-term securities during the postwar period, the relative rise in the late fifties is not as pronounced as in the case of the short-term securities nor is it as pronounced in the private long-term rates as in the Treasury rates. Table 2-5 lists the variances of the seasonal factors of a given year for selected years for all the securities considered in this study. The variance of the twelve monthly factors is a convenient measure of the over-all seasonal amplitude for a given year. The bell-shaped pattern refers to the increase in the securities from 1953 to 1957 and their decrease to 1963. (The bell is actually quite symmetrical, a fact that is hidden by the different spans of the two periods.) Except for the railroad (lowest quality) securities, the table supports the generalization stated above.

There is a curious consistency in the relations among the seasonal factors of the several long-term series, a consistency for which there is no mechanical explanation. In Table 2-5, for example, the seasonal

[38] A small amplitude does not by itself impugn the significance of the seasonal component. The seasonal amplitude for the series on the stock of money, for example, is never more than 3 per cent; although the value of the F statistic in the postwar period is a robust 281. A comparison between column 5 in Tables 2-1 and 2-4 shows that relative to the variation of the cyclical component the seasonal amplitude of long-term bond rates is typically greater than that of short-term rates.

TABLE 2-5. *Variance of Seasonal Factors for Selected Years for All Securities Considered*

Security	1953	1957	1963	1965
Long-term bonds				
Municipals				
Highest rating	2.789	6.386	1.395	1.279
Lowest rating	1.182	2.085	0.734	0.605
High grade (S & P)	2.914	3.614	1.624	1.445
Corporates				
Highest rating	0.516	2.208	0.224	0.145
Lowest rating	0.664	1.132	0.071	0.053
Industrials				
Highest rating	0.557	2.286	0.398	0.302
Lowest rating	0.588	1.014	0.112	0.075
Railroads				
Highest rating	0.386	1.350	0.115	0.062
Lowest rating	1.300	0.846	0.211	0.223
Public utilities				
Highest rating	0.762	3.580	0.260	0.144
Lowest rating	0.381	2.490	0.094	0.075
U.S. Treasury				
Long term	0.231	2.161	0.253	0.096
3–5 years	2.756	14.455	0.992	0.308
Short-term securities				
U.S. Treasury bills	15.453	92.910	5.080	2.996
Commercial paper	5.684	25.341	4.252	NA
Bankers' acceptances	12.816	67.158	1.603	0.734
U.S. Treasury 9–12 months	6.843	42.367	2.425	1.977

NOTE: Each number signifies the variance of the twelve seasonal factors computed separately for each of the years and securities shown.

NA = not available.

amplitude in 1957 for yields on lowest rated security groups is in every case less than the amplitude for the corresponding highest rated group; except for railroad bonds, this relationship holds in 1963 and 1965 as well.[39] Table 2-6 lists the correlation coefficients for the twelve monthly factors in 1957 of each of the long-term groups of securities with those of each of the other groups. In almost all cases

[39] Column 3 of Table 2-4 shows that the seasonal accounts for a smaller part of the total variation of low quality than of high quality bonds and the cyclical component accounts for a higher proportion (except for rails). This study is unable to explain the phenomenon.

TABLE 2-6. *Coefficients Among the Seasonal Factors in 1957 for All the Long-Term Securities Considered*

Series	Municipals High Grade (S&P)	Municipals Highest Rating	Corporates Highest Rating	Corporates Lowest Rating	Industrials Highest Rating	Industrials Lowest Rating	U.S. Treasury Long Term	U.S. Treasury 3–5 Years	Railroads Highest Rating	Railroads Lowest Rating	Public Utilities Highest Rating
Municipals											
Highest rating	.9627										
Lowest rating	.9385	.9596									
Corporates											
Highest rating	.9644	.9349									
Lowest rating	.7226	.7040	.8263								
Industrials											
Highest rating	.9749	.9307	.9660	.7223							
Lowest rating	.7320	.7178	.8196	.9765	.7237						
U.S. Treasury											
Long term	.9222	.9153	.8793	.7708	.8438	.8062					
3–5 years	.6553	.8514	.9036	.7914	.8440	.8251	.9400				
Railroads											
Highest rating	.9370	.8943	.9568	.8654	.8923	.8559	.9163	.9346			
Lowest rating	.7920	.6986	.8752	.9126	.8084	.9168	.7567	.8334	.8993		
Public utilities											
Highest rating	.9156	.9194	.9741	.8905	.9057	.8749	.8860	.9015	.9469	.8597	
Lowest rating	.6860	.7252	.7967	.9650	.6962	.9512	.7435	.7369	.8015	.8152	.8774

NOTE: Each coefficient, based on twelve observations, is computed by cross correlating the twelve factors of the vertical and horizontal series. Diagonal elements are omitted.

the coefficients exceed .7; in most they exceed .8; and in many they exceed .9. The high correlations denote the substantial uniformity in the seasonal patterns of the long-term yields during the period of peak seasonality. Moreover, in virtually every case the correlation between any group of securities, say corporates and industrials, is greater for comparisons among security groups of the same quality rating. Along the last row, for example, the correlation between the factors for the lowest rated version of the public utility group and those for, say, industrials-lowest rating, is greater than the correlation between the former and industrials-highest rating. In the row above, the correlations between the factors for the highest rated public utility group are greater in cases where the highest rated version of the paired group is considered in place of the lowest rated version of the same group. The correlations, of course, are not as high in years outside the period of peak seasonality; nor is the characteristic just described as conspicuous. These figures are shown in Tables 2-7 and 2-8.

By far the lowest correlations are with the long-term Treasury securities in 1965. These low coefficients help substantiate the conclusion that there is no seasonality in the series at the end of the study period. Evidence of uniformity is never more than suggestive. However, the more uniformity, the greater are the similarities among independently calculated results and the less likely are explanations of any given result that depend on alleged accidents or quirks in the computation. In this sense the similarity of the seasonal patterns and the curious relations among security groups of homogeneous rating constitute prima facie cases for the existence of a seasonal pattern, indictments, so to speak, on which it now behooves this study to obtain a conviction.

Before 1955 the typical seasonal pattern for yields on long-term securities describes low points in the first four months of the year and highs for the remainder, excepting a slight dip below 100.0 in November. The trough usually appeared in February or March, while the peak varied between July and December. The pattern changed in the 1954–56 period to one with a slight high in January, a rapid fall to a trough usually in March, continued lows through July, then a steep incline to a peak in September, and finally a gradual decline to December, still above the line. Table 2-9 lists the average seasonal factors for yields on long-term securities for selected years, computed by arithmetically averaging the monthly factors for a given year, one at a time, of the thirteen long-term series. The recorded January factor, for example, is the average of all the January factors for the

TABLE 2-7. *Coefficients Among the Seasonal Factors in 1953 for All the Long-Term Securities Considered*

Series	Municipals			Corporates		Industrials		U.S. Treasury		Railroads		Public Utilities
	High Grade (S&P)	Highest Rating	Lowest Rating	Highest Rating	Lowest Rating	Highest Rating	Lowest Rating	Long Term	3–5 Years	Highest Rating	Lowest Rating	Highest Rating
Municipals												
Highest rating	.9609											
Lowest rating	.7981	.8087										
Corporates												
Highest rating	.8679	.7863	.7454									
Lowest rating	.7224	.5943	.5041	.8114								
Industrials												
Highest rating	.8880	.8268	.8020	.9185	.5921							
Lowest rating	.6384	.5045	.4577	.7622	.9669	.5380						
U.S. Treasury												
Long term	.7881	.7092	.8303	.7772	.6281	.7944	.5338					
3–5 years	.3472	.1879	.3052	.6097	.5854	.4269	.5906	.5879				
Railroads												
Highest rating	.7056	.5705	.4289	.8722	.9021	.7061	.8373	.5518	.5505	.9619		
Lowest rating	.7316	.6001	.5127	.8660	.9774	.6681	.9407	.6040	.5792			
Public utilities												
Highest rating	.8468	.7739	.7470	.9737	.8165	.8522	.7907	.7718	.6739	.8037	.8382	
Lowest rating	.5580	.4714	.4266	.6534	.9171	.3765	.9331	.4897	.6088	.7142	.8548	.7272

NOTE: Same as Table 2-6.

TABLE 2-8. Coefficients Among the Seasonal Factors in 1965 for All the Long-Term Securities Considered

Series	Municipals			Corporates		Industrials		U.S. Treasury		Railroads		Public Utilities
	High Grade (S&P)	Highest Rating	Lowest Rating	Highest Rating	Lowest Rating	Highest Rating	Lowest Rating	Long Term	3–5 Years	Highest Rating	Lowest Rating	Highest Rating
Municipals												
Highest rating	.8655											
Lowest rating	.8308	.7063										
Corporates												
Highest rating	.6837	.7054	.8218									
Lowest rating	.7762	.7062	.8174	.9384								
Industrials												
Highest rating	.5769	.5751	.6732	.9535	.8958							
Lowest rating	.5012	.5032	.3760	.6152	.6248	.6149						
U.S. Treasury												
Long term	−.0939	−.3798	−.0377	−.1206	.0191	.0169	−.4666					
3–5 years	.2306	.0658	.5929	.5911	.5510	.6210	.1167	.5138				
Railroads												
Highest rating	.3308	.1636	.6548	.6029	.5654	.5585	.1542	.2523	.8091			
Lowest rating	.7303	.6211	.8418	.8538	.9189	.7912	.3435	.1191	.5646	.6900		
Public utilities												
Highest rating	.7939	.7504	.8317	.9216	.8983	.8833	.6508	−.1121	.4939	.3914	.7607	
Lowest rating	.5433	.3077	.4219	.6064	.7205	.7434	.4972	.4636	.5530	.4100	.5857	.6382

NOTE: Same as Table 2-6.

TABLE 2-9. *Average Seasonal Factors for Yields on Long-Term Securities for Selected Years*

	1953	1957	1963	1965
January	99.3	100.4	100.1	99.8
February	98.7	98.4	99.6	99.5
March	98.8	97.9	99.3	99.6
April	99.3	98.3	99.3	99.5
May	100.4	98.6	99.3	99.4
June	101.1	99.2	100.0	100.0
July	100.7	99.4	100.4	100.4
August	100.5	103.1	100.3	100.2
September	101.1	102.5	100.7	100.6
October	100.5	101.9	100.5	100.4
November	99.8	101.2	100.3	100.1
December	100.4	101.0	100.4	100.3

NOTE: The figures for each month are computed by arithmetically averaging the seasonal factors for that month of the thirteen long-term securities considered in this study.

given year. In addition to the change in the seasonal pattern, the differences in the seasonal amplitude between the peak period in the late fifties and that before and after the period are revealed as well.

While Table 2-9 adequately describes the general seasonal pattern, its evolution, and the order of magnitude involved, it necessarily obscures important differences in the several series. The high correlations in Table 2-6 reveal a similarity in the patterns of most series during the late fifties; although the considerable differences in amplitude revealed in Table 2-5 are not, of course, accounted for. The somewhat lower correlations in 1953 and the considerably lower ones in 1965 lessen the usefulness of the computed average pattern outside the 1955–60 period. In addition to the variety of patterns and amplitudes in the long-term series, there are also differences in the quality of the estimates of the seasonal factors. To decide on the extent of appropriate adjustment for each series it is therefore necessary to examine the familiar charts of factors and SI ratios, which we do now.

Graphic Analysis of Seasonal Variation

U.S. TREASURY SECURITIES. Chart 2-13 plots the seasonal factors and SI ratios for long-term U.S. Treasury securities (the scale is twice that used for short-term securities). The pattern prior to 1953 is very

CHART 2–13. SI Ratios and Seasonal Factors for Yields on Long-Term U.S. Bonds, 1948–65

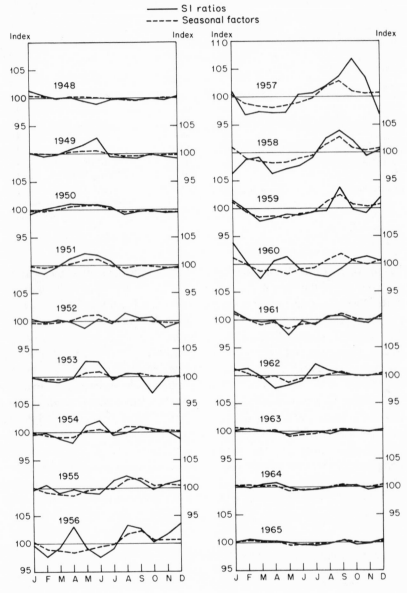

similar to the early pattern of commercial paper rates, the peak coming in midyear and the trough in the fall. Although the amplitude is small, the pattern is quite real. The reason for the asserted reality resides not only in the similarity between the curves connecting the SI ratios and the ones connecting the factors but also in the position of the factors, falling as they do between the SI ratios and the 100.0 level. The latter result is most conspicuous for 1951 and has the effect of both dampening the adjusted series and minimizing the possibility of the adjustment contributing to the random fluctuation of the series. As in the case of the Treasury bill rates during the late fifties, the assurance that all that is removed is seasonal comes at the expense of understating what seasonal influence there is. The data for 1952 provide a good example of the dilemma involved in adjusting a series with a rapidly shifting pattern: the two curves are virtually unrelated. Use of the estimated factors may then introduce random errors into the series. In 1953 the pattern assumes the shape of the average pattern of Table 2-9 and, hence, the high correlations in Table 2-7 between the long-term Treasuries and the other securities. In the following years the pattern rapidly bends into the one typical of all the rates in the late fifties. Even in this period the fit is not very good, although the pattern is clearly there; and the amplitude is among the highest of the long-term security groups. One notices, even in the late fifties, how the low part of the pattern is gradually extended through the summer, as with the short-term securities. By 1965 the pattern is very different from the average pattern and, in fact, inversely correlated with those of most of the long-term series (Table 2-8). It is clear, then, that the low F statistic noted earlier for this series is due both to a constantly shifting pattern resulting in a mediocre fit and an unstable pattern even within the periods it describes. That a seasonal pattern existed in the late fifties and even that a systematic ripple persisted to the end of the study period is, in this study's view, established. Whether there is reasonable cause to adjust the series outside the 1955–59 period is somewhat dubious; and whether it would be meaningful to adjust a series for such a short period is equally dubious. This series is perhaps one that may be profitably left alone.

Chart 2-14 plots the seasonal factors and SI ratios for U.S. Treasury securities with three- to five-year maturities. There is a fairly clear pattern for the years 1948–60 followed by several years of erratic movement—the pattern for 1953 is typical. In 1955 the pattern assumes the shape it maintains for the remainder of the decade. In

CHART 2–14. SI Ratios and Seasonal Factors for Yields on U.S. Government Three- to Five-Year Securities, 1948–65

——— S I ratios
- - - - - Seasonal factors

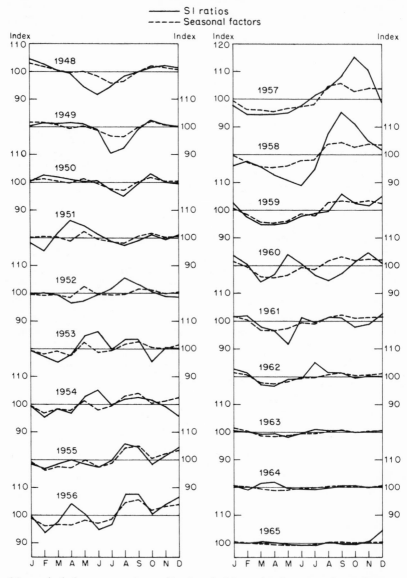

this period the seasonal amplitude of this series is somewhere between the typical amplitude of short- and long-term securities. From 1960 on, however, the seasonal pattern is too unstable to justify an adjustment.

MUNICIPAL SECURITIES. Of all the long-term securities, the F statistics are among the lowest and the amplitudes among the highest for the yields on the three municipal bond series considered. The F statistics, however, are not brought down, as in the case of long-term Treasuries, by constantly shifting patterns of small amplitude and erratic transition periods; nor is the F statistic spuriously high as a result of the attenuation of the peak seasonal in the late fifties. Chart 2-15 plots the seasonal factors and SI ratios for yields on municipal bonds of highest rating. Excluding the first two years, the pattern in the early years is quite similar to the general pattern of this period described in Table 2-9: lows during the first four months, a June peak, but then, unlike the general pattern, a rapid decline to lows in the last two months. The large gaps between the curves, implied in the unusually large irregular component recorded in column 1 of Table 2-4, reflect changes in the seasonal amplitude of the series rather than an unstable pattern. Although the greater dispersion of a given month's SI ratios results in less reliable estimates of the seasonal factors, the diagrams reveal the SI ratios for given months to fluctuate about means that clearly remain above or remain below the 100.0 line. From 1949 through 1954, every June is a high, and every January and December are lows. In 1955 the new pattern emerges, again similar to the general pattern of the late fifties, with a trough in February or March and a peak in September. The pattern changes somewhat after 1959, but persists in similar form through the end of the study period.

In this case, therefore, and in the case of the other municipal groups not shown here, a basis for seasonal adjustment exists in spite of the feeble F statistics. There is an important difference between the effects of random variations in seasonal amplitude and those in the seasonal pattern on identifying the presence of seasonality. In the former case, by narrowly defining extreme points, the program can dampen the estimated seasonal amplitudes, imposing a downward bias on the estimated means, and thereby reducing the risk of wrongly affirming the presence of seasonality. In the latter case, the danger is greater that the program will impose a seasonal pattern on the series.

PRIVATE LONG-TERM SECURITIES. Although there are differences in detail it is convenient to describe the seasonality of yields on private long-term securities for the group as a whole. This group's seasonal pattern differs from that of the municipals by its somewhat smaller amplitude and its greater stability. Table 2-4 records higher F statistics,

CHART 2–15. SI Ratios and Seasonal Factors for Yields on Municipal
Bonds, Highest Rating, 1948–65

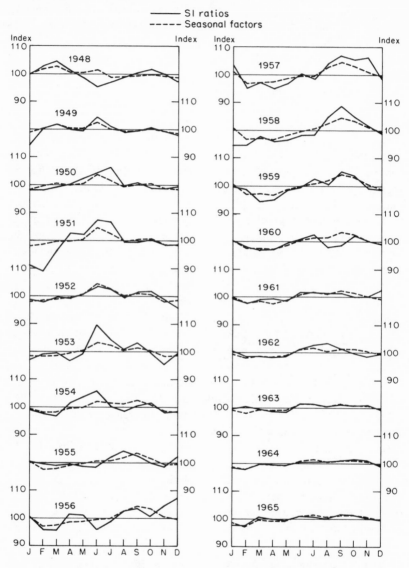

lower residual variation, and smaller peak amplitudes (columns 6, 1,
8, and 9, respectively), and Table 2-5 shows the seasonal amplitudes
of the private groups to be less than those of the municipals with very

few exceptions throughout the study period.[40] The curves connecting the SI ratios in Chart 2-16, drawn for yields on corporate securities of lowest rating, are clearly less choppy than the corresponding curves for municipal securities, and the amplitude of the corporates is smaller. The patterns are somewhat erratic through 1951, but thereafter they are quite similar to the first pattern listed in Table 2-9. In 1955 the January factor starts to rise and the low period extends into the summer, typical of the general pattern in this period. This pattern persists to the end of the study period although its amplitude at the end is barely perceptible.

The stability of the pattern and therefore the evidence of seasonality is further illustrated in Chart 2-17, where the SI ratios and the factors are plotted one month at a time across the years. There are five months for which the direction of seasonal change is consistent throughout the study period: March, April, September, October, and November. Beginning in 1950 the SI ratios for March are consistently below the 100.0 line; their amplitudes in the early fifties are as great as in the late fifties, tapering off in 1960 but persisting to the end of the study period. The factor curve is virtually identical with the curve connecting the SI ratios. Again for April, the SI ratios remain consistently below the 100.0 level, crossing it briefly in 1951 and again in 1961. Except for these two years the factor curve either coincides with the SI curve or rises above it; in any case it does not exaggerate the seasonal variation. In September, barring 1951 and 1960, and again in October the SI ratios are consistently above 100.0. Of the four months only October evinces a greater amplitude in the late fifties; and the factor curve virtually nullifies the increase. The curves for the middle months, May through August, and the one for January all cross the 100.0 line at about 1954, signifying the changed pattern.

While there are differences in the patterns of the various groups of long-term securities, a detailed account of each of the series would be almost as tedious to write as it would be to read. In lieu of that, Chart 2-18 plots time series of the seasonal factors for all the long-term series considered in this study.

---

[40] It may be that an explanation of the difference in amplitude between the two groups of securities lies in the greater ease with which private corporations can time their borrowing to correspond with periods of seasonally low yields.

CHART 2–16. SI Ratios and Seasonal Factors for Yields on Corporate Bonds, Lowest Rating, 1948–65

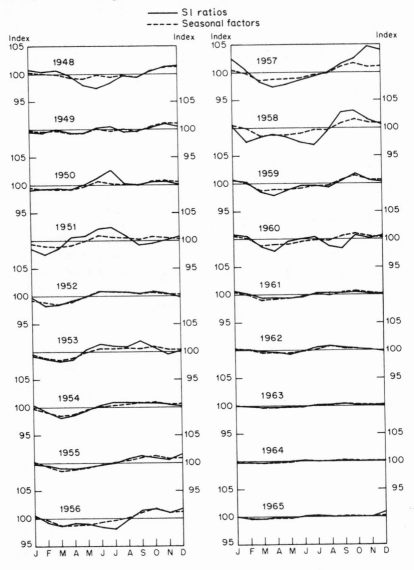

Summary of Long-Term Bonds

In spite of the low seasonal amplitudes in long-term bonds, both the summary statistics and the diagrams confirm the presence of sea-

CHART 2-17. SI Ratios and Seasonal Factors for Yields on Corporate Bonds, Lowest Rating, One Month at a Time, 1948–65

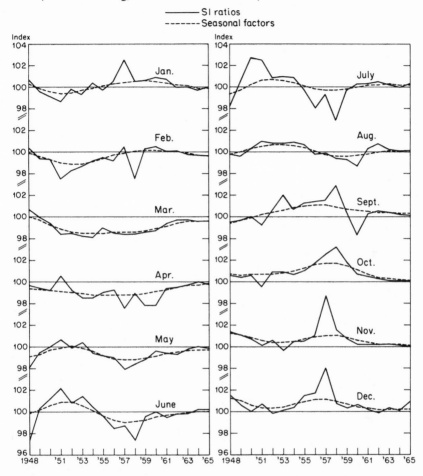

——— SI ratios
------- Seasonal factors

sonality in these series throughout most of the sample period. Starting about 1950, the seasonal factors are typically below the 100.0 line in the first four months of the year, the trough usually occurring in March, rise above the line in midyear and beyond it to a peak in September or October, then fall back to the 100.0 line in November and December. Starting in 1955, the midyear months stay below the 100.0 line, and the months at either end rise a little. The key seasonal months—March, April, September, and October—are largely unaffected by this change. The prominent bell-shaped pattern in the

CHART 2–18. Seasonal Factors for Long-Term Interest Rates, 1948–65

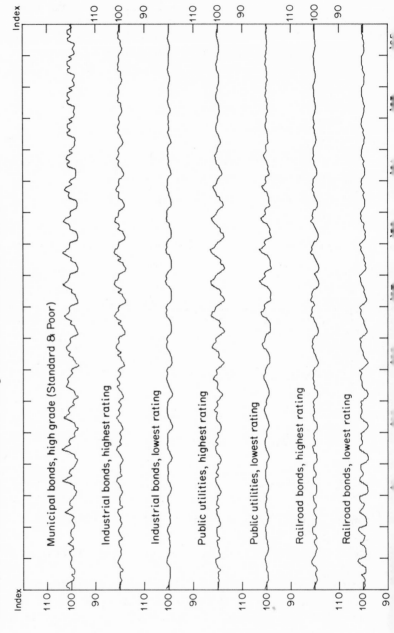

Municipal bonds, high grade (Standard & Poor)

Industrial bonds, highest rating

Industrial bonds, lowest rating

Public utilities, highest rating

Public utilities, lowest rating

Railroad bonds, highest rating

Railroad bonds, lowest rating

CHART 2–18 (concluded)

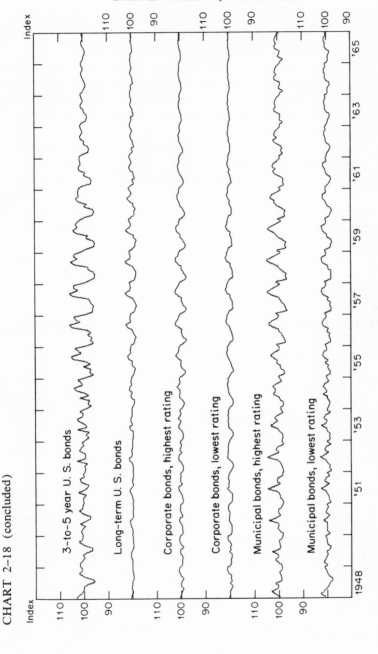

Index

3-to-5 year U. S. bonds

Long-term U. S. bonds

Corporate bonds, highest rating

Corporate bonds, lowest rating

Municipal bonds, highest rating

Municipal bonds, lowest rating

1948 '51 '53 '55 '57 '59 '61 '63 '65

seasonal factors described for the short-term rates is less prominent in the case of long-term bonds, although the seasonal factors for some of the series clearly evolve in this manner.

As in the other series considered in this study, there are some years for which there appears to be no seasonal movement at all or for which, whether present or not, the seasonal is too small and uncertain to be measured. There is no accepted method for reliably choosing the years for which an adjustment is appropriate. Nor do the necessary conditions prevail for reliable inference from the summary statistics. Although there is a large subjective element involved in the method used in this study, the primary criterion has been the apparent stability in the seasonal patterns regardless of their amplitudes. But the judgment involved in this study is restricted to the choice of accepting the results of the X-11 program. Additional judgment is required to improve this adjustment. Table 2-10 presents the suggested dates for accepting the machine adjustment. For convenience

TABLE 2-10. *Suggested Periods for Accepting Seasonally Adjusted Interest Rate Series*

Series	Period
Treasury bills	1948–65
9–12 month Treasury securities	1955–65
3–5 year Treasury securities	1955–59
Long-term Treasury securities	1955–59
Commercial paper rates	1956–63
Bankers' acceptances	1948–63
Industrial bonds[a]	1956–65
Industrial bonds[b]	1950–65
Public utility bonds[a]	1950–65
Public utility bonds[b]	1951–61
Corporate bonds[a]	1952–65
Corporate bonds[b]	1952–65
Railroad bonds[a]	1953–63
Railroad bonds[b]	1950–65
Municipal bonds[a]	1950–65
Municipal bonds[b]	1950–65
Municipal bonds[c]	1950–65

[a]Highest rating.
[b]Lowest rating.
[c]High grade Standard and Poor.

the table includes the findings for all seventeen series considered in this study.

Appendix: Alternate Adjustments of Treasury Bill Rates

There are several reasons for the differences between the curves of SI ratios and seasonal factors in Charts 2-7 and 2-8. Most important among them is, of course, the seasonal factors' intended elimination of the irregular component through its smoothing out the nonrecurring variation. One-time jumps, therefore, as in May 1960, appropriately result in gaps between the two curves. It is easy to identify these atypical (or irregular) jumps when they produce inversions (in the case of May 1960 from a low to a high), but the identification is more difficult when the atypical events exaggerate the usual fluctuation without seriously distorting the pattern. In 1958, for example, the two curves are far apart. There are no inversions, but the July trough is well below its value in adjacent years, and the October peak is high—both absolutely and relative to adjacent months. Short-term interest rates were dropping sharply in the spring of 1958 (see Chart 2-19), and investors, anticipating a continuing decline, borrowed heavily to purchase maturing Treasury bonds that earned rights to a new issue in June. Short-term capital gains on the new issue appeared certain as all the indicators agreed the decline in rates would continue. When short-term rates suddenly turned upward in June, they left many highly leveraged investors on the wrong end of the fulcrum. In addition to distorting the SI ratios, the resulting chaos invited a congressional investigation.[41]

While it is easy and proper to shield the seasonal adjustment from one-time changes in the pattern of SI ratios, it is much harder to apportion brief changes (whether lasting one or a few years) in the amplitude of a fixed pattern of SI ratios. There is no requirement that the seasonal amplitude be stable from year to year or even that it change only gradually. For example, the seasonal in the consumption of soft drinks is related to the weather; a particularly warm summer will result in an atypically large seasonal amplitude. An adjustment that is constrained to gradual changes in amplitude will arbitrarily truncate the seasonal amplitude in the above example. Alternatively,

[41] Part of the results of this investigation are recorded in a fascinating study of the crisis. See *The Treasury-Federal Reserve Study of the Government Securities Market,* Part II, Washington, D.C., February 1960.

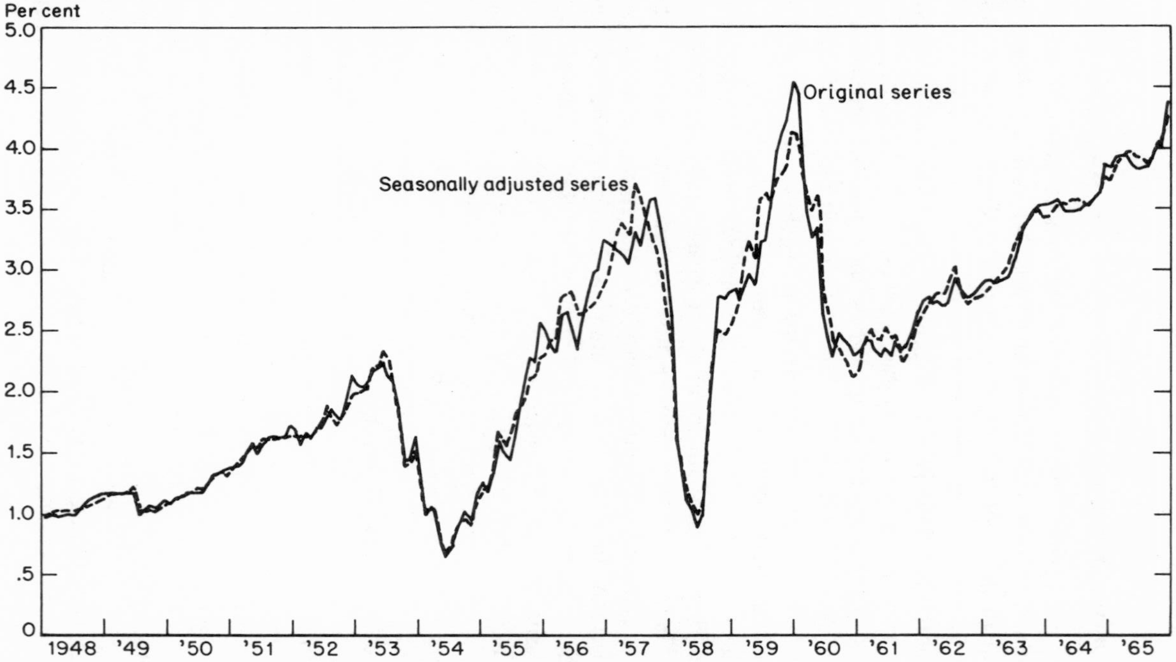

CHART 2–19. Original and Seasonally Adjusted Series of Treasury Bill Rates, 1948–65

one may argue that seasonal analysis is concerned not with the relation between climate and soft drink consumption but only with systematic intrayear changes in consumption regardless of cause. This point of view is predicated on the idea that seasonals are important because they are predictable by mechanical projections of past behavior; any variation that is not predictable in this way, even when it is caused by the same variables that cause the predictable variation, is not seasonal. In cases, such as interest rates, where there are abrupt changes in the amplitude of seasonal, or, if you will, intrayear, variation, the choice of the appropriate adjustment depends on which of the two concepts of a seasonal movement is intended.

To illustrate the practical significance of this issue the study experimented with alternate adjustments of Treasury bill rates. The Kuznets amplitude-ratio method of adjustment is convenient for dealing with an abruptly changing seasonal amplitude provided the month-to-month pattern of factors is fixed, and only the amplitude changes from year to year. The factors are computed by regressing, one year at a time, the twelve modified SI ratios[42] on the set of constant factors obtained by averaging, one month at a time, the modified SI ratios over the whole period. The more similar the particular year's pattern is to the average pattern the higher will be the correlation coefficient; when it is equal to one the regression coefficient will exactly measure the proportionate difference in amplitude between them.[43] Table 2-11 lists the coefficients of correlation and regression, as well as the latter's *t*-value, for the eighteen regressions from 1948 through 1965. All three statistics reveal the bell-shaped pattern in the seasonal amplitude that was noted earlier. Again, the seasonal in 1948 is unusually clear, its pattern being highly correlated with the average pattern. In the following two years the seasonal is still inexplicably strong, although less than in 1948, the pegged prices notwithstanding. After two dormant years in 1951 and 1952, the seasonal emerges

[42] That is, modified to eliminate extreme values. It is clearly important to eliminate the effect of extreme values on a regression computed with twelve observations, although the X-11 modifications, used here, will in some cases dampen the very changes in amplitude the Kuznets method is designed to reveal.

[43] In commenting on this method, Burns and Mitchell (*op. cit.,* pp. 48–49) recommend not accepting the estimate when the correlation coefficient falls below .7. It is clear that when the pattern changes, as in the case of commercial paper rates, the method has no value. The pattern for bill rates, however, is fairly stable; therefore, a low correlation coefficient signifies doubtful seasonality.

TABLE 2-11. *Summary Statistics for Kuznets' Amplitude–Ratio Method Regressions, 1948–56*

Year	Correlation Coefficient (1)	Regression Coefficient (2)	t value (3)	Year (4)	Correlation Coefficient (5)	Regression Coefficient (6)	t value (7)
1948	.9346	.7106	8.3102	1957	.9495	2.4562	9.5708
1949	.8826	.4643	5.9367	1958	.9434	3.0079	8.9945
1950	.7073	.2759	3.1642	1959	.9619	2.2094	11.1281
1951	.3046	.1785	1.0114	1960	.8772	1.4544	5.7780
1952	.3935	.3350	1.3534	1961	.7420	.6177	3.5004
1953	.5977	.4930	2.3575	1962	.6668	.4048	2.8294
1954	.7859	1.0771	4.0198	1963	.7134	.2911	3.2193
1955	.9130	1.5308	7.0785	1964	.6991	.2750	3.0922
1956	.9529	1.9761	9.9303	1965	.6745	.2589	2.8890

NOTE: The regression form for i^{th} year is as follows: Modified SI ratios for year $i = a + b$ (constant seasonal factors) + U. Since the mean value for both variables is 100, the constant term, a, is equal to 100 $(1-b)$. There are twelve observations for each regression.

again in 1953 and more strongly in 1954, although the erratic pattern noted earlier is reflected in a correlation coefficient that is lower than in the following years. The peak seasonal continues through 1960, after which it drops off sharply; and after 1961 the seasonal is very small.

The regression coefficients listed in Table 2-11 are convenient for evaluating the hypothesis that there is a relation between the seasonal and cyclical components. Section II noted that the X-11 method of smoothing the SI ratios over adjacent years to compute the factors necessarily obscures any relation that may exist between its seasonal and cyclical components. There is nothing, however, to prevent the Kuznets amplitude-ratios (the regression coefficients in Table 2-11) from varying with the cyclical component of the series. There is clearly nothing in columns 2 and 6 to reveal any relation between the prominence of the seasonal component and the level of the series as shown in Chart 2-19. The erratic movements in the SI ratios in 1954 and 1958 suggest that the irregular component may be more prominent during cyclical troughs, a proposition that may or may not reflect on the capacity of the Henderson curve to capture sharp turning points.

Columns 4 and 8 of Table 2-12 list the seasonal factors computed

TABLE 2-12. *Seasonal Factors of Treasury Bill Rates for July and December Computed for the Original and the Seasonally Adjusted Series, and the Kuznets' Method (per cent)*

Year	July				December			
	Original (1)	Adjusted (2)	Implicit (3)	Kuznets (4)	Original (5)	Adjusted (6)	Implicit (7)	Kuznets (8)
1948	96.8	100.0	96.9	95.1	103.7	99.8	103.5	104.9
1949	97.0	970.9	97.8	96.9	103.9	99.4	103.3	103.3
1950	97.3	102.1	99.3	98.3	104.6	99.3	103.8	102.1
1951	96.9	102.9	99.8	99.0	105.5	99.1	104.5	101.4
1952	96.2	103.5	99.6	98.1	106.9	99.2	106.0	102.7
1953	94.4	103.1	97.3	97.1	108.4	99.4	107.8	103.8
1954	92.4	102.3	94.5	92.9	110.5	100.1	110.6	107.7
1955	89.8	100.7	90.5	91.0	112.2	100.9	113.2	112.0
1956	88.3	99.8	88.1	87.8	113.8	102.0	116.1	114.8
1957	87.4	99.1	86.6	85.0	113.9	102.4	116.7	118.7
1958	87.9	99.1	87.1	80.4	113.0	102.4	115.8	121.6
1959	89.0	99.0	88.2	85.0	110.5	101.4	112.1	115.2
1960	91.1	99.6	90.8	89.9	107.9	100.3	108.2	109.8
1961	93.3	100.2	93.5	95.9	105.1	99.1	104.2	104.3
1962	95.3	100.8	96.1	97.5	103.5	98.5	101.9	103.1
1963	96.7	101.3	98.0	98.2	102.7	98.3	101.0	102.2
1964	97.6	101.7	99.3	98.3	102.7	98.4	101.1	102.0
1965	98.0	101.9	99.9	98.3	102.6	98.3	100.9	101.9

NOTE: Columns 1 and 5 are the original factors computed with the X-11. Columns 2 and 6 are the factors computed for adjusting the seasonally adjusted series. Columns 3 and 7 are the implicit factors obtained with the double adjustment.

with the Kuznets method.[44] These factors are simply the computed values of the regressions described earlier. The X-11 factors (columns 1 and 5) clearly dampen the changes in seasonal amplitudes. Excluding 1948 and 1949, the Kuznets factors show larger seasonal amplitudes from 1956 through 1960 than the X-11 factors and smaller amplitudes elsewhere. The differences are greatest in 1957 and, expectedly, in 1958. Whereas the X-11's July factors for these years are, respectively, 87.4 and 87.9, the corresponding Kuznets factors are 85.0 and 80.4; for December the X-11 factors are 113.9 and 113.0, respectively, for 1957 and 1958, and the corresponding Kuznets factors, 118.7 and 121.6.

The adjustment's sensitivity to abrupt changes in amplitude is not solely a question of preference. One condition for a perfect adjustment is the absence of seasonality in the adjusted data.[45] Perfection aside, the seasonality that remains in the adjusted data betrays the quality of the original adjustment. In other words, even allowing a gradually changing seasonal, the moving average of the X-11 may not be sufficiently elastic to expunge all the variation that by its own criteria (i.e., its response to a second round) are seasonal. The seasonally adjusted data will in this case retain some remnants of the seasonal pattern. The experiment with the Kuznets method suggests what these remnants will look like.

To illustrate the point, this study ran the seasonally adjusted data once again through the X-11. Columns 1 and 5 of Table 2-12 list the factors for July and December, respectively, obtained with the original adjustment; columns 2 and 6 list the factors with the second adjustment; and columns 3 and 6 the implicit factors computed by dividing the twice-adjusted series (i.e., the series obtained by adjusting the seasonally adjusted series) into the orignal series. When the factor in column 2 is above 100.0, the original estimate of the July factor is too low, that is, the seasonal decline is exaggerated; the implicit factor in column 3 is in this case greater (i.e., closer to 100.0) than the

[44] The other figures in Table 2-12 and curves in Chart 2-10 are explained below.
[45] While necessary, this condition is not sufficient. The adjusted data must also remain faithful to the original in all respects other than seasonality. The trend-cycle values, for example, are free of seasonality but do not otherwise qualify as properly adjusted values of the original series. Lacking perfection, an adjustment method should evince a convergence toward no-seasonality upon successive adjustments of the data, that is, adjustments of the adjusted data. The X-11 appears to satisfy this requirement, although the present study has not considered this issue in any detail.

original factor in column 1. Conversely, when the factor in 2 is below 100.0, the original estimate is too high (i.e., the seasonal trough underestimated) and the factor in 3 is below the factor in 1. When the factor in 6 is below 100.0, the original estimate of the seasonal peak is exaggerated and correspondingly reduced in 7; when above the original estimate it is too low and therefore increased in 7. From 1956 to 1960 the machine understated the seasonal low in July. Some, but very little, seasonal low remains in the adjusted data. In the other years, however, the machine converted the original seasonal lows in the July data to seasonal highs[46] in the adjusted data. In December the seasonal from 1954 to 1960 is understated in the original adjustment and in the remaining years overstated.

Table 2-13 puts the same story a little differently. In 1953 the factors computed in the second adjustment (column 2) denote, with some exceptions and with a smaller amplitude, seasonal movements in the opposite direction from those implied in the original adjustment. In 1958, the seasonal timing implied in both columns 5 and 6 is the same, reflecting the original adjustment's failure to fully remove the seasonal variance in the original series. In 1965, again the directions are reversed.

While these results confirm the expected faultiness in the machine's handling of a moving seasonal component, they emphasize even more that the magnitude of error is usually quite small; for the bill rate, with one exception, it is never more than 3 per cent of the original series and usually much less.[47] However, during the peak period the Kuznets factors differ from the original X-11 factors by up to 7 percentage points. The order of magnitude involved is shown in Chart 2-20 and again in Chart 2-21, where both the original and the

---

[46] "High" and "low" denotes positions above and below 100.0, respectively; "peak" and "trough" denotes highest and lowest, respectively. The Kuznets experiment implies the same result for July but dates the period of understatement in 1956 instead of 1954 for December.

[47] The *F* test for stable seasonality in the second adjustment indicates insignificant seasonality at any level. In adjusting the adjusted data, the machine confronts the same problem of a moving seasonal and therefore similarly underestimates the extent of the original maladjustment. The magnitudes involved there, however, are small, and one may safely ignore this point. In fact, the opposite danger exists that the machine may confuse the relatively much greater irregular component with the seasonal one and exaggerate the extent of the original maladjustment. There is no justification, for example, for the implicit lows in September, October, and November of 1965 (column 11, Table 2-13).

TABLE 2-13. *Seasonal Factors of Treasury Bill Rates for Selected Years Computed for the Original and the Seasonally Adjusted Series, and the Kuznets' Method*

Month	1953				1958				1965			
	Original (1)	Adjusted (2)	Implicit (3)	Kuznets (4)	Original (5)	Adjusted (6)	Implicit (7)	Kuznets (8)	Original (9)	Adjusted (10)	Implicit (11)	Kuznets (12)
Jan.	102.1	98.9	101.0	102.3	108.9	101.6	110.6	112.3	102.3	99.7	102.0	101.1
Feb.	97.0	98.5	95.6	100.0	98.4	99.9	98.3	98.1	102.0	100.5	102.5	99.9
March	99.2	100.8	100.0	98.9	92.1	98.4	90.6	91.8	100.8	101.7	102.5	99.3
April	98.9	101.1	100.0	98.6	91.0	98.1	89.3	89.7	99.3	101.4	100.6	99.2
May	98.7	100.7	99.4	98.5	92.6	95.0	87.9	89.4	97.9	101.4	99.3	99.1
June	94.9	100.1	95.0	97.3	89.4	99.7	89.1	81.9	97.3	101.4	98.7	98.5
July	94.4	103.1	97.3	97.1	87.9	99.1	87.1	80.4	98.0	101.9	99.9	98.3
Aug.	102.9	102.2	105.2	99.9	96.2	99.7	96.0	97.8	99.8	100.7	100.1	99.9
Sept.	103.9	98.9	102.7	102.0	107.4	100.4	107.8	110.5	99.8	97.7	97.4	100.9
Oct.	101.3	99.2	100.6	102.0	110.6	101.7	112.5	110.5	100.0	97.3	97.3	100.9
Nov.	100.0	97.7	97.7	101.9	110.9	102.8	114.0	110.1	100.1	97.9	98.0	100.9
Dec.	108.4	99.4	107.8	103.8	113.0	102.4	115.8	121.6	102.6	98.3	100.9	101.9

CHART 2–20. Unmodified SI Ratios, Original and Implicit Seasonal Factors, and Kuznets' Factors for Treasury Bill Rates

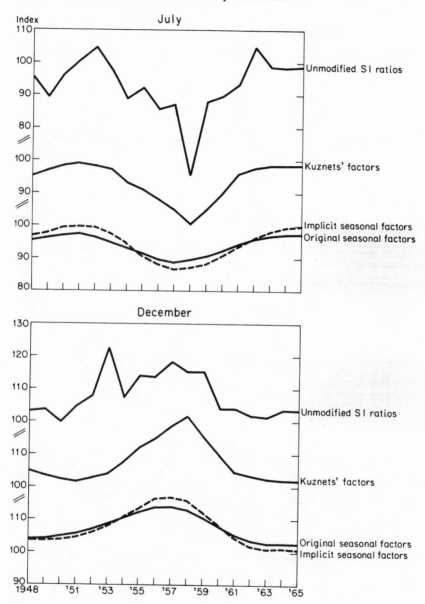

CHART 2–21. SI Ratios, Original and Implicit Seasonal Factors, and Kuznets' Factors for Treasury Bill Rates, Selected Years

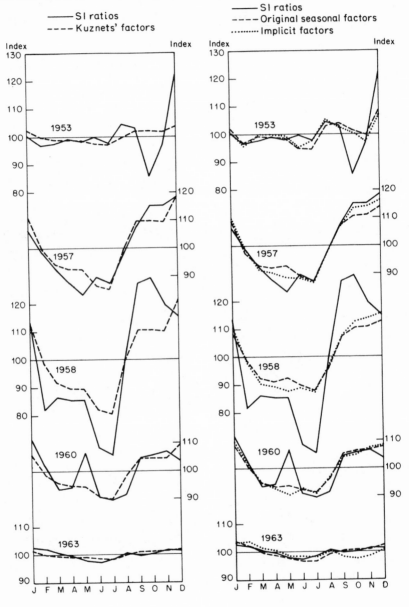

implicit factors, as well as the Kuznets factors, are plotted against the SI ratios. The implicit factors appear to follow the SI ratios slightly better than do the original factors; whether they are therefore preferable is a question on which one can argue both sides. Although the double adjustment method is used in this study for illustrative purposes, further experimentation may demonstrate its usefulness as a method of adjustment when there are abrupt changes in the seasonal amplitude. Whether the single or the double adjustment is preferred there is no compelling reason to reject the machine adjustment for any part of the sample period, although some users may prefer to take the adjusted data back only to about 1953.

IV. DETERMINANTS OF SEASONAL AMPLITUDE

This section considers some topics related to the extent and variation of seasonal amplitudes. One of the topics it deals with is the profitability of arbitrage between periods of seasonally high and low yields on long-term securities. It was found that, taking account of direct transactions and opportunity costs, a relatively small seasonal would elicit arbitrage—the more so the longer is the term to maturity, the smaller the margin requirements, and the greater the stability of the seasonal. The breakeven point for profitable arbitrage, estimated through use of hypothetical though plausible data, is below the seasonal amplitude that actually persisted through most of the study period. The result implies that a relatively high risk premium is attached to the uncertainty with which the seasonal is regarded, as well as the expected dominance of the cyclical and irregular components. The breakeven seasonal adjusted for risk would therefore be much larger. Consideration of the business and bother costs of an arbitrage operation would also raise the breakeven point.

The greater importance of term structure on short-term yield differentials complicates the question of arbitrage in the short-term segment of the securities market. Several authors have observed that the seasonal patterns of some short-term securities lead those of shorter term securities. Since these leads are evidence of investors' awareness of the seasonal movement and more generally of their attempt to forecast short-term rates, they are also evidence of what this study is calling arbitrage. Arbitrage generally implies bridging a known discrepancy between two situations, usually between two markets at a particular time; but when the two situations occur in different periods the knowledge of the later period is at best a good forecast. The unstable character of the seasonal influence on interest rates revealed in Section III implies that using the term arbitrage in connection with seasonals is somewhat misleading. Certainly, arbitrage shades into speculation as the seasonal movement becomes more problematic.

The last part of this section relates changes in the seasonal amplitude of Treasury bill rates with corresponding changes in the seasonal amplitude of other series.[48] The seasonal amplitude of Treasury bill rates is inversely related to the seasonal amplitude of the stock of money and directly related to that of total bills outstanding. This finding, relevant in its own right as a description of events, serves also to illustrate the usefulness of decomposing a series to help explain its behavior. For example, when the aggregate series of interest rates and money supply are correlated, the expected inverse relation is usually obscured by the common effect of economic activity on the cyclical components of both series; although the series frequently turn at different stages of the cycle, there are many periods during which the series are moving in the same direction. However, when the cyclical component is filtered out, the expected inverse relation materializes. By replacing the original series with their seasonal factors, this study estimates the elasticity of short-term demand for credit with respect to interest rates to be a very small but statistically significant —.0237.[49]

Arbitrage

Long-Term Securities

To determine the opportunity for arbitrage between seasonal phases, this study computed the effect on buying and selling prices, under a set of assumed conditions, of various seasonal amplitudes. Consider a twenty-year, 4 per cent bond with semiannual coupons whose

[48] "Seasonal amplitude" refers to the average departure of the monthly factors from 100.0. When the pattern of factors is approximately constant from year to year the change of a given month's factor from one year to the next is a measure of the change in seasonal amplitude.

[49] The appropriateness of the concept of elasticity in the present context is evaluated in a brief appendix to this section.

average price over the year is the $1,000 par value. Assume an investor purchases the bond at its seasonally peak yield in September and sells it, now with nineteen and one half years to maturity, the following March when yields are at their seasonal trough. The present value formula computes the prices in September and March for any desired seasonal change in yield in the following way:

$$\text{September price} = \frac{20}{(1.02 \; P.F.)} + \frac{20}{(1.02 \; P.F.)^2} + \cdots + \frac{20. + 1000}{(1.02 \; P.F.)^{40}},$$

where $P.F. =$ peak seasonal factor, e.g., 101.0; $T.F. =$ trough seasonal factor, e.g., 99.0; semiannual coupon payment is $20; principal is $1,000; and average yield is 2 per cent per half-year.

The computation leads to the result that for each one-tenth of 1 per cent in the seasonal amplitude on either side of the average value (in other words, factors equal to 100.1 and 99.9 for September and March, respectively) the price differential for a $1,000 bond comes to approximately $10.70. For an amplitude of two-tenths of a per cent (i.e., 100.2 and 99.8), the price differential is approximately $21.40.

To estimate the seasonal amplitude necessary to encourage arbitrage, this study estimated the costs and returns to this activity in two hypothetical situations: $5,000 is invested with a 5 per cent and with a 25 per cent margin requirement. In the first case the investor borrows $95,000 and purchases $100,000 worth of bonds; and in the second case $15,000 and purchases $20,000 worth of bonds. Table 2-14 lists the estimated costs in the two situations under the following assumptions:

—Foregone interest on $5,000 at annual rate of 5 per cent
—Transaction cost is $5 per $1,000 bond for combined buy and sell
—Interest cost of borrowed money exceeds bond yield by 1 percentage point per year.[50]

The required peak and trough seasonal factors are computed for breakeven, account being taken of the opportunity costs of the investment.

While the estimated returns obviously depend on the conditions assumed to prevail, the orders of magnitude are established. The smaller the margin requirements, or obversely, the greater the amount borrowed relative to capital, the smaller is the seasonal amplitude required to produce the breakeven price differential. In the example, with a 5 per

---

[50] The greater the difference between the long and short rate the greater is the incentive to arbitrage.

TABLE 2-14. *Costs and Returns of Arbitrage for Twenty-Year Securities Between Seasonal Peaks and Troughs Under Certain Hypothetical Conditions*

Part A: $5,000 Invested With 5 Per Cent Margin Requirement

Costs

Foregone interest[a] on $5,000 for six months at assumed annual rate of 5 per cent	.025 × 5,000 =	$125.
Transactions cost (buy and sell) at assumed $5 per $1,000 bond	5 × 100 =	500.
Interest cost of borrowed money for six months at assumed rate of 1 percentage point above bond yield	.5 × .01 × 95,000 =	475.
Total cost		= $1,100.

Returns

Price differential (between September and March) at assumed $10.70 per $1,000 bond for each .1 per cent of seasonal factor	100 × 10.70	= $1,070.
Required seasonal factors to cover cost	$100 + \dfrac{1,100}{1,070} \times .1$	=100.10%
	$100 - \dfrac{1,100}{1,070} \times .1 =$	99.90

(continued)

cent margin requirement the seasonal factors must exceed 0.10 per cent on either side of the level of rates to just cover the arbitrageur's costs. (While the example does not illustrate the point, it is also true that the greater the term to maturity, the greater the effect on the price differential of any given differential in yield.) When the margin requirements rise to 25 per cent, the required seasonal factors are 0.14 per cent on either side of the level of rates to just cover costs.

The long-term series considered in this study do not differentiate among terms to maturity; therefore, this study did not estimate the relation between term to maturity and the breakeven seasonal factors. However, one certainly expects the seasonal amplitude to diminish with

TABLE 2-14 (concluded)

Part B: $5,000 Invested With 25 Per Cent Margin Requirement

Costs

Foregone interest[a] on $5,000 for six months at assumed annual rate of 5 per cent	$.025 \times 5,000 =$ $125.
Transactions cost (buy and sell) at assumed $5 per $1,000 bond	$5 \times 20 =$ 100.
Interest cost of borrowed money for six months at assumed rate of 1 percentage point above bond yield	$.5 \times .01 \times 15,000 =$ 75.
Total cost	$=$ $300.

Returns

Price differential (between September and March) at assumed $10.70 per $1,000 bond for each .1 per cent of seasonal factor	20×10.70 $= $214.
Required seasonal factors to cover cost	$100 + \dfrac{300}{214} \times .1 = 100.14\%$
	$100 - \dfrac{300}{214} \times .1 = $ 99.86

[a]The capital on which the foregone interest is computed should include half the transactions cost and approximately half the borrowing cost. The greater accuracy, however, will not significantly improve the estimates.

an increasing term to maturity, since the longer the term the sooner will a given seasonal amplitude invite arbitrage. This point may explain the greater amplitude in three- to five-year Treasury securities than in the equivalent long-term securities and in the Treasury bill rates than in the nine- to twelve-month securities. It may also help explain the smaller amplitude of commercial paper rates, which are often six months to maturity, than in the short-term yields on bankers' acceptances and on 91-day Treasury bills.

While margin requirements vary over time and among borrowers, they are always lower for Treasury securities than for private and state-local issues. This point may account for the difference in the longevity of the seasonal amplitude in the two sets of securities, but the study makes only a prima facie case for the issue.

The illustrative example implies that, contrary to common opinion, there is nothing in investment behavior to preclude a seasonal influence on long-term rates provided its amplitude is sufficiently low. Since several years are required before investors perceive a seasonal, virtually any amplitude is possible for a limited period. The low breakeven points for eliciting arbitrage, 0.10 per cent and 0.14 per cent, for 5 per cent and 25 per cent margin requirements, respectively, computed in the example no doubt understate the true values because of additional business costs not incorporated in the example, as well as the point, noted in the introduction, that arbitrage is in effect at one extreme—speculation is at the other—of a continuum as the certainty of the differential between two situations becomes more remote.[51]

Perhaps the greater seasonal amplitude of municipal securities is explained by the greater prominence of their irregular components. It is tempting to generalize this point—the direct relation between seasonal amplitude and relative importance of the irregular component—into an hypothesis. Other influences on these variables, combined with the fact that the seasonal and irregular components are not independently estimated,[52] would tend to obscure the relation, however. Yet we do find that the rank correlations between the ratio of the variance of the irregular component to that of the whole series (Table 2-4, column 1) and the seasonal amplitude as measured by the variance of the factors (Table 2-5) increases from the earliest to the latest years.[53] The increasing correlations imply a movement toward an equilibrium trade-off between yield and certainty of principal. In the absence of other causes of seasonal differences among long-term securities, the observed differentials in seasonal amplitude combined with the observed differences in the relative importance of the irregular component would produce a measure of the rate of trade-off between the two or, in other words, a

---

[51] In this regard it would be better to replace at least in principle the seasonal factors in the illustrative example with confidence intervals or perhaps some form of certainty equivalents.

[52] In fact, the bias in the computation is toward an inverse relation, which strengthens the conclusion.

[53] For the years 1953, 1957, 1963, and 1965, the rank correlation coefficients are .30, .59, .76, and .82, respectively. These figures exclude the two long-term Treasury securities, although there was no attempt to determine how their inclusion would affect the results.

measure of risk premium.[54] While this suggestion helps to illustrate the potential uses of time series decomposition, it suffers from the same problem this study emphasized throughout: the difficulty in distinguishing variations in seasonal amplitude from irregular movements.

Short-Term Securities

While the cost-return analysis of seasonal arbitrage applies equally well to short- as to long-term securities, the calculation of the cost component is complicated by the greater yield differentiation among proximate maturities at the short-end of the yield curve. Whereas the nonseasonal components of the yields on twenty- and nineteen and a half-year securities are approximately the same and therefore do not affect the arbitrage, a substantial differential between a one-month and a two-month or a nine-month and a three-month security may offset any seasonal differential. The calculated costs of arbitrage must, therefore, take account of the former differential.

The tendency for yield curves, the curves relating yield to maturity with maturity, to incline at a diminishing rate is a widely observed phenomenon and its explanation a subject of considerable dispute. Some writers attribute the phenomenon to the greater number of investors with short-term liabilities who prefer to match the maturities of their assets and liabilities than investors with long-term liabilities having similar preferences—the so-called hedging theory. Others emphasize investors' preference for short-term securities to minimize their vulnerability to capital losses—the liquidity preference theory. In either case yields increase with maturity to equilibrate supply and demand. Finally, the expectations hypothesis associates the yield structure with investors' expectations of future interest rates. While this theory does not account for the observed average incline in the yield curve, it can account for the greater differentiation among shorter term yields by recognizing the greater differentiation of investors among their shorter

---

[54] In this context there is no need to consider differences in cyclical variation, which could further account for *aggregate* yield differentials among the various groups of securities, since the seasonal and irregular components abstract alike from the cyclical components of all the series. In principle, this measure of risk premium captures the true relation between the relative *dispersion* of yields and the yield differential of competitive securities as distinct from differences in the expected yields of the securities.

span forecasts, for which they have more information, than their longer
span forecasts, for which they are likely to rely more on extrapola-
tions.[55]

In evaluating the empirical basis for the expectations hypothesis,
Macaulay found evidence of market forecasting in the fact that the
seasonal peak in yields on time loans preceded the peak in call loans.[56]
Banks, he said, aware of the seasonal peak in call money rates during
December, would not tie up money in, say, November, without insur-
ing a return comparable to the average return on call money during
the two months. The yield on time money would therefore peak
earlier. With respect to this phenomenon, its amplitude would have to
be smaller, as well. Consider the same phenomenon from the borrower's point of view: To avoid the December rush he can borrow in
November for two months, perhaps lend the money for one month,
and in effect acquire a forward loan for December at the lower November rate. These transactions would have the effect Macaulay observed,
in addition to smoothing the one-month seasonal. But the borrower's
ability to avoid the peak rate depends on the nonseasonal relation between the two-month and one-month rates in November. If the former
were much greater than the latter, both rates adjusted for seasonality,
what the borrower gains by avoiding the seasonal he loses in the term
structure differential. Since this differential is known in November, it
in part determines the extent of the seasonal arbitrage and, therefore,
of the seasonal amplitude itself. This analysis, thus, suggests that a
relation exists between the slope of the yield curve and the seasonal
amplitude.

Testing for this relation obviously requires data for different but
proximate maturities. The *Treasury Bulletin* publishes series on one-,
two-, and three-month Treasury bills, but these data record the yields
on the last trading day of the month instead of weekly averages, as
in the *Federal Reserve Bulletin's* series on 91-day Treasury bills. The
Treasury Bulletin's series therefore have a considerably greater random
component distorting the estimated seasonal patterns. This study has

[55] There are, in addition, various eclectic theories of the term structure. The
literature on this subject has grown in recent years—much more, unfortunately,
than our knowledge. Two standard works are: David Meiselman, *The Term
Structure of Interest Rates,* Englewood Cliffs, N.J., 1961; and Reuben Kessel,
The Cyclical Behavior of the Term Structure of Interest Rates, Occasional Paper
91, New York, NBER, 1965, and reprinted as Chapter 6 of this volume.

[56] *Op. cit.,* p. 36. Kemmerer, *op. cit.,* p. 18, observed the same phenomenon
and had the same explanation for it.

therefore avoided the *Treasury Bulletin* data. The data do, however, illustrate this section's argument. A direct test for the relation between the seasonal amplitude of one-month rates in December and the non-seasonal yield differential between two- and one-month rates in November is available, simply, in a regression of the SI ratios for one-month bills in December on the differential in the trend-cycle components of two- and one-month rates in November. The correlation coefficient of this regression is .56; the regression coefficient, 53.56; and its *t*-value, 2.68. In general, the variance of the SI ratios for a given year (that is, the extent of seasonal amplitude) is directly related to the slope of the yield curve.[57] The converse is also true: the unadjusted term-structure data partly reflect the seasonal pattern—which was Macaulay's point.

The point is again manifest in the nonseasonal differential between nine- to twelve-month Treasury securities and 91-day Treasury bills. The average differential in July[58] is considerably greater during the period of peak seasonality, 1955–61, than during the earlier or later periods. In the period 1948–54, the mean differential in the trend-cycle values of nine- to twelve-month and 91-day Treasury securities was 6 basis points; in the period 1955–61, 45 basis points; and in 1962–65, 9 basis points (all figures are for July). The figures for

[57] It is obviously necessary to work with the SI ratios, preferably modified for extremes, instead of the seasonal factors themselves since the factors are designed to smooth out the effects of year-to-year changes in seasonal amplitude. In other words, to the extent the above analysis is relevant, the X-11 method of seasonal adjustment is inappropriate. There is nothing sacred about the December figures. In fact, the SI ratios of all seasonally high months are positively related to the slope of the yield curve, and those of all seasonally low months negatively related. In other words, the seasonal amplitude as a whole is positively related to the slope of the yield curve. While the relation for the seasonally high months is understandable, its application to the low months is less clear. Even if the principle stated in the text applied only to the high months, the observed effect on the low months would obtain due to the effect of the high months on the trend-cycle curve. This point is considered in Section II.

[58] July replaces November in this calculation because of the difference in maturities involved. Here the borrower, say the U.S. Treasury, avoids the three-month peak rate in December by borrowing for nine months in July instead of for three months in December, perhaps simultaneously purchasing a six-month security to effect the forward loan. Curiously, the point in the text is most true for July, when the combination of nine- and three-month securities is appropriate to the December peak; although, to a lesser extent it applies to all the months.

each year for the months June through November are given in Table 2-15.

As much as this analysis accurately depicts one aspect of the seasonal problem it implies still another. Typically, though not always, the slope of the yield curve is greatest when the level of rates is low.[59]

TABLE 2-15. *Differential in the Trend-Cycle Values Between Nine- to Twelve-Month and 91-Day Treasury Securities for June Through November, 1948–65 (basis points)*

Year	June	July	August	September	October	November
1948	6	10	13	14	12	11
1949	−4	12	8	6	5	4
1950	0	3	8	4	5	5
1951	24	10	10	9	10	11
1952	−1	−7	5	17	13	4
1953	11	18	23	24	42	17
1954	1	−7	−13	−12	−2	12
1955	30	14	15	11	4	13
1956	11	27	25	26	25	23
1957	13	29	38	43	31	23
1958	44	54	19	−5	2	30
1959	74	78	93	67	66	70
1960	71	62	65	51	53	55
1961	44	53	50	71	64	55
1962	25	0	16	22	19	11
1963	14	9	6	13	14	23
1964	15	16	22	23	23	22
1965	11	9	16	14	14	23

NOTE: The figures are trend-cycle values for nine- to twelve-month securities minus trend-cycle values for 91-day bills. The figures indicate the slope of the yield curve in the designated range independently of the seasonal and irregular movements. For the present purposes the differential in the seasonally adjusted rates (that is, including the irregular component) is a relevant alternative to the figures presented here.

[59] In the jargon of the expectations hypothesis, when current rates are below their normal or typical values they are expected to rise. Longer-term lenders require a higher yield in compensation for the expected capital loss. The concept is analogous to the one underlying the Keynsian liquidity preference function. Admittedly, the figures in Table 2-15 do not cast a very favorable light on this hypothesis; although, most sets of term structure data support it. Reuben Kessel, *op. cit.*, argues that the very short-term part of the yield curve is dominated by liquidity premia which, he argues, are positively related to the level of rates.

Since seasonal amplitudes should depend inversely on the slope, they should also be inversely related to the level of rates, or at least the level in relation to that of adjacent years. In Section III, we found no such relation in the data themselves. It may be, however, that this proposition works to offset a tendency in the opposite direction: In periods of tight money, during cyclical highs, it is harder or more costly to borrow money in order to arbitrage the seasonal movement. Consideration of this point concludes this section of the study.

There are as many ways to arbitrage the seasonal influence in short-term rates as there are combinations of relevant maturities. The following discussion arbitrarily selects nine- and three-month securities and deals only with the peak-to-trough and trough-to-peak relationships; although, in principle, arbitrage is feasible between any pair of months.[60] The rule in seasonal arbitrage is simply to borrow cheaply and lend dearly; that is, borrow in July and lend in December. There are two ways to effect the transaction: Borrow and sell a nine-month security in July at high prices and cover the short sale in December at low prices. Alternatively, buy a nine-month security in December and sell it, now a three-month security, the following June. The term structure would work against the arbitraguer in the first alternative and for him in the second.[61]

Given the seasonal spread, the incentive to arbitrage is determined by the cost of borrowing. In periods near cyclical peaks the incentive to purchase nine-month securities in December in order to sell them the following June is limited by the higher borrowing cost. On this ground one might expect a greater seasonal amplitude, because of

[60] In this connection, the smoothness of the seasonal patterns of interest rates, i.e., the absence of abrupt changes between adjacent months, is understandable. The major cost of seasonal arbitrage is borrowing cost, which is, of course, a linear function of the length of the loan. It is cheaper to arbitrage between adjacent months than across a six-month period, but the smoothness of the pattern reduces the opportunity. Whether the opportunity decreases at a faster rate than the costs as the span of the transaction decreases is determinable for any specific case.

[61] In addition, short positions are more costly to finance than long positions. The borrower must pay ½ of 1 per cent of the value of the security (annual rate) plus the interest that accrues to the security. See *A Study of the Dealer Market for Federal Securities, op. cit.,* p. 20. Moreover, the margin requirement is much greater on a short position than on a long position: about 2½ per cent compared with ½ of 1 per cent on a long position in certificates (*ibid.,* p. 92). It is unlikely, therefore, that this method of arbitrage would recommend itself for smoothing seasonal differentials.

the reduced arbitrage, at cyclically high rates—a consideration that is apparently offset by the one noted earlier.

Aside from the cyclical effect, however, the incentive to arbitrage is influenced by the Federal Reserve's policy toward seasonal changes in the demand for credit. The Federal Reserve's failure to meet the peak demand for credit in December would by itself produce a rise in the bill rate both directly through its own operations and indirectly through the effect on the borrowing costs of arbitraguers. Similarly, its failure to absorb redundant credit in June and July would prevent the arbitraguers' sales (to effect their capital gain) from driving the rates up. Admittedly, the failure to contract the credit supply, or more generally to diminish its rate of increase, during June and July would increase the incentive to arbitrage. This policy combined with an easy credit policy in December would, of course, lower the level of rates; but it would not eliminate the seasonal variance. Alternatively, the attempt to keep short rates high by contracting the credit supply in July and taking no action at other times would simply diminish the incentive to arbitrage and raise the December peak. In effect, it is a tight credit policy, which affects the level of rates but not the seasonality.[62] To counter the seasonal movement in interest rates, as distinct from the level of rates, requires, therefore, a relatively easy policy in December and a relatively tight one in July. The seasonal pattern in the money supply should therefore correspond with the pattern in short-term interest rates, as in fact it does. But the seasonal amplitude in money supply (that is, the extent to which the Federal Reserve alternates the relative tightness and ease) should be *inversely* related to the seasonal amplitude in short-term interest rates: The more the Federal Reserve equilibrates the supply with the demand for short-term credit, the less will interest rates vary. The final section of this report investigates this relationship.

The Effect of the Seasonal Amplitude of the Money Supply

Chart 2-22 plots time series of the seasonal factors for Treasury bills and money supply, and total bills outstanding. The relative lows in June and July and the highs in the fall months are clear evidence of

---

[62] In both cases the change is in the over-all level of rates but not the intra-month relations. By allowing the rates in December and July to fall by the same amount, the moving average is lowered and the December peak maintained. This point in a related issue was discussed in Section II.

CHART 2–22. Seasonal Factors for Treasury Bill Rates, Money Supply, and Total Treasury Bills Outstanding, 1948–65

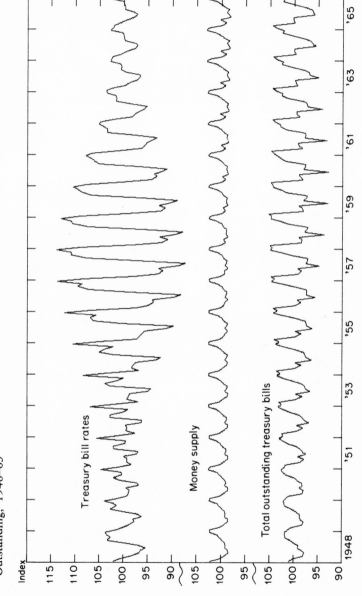

the Federal Reserve's policy of adjusting the supply to the seasonal changes in the demand for short-term credit.[63] The series on total bills outstanding is discussed later. However, if this policy were completely successful,[64] there would be no seasonal in interest rates. Figure 2-2 hypothetically depicts the situation. The demand for and

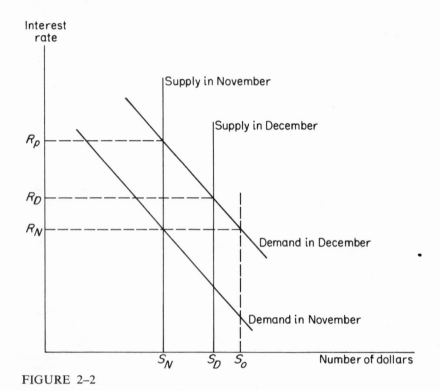

FIGURE 2–2

[63] The present section considers the monthly changes in the money supply synonymous with changes in the supply of short-term credit. The appendix to this section deals briefly with this subject to help evaluate the findings of this section.

The supply series used in this study conforms to the narrow definition of publicly held currency and demand deposits. Since time deposits do not have a significant seasonal, the broad definition of money should yield similar results; the seasonal components of both series are very similar.

[64] The word "success" is artificially vital in the current context, since the Federal Reserve did not necessarily intend to smooth out the seasonal variance in short-term rates. The desirability of eliminating the seasonal influence on interest rate is discussed in Friedman and Schwartz, *op. cit.,* pp. 292–296.

supply of short-term credit in November results in a given interest rate, R_N. In December there is an increase in the demand, depicted by the outward shift in the demand curve. If the Federal Reserve did not increase the supply at all—that is, in the present context, if there were no seasonal movement in the money supply—the rate of interest would rise to R_P. At the other extreme, if the Federal Reserve had fully anticipated the rise in demand and increased the supply of money correspondingly (to S_o), the rate of interest would remain at R_N. Again, in the present context that would imply a relatively greater seasonal amplitude in the supply of money. Finally, if the Federal Reserve anticipated part but not all of the increase in demand, the rate would move to some intermediate position—say, R_D. The necessary seasonal amplitude in the supply of money to effect any given interest rate clearly would depend on the elasticity of demand for short-term credit: The more elastic the demand for short-term credit is with respect to the interest rate, the greater must be the seasonal amplitude in money supply necessary to prevent the seasonal increases in demand from imparting a seasonal variation to interest rates.

But how sensitive is the demand for short-term credit to the interest rate? Conversely, how sensitive is the interest rate to variations in the supply of money? Discussions of these questions typically bog down in the identification problem—that of distinguishing shifts in the demand curve from movements along it. In practice one can only observe the change in the interest rate and the change in the money supply as of a given time. Since the demand curve is itself varying, there is no sure way to associate the given readings of interest rate and money supply with a particular demand curve and, therefore, to ascertain the elasticity of the curve. The problem is soluble insofar as it is feasible to specify the variables that determine the demand curve and to fix these variables while allowing the variables affecting the supply curve[65] to move freely. In this situation, since the variables

---

[65] Since the supply of new money is largely at the discretion of the Federal Reserve, to this extent the variables that affect the supply curve are those that affect the Federal Reserve's decision. This analysis presumes an autonomously determined supply of money. To the extent that the supply of money responds to interest rates apart from Federal Reserve activity, the purported separation in the determinants of supply and demand breaks down. While this point may weaken the analysis, the elasticity of supply with respect to interest rates is not likely to be sufficient to negate the substance of the analysis. In either case, the seasonal in interest rates depends on the seasonal in demand relative to supply. An endogenous supply would lessen the importance of Federal Reserve dis-

(such as income and expected changes in the price level) that determine demand are fixed, the demand curve is itself fixed, and the observed changes in interest rates and money supply may be read as points along a given demand curve. The method breaks down, however, when the same variables influence both the demand and the supply curves (such as, the preponderance of the common cyclical component in the variables affecting both curves).[66]

The study of seasonal behavior in the money market partly alleviates this problem for two reasons: (1) The use of the ratios-to-moving average of the relevant variables, or the smoothed seasonal factors, abstracts from the common cyclical component. This method is, of course, not peculiar to seasonal analysis. More importantly, (2) seasonal fluctuations in the demand for money are probably fairly stable over time; so that the seasonal shift in demand relative to the cyclical component of the shift from, say, November to December is relatively stable from year to year.[67] These seasonal shifts are determined by economic forces outside the control of the monetary authorities. Shifts

cretion in the matter of seasonality and would bias the estimated elasticity of demand for credit, since a simultaneous solution would be required. I am indebted to Walter Fisher for this point.

[66] Using averages for cyclical stages Cagan is able to show an inverse relationship between interest rates and *changes* in the money supply. (See his *Changes in the Cyclical Behavior of Interest Rates,* Occasional Paper 100, New York, NBER, 1966; reprinted as Chapter 1 of this volume.) Note he relates *changes* in money supply to levels of interest rates; whereas this study deals with *seasonal* changes in both series.

[67] Since demand per se is not observable, this proposition must be hypothesized rather than demonstrated. Some evidence in support of the proposition lies in the absence of any systematic variation in the seasonal amplitude of GNP within the study period. The implicit seasonal factors for the fourth quarter, the period of peak seasonality in the GNP, are given below. The raw data, of adjusted and nonadjusted series, are given in *The National Income and Product Accounts of the United States, 1929–1965,* pp. 11 and 30.

Year	Implicit Factors Fourth Quarter	Year	Implicit Factors Fourth Quarter
1948	107.2	1957	106.0
1949	106.7	1958	105.9
1950	105.7	1959	105.9
1951	105.3	1960	105.8
1952	105.6	1961	105.8
1953	106.0	1962	105.9
1954	105.6	1963	105.8
1955	105.3	1964	105.6
1956	105.9	1965	106.6

in supply, on the other hand, are subject to the discretion of the authorities. An estimate of the demand for short-term credit, therefore, is available from successive observations of the rate of interest necessary for people to hold the amount of money that is offered. More specifically, the analysis reveals the seasonal shift in the interest rate necessary for people to accept the seasonal shift in supply of money, given their *fixed* seasonal shift in demand.[68] The only fixity in this hypothetical system is in the demand for short-term credit; the interest rate varies as the supply varies—hence, the moving seasonal in interest rates.

The immediate purpose of this study is not to estimate the demand for short-term credit for its own sake, but rather to investigate the causes of the changing seasonal amplitudes (i.e., from year to year) of the interest rates. Given the above analysis, the first step would be to regress the seasonal factors of Treasury bills on those of money supply, one month at a time across years. In other words, regress the January factor for bill rates on the January factor for money supply in 1948, 1949, . . . , 1965: eighteen observations in each of twelve regressions. The regression coefficients, their *t* values, and the adjusted coefficients of determination are listed in Table 2-16. While the results are far from conclusive, in the five cases where the regression coefficients are statistically significant they reveal the expected inverse relation between the demand for money and the interest rate.

While the assumed stability in the seasonal demand for credit is plausible in the case of private demand, the government may have occasion to vary its demand both to meet changing fiscal requirements and, where possible, to take advantage of any seasonal in interest rates that may occur. Introduction of this factor, in the form of variation of total bills outstanding, leads to a considerable improvement in the estimates. The results, analogous to those in Table 2-16 but with the addition of total bills outstanding, are shown in Table 2-17. Eight instead of five of the money supply coefficients are significant, and each of the eight is negative. Eight of the coefficients of bills outstanding are positive, and six of these are significant. That is, in

[68] The terminology used here, admittedly awkward, does not imply that the demand is for money to hold as an asset; a demand for which there is no obvious reason for a seasonal increase in the autumn. In the present context the "demand for money" is only an abstraction that may help explain the inverse correlation between the seasonal amplitudes of money supply and Treasury bill rates. This point is considered in greater detail in the appendix to this section.

TABLE 2-16. *Regression of Seasonal Factors of Treasury Bill Rates on Those of Money Supply, 1948–65*

Month	b	t	R^2 (adj)
January	3.9474	.8381	a
February	−9.4012	−6.3215[b]	.69622
March	1.4503	.4107	a
April	−.9290	−.8665	a
May	−9.2617	−2.0270[b]	.15460
June	−4.4874	−1.6004	.08412
July	14.3076	.9028	a
August	.0644	.0279	a
September	.6536	1.3084	.04020
October	−20.6351	−4.0472[b]	.47498
November	−23.4467	−2.0905[b]	.16545
December	−8.4171	−2.0905[b]	.16545

NOTE: Each of the twelve regressions is specified as follows: seasonal factor (bill rate) = $a + b$ [seasonal factor (money supply)] +E. Each regression is run with eighteen observations.

[a]The estimated adjusted coefficients of determination are negative.

[b]Statistically significant at the 5 per cent level.

TABLE 2-17. *Regression of Seasonal Factors of Treasury Bill Rates on Those of Money Supply and Total Bills Outstanding, 1948–65*

Month	b_{MON}	t	b_{TOT}	t	R^2 (adj)
January	−7.8027	−2.6531[a]	2.4944	6.8616[a]	.73768
February	−12.6356	−11.0352[a]	−.6275	−4.9796[a]	.87787
March	.1628	.0468	1.5159	1.5604	.03512
April	−7.7407	−5.6509[a]	6.7563	5.5998[a]	.64973
May	−9.9774	−1.7788	−.3225	−.2443	.10181
June	−9.0975	−4.9189[a]	1.3450	5.5671[a]	.68138
July	18.7018	1.0639	−.8688	−.6337	−.05029
August	−12.1313	−3.0136[a]	3.2720	3.3853[a]	.35756
September	.7938	1.7885	−1.2068	−2.3739[a]	.25581
October	−25.5305	−4.6300[a]	1.8186	1.7840	.53800
November	−39.3554	−4.8579[a]	10.4859	4.7151[a]	.64137
December	−2.6776	−3.1134[a]	3.8698	19.5437[a]	.96636

NOTE: Each of the twelve regressions is specified as follows: seasonal factor (bill rate) = $a + b_1$ [seasonal factor (money supply)] + b_2 [seasonal factor (total bills outstanding)] + E. Each regression is run with eighteen observations.

[a]Statistically significant at the 5 per cent level.

most, but not all, cases where the coefficients are statistically significant they have the expected sign: Increases in the money supply reduce the bill rate; while increases in bills outstanding increase the bill rate.

To obtain these results it is obviously necessary to run the regressions one month at a time across the years (or to use the equivalent dummy variable technique described below) since the month-to-month changes in the seasonal factors of Treasury bill rates and money supply have virtually the same directions and are positively correlated. During a cyclical upturn both the demand for money and the supply of money increase, but since the demand increases faster than the supply, the interest rate increases as well. In this situation, an increase in the supply of money coincides with an increase in interest rates, and the careless observer sees a positively sloped demand curve. Similarly, over the course of the year the demand for money changes in the same direction as the supply but faster, so that the interest rate varies in the same direction as the supply. However, working with deviations from the trend-cycle component isolates the common cyclical component in the demand and the supply; and estimating the relation between interest rates and money supply for one month at a time in effect exploits the relative constancy in the seasonal shifts in demand. It is then feasible to measure the points of intersection between the fixed demand curve and the varying supply curve and, therefore, to estimate the elasticity of demand with respect to the interest rate.

Instead of estimating twelve separate regressions (one for each month) of the seasonal factors for Treasury bill rates on those of the money supply and the total number of bills outstanding, it is preferable to pool all the observations and isolate the intrayear, month-to-month movements by means of dummy variables. Table 2-18 lists the results of this regression estimated both ways, with and without dummy variables. In regression A, without dummy variables, the common seasonal patterns dominate the relation between the seasonal factors of Treasury bill rates and money supply, and thus the regression coefficient is positive. In terms of the schematic representation, both the demand and the supply curves vary together, the demand varying more than the supply; therefore, the interest rate varies with the supply. An analogous result is frequently observed in the positive correlation between interest rates and money supply over the business cycle when no allowance is made for the joint movement of supply and demand.

Essays on Interest Rates

TABLE 2-18. *Multiple Regression Statistics for the Pooled Data of the Seasonal Factors of Treasury Bill Rates on Those of the Money Supply and the Total Number of Bills Outstanding, All Months, 1948–65*

A	B
Without Dummy Variables for the Months	With Dummy Variables for the Months
b_{MON} = 1.6002 $t_{b(MON)}$ = 4.9316	b_{MON} = −3.6817 $t_{b(MON)}$ = −4.3944
b_{TOT} = .5904 $t_{b(TOT)}$ = 3.7776	b_{TOT} = 1.0767 $t_{b(TOT)}$ = 5.3460
R = .6540	R = .8471
$R^2_{(adj)}$ = .4223	$R^2_{(adj)}$ = .6993

NOTE: The regressions are computed with time series of the seasonal factors of the three variables: Treasury bill rates, money supply, and total bills outstanding. The first observation is January 1948; the second, February 1948; and the thirteenth, January 1949. Regression A is:

$$\text{Factor (bill rates)} = a + b_{MON} \text{ Factor (money)} + b_{TOT} \text{ Factor (total)} + \epsilon.$$

The constant term is not shown. Regression B is:

$$\text{Factor (bill rates)} = a + b_{MON} \text{ Factor (money)} + b_{TOT} \text{ Factor (total)} + b_i D_i + \epsilon,$$

where b_i is the regression coefficient of the dummy variable for the ith month; eleven in all. These coefficients are not listed in the table.

In regression B, however, dummy variables for each month prevent the joint movement of supply and demand from month to month from obscuring the inverse relation between interest rates and the supply of money. The dummy variables, in effect, permit the substantive co-efficients to summarize only the movement from, say, January 1956 to January 1957 and February 1951 to February 1952, instead of the movement from June 1958 to July 1958. In so doing, it allows the varying supply across all the Decembers to intersect the seasonally fixed demand for December. In this way it traces out the demand curve.[69]

An alternative estimation form to depict the seasonal influences of

[69] The higher correlation coefficient in regression B is due to the introduction of the dummy variables. Not all of the variation of the seasonal factors of Treasury bill rates is due to the variation of the two independent variables. But since the seasonal factors for bill rates are not constant throughout the period, their average values, which are reflected in the regression coefficients attached to the dummy variables (not shown), do not explain all their variation.

money supply and government borrowing makes use of the variances of the seasonal factors described in Section I. The variance of the monthly factors, computed for each year, measures the amplitude of the seasonal factors. Regressing the variance of Treasury bill rate factors (eighteen observations) on the variance of money supply and total bills outstanding factors reveals the inverse and direct relationships, respectively, of the seasonal influence of these two series on the bill rate seasonal. The results of the regression are recorded in Table 2-19.

TABLE 2-19. *Multiple Regression Statistics for the Variance of the Seasonal Factors of Treasury Bill Rates on Those of Money Supply and Total Bills Outstanding, 1948–65*

Variable	b	t_b	Constant	Partial Correlation	R	R^2 (adj)
Money supply	−75.1311	−5.1253		−.7978		
Total bill			114.4613		.8969	.7783
Outstanding	6.7873	6.8102		.8693		

NOTE: The regressions are computed with time series of the variances of the monthly seasonal factors for each series. For a given year and series the variance is computed for the twelve factors from January through December. Since the mean factor is 1, a greater seasonal amplitude implies a greater dispersion around the mean and hence a greater variance. The form of the regression is:

$$\text{Var. (fact. bill rates)} = \text{CONST.} + b_{MON}\ \text{Var (fact. money supply)}$$
$$+ b_{TOT}\ \text{Var (fact. bills outstanding)} + \text{residual.}$$

It is of course not possible to distinguish intentional changes in the seasonal variation of government borrowing to take advantage of the seasonal in interest rates from the unintentional responses to seasonal fiscal requirements.[70] The Treasury's ability to adjust the timing of its offerings to benefit from seasonal lows in interest rates is not unlimited. It is pointless to borrow merely because the rate is low. The problem here is analogous to the arbitrage issue discussed earlier in this section.

[70] In the case of the money supply, the Federal Reserve was merely assumed to have discretion over the supply. To the extent this assumption is unwarranted the distinction discussed in the text applies to the money supply as well. However, arguments against Federal Reserve control of the money supply rely to a large extent on the variability of time deposits, which, in the absence of a seasonal, are not germane to the present discussion.

From the above analysis it is a small step to compute the actual elasticity of demand for money with respect to the short-term interest rate. To do this, the variables in regression B of Table 2-18 have simply been rearranged.[71] Now the seasonal factors for money supply form the dependent variable, and the seasonal factors for Treasury bill rates form one of the independent variables. Since these variables are already expressed as percentages of the moving average, the regression coefficients signify elasticities. The elasticity of demand for short-term credit with respect to the short-term interest rate according to this method of estimation is —.0237 (Table 2-20). The puniness

TABLE 2-20. *Multiple Regression Statistics for the Pooled Data of the Seasonal Factors for Money Supply on Those of Treasury Bill Rates and Total Bills Outstanding, All Months, 1948–65*

b_{bill} = $-.0237$		$t_{b(bill)}$ = -4.3944
b_{Tot} = $.0884$		$t_{b(Tot)}$ = 5.4861
R = $.9849^a$		
$R^2_{(adj)}$ = $.9681^a$		

NOTE: The regression is computed as follows:

$$\text{Factor (money)} = a + b_{bill} \text{ Factor (bill rate)} + b_{Tot}$$
$$\text{Factor (total)} + b_i D_i + \epsilon,$$

where Factor (money) is the seasonal factors of money supply; Factor (bill rate) is the seasonal factors of Treasury bill rates; Factor (total) is the seasonal factors of total bills outstanding; and b_i is the regression coefficient of dummy variable for i^{th} month.

[a]The correlation coefficient is very high because the dummy variables explain a large part of the seasonal variation of money supply. The strength of this relationship is due to the relative stability of the seasonal factors of money supply and their susceptibility, therefore, to the dummy variable technique for seasonal adjustment. (This point is considered in Section II.)

of the estimated elasticity by no means implies its economic insignificance. On the contrary, it implies that a relatively small change in money supply may have a relatively large short run impact on interest rates. Chart 2-22 foreshadowed this result in the association it showed between the relatively small changes in the seasonal amplitude of money and the relatively large changes in the opposite direction of the seasonal amplitude of Treasury bill rates.

[71] The pooled data were used for this experiment since the regression coefficients computed with the variance data are further removed from the concept of elasticity.

Interpretation of this result, however, must take account of an important limitation of the estimation procedure used. By definition the seasonal factors for a given month are serially correlated, one year with the next. If the factor is high in December 1952, it will be high in December 1953 as well. This serial correlation in the observations severely limits the actual degrees of freedom as distinct from the nominal amount. In effect, the seasonal amplitude of Treasury bill rates is low, then high, then low; and that of the money stock high, then low, then high. In addition to these three points, there are smaller changes in between, especially with respect to the variation of the several months; but the total is not even near the nominal 202 degrees of freedom.[72] The uncertain degrees of freedom reduces the importance of the estimated test of significance of the estimated elasticities. The figures are therefore less reliable estimates, although there is no reason for thinking them biased. In any case, the relations described constitute an hypothesis that further work can corroborate or refute.

Conclusions

This section reached the following conclusions:

(1) A seasonal variation in long-term bonds can survive arbitrage so long as the amplitude does not exceed some specified amount. This amount will be greater the more important is the irregular component of the series, the shorter is the maturity of the bond, and the greater is the margin requirement for borrowing money to purchase bonds. There are, no doubt, other factors that this section did not consider.

(2) The analogous computation for short-term securities is complicated by the term structure of interest rates. Other things being the same, the seasonal amplitude for a given year will be greater, the greater is the slope of the yield curve. Since the yield curve is typically steepest when the level of rates is low, the seasonal amplitude on this account should be greatest when the level of rates is low. This consideration is apparently offset by the higher borrowing costs to arbitrageurs, when the level of rates is high.

[72] The number is computed as follows: 12 months in each of 18 years comes to 216. There are 2 independent variables, a constant term, and 11 dummy variables. $216 - 14 = 202$. Substitution of the SI ratios for the factors will not solve this problem (though it would reduce it) because the presence of seasonality implies the serial correlation of the SI ratios.

(3) The variation in the seasonal amplitude of the Treasury bill rate is closely related to the movement of the seasonal amplitudes of money supply and total bills outstanding. These relationships demonstrate the influence over the seasonal in the Treasury bill rate enjoyed by the Federal Reserve and the U.S. Treasury.

(4) There is an inverse relationship between the seasonal amplitude of Treasury bill rates and that of money stock. This relationship implies a negatively sloped demand curve for money with respect to interest rates. The elasticity of this curve is very small.

Appendix

There are at least three interpretations of what the text calls the estimated elasticity of demand for money with respect to interest rates: the slope in the observed regression of the logarithms of money supply on interest rates; the elasticity with respect to interest rates of the demand for money to hold as an asset; and the elasticity with respect to interest rates of the demand for loanable funds.

The first simply describes an observed association and is noncontroversial. The second implies the interest rate is one determinant of the demand for money-as-an-asset. However, there is no reason for a seasonal in this demand; and since the method used to estimate the elasticity assumes a seasonal shift in demand, this interpretation is not appropriate. The third assumes that the only seasonally operative component of the change in the supply of loanable funds is the supply of new money so that, given the demand for loanable funds, the shift in supply due to the change in money supply would determine the interest rate. But with a lower interest rate the demand for money-as-an-asset would rise and offset—partially, totally, or more than offset, depending on the relevant elasticities—the new money component of loanable funds. Therefore, according to the third interpretation the estimate of the elasticity of demand for loanable funds is biased downward (in absolute magnitude) because the change in loanable funds is less than the change in money supply.

This problem is only one illustration of the difficulty in specifying the conditions for which a demand curve is drawn. As already noted, the method used here avoids the problem of a cyclical component common to both the supply of and demand for money. Its reference to month-to-month variation probably alleviates other difficulties encountered in demand studies.[73] Its short-term character obviates consideration of the effect of additional supplies of money combined with lower interest rates on nominal income and, through income, the increased demand for money for transactions purposes. Depending on the relevant elasticities and periods of adjustment, additional money could conceivably raise rather than lower the interest rate by increasing the demand for money both as an asset and as a medium of exchange. With the increased income the demand for loanable funds would rise. All these effects could offset the effect on interest rates of the increased supply of money. In addition, the short run analysis obviates consideration of the effect of a change in interest rates on the proportion of income that is saved, which would, in turn, affect the supply of loanable funds. For the same reason any effect of the change in money supply on the price level and, through this effect, on interest rates is also outside the scope of this analysis.

These points have in common the difficulty of holding constant nominal (or real) income, fixing the demand curve for money while the supply of money is allowed to vary. Variation in money supply implies variation in income and that, in turn, implies shifts in the demand curve for money. The relationship among the three—money supply, income, and demand for money—is stronger the greater is the period allowed for adjustment. Choosing coeval observations of the relevant variables that span brief periods (months, for example, instead of years) limits the process of diffusion of the new money supply and alleviates the identification problem. To the extent, however, that the diffusion process is anticipated in the market, as, for example, when increases in money supply are taken to forebode inflation, estimated parameters based on short-period observations will suffer from the identification problem.

These problems in demand analysis are by no means peculiar to this study nor even to analyses of the demand for money, although the ubiquity of money may aggravate the problems of demand analysis. Ultimately, one is sure only of the first interpretation, namely, that the estimated parameters described an observed association. Depending on how the problem is set up—how the demand curve is specified, what is the source of the observations and their time dimension—and what relationship among the variables is assumed, the writer can infer

---

[73] Some of these difficulties are noted by Milton Friedman and Anna Jacobson Schwartz in *Monetary Statistics of the United States: Estimates, Sources, Methods,* New York, NBER, 1970.

behavioral parameters from the observed association. It is then his responsibility to justify the inferences.

V. SUMMARY AND CONCLUSIONS

There is compelling evidence of the presence of repetitive seasonal movements in both long- and short-term interest rates in the years between 1955 and 1960. Outside this period, both before and after, the evidence is less conclusive, and certainly the seasonal movements are smaller. Nevertheless, a seasonal pattern apparently existed in most of the rates studied over a period substantially longer than the brief period of peak seasonality. This result is largely predicated on the demonstrated similarities among the seasonal patterns of the several rates, as well as the relative uniformity of the pattern for a given rate over an extended period. The study's primary focus is on the quality of the evidence for these conclusions.

The seasonal factors for short-term rates are found typically to decline from a relative high in January through the spring months to a trough in June and then sharply increase to September, from which they rise gradually to a peak in December. This pattern is conspicuous in the late fifties but occurs with some variation throughout the postwar period. The amplitudes, however, vary considerably, rising gradually after the early fifties through 1957 or 1958 and falling off quite rapidly thereafter. By 1965 the seasonal movement had all but vanished, although recent evidence not considered in this study indicates some resurgence in the seasonal.

The seasonal pattern for yields on bankers' acceptances is, perhaps, the most stable of those examined, although its amplitude is somewhat less than that of Treasury bill rates. During part of the period of peak seasonality, the amplitudes, that is, the variation from seasonal high to seasonal low, exceeded 20 per cent of the level of the series. These amplitudes dropped sharply after 1959. By 1963, the seasonal pattern for bankers' acceptances virtually disappeared. The seasonal pattern for Treasury bills appears to have continued through 1965, the end of the study period, although its amplitude then was barely 2 per cent of the level of the series. The seasonal movement in commercial paper rates is far less stable and its amplitude smaller than those of the other two series.

While this study did not specifically evaluate the relation between seasonal amplitude and term to maturity, there is an obvious decline in both seasonal amplitude and the period over which there is a

measurable seasonal factor, as the maturity of Treasury securities increases. The patterns of the seasonal factors of long-term rates are
less stable than those of the short-term rates (except commercial
paper) and have a much smaller amplitude. In the early fifties the
pattern typically starts with a January low that falls to a trough in
March, then rises to a plateau extending from June to October,
before declining to an intermediate position for the last two months.
The patterns for all the private long-term bonds are alike with respect
to their midyear highs and January lows, the characteristic distinguishing these patterns from those of the same securities in the later
period, as well as from the patterns of the short-term rates. Starting
in 1955 the seasonal patterns of private long-term bond rates
change—the January factors from lows to highs and the June and
July factors from highs to lows. The troughs remain in March and
April and the peaks in September and October. As in the case of
the short-term rates the amplitude is greatest in the late fifties and
tapers off thereafter. By 1965, the amplitude is very low and in some
cases nonexistent.

While this evidence strongly supports the view that seasonality
exists in the interest rate series, questions relating to the methods, as
well as the desirability of adjusting the data for seasonal variations,
remain. In addition to the sampling problem of drawing from a
hypothetically stable population (a common problem of empirical
economics), the estimation of seasonal factors must cope with the
effects of a shifting population. That is, the seasonal factors for a
given month estimated for different years differ not merely because
of random fluctuations but also because the true value, apart from
randomness, may itself be varying. The difficulty in empirical seasonal
analysis is to distinguish the random from the systematic variation of
the seasonal factors. While it is possible to devise tests of the significance of differences in estimated factors for nonoverlapping periods,
a continuous reading of their accuracy from year to year is elusive.
Visual comparisons of the adjusted with the nonadjusted data (or,
correspondingly, the seasonal factors with the ratios-to-moving-aver-
age) may help to determine whether the estimated seasonal component captures the systematic seasonal movements of the raw data.
Unfortunately, this method ties the conclusions to the particular
analyst and invites differences in judgment. Because of the subjectivity
of this element, the study merely suggests the periods within which
the factors are deemed relatively accurate.

While the similarity in the patterns of all the long-term rates considered is strong evidence of a seasonal element in the rates, the patterns themselves may not be sufficiently stable to warrant an attempt to eliminate this element. The question whether a seasonal pattern exists is distinct from the question whether the seasonal movement is sufficiently stable to justify seasonally adjusting the data and risking the introduction rather than the elimination of variation. It is often maintained that a seasonal pattern in long-term rates would not persist because of the profits available to those who would arbitrage the seasonality away by buying securities in periods of seasonally high rates and selling them when the rates are seasonally low. This argument is true only to the extent the seasonal amplitude is sufficient to cover the costs of arbitrage, including the risk that on any given occasion the cyclical, trend, or random components may swamp the seasonal effect, and to the extent the seasonal movement is sufficiently stable to make the arbitrage more than a mere speculation. The greater the importance of these two effects—swamping by other components of variation and instability from year to year—the greater will be the seasonal amplitude that will survive arbitrage. Municipal bond yields, for example, a series with a large irregular component and an unstable seasonal component, has a relatively high seasonal amplitude.

The cause of the variation in seasonal amplitudes, the salient characteristic of the seasonals observed in this study, is a complex issue. At the risk of oversimplification this study considered the problem in the light of the supply of and demand for money. On the assumption that the seasonal variation in the demand for money is relatively constant from year to year, the change from year to year in the seasonal patterns for short-term interest rates would depend on that of the seasonal patterns for the supply of money. In years when the seasonal factor for, say, January in money outstanding is high the corresponding seasonal factor for interest rates would be low; and when the former is low the latter would be high. The observed relationship between the changing seasonal factors of money supply and short period interest rates is, indeed, inverse. Hence, the data are consistent with the hypothesis that the rise in the amplitude of the seasonal variations in interest rates during the 1950's and its virtual disappearance during the 1960's is attributable to changes (in the opposite direction) in the seasonal movements in money supply. This inverse relationship is more conspicuous when allowance is made

for seasonal movements in the quantity of bills outstanding
consistent with the hypothesis that the Treasury made som
to benefit from the seasonal variation in interest rates. I
take account of this effect, which involves a change in de
the same direction as the change in supply, obscures the relation
between money supply and interest rates. When this change in demand is statistically nullified the full effect of the change in supply
is observable.

3

The Influence of Call Provisions and Coupon Rate on the Yields of Corporate Bonds

Mark W. Frankena

INTRODUCTION AND SUMMARY OF FINDINGS

This study examines the effect of call provisions and the coupon rate on the yields of corporate bonds. The first section reviews the function of the call option in corporate bonds and the means of providing call protection to the investor. The second section considers the extent to which and the reasons that corporate bonds actually were called prior to maturity in the period since the Accord of 1951. The third section examines the influence of coupon rate on the yield and price

NOTE: Most of the research for this study was done in the summers of 1964 and 1965; much of the empirical material was later updated to 1966. Since this work was completed, a number of improvements have occurred to me and have been suggested by others. Unfortunately, I have had to leave several of these as footnotes.

I am greatly indebted to the late Joseph W. Conard, my teacher at Swarthmore College and director of the Bureau's Interest Rate Project until his untimely death, for suggesting the problems considered in this study and for many discussions during its earlier stages. Sidney Homer of Salomon Brothers and Hutzler provided invaluable assistance in answering questions dealing with the institutions of the corporate bond market and making available much of the data underlying this study. Albert Wojnilower of the First Boston Corporation also kindly made essential data available. Phillip Cagan, Paul Cootner, and Frank C. Jen read an earlier version of the manuscript and suggested improvements. Finally, this paper would not have been completed without the generous help and encouragement of Jack M. Guttentag.

behavior of seasoned corporate bonds. The last section considers the influence of call deferments on new issue yields.

The call option is the right of a borrowing company to redeem its debt prior to maturity, generally at a few points above par. Callability has several advantages to the borrower. Most important is the ability to reduce interest costs if new issue yields decline substantially below the coupon rate on the outstanding issue. The call option also allows the borrower to eliminate restrictive provisions in the indenture of a bond, replace an issue with stock or with a different type of debt instrument, or retire an issue completely.

However, callability has important disadvantages for the lender. If the investor is concerned with holding-period yields, and hence current market prices, callable bonds are less attractive than call-protected bonds because their price appreciation is limited. Because of the threat of call when yields are low, market prices of callable bonds do not normally rise more than a point or two above the call price. As a result, the potential capital gain on callable bonds in the event of a general decline in market yields is limited. Alternatively, when callable bonds are actually called for redemption, investors may be forced to reinvest in lower yielding bonds and incur additional transaction costs.

The benefits of the call option to borrowers and disadvantages to lenders suggests the hypothesis underlying this study, that call provisions should influence the yields to maturity of corporate bonds. There are four characteristics of a bond that influence the probability that the call option will be exercised, the size of the benefits and costs of call when it is exercised, and the extent to which capital gains are limited in periods of declining interest rates. These are (1) the coupon rate, (2) the term to maturity, (3) the call price, and (4) the call deferment, if there is one. All of the bonds used in this study were long term, and no attempt was made to determine the influence of maturity on yield which results from the existence of the call option.

Given the level of new issue yields, and assuming maturities constant, the profitability of calling an issue for refunding then depends on the call price and the coupon rate. The higher the call price and the lower the coupon rate, the less profitable is refunding to the borrower. On the other hand, the higher the call price and the lower the coupon rate, the greater is the opportunity for capital gains for the investor and the less the chance of losing a high return through call. As a result, bonds with a lower call price or higher coupon rate should bear a higher yield. In addition, a bond that is immediately

callable is less attractive to investors than a bond with a call deferment, which prevents the borrower from calling the issue for a period
of years after issue. Hence, bonds with deferments should carry lower
yields than freely callable bonds.

The empirical part of this study is limited to consideration of the
influence of coupon rate on the yields of seasoned bonds and the
influence of call deferments on the yields of seasoned and new issues.
Yield series were constructed for this study covering seasoned long-
term callable Aa-Aaa public utility bonds, separately for bonds with
a coupon rate of 2¾ to 2⅞ per cent and for bonds at each coupon
rate between 3¾ and 5¾ per cent at intervals of one-eighth per cent.
The series are monthly and cover the period from January 1957
through October 1967.

In analyzing the influence of coupon rate, yield spreads between
each series with a coupon rate of 3¾ to 5¾ per cent and the series
with a coupon rate of 2¾ to 2⅞ per cent were calculated, and
multiple regressions were run to explain the variance in the spread.
The regression covering all bonds "explained" 78 per cent of the variance in the spread. The independent variables used in the regression
were: (1) *the coupon rate* on the higher coupon bond used in measuring the yield spread—this variable had a positive regression coefficient,
indicating that a higher coupon rate is associated with a larger yield
spread. (2) *The level of yields on new issues* of callable Aa utility
bonds—this variable had a negative regression coefficient, indicating
that when yields are lower, yield spreads due to differences in coupon
rate are greater. This is partly because the price appreciation of the
higher coupon bonds is restrained by call price, so that the yields
on these bonds cannot continue to fall along with the yields on
lower coupon bonds. In addition, at lower yields investors become
more apprehensive about the greater danger of call and expect more
limited capital gains on higher coupon bonds. (3) *A weighted average
of changes in new issue yields* over the previous six months—this
variable had a negative correlation coefficient, indicating that when
yields have been falling yield spreads tend to increase. The explanation
for this is that, because of the general cyclical forces affecting interest
rates, falling yields generate the expectation that yields are likely to
continue falling in the near future. (4) *A time trend*, indicating that
yield spreads declined over the period studied—the primary explanation of the significance of trend is that the expected "normal" and
cyclical minimum levels of interest rates apparently rose over the
period. With rates no longer expected to fall to very low levels

during recessions, there was a reduction in the danger of call and of the limitation of capital gains on higher coupon bonds. A second explanation of the time trend is that the secular increase in funds channeled through institutional investors, together with a cumulative drought of publicly offered corporate bonds, reduced the spread due to coupon differences.

We also ran five separate regressions for bonds with each of the coupon rates from $4\frac{1}{2}$ to 5 per cent. The independent variables discussed above were all used except for the coupon rate, which was held constant in each regression. In addition, we included the volume of publicly offered new issues of corporate bonds for the three months preceding the observation of yield spread. All regression coefficients had the same signs as before, and the volume variable was significant with a positive regression coefficient. This supports the hypothesis that, when the volume of new corporate issues is larger, the spread due to coupon differences tends to increase. Together these variables "explained" 81 to 89 per cent of the variance in the yield spread.

To examine how refunding deferments influence the yields of seasoned bonds, yield series were constructed at each coupon rate for bonds with refunding deferments of two years or more; otherwise, these bonds were the same as those used to derive the series on freely callable bonds. The hypotheses tested were that the call protection afforded by a refunding deferment would make a bond more attractive to investors and hence reduce its yield, and that the amount by which a deferment would reduce the yield would increase as the coupon rate increased and as the level of yields decreased. These hypotheses were confirmed. On seasoned bonds with intermediate and high coupon rates, deferments reduced yields to maturity by five to nine basis points during much of the period from 1957 to 1961, and they reduced yields by more than twice that when price appreciation on the callable bonds was limited by the call price and the prices of the deferred bonds rose a few points above the call prices.

The final part of the study examines how refunding deferments have influenced the yields on new issues. Comparisons were made of the offering yields, and the yields after the termination of the underwriting syndicate, of freely callable and deferred utility bonds offered within ten days of each other and having the same quality rating (Aaa, Aa, or A). We found that, although the data for 1957 were ambiguous, the data for 1958 through 1966 consistently supported the hypothesis that deferments reduce yields unless new issue coupon rates are very low. In times of high coupons on new issues, refunding deferments of five years commonly reduced average yields by 9 to 14 basis points. This is in contrast to the finding of Hess and Winn, whose study of the influence of refunding deferments on the yield of new corporate issues offered from 1926 to 1959 concluded that the "length of call deferment did not influence yields except during the last six months of this 34-year period."[1] It is the contention of the present study that their conclusion was not justified by the data, and that in any case the conclusion does not apply to the period from 1958 to 1966.

One implication of the finding that call features do influence yields is that the capital market is considerably less imperfect than Hess and Winn and various agencies regulating the issuance of corporate securities have implied. Another implication of this study is that, because of the great effect of the coupon rate on corporate bond yields, and the smaller but nonetheless significant influence of refunding deferments (particularly on high coupon bonds in periods of low yields), many commonly used series of corporate bond yields are inaccurate indicators of the state of the corporate bond market. Furthermore, many of the calculated yield spreads between new and seasoned corporate issues,[2] between corporates and governments, and between corporate bonds of different quality are not accurate. Similarly, both the shape of yield curves and the cyclical movements of interest rates on seasoned corporate bonds depend very heavily on the levels of coupons and deferments included in the series.

THE CALL OPTION AND CALL PROTECTION

The call option is the right of a borrowing company to redeem its debt prior to maturity. Virtually all long-term corporate bonds offered publicly in the postwar period have allowed for such calls during most if not all of the period for which the bonds were issued. The

[1] Arleigh P. Hess, Jr., and Willis J. Winn, *The Value of the Call Privilege*, University of Pennsylvania, 1962, p. 80.

[2] The average yield spread between the Moody series for new and seasoned Aa public utility bonds in the period 1952 through 1963 was 17.5 basis points, but the average new-seasoned spread was reduced to 9.7 basis points when measured between the yield on new issues and the yield on seasoned bonds with the same coupon rate as the new issues. See Joseph W. Conard and Mark W. Frankena, "The Yield Spread Between New and Seasoned Corporate Bonds, 1952–63," in *Essays on Interest Rates*, Vol. I, Jack M. Guttentag and Phillip Cagan, editors, New York, NBER, 1969, pp. 143–222.

first date on which the call option may be exercised may be immediately after issue or may be deferred a number of years, usually five. The indenture of each bond specifies a call price which the borrower must pay at the time of call. Normally this is about $103 to $108 per $100 of principal for call immediately following the date of issue and declines toward par by a fraction of a point each year as the bond approaches maturity.

Advantages of Callability to the Borrower

Callability has several advantages to the borrower. The most important is the ability to reduce interest costs if new issue yields decline substantially below the coupon rate on the outstanding issue. If the yield to maturity calculated from the call price is greater than the present new issue yield, the issuer gains by calling and refunding his debt.

When new issue yields are low, such interest savings may be realized simply by refunding a bond with an issue that is identical except that the coupon rate is lower. However, in cases where the company does not intend to retire an outstanding issue at maturity, it can replace the issue with one of longer maturity. In this case, the borrower can take advantage of a new issue interest rate that is low relative both to the coupon rate on its existing issue and to the yield that it expects to prevail at the time the outstanding issue would mature.

While most called bonds are replaced by ones which are identical, except in coupon and maturity, the call option also allows the borrower to replace its issue with a different type of bond or with stock, or to retire it completely. The outstanding bond may contain restrictive provisions in its indenture that limit additional borrowing, sale of assets, merger, or dividends. Such provisions may considerably hamper the operations of a company and, hence, justify call even when interest savings are not realized. Particularly after a merger, for example, it may be considered necessary to simplify the capital structure of the company by replacing a number of existing issues with a single new issue. Similarly, bonds may be called in connection with a reorganization by court order. Finally, changed circumstances of the company may call for a change in capital structure. The call option facilitates such change, and thus provides flexibility in the face of uncertainty.[3]

---

[3] The comments above assume that if there were no call option the borrower would not be able to repurchase its debt in the open market at less than the call

Disadvantages of Callability to the Lender

Callability has important disadvantages to the lender. If the investor is concerned with holding-period yields on marketable bonds, callable bonds are less attractive than call-protected ones because the price appreciation of the former is limited. Because of the threat of call when yields are low, the prices of callable bonds do not normally rise more than a point or two above the call price.[4] As a result, in the event of a fall in yields, the potential capital gains on callable bonds, particularly those which are immediately callable and have high coupons or low call prices, are limited.

For example, a 25-year bond with a coupon rate of 5.00 per cent might have a call price of 106. If this bond were selling at its call price, its yield to maturity would be about 4.60 per cent. In order for this bond to have a yield to maturity of 4.00 per cent, its market price would have to rise to $115\frac{3}{4}$; and to have a yield of 3.50 per cent, its price would have to rise to almost 125. Because the market price never rises appreciably above 106, almost 10 points in capital gains would be lost if market yields fell from 4.60 to 4.00 per cent and almost 20 points would be lost if yields fell to 3.50 per cent.

Beyond this, when callable bonds are actually called for redemption, the investing institution may be forced to reinvest at lower yields and incur the transaction cost of reinvestment.[5]

---

price. This is a reasonable assumption, for under conditions where it is profitable to call a bond the call price would be below the price that would prevail if there were no call option. In any case, it would be impossible for a borrower to buy back all its debt in the market at a reasonable cost. The bond price would rise to an exorbitant level as bonds were purchased. Similarly, in order to remove restrictions placed on the borrower by the indenture of a bond, it might be necessary to pay a high price to bondholders.

[4] This pertains to asked prices. Bid prices rise even less above call price.

[5] The cost to the investor attributable to actual call, over and above that due to the threat of call, depends on whether or not the investor would hold the bond to maturity regardless of its market price. If the bond is nonmarketable or if the investor holding a marketable bond plans to hold it to maturity regardless of market price, the investor loses a series of payments of coupon and principal when the bond is called, and receives the call price in its place. Assuming the investor reinvests at the prevailing, and presumably low, rate of interest on low coupon bonds for the remaining term of the old bond, the cost of call to the investor will be the present discounted value of (a) the difference in the coupons received, plus (b) the cost of reinvestment and the lost interest for the period, if any, during which cash is held, minus (c) the differ-

Regardless of whether interest rates fall or the bond is actually called, the option to call introduces uncertainty about the term of the investor's holdings and the continuity of future income. It thus limits the extent to which an institution can assure itself of a given flow of interest income in the future.

Call Features

The preceding summary of the benefits of the call option to borrowers and of protection against the option to lenders suggests the hypothesis underlying this study, that call provisions should influence yields to maturity on corporate bonds. To test this hypothesis it is necessary to consider the features of a bond that are relevant to the probability that the call option will be exercised, to the size of the benefits and costs of call when it is exercised, and to the extent to which capital gains are limited in periods of declining interest rates.

The primary variables determining the profitability of refunding to reduce interest costs are the coupon rate on the outstanding issue relative to that on new issues, the call price on the outstanding bond relative to the price received for the new issue, and the maturity of the bond called. The three characteristics of the outstanding bond that influence the profitability of refunding are, thus, coupon rate, call price, and maturity. A higher call price reduces the profitability of call by increasing the present cost of replacing the outstanding issue. A lower coupon or shorter maturity reduces the profitability of call by reducing the future benefits of replacing the outstanding debt, the first by reducing the annual benefit, the second by reducing the number of years over which the benefit is received.

In addition to the above characteristics of bonds that affect the probability of call, one would expect that the length of time during which call cannot be exercised would influence yields. There are too few completely noncallable bonds to test for a difference in yields between freely callable and noncallable issues. Nevertheless, in the period since 1957 a large proportion of new issues have been non-refundable at lower interest cost, and a few noncallable for any reason,

ence between the call price received and the purchase price of the new bond. When looked at from the point of view of holding-period yields based on the market price of the bond in question, the cost of actual call would be simply the market price minus the call price.

until five years after issue.[6] On any bond with a coupon rate high enough and call price low enough that there is danger of call, a call deferment should reduce the yield.

One section of this paper examines the influence of the coupon rate on yields. Similar attention is not given to the influence of the call price for reasons noted in the text (see pp. 152–153). From a bond table it can be seen that an increase of two points in the call price of a 25-year high coupon bond has approximately the same effect on the yield to maturity calculated from call price, and hence on the profitability of call or the limitation of capital gains, as a reduction of ⅛ per cent in coupon rate with constant call price. As a result, yields should be influenced approximately the same amount by a two point difference in call price as by a ⅛ per cent difference in coupon rate in the other direction.

One may hypothesize that, if coupon and call price are held constant, bonds with longer maturity will carry higher yields in compensation for greater call risk. This effect, however, is likely to be small over the 20–40 year range covered by the bonds included in our data. The effect of callability on term structure is not studied.

THE EXERCISE OF THE CALL OPTION

In this section we examine the extent to which the call option has been exercised since 1951 and the reasons for calls. Although many types of bonds have been examined, data presented here cover publicly offered utility bonds rated A or better which were issued and called during 1951–63.

The exercise of the call option is dominated by the refunding motive, and the volume of redemptions depends largely on the level of new issue yields relative to previous peak new issue yields or coupon rates. The largest volume of redemptions took place in 1954–55, 1958, 1961, and 1962–63, when new issue yields fell below earlier peaks. Almost no calls were made during periods of high interest rates.

The first major period of refunding after the Treasury-Federal Reserve Accord of 1951 was the fifteen months from March 1954 through May 1955,[7] when new issue yields were low enough for profitable refunding of a large number of bonds that were issued during

---

[6] Between January 1957 and June 1966, 248 of the 711 new A, Aa, and Aaa utility bond issues had deferments.

[7] These are the offering dates of the new issues whose proceeds were used for refunding the issues called. The calls were actually made in May 1954 through July 1955.

April to September 1953, when yields were high. Table 3-1 shows the number of callable utility issues offered publicly in 1953 (the bottom number in each cell) and the number of these issues called for refunding in 1954–55 (upper number). None were called after 1955.

There were 72 freely callable utility bonds rated A or higher offered publicly in 1953. Of these, 32 were called in the following two years. Of the 42 bonds issued between April and September 1953, 30 were refunded. Part of the proceeds of between a third and a

TABLE 3-1. *Publicly Offered Utility Bonds Issued in 1953 and Called in 1954–55, by Quality Rating and Coupon Rate*

Coupon Rate	Aaa	Aa	A	Total
4 per cent and above	$\frac{0}{0}$	$\frac{2}{2}$	$\frac{15}{21}$	$\frac{17}{23}$
$3\frac{7}{8}$	$\frac{4}{4}$	$\frac{2}{3}$	$\frac{2}{4}$	$\frac{8}{11}$
$3\frac{3}{4}$	$\frac{1}{1}$	$\frac{2}{3}$	$\frac{0}{3}$	$\frac{3}{7}$
$3\frac{5}{8}$	$\frac{1}{2}$	$\frac{2}{4}$	$\frac{0}{8}$	$\frac{3}{14}$
$3\frac{1}{2}$ or lower	$\frac{1}{3}$	$\frac{0}{11}$	$\frac{0}{3}$	$\frac{1}{17}$
Total	$\frac{7}{10}$	$\frac{8}{23}$	$\frac{17}{39}$	$\frac{32}{72}$

NOTE: The bottom number in each cell shows the number of callable utility issues offered publicly in 1953; the upper number shows the number of these issues called for refunding in 1954-55. None were called after 1955.

SOURCE: Data from *Moody's Bond Survey* (weekly) and *Moody's Bond Record* (monthly), Moody's Investors Service, N. Y.

fourth of the A-Aaa utility issues offered publicly in the period from March 1954 to May 1955 were used for refunding.

Because of the limited variability of call prices and maturities and the absence of call deferments on all but one of the 1953 issues, the two most important variables determining whether a bond could be refunded profitably were the coupon rate and quality rating. Quality rating is important because it influences the rate at which new issues can be sold. The higher the coupon rate and the quality, the larger was the proportion of the callable bonds actually called. For example, of the 23 bonds with coupons of 4 per cent or greater, 17 were called; all those not called were rated A. Of the 17 bonds with coupons of $3\frac{1}{2}$ per cent or lower, only 1 was called and it was rated Aaa.[8]

Only four of the bonds issued in 1954 through 1956 were subse-

[8] Inclusion of bonds issued in 1951 and 1952 does not alter this general tendency.

quently called. All of these were called at a loss in connection with mergers that made it necessary to replace the debt of one of the companies involved.

In 1957, yields on new issues reached their highest level in many years. It would have been profitable to refund a great many of these bonds in early 1958 when rates were considerably lower, but in fact refunding was light. Only 7 of the 78 callable utility bonds issued publicly in 1957 and rated A or better were refunded. The reason for the extremely small number of refundings in 1958 despite the low level of new issue yields was the sudden unexpected rise in yields after June. It is clear from the contemporary financial press that a substantial further decline in new issue yields was expected and that borrowers were therefore holding off on refunding until maximum interest savings could be made. The market reversal came so quickly that a number of companies that had already announced refundings for the third quarter of 1958 were forced to abandon their plans.

As in the period from 1954 to 1956, none of the bonds issued in 1958 had a coupon high enough to justify refunding later. The only bond called was refunded at a loss in terms of interest cost in connection with a merger in 1962.

Five bonds with coupons of 5⅜ per cent or higher were refunded in the first half of 1961, but it was not until 1962–63 that refunding volume again reached large proportions. Of 105 callable bonds with coupons of 5 per cent or higher issued in 1957–61 and still outstanding, 46 were called during 1962–63. Two bonds with coupons below 5 per cent were called at a loss in connection with a merger.

Most high grade public utility bond refundings were thus designed to reduce interest costs. In many other cases the new bond issued to replace the refunded one carried a longer maturity, thus assuring low interest costs for a longer period. Considering the upward trend in interest rates through the 1950's, the ability of companies to make such advance refundings in 1954–55 and 1958 clearly reduced their interest costs appreciably. Similar conclusions apply to lower grade issues, and to industrial, railroad, and finance company obligations.

Calculation of interest savings that have been realized from refunding is complicated by the fact that outlays and savings occur at different points in time. Considering bond refunding as a risk-free investment by the firm, Bowlin[9] has made a calculation of the rates of return earned on forty bond refundings by public utilities in 1962

[9] Oswald D. Bowlin, "The Refunding Decision: Another Special Case in Capital Budgeting," *Journal of Finance,* March 1966, pp. 66–67.

and 1963. The procedure used was to discount after-tax net interest savings (for each year until the maturity date of the refunded bond) at a rate that equates their present value with the net cash investment. The range of rates of return on the investment in refunding was from 3.6 to 43.4 per cent (or 26.7 per cent on the second highest bond) and the interquartile range was 9.1 to 14.6 per cent. Because the after-tax cost of funds on refunding bonds was about 2 to 2½ per cent, none of the forty bonds was refunded at a loss and some involved very high rates of return. However, Bowlin's rate of return calculations do not indicate the magnitude of interest savings relative to total interest costs and, hence, do not shed much light on the value of the call option. We made a calculation of the difference between (a) the yield to maturity on the refunded bond calculated from the call price, which is the gross return to the company from buying back its own bond, and (b) the yield to maturity on the refunding bond calculated from the price received from the underwriter, which is the cost of funds to the company. We then averaged these yield differences over the 85 refundings of utility bonds in our sample for which the necessary data were available. The average was 50 basis points.[10]

Some refundings were for reasons other than to reduce interest costs. One reason was to refund the debt of a newly acquired subsidiary company following a consolidation or merger in order to remove restrictions from the bond indenture or to simplify and consolidate debt. In several cases such refundings raised interest costs. Refundings also were used to remove restrictive clauses or consolidate debt without any connection with mergers.[11]

---

[10] This measure of interest savings is not entirely satisfactory because it involves averaging over a nonlinear price-yield relationship and using two different discount rates. Moreover, it does not consider costs associated with the refunding other than the call premium on the outstanding issue and underwriting spread on the new issue, and it does not include the effect of taxation of increased profits.

Frank C. Jen and James E. Wert have estimated the difference between the offering yield and realized yield on funds invested in callable utility bonds issued and called during 1956–64 and the effect of call deferments on realized yields in 1956–66. See their articles, "The Effect of Call Risk on Corporate Bond Yields," *Journal of Finance,* December 1967, and "The Deferred Call Provision and Corporate Bond Yields," *Journal of Financial and Quantitative Analysis,* June 1968.

[11] In 1955–56, the Baltimore and Ohio Railroad consolidated all of the refundable mortgages of its divisional companies into a single systemwide mortgage. A company official at the time announced that this removed restrictive provisions on the railroad's dividend policy, expressed hopes that it would raise

The call option has also been used to reduce bond indebtedness pending liquidation of the firm, to retire debt with funds obtained from property condemnation settlements, and to alter a firm's capital structure. In the latter case, marketable bonds have been replaced with private placements, with bank loans, and with common stock.

These diverse reasons for exercising the call option demonstrate that the financial flexibility provided by free callability is valuable, even in the absence of expectations of declining interest rates.

THE INFLUENCE OF COUPON RATE ON SEASONED PUBLIC UTILITY BOND YIELDS

This section analyzes the effect of coupon rate on seasoned public utility bond yields. The yield series used were constructed for this project. They cover seasoned long-term callable Aa-Aaa public utility bonds during 1957–67, broken down by coupon rate. The data are shown in Appendix Table 3-A.

The Historical Record, January 1957 to October 1967

Chart 3-1 presents time series on the yield spreads between bonds with various coupon rates and bonds with a coupon rate of $2\frac{3}{4}$ to $2\frac{7}{8}$ per cent. These spreads are large and variable; the spread for the 5 per cent coupon series averages 32 basis points and ranges up to 100 basis points. The spread is larger the higher the coupon rate. This relationship can be seen more directly in Chart 3-2, which presents cross sections relating spread to coupon rate on specified dates.

Chart 3-1 also demonstrates that spreads increase as the level of yields declines. This relationship can be seen more directly in Chart 3-3, where the spread for bonds with a given coupon rate is plotted against the yield on bonds with a $2\frac{3}{4}$–$2\frac{7}{8}$ per cent coupon.

Hypotheses to Explain the Influence of Coupon Rate on Yields

The Call Option.

One reason for the coupon rate to influence yield is that, because of the threat of call, bonds do not sell at more than a point or two above

the company's credit rating, and estimated that it would also save the company an annual $2.7 million in interest payments on the $345 million debt.

CHART 3–1. Yield Differentials, Callable Aa-Aaa Utility Bonds With Specified Coupon Rates Less Bonds With Coupons of 2¾ to 2⅞ Per Cent, 1957–67

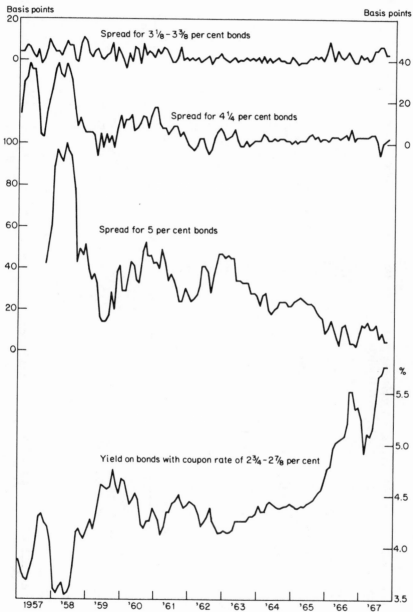

CHART 3-2. Yield Differentials, Callable Aa-Aaa Utility Bonds With Specified Coupon Rates Less Bonds With Coupons of 2¾ to 2⅞ Per Cent, Selected Months

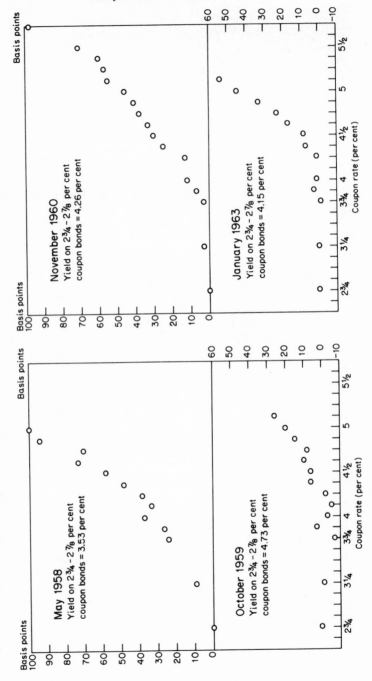

CHART 3–3. Yield Differentials, Callable Aa-Aaa Utility Bonds With Specified Coupon Rates Less Bonds With Coupons of $2\frac{3}{4}$ to $2\frac{7}{8}$ Per Cent, January 1957–September 1961

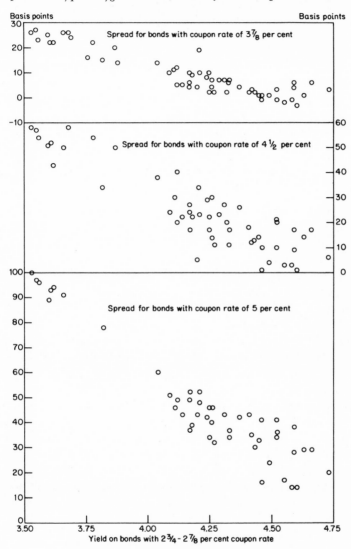

their call prices. Because of the practice of raising the call price on new issues only slightly as the coupon rate is increased, at any given yield to maturity, higher coupon bonds sell closer to call price, and hence they reach call price first as yields decline. After the price of a higher coupon bond reaches the call price, any further fall in the yield on the low coupon bond results in an equal increase in the spread between the yields of the two bonds, and the yield spread would be larger the greater the coupon on the high coupon bond.

In addition, high coupon bonds are less attractive than low coupon bonds because, if interest rates fall in the future, higher coupon bonds will have limited capital gains and may be called. We may hypothesize that this would lead investors to require higher yields to maturity on higher coupon bonds even before their price appreciation has been stopped by the call price.

Miscellaneous Reasons for a Relationship of Yield to Coupon Rate.

Apart from the call option, several reasons, most of them relatively minor, can be suggested to explain why investors might prefer low coupon bonds. Most obvious is the effect of differing tax treatment of different forms of income. Investors might be expected to prefer low coupon bonds because they sell at a discount and a larger part of any given before-tax yield to maturity is in the form of capital gains. A before-tax yield advantage would therefore be required on high coupon bonds to attract buyers.

The tax advantage of low coupon bonds would affect yield relationships only to the extent that the market for corporate bonds is dominated by investors who benefit from the substitution of capital gains for ordinary income. In fact, consideration of the tax treatment of the major investors in corporate bonds suggests that tax considerations are relatively unimportant. The corporate bond market is dominated by institutional investors, particularly life insurance companies, corporate pension funds, and state and local retirement funds. The investment income of corporate pension funds and state and local retirement funds is tax free, and hence these institutions would receive no tax advantage by holding lower coupon bonds. Until 1963, the price appreciation on discount bonds did not receive more favorable tax treatment than coupon income for life insurance companies.[12]

[12] Taxable income of life insurance companies is subject to regular corporation income taxation. Until 1963, life insurance companies were required to accrue market discounts on bonds and treat this as ordinary income for tax purposes. Since 1963 market discounts realized by insurance companies have been accorded capital gains treatment. The excess of net long-term capital

Moreover, to the extent that tax factors affect the yield differential between bonds with different coupon rates, the spread should be larger the higher the general level of yields, since the advantage of the lower coupon bonds would be greatest when their prices were lowest. In fact, one finds the opposite relation between the size of spreads and the level of yields. Tax considerations thus appear to play a negligible role in determining yield differentials between bonds with different coupon rates.

A paper by Durand and another by Durand and Winn[13] offer a variety of alleged advantages of low coupon bonds. Macaulay[14] has pointed out that a low coupon bond has a longer "duration" than a high coupon bond with the same number of years to maturity. Hickman,[15] in developing the idea of duration as a substitute for maturity,

gains over net short-term capital loss is subject to a tax rate of 25 per cent. See R. L. Denney, A. P. Rua, and R. J. Schoen, *Federal Income Taxation of Insurance Companies*, 2nd ed., New York, 1966, pp. 5.17–18, 6.2–7.

[13] David Durand, *Basic Yields of Corporate Bonds, 1900–1942*, New York, NBER, 1942, especially pp. 20–21; and David Durand and Willis J. Winn, *Basic Yields on Bonds, 1926–1947: Their Measurement and Pattern*. New York, NBER, 1947, especially Addendum pp. 31–40.

The alleged advantages are: (1) It is said that accounting procedures, sometimes adopted by legal requirement, may prevent amortization of premiums on high coupon bonds and hence force the recording of price premiums as capital losses when such bonds mature. In contrast, Sidney Homer has suggested to me that some institutional investors are attracted to high coupon bonds because the management is rated by the average current income, which is based simply on coupon receipts excluding discounts on low coupon bonds. (2) The mathematical relation between yield, price, and the coupon rate for a bond of given maturity will cause the price increase on low coupon bonds to be greater in percentage terms than that on high coupon bonds if both of their yields start at the same level and fall by the same amount, thus making the low coupon bond preferable if yields are expected to fall. However, this effect is bound to be very small. (3) It is said that "a high coupon bond, which must be purchased at a substantial premium, is far more likely to decline drastically in price than a low coupon bond, which is purchased at a small premium; traders seem to feel that in a declining market, prices fall fairly freely until they approach par, at which point they meet resistance to further decline" (Durand and Winn, *ibid.*, p. 35). This assertion has not been verified. (4) There is said to be an irrational preference for low priced and hence low coupon bonds merely because they are low priced and thought to be bargains.

[14] Frederick R. Macaulay, *Some Theoretical Problems Suggested by the Movements of Interest Rates, Bond Yields and Stock Prices in the United States Since 1856*, New York, NBER, 1938, pp. 44–53.

[15] W. Braddock Hickman, "The Term Structure of Interest Rates, An Exploratory Analysis," NBER, unpublished manuscript, 1942, Chapter 5.

argues that higher coupon bonds should sell at lower yields to maturity if the term structure of rates is upward sloping, for the same reasons that short maturity bonds carry lower yields than long maturity bonds with the same coupon.

Empirical Evidence: Multiple Regressions

The data listed in Appendix Table 3-A and presented graphically in Charts 3-1 through 3-3 were analyzed using multiple regressions. In each case, the spread between the yield of the higher coupon bonds and the average yield on the bonds with a coupon rate of 2¾ to 2⅞ per cent was used as the dependent variable whose behavior was to be explained. The 2¾ to 2⅞ per cent coupon rate is low enough that during the period under study these bonds had complete call protection. Testing was limited primarily to regression models derived from the call and capital gains hypotheses. The basic hypothesis tested was that the spread between the yields of bonds with different coupon rates depends on factors which influence the profitability of call or expectations about future movements in interest rates.

Variables for Multiple Regressions.

COUPON RATE. One independent variable should be a measure of call protection. This could be both the coupon rate and the call price. The call price is not practical as a separate variable, however, since it is set more or less equal to the offering price (usually par) plus the coupon rate. Because of this practice, there is very little independent variability in the call price: a higher call price will be associated with a higher coupon, and therefore with a higher yield, despite the hypothesis that, ceteris paribus, a higher call price leads to a lower yield.

There is a variable that reflects the call protection of both the coupon rate and the call price. This is the yield to maturity on a bond when it is purchased at the call price. Either an increase in coupon rate or a reduction in call price will reduce call protection, and this will be reflected in an increase in the yield to maturity calculated from the call price.

Because of the large amount of work required to calculate the yield to maturity from call price for all observations of all bonds used, only the coupon rate was used in the regressions as an explanatory variable measuring call protection. Since call prices tend to be higher on bonds with higher coupon rates, omission of the call price gives a downward bias to estimates of the influence of coupon rate. In Chart 3-2 we have already presented graphical evidence of the influence of the coupon rate on yields.

LEVEL OF YIELDS. A second variable which should influence spreads is the level of yields. In Chart 3-3, the spreads show a marked tendency to increase as the level of yields is decreased, even when a further price increase on the higher coupon bond has not yet been stopped by the call price.

The new issue yield is particularly relevant here because the lower it is, the greater the probability that it will fall to a level that will justify refunding. The yield on seasoned bonds with a low coupon is relevant because the lower it is, the greater the probability that it will fall to the level where price appreciation on higher coupon bonds will be halted. We used the level of yields on new issues as an independent variable.[16]

[16] The simple correlation coefficient between the new issue and seasoned yields is .78. If the yield on seasoned issues is used in the multiple regression, the R^2 and the statistical significance of the level of yields variable are increased. However, econometric considerations argue against the use of the yield on seasoned bonds with a 2¾ to 2⅞ per cent coupon rate as an independent variable, because it is used in computing the yield spread that we are seeking to explain. Because any errors of measurement or random movements in the low coupon seasoned yield series have already been transmitted to the dependent variable, part of its explanatory power in a multiple regression would be spurious and its regression coefficient would be biased.

The problem of spurious correlation and bias should be handled by transforming the regression equation and then using a consistent technique for estimating the parameters. Assume that we start with the simplified model where the dependent variable is the yield spread between seasoned bonds with a high coupon rate and bonds with a coupon rate of 2¾ to 2⅞ per cent and the only independent variable is the yield on seasoned bonds with a coupon rate of 2¾ to 2⅞ per cent. Then the regression model is:

$$(Y - X) = a + bX + E,$$

where $Y =$ the yield on high coupon seasoned bonds; $X =$ the yield on seasoned bonds with a coupon rate of 2¾ to 2⅞ per cent; and $E =$ the error term. If we add X to each side of the equation, we have:

$$Y = a + (1 + b) X + E^*.$$

Direct estimation of this by ordinary least squares would introduce simultaneous equations bias. Using a consistent method of estimation, regressing Y on a con-

The new issue series appears to be a more sensitive indicator of conditions in the capital markets.[17] The series used was compiled by Sidney Homer and covers newly issued callable Aa public utilities. This series is shown in Appendix Table 3-C.

CHANGE OF YIELDS. A third variable that might influence the size of the spread is the direction and rate of change of yields. Expectations concerning changes in interest rates will influence expectations of call and capital gains. On the hypothesis that yields are expected to continue moving in the direction they have been moved in the recent past, ceteris paribus, the yield spread due to coupon difference would be higher when interest rates have been falling.[18]

As in the case of the level of yields, a choice must be made between alternative change-in-yield variables. Because of the findings of the Conard study with regard to the primacy of the new issue market, we used the change in new issue yields.[19]

After some testing, it was decided to use a weighted average of changes in yields over the past six months. The weights were .75 for the change in yield over the past month, $(.75)^2$ for the month before that, and so forth back to $(.75)^6$ for the sixth month. This geometrically declining pattern of weights was chosen somewhat arbitrarily on the presumption that it would provide a reasonable index of past yield changes in which a greater weight is given to recent changes.[20]

stant and X, the coefficient of X will be an estimate of $(1 + b)$. The hypothesis suggests that $0 < (1 + b) < 1$.

Use of the level of yields on new issues as an independent variable introduces a similar problem of spurious correlation and bias. The coupon rates of new issues have been high enough that new issue yields are influenced by the call option. As a result, the new issue yield depends on the yield spread due to coupon differences, which is the dependent variable in the regression. This introduces simultaneous equations bias.

[17] Joseph W. Conard and Mark W. Frankena, *op. cit.*

[18] Rather than assume such a theory of expectations, one might assume the validity of the expectations theory of term structure and derive the expected change in interest rates from the yield curve. That was not done here.

[19] Simultaneous equations bias arises here again for the same reason it appears in the coefficient of the level of new issue yields. Changes in the yield on low coupon seasoned bonds proved to have more explanatory power but this is probably due to the more erratic nature of new issue rates and to spurious correlation.

[20] An alternative would be to estimate the weights using the Almon-Lagrange interpolation technique, but the reliability of the derived lag structure would

TIME TREND. Observation of the time series in Chart 3-1 suggests that there has been a downward trend in the size of yield spreads associated with differences in coupon rates. The declining trend in spreads is not due entirely to the upward trend in yield levels with constant regression coefficients. Chart 3-4 reproduces Chart 3-3 for $4\frac{1}{2}$ per cent coupon bonds with the addition of observations for the period from October 1961 through October 1967. It can be seen that the spreads for the later period (represented by X's) are substantially lower than those for the earlier period (represented by circles) at any yield on the low coupon bonds. Because of this, a time trend variable has been included in the equation. This variable is given a value of 1 for the first month's observation, 2 for the second, and so forth. The assumption of a linear time trend is of course an oversimplification.[21] The shift was probably somewhat greater in 1961 than in the other years. By 1966, spreads had reached such a low level that continued upward revision in the expected or "normal" level of yields could not cause much further reduction. As a result, at the coupon rates used in this study, one should not project the time beyond the period considered in the regressions.

Two explanations for this reduction in spreads can be suggested. The first is that there was an upward revision in the expected "normal" level of interest rates which reduced the value of call protection. If interest rates in the 1960's were no longer expected to fall to the lows that were anticipated in the 1950's, then the danger of refunding and the expected limitation of capital gains in the event of future price rises would have been reduced.

A second reason for the trend in the yield spread has been suggested by Sidney Homer. He emphasizes the role of the supply and demand for funds in determining yield spreads. On the supply side, secular growth of large institutional investors has produced an increase in competition for higher yielding investments and a tendency for yield spreads of many sorts to be reduced, including those between bonds with different coupons, bonds with different quality ratings, new and seasoned issues, and corporates and governments. He also argues that from 1961 through 1964 there was a very light volume of new corporate public offerings,

be too low for this method to be a practical improvement. See S. Almon, "The Distributed Lag between Capital Appropriations and Expenditures," *Econometrica*, January 1965, pp. 178–196.

[21] The time trend was also included as a quadratic because it seemed likely that the trend was greater in the earlier period when spreads were large. An increase in the correlation coefficients and reduction in the autocorrelation of residuals suggest that this is an improvement over the linear trend variable.

CHART 3–4. Yield Differentials on Callable Aa-Aaa Utility Bonds: Bonds With Coupon Rate of 4½ Per Cent Less Bonds With Coupon Rates of 2¾ to 2⅞ Per Cent, 1957–67

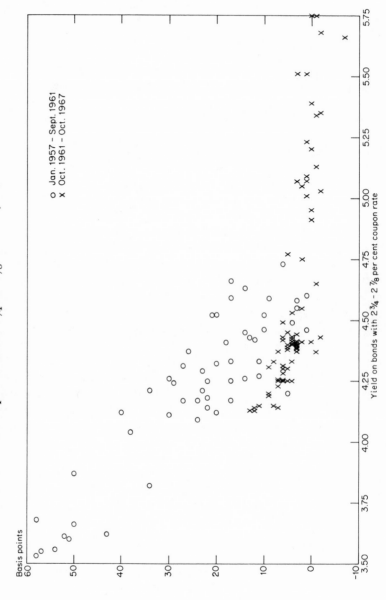

especially after allowance was made for refundings, and a cumulative drought developed. Because new issues during part of this period did not have high coupons, and because many outstanding high coupon bonds were called, the relative supply of high coupon bonds declined during 1962–63. Further, the volume of long-term governments, which are closer substitutes for low coupon than high coupon corporate bonds because of their call protection, increased. Homer believes that these changes in supply and demand factors explain the decline in the spread caused by coupon differences, particularly during the 1961–65 period.

VOLUME OF NEW CORPORATE ISSUES. A partial test of the Homer hypothesis can be made by including the volume of new corporate bonds as an independent variable in the regression equation. On the basis of our hypotheses, we should expect that, if the volume variable influences the size of the spread, it would have a positive regression coefficient. Tests of alternative measures indicated that the volume of publicly offered issues for the three months preceding the month of observation gave the best results.[22]

REGRESSIONS. Two types of regression equations were estimated. The first covered all the bonds in the sample and included the coupon rate as an independent variable. In the second set, a separate regression was run for bonds with each coupon rate, and consequently the coupon rate was not used as an independent variable.

In the first of these regressions, a linear relation between the natural logarithms of the data was used.[23] The logarithmic transformation of the data was used because our hypothesis and other analysis suggested that a purely linear relation was inappropriate because the effect that any given difference in the coupon rate or in the level of yields has on the spread depends on both the level of the coupon rate and the level of yields. A full logarithmic transformation of the data makes the first derivative of the spread with respect to each independent variable depend on the level of each of the independent variables. With two

---

[22] Inclusion of privately placed issues or the issues of one month more or less did not make much difference in the results.

[23] Because it is impossible to take the logarithm of a negative number, 1.00 per cent (100 basis points) was added to the spread and the change-in-yield variable at each observation before taking the logarithm in order to make all observations positive.

independent variables, the relation $\log y = c + b_1 \log x_1 + b_2 \log x_2$ implies a relation between the untransformed data of the form

$$y = a x_1^{b_1} x_2^{b_2}.$$

The first regression was run for all observations from January 1957 through April 1966 for bonds with coupon rates from $3\frac{3}{4}$ through $5\frac{3}{4}$ per cent. Table 3-2 provides a summary of the variables used and the results of the regression.[24]

TABLE 3-2. *Regression of Yield Spread on Explanatory Variables, $3\frac{3}{4}$ to $5\frac{3}{4}$ Per Cent Coupon Bonds, 1957–66*

Variable	b Coefficient	t Value
Constant	−.679	−10.77
X_1	1.141	55.70
X_2	−.492	−12.65
X_3	−.079	−5.87
X_4	−.0021	−30.77

NOTE: The number of observations = 1,294; the standard error of estimate = .077; R^2 = .779; F statistic for R^2 = 1,134.37; dependent variable is the logarithm of 1.00 plus the yield spread over bonds with a coupon of 2 3/4 to 2 7/8 per cent; X_1 is the logarithm of the coupon rate; X_2 is the logarithm of the level of the new issue yield; X_3 is the logarithm of 1.00 plus the weighted average of change of new issue yields; X_4 is the logarithm of e^t, where t is the time trend, or simply t since $\log (e^t)$ = t.

All regression coefficients have the signs hypothesized and are statistically significant at the .01 level. Approximately 78 per cent of the variance of the dependent variable is "explained" by the regression. It should be noted that no measure for volume of new issues was included in this regression.

Regressions were also run separately at each coupon rate for the higher coupon bonds, again using all observations available between January 1957 and April 1966. This time no logarithmic transformation of the data was made, but the level of new issue yields was included as a quadratic term. There was, therefore, one independent variable for the new issue yield and another for its square. The form of the regression equation was linear apart from this transformation. Table

[24] To provide a better test for the remaining observations, it might be desirable to run the same regression omitting all observations where the market price of the high coupon bond was close to or held at the call price.

3-3 describes the symbols used in the regression equations and gives the results.

In these regressions, the independent variables account for between 81 and 89 per cent of the variance in the yield spread. Moreover, all regression coefficients have the signs required by our hypotheses. With the exception of the change-in-yield variable in the first and last regressions, all variables are significant at the .01 level.[25]

Although these results generally support the hypotheses, the coefficient of the time trend seems implausibly large. Our interpretation of the time trend is primarily that it takes account of the upward revision in the expected "normal" and cyclical minimum levels of yields.

ZERO SPREADS. It is of some interest to know the yield level, if any, at which the yield spread for an intermediate or high coupon bond approaches zero. On the basis of our hypothesis, there is no reason to expect that the yield spread on higher coupon bonds should ever become zero as long as a fall in yields is anticipated, because the lower coupon bonds would still have an advantage in terms of call protection and capital gains potential. However, in the past decade spreads did approach to within a very few basis points of zero at a time when yields on the lower coupon bonds rose to the level of the coupon rate on the higher coupon bond and the higher coupon bond was therefore selling below par. This can be seen in Charts 3-2 and 3-4.

LIMITATIONS OF THE REGRESSION RESULTS. A statistical problem encountered in the regressions which we have discussed is autocorrelation among errors. According to the Durbin-Watson statistics for the regressions in Table 3-3, all have significant positive first-order serial correlation of the residuals. Autocorrelation alone does not introduce a bias into the estimated regression coefficients as long as the assumptions of the least squares statistical procedure hold. However, the significance levels of the regression coefficients are lower than is indicated by the calculated t values. The presence of autocorrelation also suggests that some errors have been made in the specification of the regression equation.

The reliability of the individual regression coefficients is further weakened by the likelihood of multicollinearity among the independent variables because of their related cycles and trends.

[25] Because of the autocorrelated residuals, however, the true significance levels for the regression coefficients are below those indicated by the t values.

TABLE 3-3. *Regression of Yield Spread on Explanatory Variables, for Bonds With Given Coupon Rates*

Variable	5 Per Cent Reg. Coef.	5 Per Cent t value	$4\frac{7}{8}$ Per Cent Reg. Coef.	$4\frac{7}{8}$ Per Cent t value	$4\frac{3}{4}$ Per Cent Reg. Coef.	$4\frac{3}{4}$ Per Cent t value	$4\frac{5}{8}$ Per Cent Reg. Coef.	$4\frac{5}{8}$ Per Cent t value	$4\frac{1}{2}$ Per Cent Reg. Coef.	$4\frac{1}{2}$ Per Cent t value
Constant	9.507	8.197	8.999	8.308	4.518	3.664	7.160	7.759	4.871	4.433
X_1	-3.647	-7.262	-3.521	-7.507	-1.686	-3.165	-2.928	-7.327	-1.922	-4.047
X_2	.363	6.673	.357	7.031	.166	2.885	.307	7.100	.195	3.814
X_3	-.086	-1.582	-.102	-1.996	-.133	-2.362	-.182	-4.179	-.059	-1.171
X_4	.091	4.927	.104	6.024	.120	6.120	.116	7.911	.108	6.163
X_5	-.0033	-12.763	-.0037	-15.706	-.0037	-15.314	-.0030	-14.890	-.0031	-13.983
Number of observations	103		104		111		104		109	
Mean of Y	.363		.299		.232		.181		.146	
Standard error of estimate	.071		.067		.077		.057		.069	
R^2	.876		.887		.828		.879		.808	
Durbin—Watson statistic[a]	.877		.906		.700		.867		.571	

NOTE: The dependent variable is the yield spread over bonds with a coupon of $2\frac{3}{4}$ to $2\frac{7}{8}$ per cent; X_1 is the level of the new issue yield; X_2 is the square of the level of the new issue yield, $(X_1)^2$; X_3 is the weighted average of change in the new issue yield; X_4 is the volume of publicly offered new corporate bonds; X_5 is the time trend.

[a] In computing the Durbin-Watson statistic, all first differences were taken between residuals for observations in consecutive months. Whenever an observation was missing, the corresponding first differences were omitted.

Finally, because of the inclusion of a time trend and nonlinear terms, the regression equations we have estimated do not permit extrapolation beyond the limits of the observations used in estimation.

Despite these problems all the results appear consistent with theoretical considerations of how call features should affect yields. Any gains from more exact specification of the relationships do not seem to merit the additional costs involved.

THE INFLUENCE OF CALL DEFERMENTS ON PUBLIC UTILITY BOND YIELDS[26]

Opinions and Policies of Regulatory Commissions and the Financial Community

The Securities and Exchange Commission, the Federal Power Commission, and the public service commissions of the various states regulate the sale of bonds by utility companies. Before refunding deferments came into widespread use in 1956, the SEC developed a policy designed to prevent restrictions on callability. This policy, which was in effect throughout the period under study, required that "securities be redeemable at the option of the issuer at any time upon reasonable notice and the payment of a reasonable redemption premium, if any." The purpose of this provision was "to assure that public utility companies shall be in a position, if money rates decrease materially, to refund their bonds" and thus "to ensure economies in the raising of capital." In addition to denying the use of refunding deferments, they ruled that call protection could not be provided by setting a very high call price or setting a low coupon rate and selling at a discount.[27]

---

[26] A study of this problem was made independently by Frank C. Jen and James E. Wert and reported in "The Value of the Deferred Call Privilege," *National Banking Review*, March 1966, pp. 369–378. They studied the period 1960–64 and arrived at the same conclusions reached here. See also Gordon Pye, "The Value of Call Deferment on a Bond: Some Empirical Results," *Journal of Finance*, December 1967, pp. 623–636.

[27] "The working policy of the Commission has been that the initial redemption price shall not exceed the sum of the initial public offering price plus the coupon rate on the bonds." SEC, *23rd Annual Report, Fiscal Year Ending June 30, 1957*, Washington, D.C., 1958, p. 142. Substantially the same statements are contained in every annual report through the present. See *31st Annual Report, Fiscal Year Ending June 30, 1965*, p. 91. The FPC has taken substantially the same position, denying requests for authorization of refunding deferments

In opposing restrictions on the call option, the SEC and FPC argue that the potential benefits of refunding outweigh whatever increase in the cost of funds is attributable to free callability.

The SEC stated that "issues of immediately refundable bonds have, on the whole, not been penalized in the market place as compared with those users which accepted refunding restriction."[28] As support for its position, the SEC has cited evidence on new issue yields, on the average number of underwriter bids received at competitive bidding, and on the success with which issues were marketed by the underwriter. The SEC argues that its position is supported by the study of offering yields during 1926–59 made by Hess and Winn, which found that only in the second half of 1959 was there any difference in yields on freely callable bonds and those carrying refunding deferments.[29] Moreover, the SEC reports that "studies made by the Commission's staff . . . with respect to electric and gas utility bond issues sold at competitive bidding . . . indicated that the presence or absence of a restriction on free refundability has not affected the number of bids received by an issuer at competitive bidding or the ability of the winning bidder to market the bonds."[30]

Despite the denial of deferments by the SEC and FPC since 1957, about a third of the public offerings of utility bonds (and a larger proportion of industrial issues and private placements) have had refunding deferments. This indicates that a large number of corporate borrowers

on new issues. Commissions in the states have in general issued similar statements against deferments, but in practice many have permitted them.

[28] SEC, *28th Annual Report,* p. 93. The FPC similarly stated in 1957 that, despite the value of the call option to the borrower, which would justify payment of a higher cost for funds, "our experience to date has not shown a material difference in the cost of money, on a current basis, of comparable issues with a limitation on the right of redemption and those without." *Public Utility Reports,* 19 PUR 3d, 1957, p. 187, re Puget Sound Power and Light Co.

[29] "These differences, indicating somewhat lower interest costs on bonds having refunding restrictions, were found by the Wharton School (i.e., Hess and Winn, *op. cit.*) not to have been material—at least when measured against the advantage to the issuer of being able to refund its bonds at any time." SEC, *28th Annual Report,* p. 93.

[30] This study included the period from May 14, 1957, through fiscal year 1965, and was based on simple and weighted (by volume) averages of bids by underwriters and of amounts sold at the syndicate offering price up to the date of termination of the syndicate, with the time unit over which the averages were taken in each case being a fiscal year. The only statistics that were at variance with the SEC's conclusion were the marketability indices for fiscal years 1963 and 1965. SEC, *31st Annual Report,* pp. 92–93, and earlier *Reports.*

have thought the inclusion of a deferment would increase market attractiveness and reduce the current cost of funds.

On the basis of answers to a questionnaire, Hess and Winn found that in early 1960 large institutional investors thought that on a thirty-year Aa utility issue with a $5\frac{1}{4}$ per cent coupon, "a five-year (call) deferment would be worth 15 basis points, a ten-year (call) deferment 25 basis points, and a thirty-year deferment (a nonrefundable issue) 30 to 36 basis points," though a wide range of estimates was given in each case.[31] They also found that if both the coupon on new issues and the yield on outstandings were reduced by $1\frac{1}{4}$ per cent, the median estimated value of a five-year deferment declined to about 5 basis points. This suggests that the value of the call deferments to investors is considered to be an increasing function of the coupon rate on the bond in question.[32]

In addition to borrowers and institutional investors, people acquainted with the financial market have often indicated that a call deferment on a high coupon bond reduces its yield. In 1957, 1959, and 1960, *Moody's Bond Survey* consistently recommended investment in call-protected new issues and in 1959 said: "Because interest rates are close to the highest levels seen in many years, we consider nonrefundable and noncallable provisions in bonds very important for long-term investors. . . . We expect that more of the new issues will have to incorporate protection from early redemption in order to give market attractiveness."[33] In mid-1957 *Moody's* wrote: "As in past weeks, investor preference for protection from early call showed up markedly in the receptions accorded new corporate issues. . . . Issues without protective call provisions required much higher yields."[34] Similarly, the financial section of the *New York Times* in mid-1957 said that callable bonds were selling poorly and public utilities were faced with the need to pay much more than nominally higher yields to get callable loans and that "for bonds of less than top rank . . . maintaining the unlimited call privilege means

---

[31] Hess and Winn, *op. cit.*, p. 21. Comments in parentheses were added.

[32] One problem in the interpretation of these figures is that Hess and Winn were unable to determine whether the respondents were attempting to give the true or market value of call protection. Although the Hess and Winn study did not include bonds issued in 1960, their estimates are in line with the value put on call protection by the market in early 1960, which was about 15 basis points for a five-year refunding deferment, including the effect of coupon difference due to the initial yield spread.

[33] *Moody's Bond Survey*, August 17, 1959, p. 351.

[34] *Ibid.*, June 24, 1957, p. 463.

incurring $\frac{1}{4}$ of 1 per cent more in costs," while for an Aaa bond the added cost was $\frac{1}{8}$ per cent.[35]

There has, therefore, been some difference of opinion on whether call deferments have an effect on bond yields.

Empirical Evidence

Hess and Winn's study of the influence of deferments on the yield of new corporate issues offered from 1926 to 1959 concluded that the existence of a "call deferment did not influence yields except during the last six months of this 34-year period."[36] This conclusion is misleading because the number of deferred issues before 1957 was too small to permit meaningful comparisons. Between 1926 and 1949 only 17 of the 738 bonds issued had deferments, and these included industrials and private placements as well as publicly offered utilities. The most detailed breakdown that could be made held quality rating and calendar month of issue constant. Because neither utility and industrial issues nor publicly offered and privately placed issues are sufficiently alike to warrant comparison, because private placements are not rated for quality, and because a month is too long a period in which to assume that market conditions remain constant, the data cannot justify the conclusion that "length of call deferment did not influence yields." Similarly, since there were only 12 deferred issues among the 166 new issues in the period from 1950 through 1955 and all 12 of these were on private placements, on which quality ratings are not available, no conclusion on the effect of deferments on yields is possible in this period either. Perhaps the most significant conclusion that can be drawn is that prior to 1956 there was not enough interest in deferments for investors to insist on them, except in some private placements in the early 1950's. No doubt this is explained by the fact that new issue coupons were generally so low that call protection was provided by the coupon and call price and a deferment would have added little.

The basic hypothesis tested in the present study for both new and seasoned issues is that a deferment reduces the yield on a corporate bond if the coupon rate is high enough that investors think there is a possibility of call or of capital gains limitation. This implies a positive relation between the size of the yield spread between callable and deferred issues with a given coupon rate and the size of the yield

---

[35] *New York Times,* June 23, 1957.
[36] Hess and Winn, *op. cit.,* p. 80.

spread between seasoned callable bonds with this same coupon rate and those with a very low coupon rate, since both yield spreads reflect the market valuation of call protection.

A first corollary hypothesis is that the amount by which the yield is reduced by a deferment is higher for higher coupon bonds, or it increases when the coupon rate increases relative to the expected "normal" and cyclical minimum rates of interest. If expectations about the level of future interest rates have an elasticity of less than one with respect to the present level of interest rates, then when interest rates and the new issue coupon rate increase together, borrowers and investors will believe that the probability of call or of capital gains limitation on new issues has increased. This means that when the new issue coupon rate increases, the amount by which the new issue yield is reduced by a deferment increases even though the level of yields increases simultaneously.[37]

A second corollary, which applies only to seasoned issues, is that the amount by which the yield on a bond with a given coupon rate is reduced by a deferment increases when the level of yields declines.

A third corollary is that the yield spread between callable and deferred issues with the same coupon rate is only a fraction of the yield spread between the same callable bond and a bond with a very low coupon rate. Although deferments limit the exercise of the call option, they provide less call protection than a low coupon. Most deferments restrict refunding only at a lower interest cost (call for other purposes is still permitted) and only for five years. When coupons are high enough that borrowers and investors think there is a high probability that refunding would be profitable within the first five years, they are also apt to think that there will be another chance for refunding after the deferment ends.[38]

---

[37] This would apply to comparisons for consecutive periods but not necessarily more distant periods, between which there could be major changes in expectations about the "normal" rate of interest.

[38] Thus, for example, most of the bonds issued in 1957 and since refunded were called in late 1962 and 1963, after the deferred issues had become callable. As a result, five out of the ten utility bonds rated A or better issued with deferments in 1957 and having coupons high enough (5 per cent or over) to be threatened by call in 1962–63 actually were called. On the other hand, these deferments did prevent refunding in 1958 when much greater savings could have been realized, the deferments on high coupon bonds issued in 1959–60 prevented their refunding in 1962–63, and if the bonds issued in 1953 had had deferments these deferments would have prevented refunding altogether, because after 1954–55 rates never again fell far enough to make the refunding of these bonds profitable.

Except in 1957, the evidence presented below supports the hypothesis and its corollaries concerning the influence of deferments on bond yields. Based on annual averages, deferments are found to reduce yields by up to 14 basis points.[39] This implies that the capital market is considerably less imperfect than Hess and Winn and various agencies regulating the issuance of corporate bonds have contended.

It was not until 1957 that a significant number of publicly offered corporate bonds had refunding deferments. However, during 1957–66 a substantial proportion of new issues had deferments, and therefore it is possible to compare systematically yields on freely callable and deferred issues.

For new issues, this analysis covers only long-term public utility mortgage bonds and senior debentures rated A, Aa, or Aaa by Moody and publicly offered under competitive bidding in principal amounts of $2 million or more. Quality rating is held constant in all yield comparisons. While size of issue is not held constant, all but a few issues were larger than $10 million. Most of the bonds have a maturity of about 30 years and all are within the 20 to 40 year range. Table 3-4 shows the deferment characteristics of the new issues.

In order to hold market conditions stable, yield comparisons were limited to bonds issued within a period of 10 days of each other. For the period 1957 to mid-1966, it was possible to make 108 such comparisons, each involving one or more freely callable and one or more deferred issues, but not more than one of both. Comparisons were made both between offering yields and between yields at which the bonds were selling in the open market during the first weeks after they

---

[39] We have not undertaken an independent study of the number of underwriter bids or the success of the winning bidder in marketing an issue for deferred and callable bonds. The SEC found that, in terms of yearly averages, deferred issues have not had an advantage on either count, and may have had a slight disadvantage. However, it should be pointed out that if prices are adjusted to offset any disadvantage of free callability, there would be no reason for a difference in number of bids or success in marketing. Further, superficial study indicates that the average size of deferred issues is larger than the average size of freely callable issues, and that there is an inverse relation between size of issue and number of bids, because the larger the issue the greater the number of underwriters that must combine to make a single bid. Thus, there would be a slight bias against deferred issues in terms of number of bids which was not related to the fact that they were deferred. Third, to the extent that deferred and freely callable issues are not similarly spaced within a given fiscal year, the use of yearly averages could cover up differences. In any event, we found a number of cases where the contemporary financial press said an issue had a better market reception because it had a deferment.

TABLE 3-4. *Classification of New A, Aa, and Aaa Utility Issues With Deferments, 1957–65*

Year	Total Number of Bonds	Total Number of Deferred Issues	Number of Call Deferments[a]	Deferments Other Than Five Years
1957	104	26	5	2 of 10 years
				1 of 7½ years
1958	89	23	2	None
1959	75	21	2	1 of 7 years
1960	79	28	4	None
1961	68	27	6	1 of 10 years
1962	69	29	8	None
1963	65	24	10	None
1964	49	23	2	None
1965	63	28		
Jan.–June				
1966	50	19		
Total	711	248		

[a]Call deferments restrict use of the call option not only for refunding at lower interest cost but for other purposes as well. Most deferments apply to refunding only.

were released from price maintenance agreements. The latter make it possible to eliminate a major part of any difference in yields due to differences in market conditions at the dates of offering. They also make it possible to discover the market valuation of call deferments when one of the issues was mispriced by the underwriter.

A complication arises because coupon rates on new issues are set so that the offering price will be near par: Any reduction in yield caused by a deferment will tend to lead to a reduction in coupon rate. Consequently, the coupons on the deferred bonds used in the comparisons will be systematically lower than those on the corresponding freely callable issues, and average spreads measured between such pairs will exaggerate the influence of deferments on yields by capturing the effect of differences in coupon rate. To eliminate the influence of differences in coupon rate, prior to averaging, each yield spread was adjusted for the effect of the difference in coupon rates of the deferred and callable issues in the month of issue, using the data in Appendix Table 3-A.

The average yield spreads for each year are presented in Table 3-5. Spreads are negative when the average yield on the deferred issues was lower. Columns (2) and (4) present spreads for offering yields, before and after correction for differences in coupon respectively. Columns

TABLE 3-5. *Average Yield Spreads for New A, Aa, and Aaa Utility Bonds, Callable Issues Compared to Issues With Refunding Deferments, 1957-66*

| | | Offering Yields | | | | Yields After Termination of Price Maintenance | | | | | |
| | | Uncorrected for Coupon | | Corrected for Coupon | | Uncorrected for Coupon | | Corrected for Coupon | | | |
Year	Number of Comparisons (1)	Yield Spread (2)	Signif. Level (3)	Yield Spread (4)	Signif. Level (5)	Yield Spread (6)	Signif. Level (7)	Yield Spread (8)	Signif. Level (9)	Average Coupon on Deferred Issues (10)	Yield Spread on Seasoned Bonds, Coupon of Deferred New Issue vs. $2\frac{3}{4}$ to $2\frac{7}{8}$ Per cent (11)
1957	20	-5.0	.10	NA	NA	-7.9	.05	NA	NA	4.81	NA
1958	17	-5.4	.025	-1.5	a	-7.6	.01	-4.5	.025	4.14	-23.9
1959	11	-22.5	.01	-10.4	.01	-26.5	.01	-13.8	.01	4.97	-28.8
1960	12	-15.0	.01	-9.2	.01	-15.6	.01	-9.9	.01	4.82	-32.9
1961	6	-9.2	.01	-6.8	.01	-7.2	.01	-5.2	.025	4.73	-21.2
1962	8	-1.7	a	+0.6	a	+1.1	a	+3.1	a	4.36	-3.8
1963	9	+0.2	a	+0.4	a	+0.8	a	+1.0	a	4.40	-5.7
1964	11	+2.0	a	+2.6	a	-1.5	a	-0.8	a	4.59	-3.5
1965	8	+0.3	a	+0.3	a	-4.3	.025	-4.3	.025	4.71	-7.1
1966b	6	-11.5	.025	-9.3	.025	-15.3	.01	-13.2	.01	5.27	-16.8

SOURCE: *Moody's Bond Survey* and Appendix Table 3-A.
NA = required data not available.
a = not significant at the .10 level.
b January to June.

(6) and (8) present the corresponding spreads for market yields after termination of price maintenance agreements. In the column to the right of each average yield spread is the significance level applicable to tests of the null hypothesis that the average yield spread is zero. These are based on one-tailed tests for the mean of a normally distributed random variable (the yield spread for individual pairs of bonds) with unknown variance. Column (11) presents the annual average of spreads, calculated in the month of issue for each deferred bond, between the yields of callable seasoned bonds with the same coupon rate as the deferred issue and seasoned bonds with coupon rates of $2\frac{3}{4}$ to $2\frac{7}{8}$ per cent.[40] This measures the market value of the addition of complete refunding protection (offered by a very low coupon) to a freely callable bond with the same coupon as the deferred issue, and can be compared to the market value of the five-year deferment shown in column (8).

The findings in Table 3-5 can be summarized as follows: (a) All annual average yield spreads for 1957 through 1961 and for 1966 are negative. (b) All average spreads for 1958 through 1961 and for 1966, except that for offering yields corrected for coupon in 1958, are statistically significant at the .025 level, and most are significant at the .01 level. (c) The average spreads for 1957 are only marginally significant at the .05 and .10 levels. (d) The average spreads for 1962 through 1965 are random in sign and, except for the negative average yields after termination of price maintenance in 1965, are not statistically significant. (e) Omitting 1957, average yield spreads are largest and statistically significant in the same years that the yield spread in column (11), measuring the market value at current new issue coupon rates of the addition of the complete refunding protection offered by a very low coupon, is relatively high. The yield spread in column (11) is low in each year from 1962 through 1965, indicating that for bonds with the coupon rates on new issues the market value of additional refunding protection was very low. (f) On a year-to-year basis, the direction of change for all statistically significant yield spreads corrected for coupon in columns (4) and (8) is the same as the direction of the change in the average coupon rate in column (10). (g) In every case the average reduction in yield due to deferments is a fraction of the spread in column (11) in the same year. (h) After correction for coupon, at current new issue coupons, average yield reductions due to deferments are 5 to 14 basis points in all years (except 1958) where the additional call protection provided by a low

---

[40] See Appendix Table 3-A.

coupon reduces yields by over 15 basis points compared to freely callable issues with the same coupon rate as the deferred new issues.

Except for (c), all of these findings provide clear support for the basic hypothesis, that a deferment reduces the yield on a corporate bond *if the coupon rate is high enough that investors think there is a possibility of call or capital gains limitation*. Finding (e)—the low spreads in column (11) for 1962 through 1965—explains finding (d).

A possible explanation for (c), the lack of statistical support for the hypothesis in 1957, is that market valuation of deferments was irregular because both high coupons and deferments were new to the market. This is consistent with the finding of a more uniform valuation of call protection after the market gained experience with high coupons and deferments and after the sudden decline in interest rates in 1958 demonstrated the potentials of the call option and call protection.

Finding (f) supports the first corollary hypothesis, that when the new issue coupon rate increases, the amount by which the new issue yield is reduced by a deferment increases even though the level of yields increases simultaneously.

While the second corollary does not apply to new issues, finding (g) supports the third corollary, that the yield spread between callable and deferred issues with the same coupon rate is only a fraction of the yield spread between the same callable bond and a bond with a very low coupon rate.

To test the same hypotheses concerning the influence of refunding deferments on yields on seasoned bonds, monthly series were constructed at each coupon rate for the average yield of Aa-Aaa utility bonds comparable to those used in the regressions above[41] except that the bonds in the present series have deferments of two years or longer. The yield spreads between these two sets of series for freely callable and deferred issues are presented in Appendix Table 3-B, with spreads negative when the yield on deferred bonds was lower. Table 3-6 presents averages of spreads, broken down by coupon rate, for 1957–61, 1958, 1962–65, and 1966.

No complication due to differences in coupon rates arises here because the spreads are calculated holding coupon rate constant. The spreads for seasoned issues are most similar in nature to those for new issues after termination of price maintenance and after correction for coupon differences, but they differ from the latter in two ways. First, because the seasoned bonds have been outstanding for some time,

[41] See Appendix Table 3-A.

TABLE 3-6. *Average Yield Spreads on Seasoned Aa-Aaa Utility Bonds, Callable Issues Compared to Issues With Deferments of Two Years or More, by Coupon Rate, 1957-66*

Coupon Rate (per cent)	1957–61		Jan.–Aug. 1958		1962–65		Jan.–July 1966	
	Number of Months	Yield Spread	Number of Months	Yield Spread	Number of Months	Yield Spread	Number of Months	Yield Spread
$3\frac{3}{4}$	33	−.01	—	—	—	—	—	—
$3\frac{7}{8}$	38	−.03	—	—	—	—	—	—
4	23	+.05	—	—	—	—	—	—
$4\frac{1}{4}$	—	—	—	—	41	.00	—	—
$4\frac{3}{8}$	46	−.05	—	—	48	+.01	7	+.01
$4\frac{1}{2}$	35	−.02	—	—	48	.00	7	−.02
$4\frac{5}{8}$	52	−.05	8	−.08	48	.00	7	−.02
$4\frac{3}{4}$	26	−.03	5	−.06	48	+.01	7	−.03
$4\frac{7}{8}$	51	−.06	8	−.16	13	+.01	5	−.07
5	51	−.08	8	−.18	23	−.01	4	−.06
$5\frac{1}{8}$	7	−.09	—	—	—	—	2	−.07
$5\frac{3}{8}$	4	−.06	—	—	—	—	—	—

SOURCE: Appendix Table 3-B.

deferments in the present series are for less than five years from the date of observation. The period of deferment averaged 3 to 4 years and in a number of cases the average period declined from almost five years to only two years over the set of observations. Second, while the observations for new issues were made only at times when the level of new issue yields was near the coupon rate, for seasoned issues observations were made over a wide range of yield levels.

The findings in Table 3-6 can be summarized as follows: (a) With two exceptions, both low coupon bonds, all average yield spreads in 1957–61, 1958, and 1966 are negative. (b) All spreads for 1962–65 are negligible. (c) Except in 1962–65, spreads were larger on bonds with coupons of $4\frac{7}{8}$ to $5\frac{3}{8}$ per cent than on those with lower coupon rates. (d) Spreads increased considerably in 1958. (e) Average spreads on high coupon bonds were 6 to 9 basis points during 1957 to 1961 and 1966 and twice that in 1958.

All of these findings provide support for the basic hypothesis about the effect of deferments on yields. Finding (b) is explained in the same way as the parallel finding for new issues. Finding (c) supports the first corollary hypothesis. New issue yields declined considerably in 1958, and finding (d) supports the second corollary, that the amount by which the yield on a bond with a given coupon rate is reduced by a deferment increases when the level of yields declines. The third corollary is supported by a comparison of yield spreads due to differences in coupon rate and those due to deferments.

APPENDIX TABLE 3-A. Average First-of-Month Yields on Seasoned Long-Term Callable Aa-Aaa Public Utility Bonds, by Coupon Rate, 1957-66

| Date | Coupon Rate | | | | | | | | | | | | | | | | | |
	$2\frac{3}{4}-2\frac{7}{8}$	$3\frac{1}{8}-3\frac{3}{8}$	$3\frac{3}{4}$	$3\frac{7}{8}$	4	$4\frac{1}{8}$	$4\frac{1}{4}$	$4\frac{3}{8}$	$4\frac{1}{2}$	$4\frac{5}{8}$	$4\frac{3}{4}$	$4\frac{7}{8}$	5	$5\frac{1}{8}$	$5\frac{1}{4}$	$5\frac{3}{8}$	$5\frac{1}{2}$	$5\frac{3}{4}$
1957																		
Jan.	3.88	3.92	3.93	4.02	4.01	4.00	4.02	4.25	—	—	—	—	—					
Feb.	3.76	3.80	3.79	3.92	3.92	3.95	4.05	4.15	—	—	4.42	—	—					
March	3.69	3.76	3.75	3.93	3.91	3.95	4.00	4.12	—	—	4.36	—	—					
April	3.68	3.74	3.79	3.94	3.95	3.95	4.06	4.15	4.26	—	4.35	—	—					
May	3.78	3.81	3.81	4.00	4.02	—	4.13	4.22	4.32	—	4.39	—	—					
June	3.87	3.88	—	4.07	4.10	—	4.22	4.36	4.37	—	4.44	—	—					
July	4.12	4.17	—	4.24	4.19	—	4.33	4.46	4.52	—	4.56	—	—					
Aug.	4.29	4.27	—	4.36	4.21	4.30	4.33	4.44	4.52	—	4.59	—	—					
Sept.	4.32	4.32	—	4.34	4.22	4.24	4.35	4.48	4.52	4.60	4.59	4.66	—					
Oct.	4.24	4.29	—	4.32	4.23	4.30	4.38	4.51	4.53	4.60	4.62	4.70	4.66					
Nov.	4.21	4.31	—	4.40	4.22	4.28	4.41	4.51	4.55	4.60	4.73	4.76	4.73					
Dec.	4.04	4.10	—	4.18	4.10	4.18	4.29	4.41	4.42	4.52	4.53	4.58	4.64					
1958																		
Jan.	3.60	3.64	—	3.85	3.81	3.89	3.95	4.08	4.11	4.21	4.29	4.47	4.49					
Feb.	3.55	3.59	—	3.82	3.72	3.87	3.93	4.05	4.12	4.27	4.27	4.43	4.52					
March	3.61	3.63	—	3.83	3.72	3.89	3.94	4.03	4.13	4.25	4.28	4.44	4.54					
April	3.66	3.71	3.83	3.92	3.86	3.89	3.97	4.09	4.16	4.27	4.27	4.47	4.57					
May	3.53	3.62	3.77	3.79	3.90	3.86	3.91	4.01	4.11	4.26	4.23	4.47	4.53					
June	3.56	3.63	3.76	3.79	3.85	3.85	3.91	3.99	4.10	4.20	4.20	4.47	4.52					
July	3.62	3.69	3.80	3.84	3.85	3.89	3.92	4.00	4.05	4.20	4.19	4.47	4.56					

(continued)

APPENDIX TABLE 3-A (continued)

Date	2¾–2⅞	3⅛–3⅜	3¾	3⅞	4	4⅛	4¼	4⅜	4½	4⅝	4¾	4⅞	5	5⅛	5¼	5⅜	5½	5¾
										Coupon Rate								
Aug.	3.82	3.82	3.93	3.97	3.95	4.02	3.98	4.09	4.16	4.20	4.27	4.53	4.60					
Sept.	4.14	4.13	4.21	4.19	4.16	4.18	4.22	4.35	4.36	4.32	4.29	4.50	4.57					
Oct.	4.17	4.25	4.27	4.27	4.28	4.27	4.29	4.40	4.41	4.44	4.53	4.62	4.66					
Nov.	4.11	4.22	4.18	4.22	4.20	4.25	4.18	4.30	4.41	4.39	4.41	4.56	4.57					
Dec.	4.09	4.16	4.11	4.19	4.15	4.18	4.14	4.27	4.33	4.35	4.41	4.50	4.60					
1959																		
Jan.	4.18	4.21	4.21	4.27	4.22	4.30	4.23	4.35	4.40	4.38	4.45	4.56	4.57	—				
Feb.	4.25	4.26	4.24	4.27	4.24	4.34	4.30	4.37	4.42	4.47	4.48	4.56	4.59	—				
March	4.17	4.21	4.17	4.23	4.23	4.26	4.21	4.28	4.34	4.38	4.39	4.53	4.54	—				
April	4.27	4.32	4.23	4.29	4.25	4.31	4.21	4.34	4.38	4.40	4.47	4.56	4.59	—				
May	4.46	4.47	4.38	4.45	4.39	4.45	4.50	4.50	4.47	4.56	4.55	4.68	4.62	—				
June	4.60	4.60	4.53	4.57	4.59	4.59	4.58	4.60	4.61	4.66	4.64	4.75	4.74	—				
July	4.58	4.60	4.53	4.57	4.57	4.59	4.62	4.59	4.61	4.64	4.66	4.75	4.72	—				
Aug.	4.55	4.58	4.53	4.53	4.53	4.56	4.55	4.57	4.58	4.60	4.63	4.70	4.72	—				
Sept.	4.59	4.67	4.55	4.65	4.63	4.62	4.62	4.60	4.68	4.72	4.76	4.81	4.87	4.93				
Oct.	4.73	4.72	4.66	4.76	4.70	4.68	4.71	4.79	4.79	4.83	4.81	4.88	4.93	4.99				
Nov.	4.59	4.65	4.61	4.63	4.61	4.63	4.66	4.73	4.76	4.79	4.78	4.87	4.97	4.99				
Dec.	4.52	4.55	4.54	4.55	4.58	4.65	4.65	4.71	4.73	4.80	4.78	4.87	4.93	4.98				
1960																		
Jan.	4.66	4.66	4.65	4.72	4.69	4.72	4.73	4.79	4.83	4.87	4.83	4.92	4.95	5.07	5.03	—	—	5.37
Feb.	4.63	4.59	4.61	4.64	4.64	4.72	4.74	4.76	4.77	4.84	4.85	4.92	4.92	5.01	4.99	5.02	5.17	5.32

(continued)

APPENDIX TABLE 3-A (continued)

Date	\multicolumn{18}{c}{Coupon Rate}

Date	2¾–2⅞	3⅛–3⅜	3¾	3⅞	4	4⅛	4¼	4⅜	4½	4⅝	4¾	4⅞	5	5⅛	5¼	5⅜	5½	5¾
March	4.52	4.55	4.53	4.55	4.54	4.58	4.63	4.76	4.72	4.76	4.79	4.88	4.88	4.95	4.98	5.06	5.14	5.30
April	4.41	4.40	4.38	4.43	4.48	4.53	4.54	4.57	4.59	4.65	4.68	4.81	4.84	4.89	4.89	4.94	5.04	5.24
May	4.46	4.52	4.44	4.47	4.49	4.53	4.52	4.58	4.56	4.68	4.73	4.81	4.87	4.91	4.90	4.98	5.07	5.24
June	4.52	4.57	4.47	4.51	4.53	4.60	4.59	4.65	4.62	4.72	4.75	4.82	4.86	4.93	4.94	4.99	5.07	5.24
July	4.45	4.43	4.43	4.46	4.47	—	4.54	4.61	4.59	4.63	4.69	4.73	4.78	4.86	4.89	4.93	5.03	5.24
Aug.	4.21	4.29	4.20	4.31	4.27	—	4.34	4.38	4.44	4.49	4.54	4.64	4.69	4.75	4.82	4.86	4.97	5.24
Sept.	4.17	4.19	4.14	4.21	4.14	—	4.29	4.35	4.44	4.46	4.50	4.62	4.69	4.76	4.81	4.86	4.95	5.24
Oct.	4.25	4.29	4.27	4.35	4.20	—	4.32	4.45	4.47	4.57	4.61	4.66	4.71	4.78	4.80	4.87	4.98	5.24
Nov.	4.26	4.29	4.29	4.33	4.38	—	4.39	4.51	4.56	4.59	4.64	4.67	4.72	4.81	4.83	4.86	4.98	5.24
Dec.	4.37	4.38	4.39	4.41	4.41	—	4.54	4.59	4.63	4.71	4.75	4.77	4.79	4.84	4.88	4.97	5.01	—
1961																		
Jan.	4.31	4.36	4.36	4.38	4.38	—	4.48	4.45	4.58	4.61	4.64	4.70	4.74	4.80	4.86	4.89	5.00	
Feb.	4.26	4.29	4.30	4.30	4.30	—	4.35	4.37	4.40	4.48	4.52	4.60	4.66	4.74	4.83	4.81	4.97	
March	4.12	4.18	4.16	4.17	4.14	—	4.19	4.27	4.32	4.37	4.42	4.53	4.61	4.69	4.80	4.81	4.96	
April	4.20	4.25	4.24	4.24	4.22	—	4.27	4.35	4.25	4.41	4.47	4.55	4.63	4.71	4.79	4.83		
May	4.33	4.35	4.36	4.40	4.39	—	4.37	4.42	4.50	4.56	4.59	4.64	4.67	4.73	4.82	4.85		
June	4.33	4.32	4.34	4.39	4.36	—	4.39	4.45	4.44	4.61	4.63	4.66	4.70	4.74	4.82	4.84		
July	4.42	4.41	4.44	4.45	4.46	—	4.50	4.50	4.54	4.64	4.69	4.72	4.77	4.81	4.85			
Aug.	4.45	4.44	4.45	4.45	4.46	—	4.51	4.51	4.56	4.62	4.65	4.69	4.73	4.79	4.86			
Sept.	4.49	4.55	4.49	4.50	4.53	—	4.52	4.53	4.53	4.62	4.61	4.68	4.73	4.79	4.85			
Oct.	4.43	4.43	4.43	4.43	4.42	—	4.48	4.45	4.47	4.51	4.55	4.59	4.67	4.73	4.82			
Nov.	4.37	4.38	4.38	4.43	4.39	—	4.39	4.39	4.44	4.46	4.50	4.59	4.67	4.73	4.82			
Dec.	4.40	4.40	4.38	4.39	4.38	—	4.39	4.41	4.44	4.47	4.51	4.59	4.67	4.73	4.82			

(continued)

APPENDIX TABLE 3-A (continued)

Date	2¾–2⅞	3⅛–3⅜	3¾	3⅞	4	4⅛	4¼	4⅜	4½	4⅝	4¾	4⅞	5	5⅛	5¼	5⅜	5½	5¾
1962																		
Jan.	4.44	4.45	4.43	4.45	4.41	—	4.42	4.42	4.47	4.51	4.52	4.62	4.68	4.73	4.82			
Feb.	4.42	4.42	4.40	4.41	4.37	—	4.39	4.42	4.46	4.50	4.50	4.59	4.67	4.73	4.81			
March	4.40	4.41	4.39	4.42	4.37	—	4.39	4.41	4.45	4.49	4.48	4.59	4.67	4.73	4.81			
April	4.31	4.30	4.30	4.31	4.32	—	4.33	4.35	4.40	4.42	4.44	4.53	4.62	4.70	4.81			
May	4.20	4.20	4.22	4.24	4.23	—	4.22	4.25	4.29	4.35	4.41	4.49	4.61	4.70	4.80			
June	4.23	4.24	4.22	4.27	4.14	—	4.21	4.27	4.30	4.37	4.41	4.50	4.64	4.72	4.78			
July	4.28	4.30	4.29	4.32	4.19	—	4.23	4.31	4.34	4.42	4.42	4.53	4.66	4.73	4.79			
Aug.	4.37	4.35	4.35	4.39	4.33	—	4.34	4.33	4.36	4.44	4.46	4.52	4.65	4.73	4.79			
Sept.	4.25	4.26	4.26	4.29	4.26	—	4.27	4.25	4.30	4.37	4.43	4.51	4.61	4.71	—			
Oct.	4.19	4.20	4.21	4.26	4.23	—	4.24	4.24	4.28	4.35	4.41	4.51	4.62	4.71	—			
Nov.	4.13	4.16	4.16	4.19	4.16	—	4.20	4.24	4.26	4.35	4.40	4.50	4.60	4.70	—			
Dec.	4.13	4.14	4.12	4.20	4.16	—	4.18	4.21	4.25	4.32	4.38	4.49	4.60	4.69	—			
1963																		
Jan.	4.15	4.15	4.14	4.17	4.16	—	4.16	4.22	4.23	4.32	4.38	4.48	4.60	4.69				
Feb.	4.14	4.13	4.14	4.15	4.10	—	4.16	4.21	4.21	4.30	4.38	4.49	4.60	4.71				
March	4.14	4.14	4.17	4.15	4.07	4.19	4.17	4.23	4.26	4.31	4.37	4.49	4.59	4.71				
April	4.15	4.16	4.16	4.16	4.13	4.23	4.21	4.24	4.26	4.31	4.35	4.49	4.60	4.71				
May	4.25	4.24	4.24	4.22	4.15	4.26	4.26	4.31	4.32	4.37	4.39	4.49	4.59	4.72				
June	4.25	4.25	4.23	4.25	4.15	4.26	4.24	4.28	4.31	4.35	4.38	4.49	4.59	4.72				
July	4.25	4.25	4.24	4.23	4.20	4.23	4.24	4.27	4.29	4.34	4.37	4.49	4.58	4.72				
Aug.	4.25	4.26	4.26	4.26	4.26	4.26	4.26	4.31	4.31	4.37	4.40	4.50	4.58	4.73				

Coupon Rate

(continued)

APPENDIX TABLE 3-A (continued)

Date	Coupon Rate																	
	$2\frac{3}{4}-2\frac{7}{8}$	$3\frac{1}{8}-3\frac{3}{8}$	$3\frac{3}{4}$	$3\frac{7}{8}$	4	$4\frac{1}{8}$	$4\frac{1}{4}$	$4\frac{3}{8}$	$4\frac{1}{2}$	$4\frac{5}{8}$	$4\frac{3}{4}$	$4\frac{7}{8}$	5	$5\frac{1}{8}$	$5\frac{1}{4}$	$5\frac{3}{8}$	$5\frac{1}{2}$	$5\frac{3}{4}$
Sept.	4.25	4.25	4.25	4.26	4.26	4.24	4.24	4.31	4.32	4.36	4.39	4.50	4.58	4.73				
Oct.	4.30	4.31	4.30	4.32	4.31	4.33	4.30	4.33	4.36	4.38	4.41	4.50	4.58	4.73				
Nov.	4.30	4.30	4.30	4.30	4.31	4.33	4.31	4.33	4.35	4.39	4.42	4.50	4.58	4.71				
Dec.	4.31	4.32	4.31	4.31	4.29	4.39	4.32	4.34	4.37	4.42	4.44	4.51	4.58	4.70				
1964																		
Jan.	4.39	4.38	4.39	4.39	4.41	4.44	4.40	4.40	4.44	4.46	4.47	4.53	4.61	4.70				
Feb.	4.33	4.35	4.35	4.36	4.41	4.37	4.37	4.37	4.41	4.42	4.45	4.53	4.60	4.70				
March	4.33	4.32	4.33	4.34	4.35	4.39	4.36	4.35	4.37	4.39	4.43	4.52	4.61	4.70				
April	4.41	4.42	4.41	4.40	4.40	4.39	4.42	4.41	4.41	4.45	4.49	4.54	4.61	4.69				
May	4.43	4.42	4.43	4.41	4.40	4.48	4.44	4.41	4.41	4.45	4.49	4.54	4.61	4.73				
June	4.41	4.41	4.41	4.40	4.40	4.44	4.43	4.41	4.43	4.45	4.48	4.54	4.61	4.71				
July	4.40	4.41	4.39	4.38	4.41	4.41	4.41	4.41	4.44	4.45	4.48	4.53	4.61	4.71				
Aug.	4.38	4.38	4.38	4.37	4.38	4.41	4.40	4.39	4.43	4.43	4.47	4.53	4.62	4.73				
Sept.	4.38	4.38	4.38	4.37	4.38	4.41	4.40	4.39	4.41	4.43	4.47	4.53	4.62	4.73				
Oct.	4.40	4.39	4.40	4.39	4.40	4.41	4.41	4.40	4.43	4.44	4.48	4.53	4.64	4.73				
Nov.	4.40	4.39	4.39	4.38	4.40	4.43	4.41	4.40	4.43	4.44	4.47	4.53	4.62	4.71				
Dec.	4.41	4.43	4.40	4.40	4.41	4.40	4.41	4.41	4.45	4.45	4.48	4.54	4.63	4.73				
1965																		
Jan.	4.39	4.39	4.39	4.39	4.42	4.40	4.40	4.39	4.42	4.43	4.48	4.54	4.63	4.73				
Feb.	4.37	4.35	4.36	4.37	4.40	4.38	4.37	4.38	4.40	4.40	4.46	4.54	4.62	4.73				
March	4.38	4.37	4.38	4.38	4.41	4.41	4.39	4.39	4.41	4.44	4.47	4.54	4.64	4.73				

(continued)

APPENDIX TABLE 3-A (concluded)

Date	\(2\frac{3}{4}\)–\(2\frac{7}{8}\)	\(3\frac{1}{8}\)–\(3\frac{3}{8}\)	\(3\frac{3}{4}\)	\(3\frac{7}{8}\)	4	\(4\frac{1}{8}\)	\(4\frac{1}{4}\)	\(4\frac{3}{8}\)	\(4\frac{1}{2}\)	\(4\frac{5}{8}\)	\(4\frac{3}{4}\)	\(4\frac{7}{8}\)	5	\(5\frac{1}{8}\)	\(5\frac{1}{4}\)	\(5\frac{3}{8}\)	\(5\frac{1}{2}\)	\(5\frac{3}{4}\)
April	4.39	4.38	4.39	4.39	4.41	4.41	4.40	4.40	4.42	4.44	4.48	4.54	4.64	4.74				
May	4.40	4.39	4.40	4.40	4.41	4.41	4.41	4.41	4.43	4.44	4.48	4.54	4.64	4.75				
June	4.42	4.43	4.45	4.44	4.47	4.46	4.45	4.44	4.48	4.48	4.51	4.56	4.65	4.76				
July	4.43	4.44	4.43	4.44	4.47	4.47	4.47	4.46	4.49	4.49	4.53	4.47	4.66	4.76				
Aug.	4.45	4.47	4.44	4.45	4.48	—	4.47	4.45	4.50	4.50	4.52	4.58	4.67	—				
Sept.	4.49	4.50	4.50	4.52	4.52	—	4.52	4.54	4.55	4.56	4.59	4.65	4.68	—				
Oct.	4.53	4.55	4.52	4.54	4.54	—	4.54	4.55	4.57	4.60	4.60	4.67	4.70	—				
Nov.	4.55	4.55	4.52	4.55	4.57	—	4.57	4.57	4.57	4.61	4.63	4.69	4.71	—				
Dec.	4.65	4.68	4.66	4.67	4.67	—	4.67	4.66	4.64	4.69	4.71	4.73	4.74	—				
1966																		
Jan.	4.75	4.84	4.74	4.75	4.77	—	4.76	4.78	4.77	4.79	4.76	4.81	4.86	—				
Feb.	4.77	4.81	4.79	4.80	4.84	4.82	4.80	4.82	4.82	4.82	4.77	4.88	4.92	4.94				
March	4.95	4.95	4.96	4.99	4.95	5.03	4.98	4.97	4.95	5.01	4.99	5.03	5.05	5.11				
April	5.01	5.06	5.00	5.04	5.09	5.05	5.04	5.03	5.02	5.05	5.03	5.07	5.07	5.09				
May	5.03	5.05	5.02	5.01	4.99	5.10	5.05	5.03	5.01	5.04	5.04	5.06	5.06	5.16				
June	5.05	5.06	5.02	5.03	5.06	5.10	5.08	5.04	5.07	5.08	5.10	5.15	5.17	5.20				
July	5.07	5.09	5.03	5.07	5.06	5.10	5.11	5.11	5.10	5.11	5.11	5.22	5.20	5.27				
Aug.	5.20	5.24	5.19	5.22	5.15	5.25	5.22	5.24	5.20	5.24	5.26	5.31	5.29	5.38	5.37			
Sept.	5.51	5.52	5.48	5.47	5.15	5.55	5.58	5.59	5.54	5.52	5.52	5.66	5.55	5.58	5.64			
Oct.	5.51	5.49	5.50	5.49	5.49	5.48	5.52	5.50	5.52	5.50	5.54	5.63	5.55	5.52	5.55			
Nov.	5.34	5.32	5.34	5.32	5.36	5.35	5.37	5.36	5.33	5.35	5.35	5.40	5.37	5.35				
Dec.	5.35	5.38	5.35	5.30	5.29	5.38	5.38	5.35	5.33	5.39	5.37	5.42	5.44	5.40				

NOTES TO APPENDIX TABLE 3-A

NOTE: Quotations were taken from the daily public utility quotation sheets of Solomon Brothers and Hutzler and The First Boston Corporation, and are calculated from the asked price for individual bonds on the business day closest to the beginning of the month. Yields are therefore a few basis points lower than if they had been calculated in the more conventional manner from the mid-point of the bid and asked prices. The series for 3 1/8 to 3 3/8 bonds was constructed by Sidney Homer. The averages include all Aa-Aaa utility bonds maturing between 1980 and 2010, except convertibles and sinking fund debentures, issues smaller than $10 million, and issues outstanding less than four months. Gaps in the series arise when there were no observations for bonds with the specified coupon rate.

APPENDIX TABLE 3-B. *Spreads Between Average First-of-Month Yields on Seasoned Long-Term Callable Aa-Aaa Public Utility Bonds and Similar Bonds With Refunding Deferments of Two Years or More, by Coupon Rate, 1957–66*

Date	Coupon Rate															
	$3\frac{3}{4}$	$3\frac{7}{8}$	4	$4\frac{1}{8}$	$4\frac{1}{4}$	$4\frac{3}{8}$	$4\frac{1}{2}$	$4\frac{5}{8}$	$4\frac{3}{4}$	$4\frac{7}{8}$	5	$5\frac{1}{8}$	$5\frac{1}{4}$	$5\frac{3}{8}$	$5\frac{1}{2}$	$5\frac{3}{4}$
1957																
Jan.																
Feb.																
March																
April																
May																
June						−.03										
July						−.12										
Aug.						−.06										
Sept.						−.07		−.04								
Oct.						−.07		−.01	+.06	+.05	+.01					
Nov.						−.07		+.04	−.02	+.02	−.02					
Dec.						−.03		−.05	−.08	−.05	−.06					
1958																
Jan.						−.10		−.04	−.10	−.13	−.10					
Feb.						−.11		−.08	−.08	−.13	−.16					
March								−.08	−.06	−.12	−.19					
April		−.14						−.12	−.05	−.14	−.21					
May		−.05						−.14	−.01	−.19	−.20					
June		−.06						−.11		−.22	−.20					
July	−.03	−.08	−.01					−.08		−.19	−.25					

(continued)

APPENDIX TABLE 3-B (continued)

	Coupon Rate															
Date	$3\frac{3}{4}$	$3\frac{7}{8}$	4	$4\frac{1}{8}$	$4\frac{1}{4}$	$4\frac{3}{8}$	$4\frac{1}{2}$	$4\frac{5}{8}$	$4\frac{3}{4}$	$4\frac{7}{8}$	5	$5\frac{1}{8}$	$5\frac{1}{4}$	$5\frac{3}{8}$	$5\frac{1}{2}$	$5\frac{3}{4}$
Aug.	−.01	−.07	+.05					−.01		−.13	−.15					
Sept.	.00	+.03	+.12					+.06		−.02	−.05					
Oct.	−.03	+.07	+.05					−.06		−.14	−.09					
Nov.	−.04	−.02	+.01					−.13		−.14	−.09					
Dec.	−.03	−.04	+.03			−.05		−.08		−.13	−.15					
1959																
Jan.	+.03	−.04	+.08			−.09		−.07		−.13	−.05					
Feb.	+.02	.00	+.12			−.06	−.01	−.15		−.09	−.04					
March	+.03	−.03	+.06			−.09	−.05	−.10		−.10	−.06					
April	+.01	−.03	+.09			−.07	−.06	−.09		−.08	−.08					
May	−.04	−.05	+.03			−.10	+.08	−.05		−.01	+.02					
June	−.07	−.04	+.01			−.15	−.04	−.08		+.02	.00					
July	−.01	−.03	+.02			−.12	−.07	−.08		−.01	.00					
Aug.	−.03	+.03	+.04			−.09	+.01	−.03		−.04	−.02					
Sept.	+.01	−.07	−.01			−.03	−.03	−.09		.00	−.06					
Oct.	+.02	−.06	+.06			−.07	+.02	−.01		−.03	−.03					
Nov.	.00	−.01	−.02			−.03	−.01	.00		+.01	−.03					
Dec.	−.05	−.01	+.07			−.04	+.02	−.09		−.02	−.08					
1960																
Jan.	−.02	−.07	+.10			−.09	−.11	−.11		−.04	−.07	−.14				
Feb.	−.03	+.01	+.11			−.02	−.01	−.10		−.04	−.03	−.12		−.04		

(continued)

APPENDIX TABLE 3-B (continued)

	Coupon Rate															
Date	$3\frac{3}{4}$	$3\frac{7}{8}$	4	$4\frac{1}{8}$	$4\frac{1}{4}$	$4\frac{3}{8}$	$4\frac{1}{2}$	$4\frac{5}{8}$	$4\frac{3}{4}$	$4\frac{7}{8}$	5	$5\frac{1}{8}$	$5\frac{1}{4}$	$5\frac{3}{8}$	$5\frac{1}{2}$	$5\frac{3}{4}$
March	-.04	-.04	+.05			-.10	+.01	-.04		-.03	-.01	-.02		-.13		
April	-.02	-.02	+.05			-.01	+.02	-.03		-.08	-.14	-.11		-.02		
May	+.05	-.01	+.04			.00	+.05	-.05		-.07	-.14	-.10		-.03		
June	+.01	-.02				-.06	.00	-.03		-.04	-.12	-.08				
July	.00	-.01				-.05	-.06	-.01		-.02	-.09	-.08				
Aug.	.00	-.06				+.01	.00	-.06	.00	-.07	-.11					
Sept.	.00	-.03				.00	-.03	-.09	-.03	-.08	-.11					
Oct.	.00	-.09				-.08	.00	-.06	-.05	-.03	-.08					
Nov.	.00	-.04				-.11	-.06	-.06	-.06	-.02	-.09					
Dec.	+.01	.00				-.04	+.01	-.03	-.04	-.02	-.13					
1961																
Jan.	+.01	+.01				+.06	-.08	-.04	-.04	-.09	-.09					
Feb.	.00	-.02				+.02	-.02	-.06	.00	-.05	-.04					
March	.00	-.01				-.03	-.04	-.05	-.01	-.03	-.08					
April		-.04				-.05	+.06	-.06	-.01	+.02	-.07					
May		-.06				-.01	-.04	-.03	-.14	+.03	-.02					
June						-.05	+.03	-.03	-.05	+.03	-.03					
July						-.03	.00	-.03	-.01	+.03	-.03					
Aug.						-.06	-.06	-.01	-.02	.00	-.03					
Sept.						-.07	-.03	-.02	-.02	-.06	-.03					
Oct.						-.02	-.04	-.01	-.02	-.04	-.01					
Nov.						-.01	-.07	.00	-.01	-.04	-.02					
Dec.						-.01	-.04	-.01	-.02	-.03	-.03					

(continued)

APPENDIX TABLE 3-B (continued)

Date									Coupon Rate							
	$3\frac{3}{4}$	$3\frac{7}{8}$	4	$4\frac{1}{8}$	$4\frac{1}{4}$	$4\frac{3}{8}$	$4\frac{1}{2}$	$4\frac{5}{8}$	$4\frac{3}{4}$	$4\frac{7}{8}$	5	$5\frac{1}{8}$	$5\frac{1}{4}$	$5\frac{3}{8}$	$5\frac{1}{2}$	$5\frac{3}{4}$
1962																
Jan.						−.02	−.07	−.05	−.01	−.06	−.03					
Feb.						−.02	−.04	−.02	+.02	−.03	−.03					
March						−.01	−.05	−.03	+.02	−.03	−.04					
April						−.03	−.05	−.02	−.01	.00	−.01					
May						+.03	+.01	.00	−.02	+.04	−.03					
June						+.03	+.02	−.02	.00	.00	−.02					
July						+.02	+.01	−.02	+.02	+.02	−.03					
Aug.					−.01	+.03	+.03	−.05	.00	+.03	−.02					
Sept.					−.03	+.01	.00	−.02	−.02	+.04	−.01					
Oct.					−.01	+.02	−.01	−.01	.00	+.01	−.02					
Nov.					.00	.00	+.01	−.02	+.01	+.02	.00					
Dec.					+.01	+.02	−.02	.00	+.02	+.03	.00					
1963																
Jan.					+.04	+.01	+.02	−.01	+.02	+.04	.00					
Feb.					+.05	.00	+.03	+.01	.00		.00					
March					+.04	.00	+.01	+.02	+.02		+.01					
April					+.01	−.01	+.02	+.02	+.02		.00					
May					.00	−.02	.00	−.02	+.01		+.01					
June					.00	.00	+.01	.00	+.01		+.02					
July					.00	+.01	+.01	.00	+.02		−.02					
Aug.					+.01	.00	+.01	.00	−.01		−.01					

(continued)

APPENDIX TABLE 3-B (continued)

Date	\(3\frac{3}{4}\)	\(3\frac{7}{8}\)	4	\(4\frac{1}{8}\)	\(4\frac{1}{4}\)	\(4\frac{3}{8}\)	\(4\frac{1}{2}\)	\(4\frac{5}{8}\)	\(4\frac{3}{4}\)	\(4\frac{7}{8}\)	5	\(5\frac{1}{8}\)	\(5\frac{1}{4}\)	\(5\frac{3}{8}\)	\(5\frac{1}{2}\)	\(5\frac{3}{4}\)
Sept.					+.03	.00	+.01	.00	+.01		-.01					
Oct.					+.02	+.01	-.01	+.01	+.01		.00					
Nov.					+.01	+.01	+.01	.00	+.01		.00					
Dec.					+.01	+.02	+.01	.00	.00							
1964																
Jan.					+.02	+.01	+.01	+.01	.00							
Feb.					+.01	+.02	.00	+.02	+.01							
March					.00	+.01	.00	+.02	.00							
April					.00	-.01	+.02	+.01	.00							
May					-.02	.00	+.02	-.01	.00							
June					-.01	.00	.00	.00	+.01							
July					.00	.00	.00	-.01	+.01							
Aug.					-.01	+.01	-.01	-.02	+.02							
Sept.					-.01	+.01	+.01	-.01	+.02							
Oct.					-.02	+.01	+.01	-.01	+.01							
Nov.					-.01	+.01	+.01	.00	+.02							
Dec.					+.01	+.01	-.01	+.01	+.01							
1965																
Jan.					.00	.00	+.01	+.01	+.01							
Feb.					+.02	.00	.00	+.02	-.01							
March					.00	.00	.00	+.01	-.01							

(continued)

APPENDIX TABLE 3-B (concluded)

| Date | Coupon Rate | | | | | | | | | | | | | | | |
	$3\frac{3}{4}$	$3\frac{7}{8}$	4	$4\frac{1}{8}$	$4\frac{1}{4}$	$4\frac{3}{8}$	$4\frac{1}{2}$	$4\frac{5}{8}$	$4\frac{3}{4}$	$4\frac{7}{8}$	5	$5\frac{1}{8}$	$5\frac{1}{4}$	$5\frac{3}{8}$	$5\frac{1}{2}$	$5\frac{3}{4}$
April					.00	.00	+.01	−.01	.00							
May					−.01	+.01	.00	−.02	.00							
June					−.03	+.01	.00	.00	+.02							
July					−.04	+.01	−.01	.00	.00							
Aug.					−.03	+.01	−.01	−.02	+.01							
Sept.					+.01	+.01	−.01	+.02	−.02							
Oct.					.00	.00	−.01	+.02	+.01							
Nov.					−.02	.00	−.01	+.01	.00							
Dec.					−.01	.00	−.01	−.02	.00							
1966																
Jan.						+.01	−.05	−.03	−.02							
Feb.						+.03	−.03	−.01	−.01							
March						+.01	−.04	−.02	−.02	−.02	−.08					
April						.00	.00	−.02	−.04	−.11	−.05					
May						+.03	.00	−.01	−.04	−.09	−.07					
June						+.03	−.01	.00	−.01	−.10	−.03	−.12				
July						−.05	−.03	−.05	−.08	−.01		−.02				

NOTE: Spreads are measured as the yield on deferred issues minus the yield on callable issues.
SOURCE: See Table 3-1.

Essays on Interest Rates

APPENDIX TABLE 3-C. *First-of-Month Yield on New Issues, Callable Aa Public Utility Bonds, 1956-66*

Year	Jan.	Feb.	March	April	May	June	July	Aug.	Sept.	Oct.	Nov.	Dec.
1956	3.25	3.20	3.15	3.45	3.70	3.57	3.73	3.90	4.07	4.01	4.20	4.30
1957	4.50	4.40	4.22	4.29	4.35	4.62	4.85	5.00	4.81	4.78	4.97	4.47
1958	3.94	3.70	4.00	4.00	3.90	3.85	3.95	4.25	4.60	4.57	4.42	4.55
1959	4.60	4.65	4.37	4.47	4.59	5.05	4.95	4.85	5.00	5.25	5.15	5.15
1960	5.25	4.95	5.10	4.85	4.88	4.90	4.80	4.60	4.47	4.65	4.75	5.00
1961	4.60	4.32	4.32	4.52	4.75	4.75	4.85	4.65	4.75	4.55	4.52	4.60
1962	4.65	4.55	4.55	4.40	4.29	4.29	4.39	4.47	4.30	4.30	4.26	4.28
1963	4.28	4.19	4.27	4.27	4.39	4.35	4.32	4.35	4.35	4.38	4.40	4.43
1964	4.50	4.42	4.39	4.50	4.48	4.48	4.44	4.42	4.45	4.47	4.47	4.50
1965	4.45	4.39	4.47	4.48	4.48	4.59	4.56	4.60	4.67	4.70	4.66	4.80
1966	4.90	4.98	5.30	5.15	5.50	5.67	5.67	5.77	6.35	6.05	6.00	6.20

SOURCE: Sidney Homer, "An Analytic Record of Yields and Yield Spreads," Salomon Brothers and Hutzler, New York.

4

The Geographic Structure of
Residential Mortgage
Yields

INTRODUCTION: SCOPE AND FOCUS

This paper reports some results of an exploratory study of the influence of property location on yields of conventional, residential mortgage loans. It provides new benchmark data on comparative average mortgage yields and contract terms for regions, states, and metropolitan areas in 1963; loan originations by five types of lenders for three categories of loan purpose are included in the sample data provided by the Federal Home Loan Bank Board.

Some of the questions dealt with here are: Is property location a mortgage yield determinant? What is the absolute level of differentials between average mortgage interest rates in various regions of the United States? How do these interregional differentials compare in magnitude to those that may arise within various geographical regions— for example, between two eastern metropolitan areas? Since aggregate data include three categories of loan purpose, we may ask whether loan purpose affects the size of differentials. Because of the diverse institutional structure and lending patterns of the several types of financial intermediary, it is of interest to inquire whether the regional pattern of mortgage yields is generally similar for each of the five lender groups.

Finally, we study the effect of variations in contract terms on com-

NOTE: I am deeply indebted to Jack Guttentag for his continued guidance during this project.

parative mortgage yield differentials. With the data at hand we are able to measure yield differentials in the raw data and, in addition, to take account of differences in key contract terms, obtaining thereby a second estimate of the yield differential between two areas. Inspection of the two sets of differentials provides a basis for determining whether comparisons of simple average yields in different sections of the country are valid, or whether, in contrast, geographic differences in contract terms that affect yield are so large that they require a statistical correction. Because unadjusted national figures are compiled and distributed monthly by the Federal Home Loan Bank Board, and presumably influence policy decisions at various levels of government, interest in this question transcends the academic.

The Data

The data underlying the statistical results are unique in both geographic scope and detail; thus, a brief description is appropriate at this point. Since December 1962, the Federal Home Loan Bank Board (FHLBB) has been compiling records of individual, conventional mortgage commitments on one-family, nonfarm homes on a sample basis from lenders located throughout the United States. Roughly 14,000 mortgage transactions are reported monthly by a sample of lenders that numbered approximately 3,000 during 1963. The magnetic tape record for each loan includes the date, the amount of the loan, the value or purchase price of the property, the maturity, the contract interest rate, fees and charges, the type of lender, the loan purpose, and coded location of both property and lender by Standard Metropolitan Statistical Area (SMSA) or non-SMSA, state, Home Loan Bank District (11 during the period of this study), census division (9), and region (4). Effective interest rates were computed for this study on the assumption that the unamortized principal is prepaid after one half of the original maturity has expired.[1] The weight used in all calculations is the number of loans in the area under study rather than the dollar amount of the loan.

The loans included in the present study represent commitments made by selected lenders during the eight-month period of May–December

---

[1] For a discussion of alternative methods of computing effective rate, see Jack M. Guttentag and Morris Beck, *Mortgage Interest Rates Since 1951*, New York, NBER, 1970, Chapter 5.

1963, inclusive, a period of relative yield stability in the mortgage market. Nearly 110,000 loans are included in this sample. Of these, 46 per cent were made on properties located in 18 large SMSAs.[2] Much of the analysis in this paper, including all of the regression runs, is based on the data for these 18 SMSAs.

Mortgages examined during this study are distinguished according to the loan purpose or the type of property being mortgaged. The "new construction" category represents permanent building loans for individuals and homebuilders who do not utilize interim financing. The "newly built" category refers to loans for the purchase of a newly constructed (never occupied) home from a builder. The "previously occupied" category includes loans for the purchase of existing houses.

The composition of the sample, by both loan purpose and lender type, is presented below (all figures are a percentage of the total):

	Previously Occupied	Newly Built	New Construction	Total
Life insurance companies	1.2	1.9	1.3	4.4
Mortgage companies	1.3	1.7	0.8	3.8
Savings and loan associations	40.5	14.2	14.3	69.0
Mutual savings banks	6.1	2.3	1.1	9.5
Commercial banks	9.6	1.7	2.1	13.4
Total	58.7	21.8	19.6	100.0

It is obvious that loans by savings and loan associations, representing more than two-thirds of the sample, dominate the data. Among types of loan purpose, the total sample includes comparable weighting for the newly built and new construction categories, while nearly 60 per cent of the loans recorded represent mortgages issued for the purchase of previously occupied homes. Because of the unequal weights accorded the different categories of loan purpose and lender type, mean statistics are presented, where available, for each group separately. In many cases, mean data for each of the 15 combinations of lender type and loan purpose are also presented.

When national or regional data are the subject of the analysis, the number of observations in each cell generally ranges from a hundred to several thousand. However, when the geographic area of interest is the state or standard metropolitan area, the number of observations

[2] The Home Loan Bank Board issues a monthly time series of average interest rates on properties in each of these areas.

recorded for a given property and lender type may be small or even zero. In particular, the regional concentration of mortgage companies and mutual savings banks gives rise to many blank cells. Additionally, even where all lender types are represented, the statistical significance of some results may be limited by possible deficiencies in the original sample and by nonuniform response rates by institutions included in the survey group. Generally, the savings and loan associations, which are directly regulated by the Federal Home Loan Bank Board, and the mutual savings banks have had the highest response rate.

The loans analyzed in this paper are loans to original borrowers involving the creation of a new mortgage instrument. No information regarding the ultimate disposition of the loans is available. It may be assumed, however, that virtually all mortgage company loans were originated for sale to ultimate lenders, principally life insurance companies and mutual savings banks. Some commercial bank loans also represent temporary commitments.

All of the loans in the FHLBB's sample were scheduled to be fully amortized over the mortgage term, which was limited to maturities of between five and forty years, inclusive. The five-year minimum term was imposed principally to exclude construction loans by builders who had not arranged for permanent owner financing.[3]

Method of Analysis

Two methods of analysis are used in this paper to measure yield differentials. First, average yields in different areas are simply compared. Because the records are coded by both region and metropolitan area, it is possible to determine the approximate magnitude of both inter- and intraregional yield differentials by examining mean rates for various geographic subsets of the total sample. Further refinement is made possible by classifying loans by either loan purpose or lender type, or both. This procedure does not, however, fully utilize the available data. Information on yield determinants such as the loan-value ratio cannot be employed effectively by comparing averages.

[3] Before any calculations were made for this study, all observations were subjected to a screening program, designed to eliminate apparently erroneous records on the tapes, which limited the acceptable terms as follows: loan-value ratio, less than 1.00 and greater than .06; principal amount, $1,000 to $99,999; purchase price, less than $100,000; contract interest rate, 3.00 to 9.99 per cent; fees and charges, less than 6.0 per cent.

The second statistical method is multiple regression analysis, with either effective interest rate or contract rate as the dependent variable. From the entire sample, a subset representing 50,000 loans on properties in 18 principal SMSAs was drawn. In regressions covering all 50,000 loans, both lender type and loan purpose were held constant with dummy variables in order to remove their specific effects. Then 17 dummy variables representing the SMSAs were introduced. The resulting *b*-coefficients for the individual SMSAs provide an indication of the differentials in mortgage interest rates between the metropolitan areas included in the regression on loans standardized for loan purpose and lender type. Three risk variables—purchase price, loan-value ratio, and maturity—were then introduced in the regression and their impact on yield differentials between metropolitan areas was assessed. Separate regressions were run for each of the different lender type and loan purpose groups.

The area differentials calculated from the regressions, while allowing for the influence of some important yield determinants that are correlated with area, may be influenced by others for which no allowance could be made. These include the socioeconomic characteristics of the neighborhood or broader area, which may be deteriorating or developing, integrated or segregated, residential or semicommercial. Transaction characteristics that may be correlated with both yield and area include the borrower's present and expected income and wealth, his age and family size, and (on previously occupied homes) the age of the property. Despite these shortcomings, the data presented in this paper remain the most comprehensive available, or likely to be available, for examining yield differentials on residential mortgages.

PROPERTY LOCATION AS A YIELD DETERMINANT

The multiple regression procedure permits a statistical determination of the importance of property location as a mortgage yield determinant. After the lender type and loan purpose had been introduced into the regression, explained variance, as represented by the coefficient of multiple determination (R^2), was .3303. With the subsequent introduction of the 17 property location dummy variables, R^2 rose to .5124, indicating that over 18 per cent of variance was explained by the metropolitan area variables after both lender and property type were taken into account. To determine whether some of the contribution attributed to property location in fact derived from differences in contract terms, additional regressions in which the three risk variables were introduced after the loan purpose and lender type variables and before the SMSA variables were run. In this regression the introduction of property location increased explained variation of effective yields by 21 per cent, again indicating clearly the significance of the SMSA variables.

When the same regression format was employed on individual lender type and loan purpose groups, similar results were obtained. After lender type and contract terms were held constant, the increase in R^2 on the loan purpose runs ranged from 17 per cent on newly built homes to 26 per cent on loans for new construction.

Regressions covering the lender type series showed wide differences in the significance of property location as a determinant of effective interest rate. Contributions to explained variance, after holding contract terms and loan purpose constant, ranged from 14 per cent for life insurance company loans to 41 per cent for the mutual savings bank sample. The complete tabulation (in per cent) of the contribution of property location after the inclusion of lender type and loan purpose, both before and after the inclusion of the three risk variables, appears in the table below.

Increase in R^2 Resulting From Introduction
of Property Location Variables
Into Effective Interest Rate Regressions

	Before Risk Variables	After Risk Variables
All loans	18	21
New construction	26	26
Newly built	18	17
Previously occupied	20	24
Life insurance companies	15	14
Mortgage companies	32	23
Savings and loans	31	37
Mutual savings banks	46	41
Commercial banks	26	23

A tabulation of R^2 and the standard error after each step for both contract rate and effective rate regressions appear in Appendix Tables 4-A5 and 4-A6. The location coefficients appear in Tables 4-A12 and 4-A15.

STRUCTURE OF INTERREGIONAL DIFFERENTIALS

Prior Research

Several previous researchers, using much less comprehensive data, examined the broad structure of the national mortgage market and drew tentative conclusions regarding the general nature of regional differentials.

J. E. Morton's analysis of loans outstanding in 1947 provides the following conclusions of interest, which are generally confirmed by the present study: (1) Interest rates on nonfarm mortgage loans are highest in the West and lowest in the North, with rates on Southern properties falling in between. (2) Differences between rates charged by various lender types are apparently greatest in the West and South, as compared with the North. (3) Rates on loans by life insurance companies showed less regional variation than those on commercial bank loans.[4]

Morton's data differ from those included in the present study in two important respects. First, Morton's data reflect loans outstanding, rather than the commitment data underlying this study. Loans outstanding reflect net acquisitions over a period of years so that regional yield differentials are influenced by dissimilarities in the time pattern of acquisitions by different institutions in different areas.[5] (The next two studies referred to below also employ data on outstanding loans.) Second, Morton's data only cover broad regions, while the data below cover states and metropolitan areas as well.

Grebler, Blank, and Winnick considered the regional structure of residential mortgage rates in historical perspective. Their conclusion that interregional rate differentials have diminished since the late nineteenth century is based upon Table 4-1 (updated here with data from the 1960 Census of Residential Housing).[6] In 1890 the interest rate on urban mortgages was nearly 4 or 5 percentage points higher in some sections of the country than in other sections because of the localization

[4] J. E. Morton, *Urban Mortgage Lending: Comparative Markets and Experience*, Princeton, Princeton University Press for NBER, 1956, pp. 82–83.

[5] For a discussion of the timing aspects of mortgage yield series, see Guttentag and Beck, *op. cit.*

[6] Leo Grebler, David M. Blank, and Louis Winnick, *Capital Formation in Residential Real Estate: Trends and Prospects,* Princeton, Princeton University Press for NBER, 1956, Chapter 15.

TABLE 4-1. *Average Interest Rate on Residential Mortgages Outstanding by Region, for Selected Years, 1890–1960 (per cent)*

Region	All Mortgages on Owner Occupied Houses		First Mortgages in Various Cities, 1934		First Mortgages on Owner Occupied One-Family Houses, 1940	Conventional Mortgages on One-Unit Homeowner Mortgaged Properties, 1960	All Mortgages on One-Unit Homeowner Mortgaged Properties, 1960
	1890	1920	Owner Occupied Houses	Rented Houses			
Northeast							
New England	5.5	5.8	5.93	5.88	5.38	5.1	5.0
Middle Atlantic	5.5	5.7	5.65	5.72	5.47		
North Central							
East North Central	6.8	6.1	6.18	6.15	5.45	5.6	5.1
West North Central	7.8	6.5	6.09	6.08	5.48		
South							
South Atlantic	6.3	6.3	6.25	6.32	5.63	6.0	6.1
East South Central	7.0	6.4	6.59	6.39	5.64		
West							
West South Central	9.0	7.9	6.99	7.07	5.97	6.0	5.0
Mountain	9.3	7.5	7.02	7.06	5.79		
Pacific	8.6	6.8	6.34	6.42	5.73		

SOURCE: 1890–1940 – Grebler, Blank, and Winnick, *Capital Formation in Residential Real Estate*, Princeton University Press for NBER, 1956, Table 65, page 230; 1960 – *1960 Census of Housing*; Vol. V, Residential Finance, Part 1, Homeowner Properties, pp. 53, 67, 81, 95.

of mortgage markets.[7] Since 1940, yields on Western mortgages have continued to exceed those on Eastern properties, but the differential has been a percentage point or less.

The Wickens study[8] was based upon detailed data accumulated by the Financial Survey of Urban Housing, conducted by the Commerce Department in 1934. It reported both contract and effective interest rates in 52 cities, thus allowing the measurement of selected intra-regional as well as interregional differentials. The survey data were drawn principally from owner reports, which rely on the borrower's recollection of distant events. Because of the statistical limitations of Wickens' data on rates in specific metropolitan areas, they are not presented here. However, the 1934 data for regions in Table 4-1 are computed from Wickens' statistics on interest rates in 52 cities.

More recently, A. H. Schaaf attempted to explain regional differences in mortgage yields by employing the monthly mean rates on mortgage loans in 18 metropolitan areas reported by the Federal Home Loan Bank Board since 1963. Schaaf's qualified conclusion is that a large part of total regional variation, as indicated in the series, is accounted for by "the distance of the borrower from the northeastern capital markets, the risk of mortgage default, and the relative intensity of local demands for local savings."[9] The results of the present study suggest that Schaaf's model greatly oversimplifies the complex, fragmented nature of local mortgage markets.

Differentials Between Four Major Regions in 1963

Loans sampled in 1963 support the historical finding that yields on conventional mortgage loans are typically lower in the East and Midwest than in the South and West. The following are mean effective interest rates on all loans sampled, classified by four regions, which together embrace the 50 states and the District of Columbia (standard deviation in parentheses):[10]

[7] See D. N. Frederiksen, "Mortgage Banking in America," *Journal of Political Economy*, March 1894, p. 209.

[8] David L. Wickens, *Residential Real Estate: Its Economic Position as Shown by Values, Rents, Family Incomes, Financing, and Construction, Together with Estimates for All Real Estate*, New York, NBER, 1941.

[9] A. H. Schaaf, "Regional Differences in Mortgage Financing Costs," *Journal of Finance*, March 1966, p. 93.

[10] A list of states in each region appears in Appendix Table 4-A1.

Mean Effective Interest Rate

East	5.71 (.32)
Midwest	5.94 (.39)
South	6.10 (.46)
West	6.40 (.48)

An analysis of the variance test provided an *F*-ratio far in excess of that required to reject, at the one per cent level, the null hypothesis that the means are not significantly different. (These data reflect loans on all property types by all lender groups. Analysis of a number of subsets of the total sample will be provided later.)

During the period under study, a differential of approximately 70 basis points was evident between average mortgage interest rates in the Northeast and West, the lowest and highest yield regions, respectively. This compares with a yield differential of between 3 and 4 percentage points in 1890 and approximately 60 basis points in 1940 (Table 4-1).

While it is clear that interregional yield differentials diminished greatly during the half century ending in 1940, the small increase between 1940 and 1963 is not necessarily meaningful. The two sets of data are not at all comparable. The 1940 statistics refer to contract interest rates on outstanding loans on all owner-occupied housing, including FHA-insured loans, as reported by the 1940 Census of Housing. Our data, in contrast, represent average effective rates on new commitments and cover only conventional mortgages.

Regional Differentials by States and Metropolitan Areas

Regional yield differentials are very sensitive to the mix of areas within regions. This is illustrated in the tabulation below, which shows the effective yield difference between the East and West regions, and between two states and two metropolitan areas in these regions deliberately selected so as to provide large differentials.

Difference in Effective Yield Between	Basis Points
West and East	69
California and Massachusetts	98
San Diego and Boston	126

By a different selection of states and metropolitan areas we can obtain state and metropolitan area differentials considerably smaller than the regional average, as the reader can see by consulting Appendix Tables 4-A2 and 4-T1. This reflects the wide variation in yields within regions, a topic discussed further below.

Distinction Between Contract and Effective Rate Differentials

It is important to distinguish differentials based on effective rate from differentials based on contract rate. The 1963 regional differences on the two bases are shown below (basis points):

Difference Between East and	Contract Rate	Effective Rate
Midwest	15	23
South	29	39
West	52	69

In each case the effective rate differential exceeds that of the contract rate. The East-West spread falls by 17 basis points to 52 basis points. The divergence is explained by the fact that the average level of borrower fees and charges is lowest in the East and progressively higher in the Midwest, South, and West. Fees average .26 per cent of loan amount in the East and 1.12 per cent of the loan amount in the Western states.

Similar comparisons can be made for yield differentials between selected metropolitan areas in different regions. These differentials are measured as the difference between the b-coefficients of the dummy variables representing the 18 metropolitan areas included in the multiple regression, as explained previously. The cities were paired by ranking them from 1 to 18 on the basis of their coefficients in the all-loan regressions with risk variables held constant. Then the lowest yield city was paired with the 10th, the second with the 11th, and so on. Since in one pair the two cities were in the same region (New York and Boston) only eight pairs are shown in Table 4-2.

It is again clear from Table 4-2 that effective yield differentials exceed those in contract rate, whether or not risk variables are taken into account. Of the 122 figures in this table, only 29 are negative, and 22 of these represent comparisons between two sets of the paired cities, Dallas-Chicago and Los Angeles-Miami. In these comparisons the contract yield differentials exceed those in effective yield for all categories of loan purpose, with one exception: the Los Angeles-Miami differential for new construction loans widens by 15 basis points when effective rate

TABLE 4-2. *Interregional Yield Differential Measured by Effective Interest Rate Minus Yield Differential Measured by Contract Rate (per cent)*

	Loan Purpose				Type of Lender			
	All Loans	New Construction	Newly Built	Previously Occupied	Life Insurance	Mortgage Companies	Savings and Loan	Commercial Banks
Before Risk Variables								
Memphis less Baltimore	.107	(.024)	.115	.113	(.025)	NA	.101	.228
Houston less Philadelphia	.071	.005	.097	.093	(.004)	.038	.088	.193
Seattle less Detroit	.124	.219	.033	.106	.010	(.045)	.180	.054
Atlanta less Minneapolis	.139	.130	.119	.174	.061	.083	.138	.394
Dallas less Chicago	(.112)	(.184)	(.086)	(.094)	.013	NA	(.119)	(.136)
Denver less Cleveland	.112	.128	.095	.108	.091	.034	.121	.049
San Francisco less New Orleans	.179	.262	.113	.168	.005	.042	.214	.078
Los Angeles less Miami	(.099)	.141	(.231)	(.110)	.024	(.143)	(.093)	NA
After Risk Variables[a]								
Memphis less Baltimore	.140	(.002)	.129	.170	(.021)	NA	.146	.200
Houston less Philadelphia	.076	.005	.108	.097	.001	.049	.092	.181
Seattle less Detroit	.113	.203	.032	.094	.009	(.042)	.154	.055
Atlanta less Minneapolis	.123	.114	.114	.155	.058	.103	.119	.368
Dallas less Chicago	(.127)	(.191)	(.087)	(.117)	.011	NA	(.137)	(.161)
Denver less Cleveland	.108	.121	.098	.103	.108	.145	.117	.049
San Francisco less New Orleans	.197	.272	.119	.202	(.005)	.043	.244	.105
Los Angeles less Miami	(.075)	.155	(.221)	(.083)	(.030)	(.143)	(.062)	NA

NOTE: Figures in parentheses are negatives. Data are fractions of one percentage point; for differential in basis points, move decimal right two places.

NA = not applicable.

[a]Risk variables: loan-value ratio, purchase price, maturity.

is measured, reflecting the high level of fees and charges on home construction loans in Los Angeles. For loans by life insurance companies, the Miami rate exceeds the Los Angeles rate, but the contract rate differential is greater than the effective rate differential; thus, the difference is positive whether or not risk variables are included.

Interregional Differentials by Purpose of Loan

Interregional yield differentials are not uniform for the three types of loan purpose, as shown below (basis points):

Difference Between East and	New Construction	Newly Built	Previously Occupied
Midwest	17	16	25
South	38	32	44
West	76	47	70

Yield differentials are smallest in the newly built category of loan purpose. This reflects the fact that effective yields are generally lower for newly built homes because of the lower property risk. In general, geographical differentials tend to be smaller for subcategories of loans which carry less risk.[11]

In the regressions run separately for each category of loan purpose, the newly built class also appears the most homogeneous with respect to area. This is true whether or not risk variables are taken into account. In five of the eight pairings here, the newly built differential is lowest of the three types of loan purpose. Moreover, for certain sets of paired cities, the loan purpose affects the magnitude of the regression differential sharply. In several cases the yield differential on new construction loans exceeds that on loans for newly built homes by approximately one-half of a percentage point. The following differentials (shown in basis points) hold risk variables and lender type constant.

[11] Yield levels are summarized below:

	New Construction	Newly Built	Previously Occupied
East	5.78	5.68	5.71
Midwest	5.95	5.84	5.96
South	6.16	6.00	6.15
West	6.54	6.15	6.41

Effective Yield Differential

	New Construction	Newly Built	Previously Occupied
Memphis less Baltimore	15	36	46
Houston less Philadelphia	21	46	48
Seattle less Detroit	58	14	36
Atlanta less Minneapolis	27	27	41
Dallas less Chicago	3	29	44
Denver less Cleveland	34	24	29
San Francisco less New Orleans	46	14	37
Los Angeles less Miami	67	14	45

Interregional Differentials by Lender Type

Since the lending activities of four of the five lender groups are over-shadowed in the statistical data by the savings and loan association loans, which comprise nearly 70 per cent of the observations, it is instructive to examine separately the results for each group. This allows us to determine whether the type of lender that a prospective borrower contacts is likely to affect the premium over the East Coast rate that he pays.[12] Effective yield differentials by region for the lender groups follow (basis points; figures in parentheses are negatives):

[12] Effective interest rates for the five lender groups are:

	Life Insurance	Mortgage Company	Savings and Loan	Mutual Savings	Commercial Banks
East	5.51	5.78	5.84	5.59	5.67
Midwest	5.50	5.55	6.04	5.66	5.73
South	5.54	5.71	6.20	NA	5.93
West	5.62	5.76	6.49	5.87	6.01

NA = not applicable.

As noted above, in these tabulations loans are classified by location of property. Mean rates in each region were also computed on loans by lenders located within the same region as the property. Because direct interregional lending activities are unusual, the number of observations in the two data sets, and the mean interest rates, were nearly identical. The principal exception was the life insurance category, in which the mean rate on Western properties is raised by 30 to 40 basis points, depending on loan purpose, when loans in the West by Eastern lenders are excluded. A complete tabulation of both effective and contract rates by regions, for all property and lender types and all combined categories, appears in Appendix Tables 4-A7 and 4-A8.

Difference Between East and	Life Insurance	Mortgage Company	Savings and Loan	Mutual Savings	Commercial Banks
Midwest	(1)	(23)	20	7	6
South	3	(7)	36	NA	26
West	11	(2)	65	28	34

NA = not applicable.

It is clear that much of the variation in mortgage interest rates is indeed attributable to the savings and loan group, for which the East-West differential is 65 basis points. For the remaining lenders, the spread ranges from 11 basis points in the life insurance category to 34 basis points in the commercial bank group. When measured between average contract rates on commercial bank loans, the East-West differential is only 29 basis points, and on bank loans for newly built homes, only 22 basis points. On mortgage company loans, the yield is higher in the East than in any other region. Yield differentials between metropolitan areas in different regions are also significantly different for different lender types. This is true in the raw data as well as in the regression results. Lender group yield differentials between cities based upon the effective rate regression that held loan purpose, maturity, purchase price and loan-value ratio constant are as follows (basis points; figures in parentheses are negatives):

	All Loans	Life Insurance Companies	Mortgage Companies	Savings and Loans	Commercial Banks
Memphis less Baltimore	40	18	NA	44	42
Houston less Philadelphia	41	15	13	45	69
Seattle less Detroit	37	15	2	44	37
Atlanta less Minneapolis	31	11	12	36	70
Dallas less Chicago	32	3	NA	31	68
Denver less Cleveland	29	14	25	27	27
San Francisco less New Orleans	35	11	6	44	32
Los Angeles less Miami	42	(03)	1	47	NA

NA = not applicable.

Differentials based on pairings of all cities with Boston, presented in Appendix Table 4-A14, further illustrate the lender group differences. For example, when loan purpose and the three risk variables are held constant, the savings and loan yield coefficient for Los Angeles exceeds the Boston coefficient by 1.07 percentage points; the life insurance differential is only 39 basis points, and the commercial bank, 82. Atlanta's coefficient in the commercial bank regression suggests a rate one percentage point above that in Boston; in the savings and loan regression it is 76 basis points, and only 35 basis points in the life insurance regression. Contract rate differentials appear in Appendix Table 4-A17.

Because of the weight of savings and loans in the total sample, the coefficients in the savings association regression parallel most closely those in the all loan regression. The savings and loan coefficients are generally larger than those in the all loan regression, indicating that the net effect of the activities of the other lender groups is to reduce the differential in mean mortgage yields between Boston and other metropolitan areas. The city coefficients in the commercial bank regression are the most variable relative to the total sample. Some of the coefficients in the commercial bank regressions are substantially larger than those in the total sample and some are considerably smaller.

All city coefficients in the life company regression are exceeded by those in the all loan regression. If we exclude Boston and Baltimore, the lowest rate cities, all remaining city coefficients fall within a range of less than one-quarter of a percentage point.

The most interesting result of the mortgage company regressions is the apparent reversal of the typical regional pattern of mortgage yields. New York has the highest coefficient, 51 basis points higher than Chicago and 31 higher than San Francisco. Apparently this reflects a difference in the intermediary role assumed by Eastern mortgage companies, as opposed to those in other areas. Mortgage companies in the South and West originate loans for Eastern life insurance companies and mutual savings banks. Thus, terms on mortgage company loans in the South and West reflect lending limitations on these institutions, as well as their generally conservative investment preferences. In the East, mortgage companies are more likely to serve local savings and loan associations, which prefer higher risk loans at higher yields. In short, mortgage companies earn a yield that is generally higher than that of their clients, but their clients in the East are relatively high-yield lenders while their clients in other areas tend to be relatively low-yield lenders. The high effective yield on mortgage company loans in the East is primarily traceable to the fees that borrowers pay for the mortgage company's services in placing the loan. For all loans these average .66 per cent of the loan amount on mortgage company loans in the East; on new construction loans, the mean fee is 1.7 per cent of the loan amount. The comparable figures for savings and loan associations are .31 and .55 per cent.

Impact of Risk Variables on Interregional Differentials

An important question is whether regional yield differentials are significantly influenced by differences in mortgage risk characteristics. Table 4-3 indicates that both increases and decreases in yield differentials between paired cities can be expected to arise with the introduction of risk variables, but that for all loans combined the changes will ordinarily be small. The differential widened in four cases and narrowed in four cases in the effective rate comparisons, with changes ranging up to 12 basis points but averaging only 7 basis points. Among categories of loan purpose, the largest increase, 16 basis points, arose in the previously occupied group.

The influence of risk variables on yield differentials is clearly dependent upon the lender category. Differentials between interest rates in paired cities generally increased slightly, when differences in contract terms were taken into account, for loans by life insurance companies and mortgage companies. For loans by savings and loan associations, the changes were greater, averaging over 9 basis points, representing four increases and four declines. On commercial bank loans five of the differentials decreased and only two increased. Changes averaged 12.5 basis points, with three decreases ranging to over 20 basis points.

For all lender groups and categories of loan purpose the changes that result when risk variables are considered are slightly lower in the contract rate data than in the effective rate data.

Yield differentials between paired cities as measured from regression coefficients were also compared with the raw data, in which neither loan purpose nor lender type is held constant. The yield differential was larger in the unadjusted data for six of the eight sets of paired cities; the average of the eight differences was nearly 10 basis points, and the largest was 16 basis points.

INTRAREGIONAL MORTGAGE YIELD DIFFERENTIALS

Chart 4-1 presents frequency distributions of average effective interest rates in 100 SMSAs, divided into four regions. Data appear in Table 4-4. These distributions show that yield differentials of 50 basis points or more between cities in the same region are not uncommon. Moreover, although there are more low rate cities in the East than in the

TABLE 4-3. *Change in Yield Differential Between Paired Cities From Inclusion of Risk Variables*

	Loan Purpose				Type of Lender			
	All Loans	New Construction	Newly Built	Previously Occupied	Life Insurance	Mortgage Companies	Savings and Loan	Commercial Banks
Effective Rate								
Number of differentials increased	4	3	5	4	6	6	4	2
Largest increase (basis points)	12.0	5.2	7.0	16.2	7.9	7.9	14.7	14.8
Number of differentials decreased	4	5	3	4	2	0	4	5
Largest decrease (basis points)	8.7	7.5	9.8	8.7	0.3	NA	10.6	20.6
Average absolute change (basis points)	7.1	5.1	4.7	8.8	2.4	3.5	9.4	12.5
Contract Rate								
Number of differentials increased	4	3	4	4	5	5	4	2
Largest increase (basis points)	8.7	3.0	5.9	12.5	4.7	4.8	9.2	12.1
Number of differentials decreased	4	5	4	4	3	1	4	5
Largest decrease (basis points)	7.2	6.9	9.9	9.6	2.0	3.2	8.0	17.8
Average absolute change (basis points)	5.6	4.0	4.0	7.0	1.7	3.0	7.0	10.8

SOURCE: Appendix Table 4-A11.
NA = not applicable.

CHART 4–1. Distribution of Effective Interest Rate for All Loans by Geographic Area, 100 Metropolitan Areas

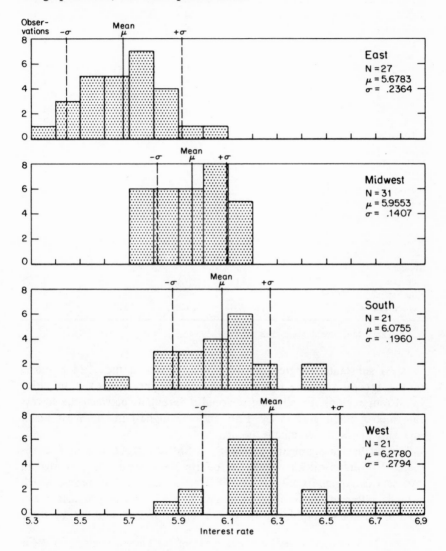

TABLE 4-4. *Distribution of Mean Effective Interest Rates on All Loans in 100 Metropolitan Areas, by Geographic Areas, May–December 1963 (number of observations)*

Rate Class	East	Midwest	South	West	All Areas
5.30–5.39	1	–	–	–	1
5.40–5.49	3	–	–	–	3
5.50–5.59	5	–	–	–	5
5.60–5.69 →	5	–	–	–	6
5.70–5.79	7	6	1	–	13
5.80–5.89	4	6	3	1	14
5.90–5.99	1 →	6	3	2	→ 12
6.00–6.09	1	8	→ 4	–	13
6.10–6.19	–	5	6	6	17
6.20–6.29	–	–	2	→ 6	8
6.30–6.39	–	–	–	–	–
6.40–6.49	–	–	2	2	4
6.50–6.59	–	–	–	1	1
6.60–6.69	–	–	–	1	1
6.70–6.79	–	–	–	1	1
6.80–6.89	–	–	–	1	1
Mean rate	5.678	5.955	6.076	6.278	5.974
Standard deviation	.236	.141	.196	.279	.300
Number of observations	27	31	21	21	100

NOTE: → indicates median class.

West, a substantial degree of overlapping exists in the yield patterns of the several regions. Rates of 5.8 to 6.1 per cent exist in cities in all four regions. Finally, the regional differentials between the lowest rate metropolitan area in the East and the highest in the West reach one and one-half percentage points.

We further disaggregate data for 42 SMSAs grouped into five regions.[13] Average rates and other terms for these areas are presented in two sets of Appendix tables, the "T" series and the "S" series, which provide different levels of aggregation. The "T" series provides mean data for all loans combined, for all five lender groups, and for the three

[13] The New England states were broken out of the Eastern grouping to create five regions instead of four.

categories of loan purpose. The "S" series further disaggregates the data, so that terms on loans in each loan purpose group by members of each lender group can be compared. Both series provide mean values of the seven available contract terms for any cell in which at least six observations were recorded. Cells in which 6–10 observations were available are starred.[14]

These tabulations demonstrate that a map of mortgage yields presents a checkered, rather than an orderly, regional pattern even within a given category of lender type and loan purpose. This point is illustrated below by selected comparisons from Appendix Table 4-S1 of some intraregional and interregional yield differentials covering loans on newly built homes by savings and loan associations.

Geographical Yield Differentials

Intraregional	*Basis Points*	*Interregional*	*Basis Points*
Boston-Hartford	43	Boston-New York	42
Providence-New Haven	38	Chicago-New York	4
Detroit-Indianapolis	22	Chicago-New Orleans	15
Cincinnati-Cleveland	12	Kansas City-Atlanta	27
Houston-Ft. Worth	21	St. Louis-Seattle	21
Louisville-Atlanta	30	Cleveland-Houston	30
Seattle-Portland	17	Boston-San Francisco	76
Denver-San Diego	31	Atlanta-Los Angeles	5

Intraregional yield differentials also can be measured by the regressions covering 18 major metropolitan areas. Effective yield differentials (in basis points) between four pairs of cities, one pair in each of the major regions, are shown below for both all loans and loans on newly built homes by savings and loan associations:

---

[14] The terms presented are mean effective interest rate (Appendix Tables 4-T1, 4-S1), mean contract rate (4-T2, 4-S2), average fees and charges (4-T3, 4-S3), average loan-value ratio (4-T4, 4-S4), mean purchase price (4-T5, 4-S5), mean loan amount (4-T6, 4-S6), and average maturity (4-T7, 4-S7). Ordering of cities within each region in the T and S series is based upon mean effective interest rate secured by savings and loan associations for mortgages on previously occupied properties (Appendix Table 4-S1, col. 1).

		All Loans, Differential Based on		Savings and Loan on Newly Built Homes, Differential Based on	
Region	Cities	Average Rate	Regressions With Risk Variables	Average Rate	Regressions With Risk Variables
East	New York less Philadelphia	12	32	17	29
Midwest	Cleveland less Detroit	4	11	3	24
South	Dallas less New Orleans	27	21	23	22
West	Los Angeles less Seattle	27	24	13	28

It is clear that the risk variables included in the regression do not explain these intraregional differentials. In both sets of pairings the yield differentials are larger after inclusion of risk variables for three of the four sets of paired cities. Differences in mortgage yield determinants not included in our data, including factors bearing on local market structure, may be responsible for this.

FACTORS UNDERLYING YIELD DIFFERENTIALS

The existence and approximate magnitude of mortgage yield differentials both between and within regions have been established; we now consider possible factors underlying these differences.

The mortgage market is essentially a local market, matching local savings with local housing demands. Assuming no capital flows between markets, uniform mortgage yields would arise only if demand and supply curves for mortgage capital intersected at the identical interest rate in all areas. This would require essentially uniform local demand and supply curves throughout the United States, which implies, among other things, uniform rates of population and economic growth; such conditions are not met in the American economy.

Guttentag has reduced the situation to its essentials: "The most important determinant of the demand for mortgage funds is growth in the number of households, while the supply of funds is largely determined by the size of the sitting population. For this reason, the demand in areas experiencing a large net immigration of population will be greater, relative to supply, and interest rates will be higher than in 'old' areas where population is growing slowly or not at all. This is the principal cause of regional yield differentials."[15]

The major question is why the market does not entirely eliminate the differentials through intermarket flow.

High Cost of Information

Information on average loan characteristics for various areas is not difficult to obtain. Average terms on new commitments in major cities are published monthly by both *House and Home* and the Federal Home Loan Bank Board. Additionally, mortgage investors are a gregarious group, frequently meeting with colleagues in the city, county, state, region, and nation. Consequently, most competent mortgage lenders have a fairly accurate picture of interest rate patterns in the areas in which they operate. For life insurance companies and some large savings banks, this area encompasses most of the United States.

Information on specific loans, however, is costly to obtain. Although some economists may be surprised by the fact, most national lenders in the mortgage market insist upon personally visiting every residential property upon which they make conventional loans. They are reluctant to surrender authority for firm commitments to agents.[16] To many lenders a personal assessment of the borrower's willingness to fulfill his obligation is the most important factor in a mortgage commitment. The cost of personal interviews increases with both distance and the number of areas selected for foreign investment. Thus, information regarding the quality of a loan in a distant area is likely to cost more than comparable information on local conditions.

[15] Jack M. Guttentag, "The Federal National Mortgage Association," in *Federal Credit Agencies,* Englewood Cliffs, 1963, p. 135.

[16] An investor who has corresponded for some years with a mortgage banker may purchase the loan without inspecting the property, but he will visit it within six months, with an option to return the loan to the originator.

Legal Constraints

Legal factors that affect lenders' ability and willingness to make out-of-state conventional mortgage loans may be classified into two categories—those that serve as a barrier to capital flowing from the state, and those that inhibit or influence the flow of foreign mortgage funds into the state.

The first category of statutes governs out-of-state lending by domestic institutions. In general, these statutes allow life insurance companies nationwide lending powers, but restrict out-of-state lending by other types of financial institutions. Savings and loan associations have generally been limited to an area bounded by a 50 or 100 mile radius from the home office.

The 19 states that have chartered mutual savings banks fall into three groups. Connecticut, Massachusetts, and New Jersey allow out-of-state lending within only a limited radius. Currently, the range in New Jersey is 50 miles from the state border and, in Connecticut and Massachusetts, 50 miles from the home office.[17] Five states limit out-of-state lending by mutual savings banks to a group of states, usually contiguous states. The remaining states permit virtually unlimited out-of-state lending powers, although maximum contract terms may be specified. Although the principal savings bank state, New York, presently falls within this category, in 1963 lending activities were restricted to New York and adjoining states.

The second category of statutes, which may influence the transfer of funds to a foreign state, is more complex. A lender must consider the doing business statutes, registration and qualification requirements, and franchise and income taxes. Some states make it relatively easy for a foreign corporation to engage in mortgage lending, others require some comparatively simple and inexpensive procedures, some require onerous and/or expensive procedures, and a number of states prohibit entirely loans by certain types of foreign lenders. For example, Alabama, Arizona, Colorado, and New Hampshire do not permit out-of-state savings and loan associations to make mortgage loans.[18]

[17] The permissible area for both Connecticut and New Jersey savings banks has been broadened since 1963.

[18] See Malcolm C. Sherman, *Mortgage and Real Estate Investment Guide*, which is published annually by Helen B. Sherman, Boston, Massachusetts. Much of the material in this section is drawn from the 1967 edition of the *Guide*. Sherman includes (on pp. 407–408 of the 1967 edition) a summary of the ease

Legal limits on loan characteristics may affect foreign lending in a state. Both maximum allowable interest charges and penalties for usurious rates differ widely among states. In early 1967, maximum interest rates ranged from 6 per cent (10 states) to 21 per cent (1 state).[19] Some states impose civil penalties only, but these range from loss of excess interest, to loss of all interest, to loss of principal and interest. The effect of fees and charges on the determination of usury varies in similar fashion. Finally, in some states interest on interest is prohibited, which causes complications for the lender in the assessment of penalties for delinquent payments. Statutory limits on loan size, loan-value ratio, and maturity also vary from state to state.

The foreign lender must be familiar with the detail of the real property laws, because of the importance of assuring adequate security. "The rights of husband and wife, courtesy, dower and homestead are pertinent in making mortgage loans in the various states, especially where one of the parties does not execute the mortgage and the other claims sole ownership of the security."[20]

Of major importance are the remedies available to the mortgagee in the event of default and/or foreclosure. For example, in Louisiana, if a monthly payment is not paid within 31 days of the due date, the property may be immediately foreclosed and sold; there is no equity of redemption. In other states, it may be several years before the

of making out-of-state mortgages by foreign corporations. He rates each state, on an A (easiest) to E (prohibited) scale, on the basis of the aggregate effect of state statutes, in his opinion, on mortgage loan activities of seven types of lending institutions. See also John J. Redfield, "Out-of-State Mortgage Investments by Savings Banks," *Commercial and Financial Chronicle,* January 5, 1956.

[19] The complete distribution follows: 6 per cent—10 states; 7 per cent—6 states; 8 per cent—12 states and D.C.; 9 per cent—1 state; 10 per cent—11 states; 12 per cent—6 states; 21 per cent—1 state; no limit—Maine, New Hampshire, Massachusetts. (Source: memorandum from the legal department, National Association of Mutual Savings Banks, March 29, 1967.) Since credit was relatively easy during the period under study, usury statutes were of limited significance. In 1967, however, foreign residential mortgage capital virtually ceased flowing into a number of Southern states with 6 per cent ceilings. North Carolina, under pressure from mortgage bankers and home builders, raised the rate limit to 7 per cent in June of 1967.

During the extremely tight credit conditions that obtained during 1967, usury statutes probably contributed to interstate capital flows. New York savings banks, faced with a 6 per cent limit on conventionals when FHA-insured loans were selling at 6 per cent plus five to eight points, took advantage of legislation allowing nationwide conventional lending and poured mortgage money into states allowing higher yields. The situation was comparable in Pennsylvania.

[20] Sherman, *op. cit.,* p. 4.

redemption period has expired and a clear title can be passed to a subsequent purchaser. Discussions with a large number of mortgage bankers indicate that the diversity of foreclosure and equity of redemption statutes is the single most important barrier, if one is to be singled out, to a larger interstate flow of mortgage capital, and certainly to the development of a secondary mortgage market.

Varying Costs of Acquisition and Servicing

Facilities for the acquisition and servicing of residential mortgages are not uniformly available. A sparsely settled area may simply not justify the cost of establishing a mortgage company or branch office of a bank or life company. The consequence is pockets of capital scarcity that can be found in rural areas and small cities throughout the United States. They are often characterized by a local financial monopoly, perhaps a single savings and loan association, or a commercial bank and savings and loan with close ties. This lack of technical facilities for capital transfers is the principal source of intraregional differentials.

Facilities do exist for interregional fund transfers to capital-deficit areas, but in mortgage lending they often involve higher processing costs than local lending. This is largely a result of duplication of facilities and services when a mortgage banker is retained; the amount depends upon the degree to which the lender is willing to delegate lending authority. Auditing procedures for assuring the financial soundness of the servicing agent also increase the total cost of foreign lending.

SUMMARY AND CONCLUSIONS

This paper has considered the influence of property location on effective yields of conventional, residential mortgage yields during 1963. Property location is shown to be a statistically significant yield determinant. This is true of loans by five types of lender and for three categories of loan purpose. Property location is least significant for loans on newly built homes, which represent a more homogenous class than the new construction and previously occupied categories.

Interregional mortgage yield differentials are largest in magnitude when measured between average interest rates prevailing in the East and West. The differential of approximately 70 basis points in effective mortgage yields in these regions does not differ markedly from that which existed in 1940. On the most standardized property type, newly built homes, the differential between Eastern and Western average rates is slightly less than one-half of one percentage point.

A large part of the East-West differential in mortgage yields is attributable to differences in mean rates on loans by savings and loan associations. For this lender group, effective interest rate in the West averages 65 basis points higher than in the East. In contrast, the average differential for three other lender groups—life insurance companies, mutual savings banks, and commercial banks—is only one-quarter of a percentage point.

This would appear to enlarge, rather than diminish, the economic significance of the interregional differential because savings and loan associations represent the principal source of conventional residential mortgage financing. For many borrowers they may be the only practical source. The most important consideration to most borrowers seeking home financing is the down payment required, and savings associations typically are authorized to allow a higher loan-value ratio than competing lenders. There is some evidence that borrowers who require a loan in excess of 75 per cent of property value pay a market premium for the privilege, particularly in areas where capital demand exceeds supply. Whether lender risk exposure rises correspondingly is questionable.

The continued existence of interregional yield differentials appears to represent a manifestation of allocational inefficiency within an important segment of the financial markets.[21] Whether it is serious enough to warrant official concern is a matter of personal determination. There are indications, however, that some mortgage interest rate variation could be reduced if existing obstacles in the path of interstate mortgage capital transfers were removed. Specifically, state laws should be redrawn to increase the mobility of mortgage capital. A uniform real property code would reduce the reluctance of lenders to engage in widespread out-of-state mortgage lending activities. A corresponding requirement is that geographical lending authority of the various financial institutions be broadened to permit nationwide mortgage lending.

---

[21] Without knowledge of transaction costs, of which information costs relating to the lender's risk are often the most important, we cannot make a conclusive determination of allocative inefficiency. George J. Stigler's remarks in "Imperfections in the Capital Market," *Journal of Political Economy*, June 1967, pp. 287–292, are most relevant here. But the local-monopoly-structure of a good deal of the residential mortgage market does suggest the opportunity for inefficiency.

Intraregional yield differentials of substantial magnitude were also established. These arise not only across state lines but also between neighboring cities within individual states. Additionally, within individual metropolitan areas, significant differences in rates charged by different types of lenders are evident. In conclusion, it would seem that structural changes are required in a relatively large number of local residential mortgage markets.

APPENDIX TABLE 4-A1. *States Included in Regions*

REGION ONE – East	REGION THREE (cont'd)
Connecticut	Georgia
Maine	Kentucky
Massachusetts	Louisiana
New Hampshire	Maryland
New Jersey	Mississippi
New York	North Carolina
Pennsylvania	Oklahoma
Rhode Island	South Carolina
Vermont	Tennessee
	Texas
REGION TWO – Midwest	Virginia
Illinois	Washington D. C.
Indiana	West Virginia
Iowa	
Kansas	
Michigan	REGION FOUR – West
Minnesota	Alaska
Missouri	Arizona
Nebraska	California
North Dakota	Colorado
Ohio	Hawaii
South Dakota	Idaho
Wisconsin	Montana
	Nevada
REGION THREE – South	New Mexico
Alabama	Oregon
Arkansas	Washington
Delaware	Wyoming
Florida	Utah

APPENDIX TABLE 4-A2. *Mean Effective Interest Rate for States, Grouped by Region, Loan Purpose, and Lender Type (standard deviations in parentheses)*

		Loan Purpose			Type of Lender				
	All Loans	New Construction	Newly Built	Previously Occupied	Life Insurance	Mortgage Companies	Savings and Loan	Mutual Savings	Commercial Banks
Northeast									
Connecticut	5.67 (.25)	5.69 (.24)	5.67 (.25)	5.67 (.25)	5.52 (.10)	—	5.84 (.27)	5.62 (.22)	5.62 (.20)
Maine	5.86 (.29)	5.84 (.23)	—	5.87 (.30)	—	—	5.89 (.20)	5.84 (.24)	5.89 (.48)
Massachusetts	5.43 (.27)	5.46 (.27)	5.37 (.27)	5.44 (.27)	5.22 (.08)	—	5.58 (.28)	5.40 (.25)	5.31 (.26)
New Hampshire	5.89 (.22)	5.86 (.29)	5.89 (.19)	5.89 (.20)	—	—	5.93 (.19)	5.89 (.22)	5.84 (.22)
Rhode Island	5.63 (.27)	5.65 (.27)	5.62 (.25)	5.63 (.27)	—	—	5.76 (.32)	5.52 (.14)	5.53 (.17)
Vermont	5.86 (.25)	—	—	5.89 (.24)	—	—	5.88 (.22)	—	5.81 (.31)
Middle Atlantic									
Delaware	5.52 (.35)	5.53 (.40)	5.50 (.30)	5.54 (.36)	5.32 (.15)	—	6.22 (.22)	5.38 (.24)	5.64 (.28)
Maryland	5.70 (.33)	6.00 (.28)	5.61 (.28)	5.66 (.33)	5.44 (.15)	5.54 (.16)	5.83 (.31)	5.39 (.16)	5.68 (.32)
New Jersey	5.73 (.29)	5.76 (.29)	5.68 (.28)	5.75 (.29)	5.52 (.08)	5.72 (.33)	5.80 (.27)	5.74 (.31)	5.63 (.29)
New York	5.79 (.28)	5.86 (.28)	5.82 (.27)	5.76 (.27)	5.55 (.11)	5.98 (.24)	5.90 (.24)	5.75 (.25)	5.69 (.28)

(continued)

APPENDIX TABLE 4-A2 (continued)

	All Loans	Loan Purpose			Type of Lender				
		New Construction	Newly Built	Previously Occupied	Life Insurance	Mortgage Companies	Savings and Loan	Mutual Savings	Commercial Banks
Pennsylvania	5.73 (.35)	5.86 (.33)	5.58 (.32)	5.76 (.35)	5.44 (.22)	5.54 (.29)	5.89 (.32)	5.40 (.18)	5.76 (.32)
Great Lakes									
Illinois	5.91 (.42)	5.95 (.45)	5.81 (.39)	5.92 (.41)	5.49 (.24)	5.42 (.17)	6.01 (.38)	—	5.57 (.35)
Indiana	6.01 (.34)	6.02 (.36)	5.90 (.31)	6.03 (.33)	5.48 (.22)	5.58 (.14)	6.11 (.27)	—	5.79 (.35)
Michigan	5.85 (.34)	5.79 (.33)	5.75 (.29)	5.90 (.36)	5.50 (.16)	5.79 (.29)	5.86 (.29)	—	5.94 (.46)
Ohio	5.96 (.40)	6.03 (.39)	5.82 (.35)	5.98 (.41)	5.52 (.18)	5.51 (.15)	6.12 (.35)	—	5.67 (.32)
Wisconsin	5.85 (.32)	5.81 (.34)	5.88 (.29)	5.86 (.31)	5.38 (.17)	5.45 (.21)	5.93 (.28)	6.04 (.14)	5.70 (.32)
Upper South									
Kentucky	6.00 (.26)	6.02 (.25)	5.93 (.25)	6.04 (.25)	5.62 (.15)	—	6.04 (.23)	—	5.83 (.31)
Tennessee	6.03 (.31)	5.94 (.34)	6.02 (.31)	6.08 (.29)	5.50 (.22)	5.71 (.19)	6.13 (.24)	—	6.05 (.30)
Virginia	5.90 (.30)	6.00 (.28)	5.84 (.31)	5.88 (.29)	5.53 (.22)	5.50 (.11)	5.98 (.26)	5.25 (.00)	5.83 (.28)
West Virginia	6.05 (.23)	6.02 (.24)	5.99 (.21)	6.10 (.23)	5.72 (.18)	—	6.11 (.18)	—	5.93 (.28)

(continued)

APPENDIX TABLE 4-A2 (continued)

	All Loans	Loan Purpose			Type of Lender				
		New Construction	Newly Built	Previously Occupied	Life Insurance	Mortgage Companies	Savings and Loan	Mutual Savings	Commercial Banks
Lower South									
Alabama	6.35 (.58)	6.42 (.59)	6.19 (.48)	6.55 (.67)	5.43 (.21)	5.72 (.16)	6.59 (.35)	—	7.22 (.79)
Arkansas	6.60 (.51)	6.70 (.56)	6.38 (.46)	6.75 (.46)	5.64 (.16)	—	6.69 (.41)	—	—
Florida	6.17 (.33)	6.20 (.35)	6.14 (.29)	6.17 (.34)	5.74 (.31)	5.95 (.23)	6.21 (.31)	—	6.39 (.48)
Georgia	6.29 (.47)	6.29 (.45)	6.15 (.40)	6.44 (.50)	5.55 (.29)	5.67 (.11)	6.37 (.40)	—	6.47 (.68)
Louisiana	6.22 (.60)	6.22 (.62)	5.94 (.43)	6.31 (.62)	5.42 (.25)	5.56 (.19)	6.34 (.56)	—	5.92 (.57)
Mississippi	6.41 (.62)	6.21 (.60)	6.23 (.59)	6.68 (.56)	5.45 (.31)	—	6.58 (.49)	—	—
North Carolina	6.05 (.22)	6.03 (.24)	6.04 (.25)	6.08 (.17)	5.47 (.26)	—	6.09 (.15)	—	5.73 (.23)
South Carolina	6.20 (.41)	6.21 (.37)	6.02 (.31)	6.28 (.46)	—	—	6.21 (.40)	—	—
Plains									
Iowa	6.05 (.34)	5.98 (.37)	6.11 (.43)	6.06 (.29)	5.55 (.13)	5.69 (.29)	6.15 (.28)	—	5.87 (.30)
Kansas	6.09 (.35)	6.05 (.35)	5.99 (.34)	6.14 (.34)	5.53 (.21)	5.65 (.17)	6.13 (.31)	—	5.96 (.50)

(continued)

APPENDIX TABLE 4-A2 (continued)

	All Loans	Loan Purpose			Type of Lender				
		New Construction	Newly Built	Previously Occupied	Life Insurance	Mortgage Companies	Savings and Loan	Mutual Savings	Commercial Banks
Minnesota	5.83 (.33)	5.90 (.33)	5.70 (.28)	5.83 (.33)	5.49 (.16)	5.58 (.24)	5.95 (.25)	5.56 (.13)	5.68 (.39)
Missouri	6.12 (.49)	6.24 (.53)	5.93 (.37)	6.18 (.50)	5.44 (.17)	5.77 (.21)	6.20 (.41)	—	6.08 (.63)
Nebraska	6.00 (.33)	5.93 (.23)	5.92 (.36)	6.07 (.37)	5.58 (.15)	—	6.04 (.29)	—	6.08 (.57)
North Dakota	6.19 (.31)	6.41 (.34)	6.04 (.14)	6.15 (.29)	—	—	6.20 (.30)	—	6.24 (.41)
South Dakota	6.12 (.30)	6.06 (.34)	6.05 (.26)	6.18 (.28)	—	5.71 (.17)	6.16 (.24)	—	—
South West									
Arizona	6.31 (.45)	6.29 (.64)	6.24 (.34)	6.35 (.44)	5.48 (.24)	—	6.43 (.34)	—	—
New Mexico	6.12 (.42)	5.94 (.32)	6.10 (.32)	6.39 (.64)	5.48 (.24)	—	6.25 (.32)	—	—
Oklahoma	6.07 (.51)	6.08 (.51)	5.87 (.39)	6.28 (.54)	5.45 (.23)	—	6.21 (.43)	—	5.82 (.63)
Texas	6.29 (.56)	6.19 (.48)	6.17 (.43)	6.45 (.67)	5.54 (.22)	5.77 (.21)	6.35 (.52)	—	6.42 (.78)
Rocky Mountains									
Colorado	6.25 (.52)	6.33 (.55)	6.13 (.43)	6.29 (.54)	5.60 (.15)	5.76 (.18)	6.41 (.47)	—	5.91 (.45)

(continued)

APPENDIX TABLE 4-A2 (concluded)

	All Loans	Loan Purpose			Type of Lender				
		New Construction	Newly Built	Previously Occupied	Life Insurance	Mortgage Companies	Savings and Loan	Mutual Savings	Commercial Banks
Idaho	6.08 (.23)	6.09 (.13)	—	—	6.05 (.16)	—	—	—	—
Montana	6.11 (.49)	6.20 (.43)	5.84 (.21)	6.21 (.64)	6.05 (.13)	—	6.20 (.53)	—	5.67 (.12)
Utah	6.23 (.39)	6.35 (.29)	6.19 (.37)	6.20 (.43)	5.76 (.36)	—	6.35 (.26)	—	6.14 (.53)
Wyoming	6.42 (.61)	—	—	6.49 (.58)	—	—	6.13 (.33)	—	6.78 (.53)
Far West									
California	6.41 (.49)	6.70 (.58)	6.16 (.43)	6.41 (.45)	5.58 (.25)	5.70 (.34)	6.51 (.42)	—	5.99 (.34)
Nevada	6.20 (.39)	—	6.07 (.03)	—	—	—	—	—	6.14 (.23)
Oregon	6.19 (.47)	6.23 (.49)	5.97 (.30)	6.23 (.49)	5.65 (.23)	5.60 (.12)	6.30 (.44)	—	5.92 (.30)
Washington	6.20 (.44)	6.30 (.37)	5.96 (.34)	6.22 (.50)	5.70 (.33)	5.89 (.33)	6.37 (.39)	5.87 (.22)	6.10 (.50)

NOTE: Cells with less than 15 observations are excluded. This nine-region breakdown is that recommended by the Conference on Research in Income and Wealth, *Regional Income*, Vol. 21, Princeton, Princeton University Press for NBER, 1957, pp. 103-104.

APPENDIX TABLE 4-A3. *Average Terms on Conventional Residential Mortgage Loan by Loan Purpose and Type of Lender for 18 Principal Metropolitan Areas Combined, May-December, 1963 (standard deviations in parentheses)*

	Maturity (years)	Loan Amount (dollars)	Loan/Value Ratio (per cent)	Purchase Price (dollars)	Contract Interest Rate (per cent)	Fees and Charges (per cent)	Effective Interest Rate (per cent)
All observations	22.57	16,508	72.19	23,149	5.84	0.80	5.98
	(4.96)	(7,815.6)	(13.40)	(11,088)	(.420)	(.787)	(.494)
Life insurance	25.37	20,602	66.92	31,029	5.50	0.18	5.53
	(4.01)	(7,751.3)	(11.11)	(11,453)	(.190)	(.321)	(.210)
Mortgage companies	24.28	19,229	68.49	28,561	5.56	0.59	5.65
	(4.04)	(7,596.5)	(12.91)	(11,879)	(.257)	(.543)	(.284)
Savings and loan	23.19	16,270	75.78	21,527	6.00	1.03	6.18
	(4.59)	(7,589.3)	(11.43)	(9,948)	(.388)	(.802)	(.444)
Mutual savings	22.78	15,098	67.01	22,595	5.46	0.19	5.49
	(4.87)	(6,673.4)	(13.98)	(9,255)	(.235)	(.396)	(.266)
Commercial banks	18.09	16,609	61.56	27,265	5.57	0.34	5.64
	(4.80)	(9,122.1)	(14.55)	(14,143)	(.329)	(.503)	(.357)
New construction	23.29	18,514	71.04	26,448	5.84	1.21	6.04
	(4.29)	(8,171.5)	(12.84)	(11,865)	(.385)	(1.066)	(.492)
Newly built	24.59	17,616	73.20	24,358	5.76	0.69	5.87
	(4.38)	(6,797.0)	(14.03)	(9,280)	(.365)	(.701)	(.415)
Previously occupied	21.75	15,695	72.12	22,011	5.87	0.74	6.00
	(5.07)	(7,919.3)	(13.26)	(11,258)	(.440)	(.707)	(.510)

APPENDIX TABLE 4-A4. *Standard Deviation of Average Contract Terms in 18 Metropolitan Areas*

SMSA	Maturity (years)	Loan Amount (dollars)	Loan/Value Ratio (per cent)	Purchase Price (dollars)	Contract Interest Rate (per cent)	Fees and Charges (per cent)	Effective Interest Rate (per cent)
East							
Baltimore	5.68	6,806.8	14.99	9,591	.279	.469	.332
Boston	4.11	7,254.5	15.02	10,782	.214	.229	.215
New York	5.35	7,817.3	13.30	12,018	.248	.556	.276
Philadelphia	5.08	6,166.9	15.22	8,633	.315	.425	.345
Midwest							
Chicago	4.54	6,574.9	14.90	10,054	.329	.787	.425
Cleveland	4.76	6,843.1	16.83	9,999	.331	.562	.394
Detroit	5.40	6,759.8	13.64	9,849	.259	.523	.314
Minneapolis	4.81	6,585.1	12.99	9,865	.258	.791	.292
South							
Atlanta	5.11	7,019.3	10.13	9,552	.395	1.016	.460
Memphis	4.88	6,417.5	12.79	8,261	.214	.484	.272
Miami	3.51	8,738.9	10.52	12,170	.167	.943	.287
New Orleans	4.39	8,532.1	14.07	11,548	.301	.254	.299
West							
Dallas	5.31	8,943.4	11.60	12,130	.543	.513	.606
Denver	5.24	6,777.1	12.27	9,861	.415	.728	.507
Houston	4.36	9,221.7	10.17	12,266	.381	.630	.449
Los Angeles	3.64	8,698.0	8.52	11,952	.352	.702	.406
San Francisco	4.13	7,444.1	10.85	11,190	.383	.640	.453
Seattle	4.47	7,085.1	12.99	10,325	.367	.809	.465

NOTE: Mean values for these terms appear in Appendix Tables 4-T1 through 4-T7.

APPENDIX TABLE 4-A5. *Coefficient of Multiple Determination and Standard Error of the Estimate for Successive Regression Steps, by Loan Purpose and Region and Lender Type; Dependent Variable Is Effective Interest Rate*

Category		Variables Introduced					
		Lender Type[a]	Loan Purpose[a]	Loan/Value Ratio	Purchase Price	Maturity	Property Location[a]
All Loans	R^2	.3263	.3303	.3589	.3884	.4044	.6193
	Standard error	.4054	.4042	.3954	.3862	.3811	.3047
By Region							
Midwest	R^2	.2484	.2510	.2905	.3795	.4373	.4478
	Standard error	.3330	.3324	.3235	.3025	.2881	.2854
Western	R^2	.2679	.2918	.2932	.3834	.4364	.4894
	Standard error	.3964	.3898	.3895	.3638	.3478	.3310
Southern	R^2	.2138	.2167	.2167	.3197	.4035	.4373
	Standard error	.3373	.3367	.3367	.3138	.2938	.2854
Eastern	R^2	.2312	.2428	.3662	.3961	.3966	.5496
	Standard error	.2938	.2916	.2668	.2604	.2603	.2249
By Loan Purpose							
New construction	R^2	.2921		.3160	.3424	.3705	.6271
	Standard error	.4139		.4068	.3989	.3903	.3004
Previously occupied	R^2	.3305		.3472	.3806	.3995	.6424
	Standard error	.4173		.4121	.4014	.3953	.3050
Newly built	R^2	.3550		.4492	.4632	.4645	.6336
	Standard error	.3332		.3079	.3040	.3036	.2512

(continued)

APPENDIX TABLE 4-A5 (concluded)

		Variables Introduced					
		Lender Type[a]	Loan Purpose[a]	Loan/Value Ratio	Purchase Price	Maturity	Property Location[a]
By Lender Types							
Commercial banks	R^2	—	.0219	.0249	.1658	.2282	.4605
	Standard error	—	.3526	.3521	.3257	.3132	.2619
Mortgage companies	R^2	—	.0324	.2209	.2231	.2252	.4599
	Standard error	—	.2794	.2507	.2504	.2501	.2088
Mutual savings	R^2	—	.0162	.1874	.1899	.2087	.6188
	Standard error	—	.2638	.2397	.2394	.2366	.1642
Savings and loan	R^2	—	.0123	.0552	.0975	.1310	.4972
	Standard error	—	.4415	.4318	.4220	.4141	.3150
Life insurance	R^2	—	.0090	.0144	.0184	.0482	.1920
	Standard error	—	.2094	.2088	.2084	.2052	.1891

[a]Dummy variables.

APPENDIX TABLE 4-A6. *Coefficient of Multiple Determination and Standard Error of the Estimate for Successive Regression Steps, by Loan Purpose and Region and Lender Type; Dependent Variable Is Contract Interest Rate*

		Lender Type[a]	Loan Purpose[a]	Loan/Value Ratio	Purchase Price	Maturity	Property Location[a]
All Loans	R^2	.2855	.2903	.3291	.3616	.3728	.6154
	Standard error	.3552	.3540	.3442	.3357	.3328	.2606
By Region							
Midwest	R^2	.1755	.1778	.2438	.3369	.3813	.4299
	Standard error	.2821	.2817	.2701	.2529	.2443	.2345
Western	R^2	.2469	.2639	.2641	.3574	.4031	.4600
	Standard error	.3469	.3429	.3429	.3204	.3088	.2937
Southern	R^2	.1888	.1933	.1944	.3066	.3686	.4426
	Standard error	.2854	.2846	.2844	.2639	.2518	.2366
Eastern	R^2	.2117	.2173	.3704	.4109	.4127	.5239
	Standard error	.2623	.2614	.2344	.2268	.2264	.2038
By Loan Purpose							
New construction	R^2	.2523		.2867	.3196	.3487	.5806
	Standard error	.3331		.3254	.3178	.3109	.2495
Previously occupied	R^2	.2925		.3164	.3520	.3644	.6375
	Standard error	.3704		.3641	.3545	.3511	.2651
Newly built	R^2	.2963		.4229	.4384	.4391	.6131
	Standard error	.3060		.2771	.2733	.2731	.2269

(continued)

APPENDIX TABLE 4-A6 (concluded)

	Variables Introduced					
	Lender Type[a]	Loan Purpose[a]	Loan/Value Ratio	Purchase Price	Maturity	Property Location[a]
By Lender Types						
Commercial banks R^2		.0176	.0231	.1721	.2361	.4507
Standard error		.3258	.3249	.2991	.2873	.2436
Mortgage companies R^2		.0546	.2678	.2692	.2698	.4623
Standard error		.2500	.2200	.2198	.2197	.1885
Mutual savings R^2		.0120	.2129	.2197	.2314	.5828
Standard error		.2333	.2083	.2073	.2058	.1516
Savings and loan R^2		.0139	.0723	.1137	.1330	.5202
Standard error		.3852	.3736	.3652	.3612	.2687
Life insurance R^2		.0092	.0140	.0156	.0525	.1857
Standard error		.1891	.1886	.1885	.1849	.1714

[a]Dummy variables.

APPENDIX TABLE 4-A7. *Mean Effective Interest Rate on Conventional Residential Mortgage Loans by Loan Purpose and Region and Lender Type, May–December, 1963 (per cent)*

	East	North Central	South	West
Life insurance				
New construction	5.47	5.48	5.54	5.62
Newly built homes	5.53	5.53	5.54	5.63
Previously occupied	5.50	5.50	5.52	5.62
All loans	5.51	5.50	5.54	5.62
Mortgage companies				
New construction	6.16	5.49	5.75	5.93
Newly built homes	5.79	5.59	5.70	5.68
Previously occupied	5.60	5.56	5.67	5.75
All loans	5.78	5.55	5.71	5.76
Savings and loan				
New construction	5.89	6.07	6.24	6.71
Newly built homes	5.76	5.98	6.12	6.31
Previously occupied	5.86	6.05	6.24	6.49
All loans	5.84	6.04	6.20	6.49
Mutual savings				
New construction	5.65	5.95	–	5.91
Newly built homes	5.58	5.59	–	5.79
Previously occupied	5.58	5.66	–	5.87
All loans	5.59	5.66	–	5.87
Commercial banks				
New construction	5.72	5.78	5.90	6.13
Newly built	5.56	5.57	5.66	5.83
Previously occupied	5.68	5.74	6.03	6.01
All loans	5.67	5.73	5.93	6.01
New construction	5.78	5.95	6.16	6.54
Newly built	5.68	5.84	6.00	6.15
Previously occupied	5.71	5.96	6.15	6.41
All loans	5.71	5.94	6.10	6.40

APPENDIX TABLE 4-A8. *Mean Contract Interest Rate on Conventional Residential Mortgage Loans by Loan Purpose and Region and Lender Type, May–December, 1963 (per cent)*

	East	North Central	South	West
Life insurance				
New construction	5.46	5.45	5.52	5.56
Newly built	5.51	5.50	5.52	5.58
Previously occupied	5.49	5.47	5.50	5.57
All loans	5.49	5.48	5.52	5.57
Mortgage companies				
New construction	5.91	5.35	5.66	5.77
Newly built	5.69	5.50	5.61	5.59
Previously occupied	5.58	5.48	5.57	5.68
All loans	5.69	5.45	5.62	5.67
Savings and loan				
New construction	5.80	5.89	6.04	6.36
Newly built	5.72	5.85	5.97	6.16
Previously occupied	5.82	5.91	6.08	6.29
All loans	5.79	5.90	6.03	6.28
Mutual savings				
New construction	5.62	5.88	–	5.70
Newly built	5.55	5.59	–	5.71
Previously occupied	5.55	5.64	–	5.77
All loans	5.56	5.64	–	5.74
Commercial banks				
New construction	5.68	5.68	5.87	5.96
Newly built	5.54	5.53	5.65	5.76
Previously occupied	5.63	5.71	5.98	5.94
All loans	5.63	5.69	5.89	5.92
New construction	5.72	5.81	5.98	6.23
Newly built	5.64	5.74	5.87	6.02
Previously occupied	5.67	5.85	6.01	6.22
All loans	5.67	5.82	5.96	6.19

APPENDIX TABLE 4-A9. *Frequency Distribution of Mean Effective Interest Rates on Conventional Residential Mortgage Loans in 100 Metropolitan Areas, by Loan Purpose, May–December, 1963*

Rate Class	New Construction	Newly Built	Previously Occupied
5.20 – 5.29	1	1	–
5.30 – 5.39	1	–	1
5.40 – 5.49	2	3	1
5.50 – 5.59	7	11	5
5.60 – 5.69	11	12	8
5.70 – 5.79	5	13	9
5.80 – 5.89	19 →	14	14
5.90 – 5.99 →	10	13	11
6.00 – 6.09	17	11 →	14
6.10 – 6.19	8	14	14
6.20 – 6.29	9	3	8
6.30 – 6.39	5	2	4
6.40 – 6.49	–	1	2
6.50 – 6.59	1	–	4
6.60 – 6.69	3	1	3
6.70 and over	1	–	2
Mean rate (per cent)	5.97	5.87	6.02

NOTE: → indicates median class. Data for loans on newly built properties available for only 99 SMSAs.

APPENDIX TABLE 4-A10. *Frequency Distribution of Mean Effective Interest Rates on Conventional Residential Mortgage Loans in 100 Metropolitan Areas, by Type of Lender, May–December, 1963 (per cent)*

Rate Class	Life Insurance	Mortgage Companies	Savings and Loan	Mutual Savings	Commercial Banks
5.10 – 5.19	1.1	–	–	–	–
5.20 – 5.29	5.4	2.1	–	7	2.4
5.30 – 5.39	6.5	–	–	11	3.6
5.40 – 5.49	26.9	4.2	2.0	18	9.6
5.50 – 5.59	39.8	31.3	1.0	21	10.8
5.60 – 5.69	12.9	16.7	4.0	11	12.0
5.70 – 5.79	5.4	12.5	4.0	14	14.5
5.80 – 5.89	1.1	8.3	13.1	7	9.6
5.90 – 5.99	–	12.5	14.1	–	14.5
6.00 – 6.09	1.1	6.3	14.1	7	14.5
6.10 – 6.19	–	2.1	18.2	–	1.2
6.20 – 6.29	–	4.2	6.1	4	2.4
6.30 – 6.39	–	–	11.1	–	1.2
6.40 – 6.49	–	–	4.0	–	2.4
6.50 – 6.59	–	–	2.0	–	–
6.60 – 6.69	–	–	3.0	–	1.2
6.70 and over	–	–	3.0	–	–
Mean rate	5.51	5.72	6.14	5.60	5.79

NOTE: Detail may not add to 100 per cent because of rounding. No lender group was represented in all 100 SMSAs.

APPENDIX TABLE 4-A11. *Yield Differential Before Inclusion of Risk Variable Less Yield Differential After Inclusion of Risk Variable*

	Loan Purpose				Type of Lender			
	All Loans	New Construction	Newly Built	Previously Occupied	Life Insurance	Mortgage Companies	Savings and Loan	Commercial Banks
Effective rate								
Memphis less Baltimore	(.120)	(.052)	(.012)	(.162)	(.008)	—	(.147)	.206
Houston less Philadelphia	(.032)	.043	(.031)	(.038)	(.079)	(.015)	(.028)	.081
Seattle less Detroit	.045	.075	(.007)	.046	(.008)	(.046)	.106	(.009)
Atlanta less Minneapolis	.067	.075	.036	.087	(.012)	(.012)	.088	.202
Dallas less Chicago	.087	.037	.098	.119	(.008)	—	.089	.201
Denver less Cleveland	.057	.064	.096	.042	.003	(.079)	.072	.030
San Francisco less New Orleans	(.077)	(.015)	(.025)	(.106)	.002	(.009)	(.108)	(.148)
Los Angeles less Miami	(.086)	(.044)	(.070)	(.110)	(.074)	(.048)	(.117)	—
Contract rate								
Memphis less Baltimore	(.087)	(.030)	.002	(.125)	.005	—	(.092)	.178
Houston less Philadelphia	(.027)	.038	(.020)	(.036)	(.031)	(.004)	(.024)	.069
Seattle less Detroit	.034	.069	(.008)	.034	(.009)	(.043)	.080	(.008)
Atlanta less Minneapolis	.051	.059	.031	.068	(.015)	(.042)	.069	.176
Dallas less Chicago	.072	.030	.087	.096	.000	—	.071	.176
Denver less Cleveland	.053	.057	.099	.047	.020	.032	.068	.030
San Francisco less New Orleans	(.058)	(.005)	(.019)	(.072)	(.006)	(.009)	(.078)	(.121)
Los Angeles less Miami	(.062)	(.030)	(.059)	(.084)	(.047)	(.048)	(.075)	—

NOTE: Figures in parentheses are negative, indicating that the differential was greater with risk variables taken into account. Data are fractions of one percentage point; for differential in basis points, move decimal point right two places.

APPENDIX TABLE 4-A12. *Coefficients for Dummy Variables Representing SMSAs, for All Loans, and by Type of Lender and Loan Purpose; Dependent Variable Is Effective Interest Rate*

SMSA	All Observations	Loan Purpose			Type of Lender				
		New Construction	Previously Occupied	Newly Built	Life Insurance	Commercial Banks	Mortgage Companies	Mutual Savings	Savings and Loan
Atlanta	0	0	0	0	0	0	0	0	0
Baltimore	-.492 (.00999)	-.306 (.02832)	-.602 (.01471)	-.484 (.01392)	-.306 (.05564)	-.805 (.04521)	—	.811 (.56466)	-.468 (.01283)
Boston	-.620 (.01117)	-.646 (.03243)	-.687 (.01536)	-.648 (.01897)	-.346 (.07463)	-1.030 (.04440)	—	.695 (.56470)	-.756 (.02092)
Chicago	-.272 (.00818)	-.137 (.01727)	-.376 (.01252)	-.255 (.01305)	-.139 (.02990)	-.754 (.04261)	-.240 (.0269)	—	-.250 (.00929)
Cleveland	-.230 (.00938)	-.116 (.02843)	-.320 (.01339)	-.225 (.01550)	-.095 (.02618)	-.738 (.04206)	-.159 (.02713)	—	-.164 (.01184)
Dallas	.044 (.01073)	-.109 (.02270)	.064 (.01644)	.037 (.01512)	-.107 (.02586)	-.072 (.05326)	—	—	.056 (.01188)
Denver	.056 (.01063)	.222 (.02663)	-.029 (.01538)	.014 (.01560)	.045 (.02710)	-.464 (.04427)	.091 (.03019)	—	.108 (.01260)
Detroit	-.338 (.00987)	-.413 (.02016)	-.408 (.01470)	-.233 (.01636)	-.106 (.02328)	-.625 (.04462)	.069 (.02549)	—	-.407 (.01171)
Houston	-.024 (.01089)	-.058 (.02213)	-.053 (.01940)	.011 (.01364)	-.022 (.02709)	-.041 (.06515)	-.047 (.04831)	—	-.009 (.01202)
Los Angeles	.273 (.00800)	.551 (.01964)	.202 (.01214)	.111 (.01275)	.044 (.02330)	-.211 (.04793)	.083 (.02442)	—	.319 (.00906)
Memphis	-.085 (.01381)	-.159 (.04178)	-.144 (.02163)	-.123 (.01706)	-.127 (.04556)	-.385 (.10750)	-.027 (.03071)	—	-.025 (.01568)

(continued)

APPENDIX TABLE 4-A12 (concluded)

SMSA	Loan Purpose				Type of Lender				
	All Observations	New Construction	Previously Occupied	Newly Built	Life Insurance	Commercial Banks	Mortgage Companies	Mutual Savings	Savings and Loan
Miami	-.143 (.01084)	-.118 (.02115)	-.247 (.01616)	-.030 (.01811)	.069 (.05440)	—	.077 (.04376)	—	-.146 (.01171)
Minneapolis	-.314 (.00957)	-.269 (.02048)	-.409 (.01389)	-.270 (.01728)	-.114 (.02682)	-.695 (.04291)	-.120 (.02523)	.985 (.56489)	-.355 (.01161)
New Orleans	-.167 (.01243)	-.145 (.02264)	-.239 (.01839)	-.117 (.02354)	-.060 (.03226)	-.659 (.06205)	-.098 (.03555)	—	-.164 (.01396)
New York	-.115 (.00868)	-.156 (.01947)	-.233 (.01331)	-.084 (.01264)	-.036 (.02809)	-.589 (.04200)	.271 (.02352)	1.142 (.56467)	-.172 (.01158)
Philadelphia	-.438 (.00851)	-.265 (.02457)	-.531 (.01275)	-.450 (.01234)	-.169 (.02644)	-.730 (.04271)	-.175 (.02301)	.838 (.56465)	-.462 (.01032)
San Francisco	.183 (.00892)	.316 (.02374)	.132 (.01305)	.019 (.01424)	.054 (.02328)	-.337 (.04371)	-.043 (.02280)	—	.274 (.01040)
Seattle	.030 (.01062)	.167 (.01940)	-.046 (.01705)	-.092 (.01666)	.045 (.03159)	-.258 (.04767)	.084 (.02357)	1.282 (.56484)	.037 (.01325)
Standard error of est.	.3046	.3001	.3048	.2511	.1869	.2618	.2082	.1640	.3148
R^2	.6195	.6277	.6428	.6339	.2101	.4608	.4629	.6196	.4977
F ratio	2428.29	368.97	1839.29	578.21	13.72	199.92	87.50	283.09	1122.14
Degrees of freedom	49216	7114	31688	10352	1495	6783	2944	5040	32838

NOTE: Standard errors are in parentheses under each variable. Each column represents a separate regression. Purchase price, maturity, and loan/value ratio are held constant in all regressions. Dummy variables for lender types were included in the loan purpose series; and for loan purpose in the lender series. The all loan regression holds both loan purpose and lender type constant.

APPENDIX TABLE 4-A13. *T Values for Coefficients in Appendix Table 4-A12*

SMSA	All Observations	Loan Purpose			Type of Lender				
		New Construction	Previously Occupied	Newly Built	Life Insurance	Commercial Banks	Mortgage Companies	Mutual Savings	Savings and Loan
Atlanta	—	—	—	—	—	—	—	—	—
Baltimore	49.249	10.805	40.925	34.770	5.500	17.806	—	1.436[a]	36.477
Boston	55.506	19.920	44.727	34.159	4.636	23.198	—	1.231[a]	36.138
Chicago	33.252	7.933	30.032	19.540	4.649	17.695	10.577	—	26.911
Cleveland	24.520	4.080	23.898	14.516	3.629	17.546	5.861	—	13.851
Dallas	4.101	4.802	3.893	2.447[b]	4.138	1.352[a]	—	—	4.714
Denver	5.268	8.336	1.886[a]	0.897[a]	1.661[a]	10.481	3.014	—	8.571
Detroit	34.245	20.486	27.755	14.242	4.553	14.007	2.707	—	34.757
Houston	2.204[b]	2.621	2.732	0.806[a]	0.812[a]	0.629[a]	0.973[a]	—	0.749[a]
Los Angeles	34.125	28.055	16.639	8.706	1.888[a]	4.402	3.399	—	35.210
Memphis	6.155	3.806	6.657	7.210	2.788	3.581	0.879[a]	—	1.594[a]
Miami	13.192	5.579	15.285	1.657[a]	1.268[a]	—	1.760[a]	—	12.468
Minneapolis	32.811	13.135	29.446	15.625	4.251	16.197	4.756	1.744[a]	30.577
New Orleans	13.435	6.405	12.996	4.970	1.860[a]	10.620	2.757	—	11.748
New York	13.249	8.012	17.506	6.646	1.282[a]	14.024	11.522	2.022[b]	14.853
Philadelphia	51.469	10.786	41.647	36.467	6.392	17.092	7.605	1.484[a]	44.767
San Francisco	20.516	13.311	10.115	1.334[a]	2.320[b]	7.710	1.886[a]	—	26.346
Seattle	2.824	8.608	2.698	5.522	1.425[a]	5.412	3.564	2.270[b]	2.792

NOTE: All values are significant at the 99 per cent level, unless otherwise indicated by footnote.

[a]Not significant at the 95 per cent level.

[b]Significant at the 95 per cent level, not at the 99 per cent level.

APPENDIX TABLE 4-A14. *Effective Interest Rate Differential Based Upon Multiple Regression Analysis, Between Loans on Boston Properties and Loans in 17 Other SMSAs*

	All Observations	Loan Purpose			Type of Lender				
		New Construction	Previously Occupied	Newly Built	Life Insurance	Commercial Banks	Mortgage Companies[a]	Mutual Savings	Savings and Loan
Atlanta	.620	.646	.687	.648	.346	1.030	.240	—	.756
Baltimore	.128	.340	.085	.164	.040	.225	—	.116	.288
Boston	0	0	0	0	0	0	0	0	0
Chicago	.348	.509	.311	.393	.207	.276	0	—	.506
Cleveland	.390	.530	.367	.423	.251	.292	.081	—	.592
Dallas	.664	.537	.751	.685	.239	.958	—	—	.812
Denver	.676	.868	.658	.662	.391	.566	.331	—	.864
Detroit	.282	.233	.279	.415	.240	.405	.309	—	.349
Houston	.596	.588	.634	.659	.324	.989	.193	—	.747
Los Angeles	.893	1.197	.889	.759	.390	.819	.323	—	1.075
Memphis	.535	.487	.543	.525	.219	.645	.213	—	.731
Miami	.477	.528	.440	.618	.415	—	.317	—	.610
Minneapolis	.306	.377	.278	.378	.232	.335	.120	.290	.401
New Orleans	.453	.501	.448	.531	.286	.371	.142	—	.592
New York	.505	.490	.454	.564	.310	.441	.511	.447	.584
Philadelphia	.182	.381	.156	.198	.177	.300	.065	.143	.294
San Francisco	.803	.962	.819	.667	.400	.693	.197	—	1.030
Seattle	.650	.813	.641	.556	.391	.772	.324	.587	.793

[a] No Boston observations. Data represent basis points higher than Chicago rate.

APPENDIX TABLE 4-A15. *Coefficients for Dummy Variables Representing SMSAs, for All Loans, by Type of Lender and Loan Purpose; Dependent Variable Is Contract Interest Rate*

SMSA	Loan Purpose				Type of Lender				
	All Observations	New Construction	Previously Occupied	Newly Built	Life Insurance	Commercial Banks	Mortgage Companies	Mutual Savings	Savings and Loan
Atlanta	0	0	0	0	0	0	0	0	0
Baltimore	−.347	−.211	−.421	−.340	−.263	−.423	—	−.331	−.344
	(.00854)	(.02353)	(.01279)	(.01257)	(.05046)	(.04206)		(.52162)	(.01094)
Boston	−.471	−.475	−.516	−.494	−.290	−.663	—	−.461	−.541
	(.00954)	(.02694)	(.01335)	(.01713)	(.06768)	(.04130)		(.52167)	(.01784)
Chicago	−.296	−.177	−.374	−.264	−.076	−.517	−.193	—	−.290
	(.00700)	(.01434)	(.01088)	(.01179)	(.02711)	(.03964)	(.02050)		(.00792)
Cleveland	−.106	−.072	−.161	−.098	−.040	−.366	−.015	—	−.052
	(.00802)	(.02361)	(.01164)	(.01400)	(.02375)	(.03913)	(.02451)		(.01009)
Dallas	.148	.041	.182	.114	−.054	.326	—	—	.153
	(.00917)	(.01886)	(.01429)	(.01366)	(.02345)	(.04954)			(.01013)
Denver	.073	.146	.026	.043	.008	−.140	.096	—	.102
	(.00909)	(.02212)	(.01337)	(.01409)	(.02459)	(.04119)	(.02728)		(.01074)
Detroit	−.224	−.252	−.272	−.166	−.062	−.324	.073	—	−.270
	(.00844)	(.01675)	(.01278)	(.01477)	(.02111)	(.04151)	(.02303)		(.00998)
Houston	.063	.092	.045	.065	.028	.154	.082	—	.075
	(.00931)	(.01839)	(.01686)	(.01232)	(.02456)	(.06061)	(.04365)		(.01025)
Los Angeles	.305	.401	.263	.214	.082	.034	.170	—	.335
	(.00684)	(.01632)	(.01056)	(.01151)	(.02113)	(.04459)	(.02207)		(.00772)
Memphis	−.079	−.061	−.134	−.107	−.063	−.202	.033	—	−.046
	(.01181)	(.03470)	(.01880)	(.01541)	(.04132)	(.10000)	(.02774)		(.01337)

(continued)

APPENDIX TABLE 4-A15 (concluded)

	Loan Purpose				Type of Lender				
SMSA	All Observations	New Construction	Previously Occupied	Newly Built	Life Insurance	Commercial Banks	Mortgage Companies	Mutual Savings	Savings and Loan
Miami	-.187 (.00927)	-.114 (.01757)	-.269 (.01404)	-.148 (.01636)	.137 (.04933)	—	.022 (.03953)	—	-.192 (.00998)
Minneapolis	-.191 (.00819)	-.156 (.01702)	-.254 (.01208)	-.156 (.01561)	-.054 (.02432)	-.327 (.03991)	.019 (.02279)	-.158 (.52184)	-.236 (.00990)
New Orleans	.050 (.01063)	.076 (.01880)	.007 (.01599)	.062 (.02126)	-.026 (.02925)	-.261 (.05773)	.062 (.03212)	—	.068 (.01191)
New York	-.076 (.00742)	-.078 (.01618)	-.170 (.01157)	-.038 (.01141)	.021 (.02548)	-.332 (.03907)	.251 (.02124)	-.081 (.52163)	-.103 (.00987)
Philadelphia	-.274 (.00728)	-.115 (.02041)	-.336 (.01108)	-.289 (.01114)	-.118 (.02398)	-.354 (.03973)	.004 (.02078)	-.306 (.52162)	-.285 (.00880)
San Francisco	.201 (.00763)	.266 (.01972)	.175 (.01134)	.078 (.01286)	.083 (.02111)	-.046 (.04066)	.070 (.02060)	—	.261 (.00887)
Seattle	.031 (.00908)	.124 (.01611)	-.005 (.01482)	-.058 (.01505)	.081 (.02865)	-.012 (.04435)	.133 (.02129)	.012 (.52179)	.019 (.01130)
Standard error of est.	.2605	.2493	.2650	.2268	.1695	.2436	.1881	.1515	.2685
R^2	.6157	.5812	.6380	.6135	.2034	.4510	.4648	.5833	.5210
F ratio	2389.89	318.52	1801.16	529.98	13.16	192.12	88.16	243.24	1231.52
Degrees of freedom	49216	7114	31688	10352	1495	6783	2944	5040	32838

NOTE: Standard errors are in parentheses under each variable. Each column represents a separate regression. Purchase price, maturity, and loan/value ratio are held constant in all regressions. Dummy variables for lender types were included in the loan purpose series; and for loan purpose in the lender series. The all loan regression holds both loan purpose and lender type constant.

APPENDIX TABLE 4-A16. *T Values for Coefficients in Appendix Table 4-A15*

SMSA	All Observations	Loan Purpose			Type of Lender				
		New Construction	Previously Occupied	Newly Built	Life Insurance	Commercial Banks	Mortgage Companies	Mutual Savings	Savings and Loan
Atlanta	–	–	–	–	–	–	–	–	–
Baltimore	40.632	8.967	32.916	27.048	5.212	10.057	–	0.635[a]	31.444
Boston	49.371	17.632	38.652	28.838	4.285	16.053	–	0.884[a]	30.325
Chicago	42.286	12.343	34.375	22.392	2.803	13.042	9.415	–	36.66
Cleveland	13.217	3.049	13.832	7.000	1.684[a]	9.353	0.612	–	5.154
Dallas	16.140	2.174[b]	12.735	8.346	2.303[b]	6.580	–	–	15.104
Denver	8.031	6.600	1.945[a]	3.052	0.326[a]	3.399	3.519	–	9.497
Detroit	26.540	15.045	21.283	11.240	2.937	7.805	3.170	–	27.054
Houston	6.767	5.003	2.669	5.276	1.140[a]	2.541[b]	1.880[a]	–	7.317
Los Angeles	44.591	24.571	24.905	18.592	3.881	0.763[a]	0.770[a]	–	43.394
Memphis	6.689	1.758[a]	7.128	6.943	1.528[a]	2.020[b]	1.190[a]	–	3.441
Miami	20.173	6.488	19.160	9.046	2.777	–	0.557[a]	–	19.238
Minneapolis	23.321	9.166	21.026	9.994	2.220[b]	8.193	0.834[a]	0.303[a]	23.844
New Orleans	4.704	4.043	0.438[a]	2.916	0.889[a]	4.521	1.930[a]	–	5.709
New York	10.246	4.821	14.693	3.330	0.824[a]	8.497	11.817	0.155[a]	10.436
Philadelphia	37.637	5.634	30.325	25.943	4.921	8.910	0.193[a]	0.587[a]	32.386
San Francisco	26.343	13.488	15.432	6.065	3.932	1.131[a]	3.398	–	29.425
Seattle	3.414	7.697	0.337[a]	3.854	2.827	0.271[a]	6.247	0.023[a]	1.681[a]

NOTE: All values are significant at the 99 per cent level, unless otherwise indicated by footnote.

[a]Not significant at the 95 per cent level.

[b]Significant at the 95 per cent level, not at the 99 per cent level.

APPENDIX TABLE 4-A17. *Contract Interest Rate Differential Based Upon Multiple Regression Analysis, Between Loans on Boston Properties and Loans in 17 Other SMSAs*

	All Observations	Loan Purpose			Type of Lender				
		New Construction	Previously Occupied	Newly Built	Life Insurance	Commercial Banks	Mortgage Companies [a]	Mutual Savings	Savings and Loan
Atlanta	.471	.475	.516	.494	.290	.663	.193	—	.541
Baltimore	.124	.264	.095	.154	.027	.240	—	.130	.197
Boston	0	0	0	0	0	0	—	0	0
Chicago	.175	.298	.142	.230	.214	.146	0	—	.251
Cleveland	.366	.403	.355	.396	.250	.297	.178	—	.489
Dallas	.619	.516	.696	.608	.236	.989	—	—	.694
Denver	.544	.621	.542	.537	.298	.523	.289	—	.643
Detroit	.247	.223	.244	.328	.228	.339	.266	—	.271
Houston	.534	.567	.561	.559	.318	.817	.275	—	.616
Los Angeles	.776	.876	.779	.708	.372	.697	.363	—	.876
Memphis	.392	.414	.382	.387	.227	.461	.226	—	.495
Miami	.284	.361	.247	.346	.427	—	.215	—	.349
Minneapolis	.280	.319	.262	.338	.236	.336	.212	.303	.305
New Orleans	.521	.551	.523	.556	.264	.402	.255	—	.609
New York	.395	.397	.346	.456	.311	.331	.444	.380	.438
Philadelphia	.197	.360	.180	.205	.172	.309	.197	.157	.256
San Francisco	.672	.741	.691	.572	.373	.617	.263	—	.802
Seattle	.502	.599	.511	.436	.371	.651	.326	.473	.560

[a] No Boston observations. Data represent basis points higher than Chicago rate.

APPENDIX TABLE 4-S1. *Mean Effective Interest Rate, Selected Cities, by Loan Purpose and Lender Type Category (per cent)*

City	Previously Occupied					Newly Built					New Construction				
	S&L	M.C.	C.B.	M.S.	L.I.	S&L	M.C.	C.B.	M.S.	L.I.	S&L	M.C.	C.B.	M.S.	L.I.
Northeast															
Boston	5.48	—	5.24	5.29	—	5.45	—	5.16	5.20	—	5.46	—	5.22	5.28	—
Bridgeport	5.72	—	5.59	5.51	—	5.63	—	—	5.50	—	5.62	—	—	5.51	—
Providence	5.77	—	5.50	5.54	—	5.69	—	5.33	5.46	—	5.77	—	5.43	5.51	—
Hartford	5.93	—	5.44[a]	5.58	—	5.88	—	—	5.53	—	5.83	—	5.50[a]	5.52	—
New Haven	6.05	—	5.59	5.52	—	6.07[a]	—	—	5.46	5.47[a]	—	—	5.87[a]	5.50[a]	—
Middle Atlantic															
Washington, D. C.	5.75	—	5.84	5.25	5.47	5.68	5.50	5.43	5.25	5.47	6.09	—	5.83	—	5.37
Newark	5.80	—	5.45	5.74	5.51	5.68	5.85[a]	5.48	5.68	5.52	5.73	—	5.49	5.64	5.50[a]
Philadelphia	5.84	5.56	5.66	5.40	5.35	5.70	5.51	5.44	5.41	5.47	5.98	—	5.72	5.87[a]	5.37
Pittsburgh	5.86	—	5.80	5.39	—	5.67	—	5.56	—	—	5.90	—	5.70	5.36[a]	5.21[a]
Baltimore	5.87	—	5.61	5.38	—	5.71	—	5.40	5.43	—	5.93	—	5.76	—	—
Rochester	5.88	—	5.62	5.67	—	5.78	—	5.44[a]	5.67	—	5.74	—	5.50	5.63	—
New York City	5.94	5.49	5.61	5.68	5.52	5.87	5.97	5.63	5.84	—	6.01	—	5.75	5.73	5.52
Buffalo	5.95	—	5.76	5.71	—	5.87	6.00[a]	5.63[a]	5.66	5.56	5.88	6.26	5.81	5.64	—
Norfolk	6.05	—	6.00	—	—	6.00	—	—	—	5.62[a]	6.01	—	—	—	5.60
Harrisburg	6.17	—	5.99	—	—	6.12	—	—	—	5.73[a]	6.17	—	5.94	—	—
South															
Miami	6.10	—	—	—	—	6.17	5.77	—	—	—	6.09	5.75	—	—	—
Louisville	5.92	—	5.59	—	—	5.92	—	5.56[a]	—	5.73	5.89	—	—	—	—
New Orleans	6.10	5.63[a]	5.75	—	—	6.06	5.60	—	—	5.46	6.08	5.50	—	—	5.55

(continued)

APPENDIX TABLE 4-S1 (continued)

City	Previously Occupied					Newly Built					New Construction				
	S&L	M.C.	C.B.	M.S.	L.I.	S&L	M.C.	C.B.	M.S.	L.I.	S&L	M.C.	C.B.	M.S.	L.I.
Ft. Lauderdale	6.12	–	–	–	–	6.16	–	–	–	–	6.10	–	–	–	–
Memphis	6.12	5.61	–	–	5.39a	6.09	5.68	–	–	–	5.95	5.55	–	–	5.47a
Tampa	6.19	–	6.74	–	–	6.12	–	–	–	5.59	6.20	–	–	–	5.54
Houston	6.26	5.69a	6.79	–	5.55	6.18	–	–	–	5.51	6.28	5.65	5.87a	–	5.51
Atlanta	6.44	5.69	6.61	–	5.55	6.22	5.64	5.87a	–	5.60	6.33	5.68a	–	–	5.52
Dallas	6.47	–	6.58	–	5.51	6.29	–	5.91	–	5.37	6.14	–	6.19	–	5.51
Ft. Worth	6.83	5.73a	–	–	5.70	6.39	5.88	–	–	5.63	6.21	–	–	–	5.59
North Central															
Detroit	5.83	5.81	5.80	–	5.50	5.85	5.78	5.49	–	5.49	5.71	–	5.64	–	5.42
Milwaukee	5.86	5.54	5.43	–	5.33	5.71a	–	5.45a	–	–	5.73	5.35	5.56	–	5.27
Minneapolis	5.91	5.64	5.59	5.56	5.52	5.88	5.48	5.59	5.57	5.48	5.93	5.59	5.61	–	5.41
Cincinnati	5.93	–	5.45	–	5.50a	5.76	–	5.39	–	5.46a	5.92	–	5.40	–	–
Chicago	5.94	5.41	5.50	–	5.41	5.91	5.37	5.41	–	5.44	6.11	5.44	5.58	–	5.42
Cleveland	6.07	5.52	5.57	–	5.44	5.88	5.47	5.50	–	5.53	6.24	–	5.59	–	5.49
Kansas City	6.08	5.78	6.04	–	5.42	5.95	5.69	–	–	5.50	6.14	5.84a	5.63	–	5.30a
St. Louis	6.22	–	5.73	–	5.45	5.93	–	5.54	–	5.38	6.12	–	6.02	–	5.25a
Indianapolis	6.38	–	5.41	–	5.37	6.07	–	–	–	5.46	6.23	–	5.36	–	5.38
West															
Seattle	6.31	5.78	6.07	5.86	5.55	6.14	5.75	5.88	5.79	5.51	6.47	5.78	6.11	5.91	5.75
Denver	6.38	5.76	5.90	–	5.64	6.28	5.77	5.70	–	5.62	6.60	5.65a	5.89	–	5.60
San Francisco	6.41	5.59	5.88	–	5.65	6.21	5.56	5.85	–	5.66	6.64	5.69	6.13	–	5.40

(continued)

APPENDIX TABLE 4-S1 (concluded)

City	Previously Occupied					Newly Built					New Construction				
	S&L	M.C.	C.B.	M.S.	L.I.	S&L	M.C.	C.B.	M.S.	L.I.	S&L	M.C.	C.B.	M.S.	L.I.
San Jose	6.42	5.56	5.95	—	5.56	6.18	5.55	5.78	—	5.56	6.38	5.66[a]	6.08[a]	—	5.38
Portland, O.	6.42	5.59	5.93	—	5.50	5.97	—	—	—	—	6.37	—	—	—	5.54
Los Angeles	6.45	5.73	6.08	—	5.60	6.27	5.56	5.65[a]	—	5.63	6.78	5.76	6.05	—	5.56
San Diego	6.63	—	6.16	—	5.28[a]	6.59	—	—	—	5.45	6.83	—	6.08[a]	—	5.20
Honolulu	6.67	—	6.31[a]	—	—	6.63	—	—	—	—	6.63	—	6.23[a]	—	—

[a]6–10 observations. All other cells represent 11 or more observations. Less than 6 left out.

APPENDIX TABLE 4-S2. *Mean Contract Interest Rate, Selected Cities, by Loan Purpose and Lender Type Category (per cent)*

City	Previously Occupied					Newly Built					New Construction				
	S&L	M.C.	C.B.	M.S.	L.I.	S&L	M.C.	C.B.	M.S.	L.I.	S&L	M.C.	C.B.	M.S.	L.I.
Northeast															
Boston	5.47	—	5.23	5.28	—	5.43	—	5.16	5.20	—	5.44	—	5.22	5.28	—
Bridgeport	5.72	—	5.58	5.51	—	5.61	—	—	5.50	—	5.62	—	—	5.50	—
Providence	5.76	—	5.50	5.54	—	5.69	—	5.33	5.46	—	5.72	—	5.43	5.51	—
Hartford	5.93	—	5.44ª	5.58	—	5.88	—	—	5.53	—	5.83	—	5.50ª	5.52	—
New Haven	6.04	—	5.59	5.52	—	6.07ª	—	—	5.46	5.46ª	—	—	5.86ª	5.50ª	—
Middle Atlantic															
Washington, D.C.	5.73	—	5.78	5.25ª	5.45	5.68	5.50	5.43	5.25	5.45	5.91	—	5.81	—	5.36
Newark	5.78	—	5.43	5.65	5.50	5.66	5.71ª	5.44	5.62	5.50	5.70	—	5.46	5.57	5.50ª
Philadelphia	5.79	5.56	5.66	5.40	5.34	5.65	5.51	5.44	5.41	5.45	5.87	—	5.70	5.69ª	5.35
Pittsburgh	5.75	—	5.74	5.39	—	5.58	—	5.51	—	—	5.70	—	5.64	5.36ª	5.21ª
Baltimore	5.77	—	5.60	5.38	—	5.63	—	5.40	5.43	—	5.72	—	5.74	—	—
Rochester	5.88	—	5.62	5.67	—	5.78	—	5.44ª	5.67	—	5.74	—	5.50	5.63	—
New York City	5.81	5.43	5.50	5.61	5.51	5.77	5.81	5.55	5.73	5.54	5.82	—	5.67	5.67	5.52
Buffalo	5.95	—	5.76	5.71	—	5.87	6.00ª	5.63ª	5.65	5.61ª	5.88	6.00	5.75	5.64	—
Norfolk	5.95	—	6.00	—	—	5.88	—	—	—	5.42ª	5.89	—	—	—	—
Harrisburg	5.99	—	5.99	—	—	6.00	—	—	—	5.68ª	5.99	—	5.94	—	5.56
South															
Miami	5.82	—	—	—	—	5.84	5.55	—	—	—	5.83	5.54	—	—	—
Louisville	5.92	—	5.59	—	—	5.92	—	5.56ª	—	5.73	5.89	—	—	—	—
New Orleans	6.10	5.61ª	5.75	—	—	6.06	5.56	—	—	5.44	6.05	5.48	—	—	5.52

(continued)

APPENDIX TABLE 4-S2 (continued)

City	Previously Occupied					Newly Built					New Construction				
	S&L	M.C.	C.B.	M.S.	L.I.	S&L	M.C.	C.B.	M.S.	L.I.	S&L	M.C.	C.B.	M.S.	L.I.
Ft. Lauderdale	5.88	—	—	—	—	5.80	—	—	—	—	5.84	—	—	—	—
Memphis	5.90	5.54	—	—	5.39[a]	5.91	5.55	—	—	—	5.81	5.50	—	—	5.47[a]
Tampa	6.02	—	6.66	—	—	5.98	—	—	—	5.59	5.96	—	—	—	5.54
Houston	6.12	5.69[a]	6.48	—	5.51	6.03	—	—	—	5.50	6.15	5.59	5.83[a]	—	5.50
Atlanta	6.16	5.53	6.18	—	5.50	6.01	5.49	5.64[a]	—	5.53	6.04	5.53[a]	—	—	5.45
Dallas	6.32	—	6.58	—	5.49	6.15	—	5.91	—	5.36	6.02	—	6.19	—	5.50
Ft. Worth	6.60	5.59[a]	—	—	5.64	6.21	5.73	—	—	5.60	6.05	—	—	—	5.57
North Central															
Detroit	5.74	5.65	5.71	—	5.47	5.74	5.62	5.45	—	5.46	5.64	—	5.55	—	5.42
Milwaukee	5.72	5.46	5.40	—	5.33	5.56[a]	—	5.38[a]	—	—	5.60	5.34	5.52	—	5.26
Minneapolis	5.81	5.58	5.59	5.56	5.49	5.75	5.48	5.59	5.57	5.48	5.77	5.54	5.59	—	5.41
Cincinnati	5.87	—	5.29	—	5.50[a]	5.72	—	5.28	—	5.46[a]	5.87	—	5.24	—	—
Chicago	5.69	5.31	5.37	—	5.41	5.68	5.28	5.27	—	5.44	5.80	5.27	5.42	—	5.41
Cleveland	5.97	5.50	5.57	—	5.43	5.80	5.44	5.50	—	5.51	5.99	—	5.50	—	5.49
Kansas City	5.92	5.61	5.84	—	5.38	5.80	5.54	—	—	5.50	5.96	5.69[a]	5.50	—	5.30[a]
St. Louis	6.02	—	5.72	—	5.45	5.80	—	5.53	—	5.38	5.92	—	6.00	—	5.25[a]
Indianapolis	6.11	—	5.41	—	5.37	5.90	—	—	—	5.40	5.97	—	5.36	—	5.35
West															
Seattle	6.07	5.69	5.96	5.77	5.54	5.95	5.62	5.75	5.71	5.51	6.14	5.64	5.94	5.70	5.68
Denver	6.16	5.60	5.85	—	5.54	6.10	5.62	5.65	—	5.52	6.21	5.50[a]	5.77	—	5.50
San Francisco	6.21	5.55	5.81	—	5.60	6.05	5.53	5.78	—	5.62	6.29	5.56	5.98	—	5.40

(continued)

APPENDIX TABLE 4-S2 (concluded)

City	Previously Occupied					Newly Built					New Construction				
	S&L	M.C.	C.B.	M.S.	L.I.	S&L	M.C.	C.B.	M.S.	L.I.	S&L	M.C.	C.B.	M.S.	L.I.
San Jose	6.23	5.52	5.86	—	5.54	6.00	5.50	5.73	—	5.54	6.09	5.53[a]	5.93[a]	—	5.38
Portland, O.	6.21	5.59	5.88	—	5.50	5.91	—	—	—	—	6.11	—	—	—	5.52
Los Angeles	6.28	5.68	5.96	—	5.58	6.18	5.53	5.60[a]	—	5.61	6.36	5.59	5.87	—	5.53
San Diego	6.32	—	5.95	—	5.28[a]	6.28	—	—	—	5.42	6.37	—	5.83[a]	—	5.17
Honolulu	6.47	—	6.14[a]	—	—	6.46	—	—	—	—	6.46	—	6.10[a]	—	—

[a]6–10 observations. All other cells represent 11 or more observations. Less than 6 left out.

APPENDIX TABLE 4-S3. *Average Fees and Charges, Selected Cities, by Loan Purpose and Lender Type Category (per cent)*

City	Previously Occupied					Newly Built					New Construction				
	S&L	M.C.	C.B.	M.S.	L.I.	S&L	M.C.	C.B.	M.S.	L.I.	S&L	M.C.	C.B.	M.S.	L.I.
Northeast															
Boston	.06	—	.02	.10	—	.08	—	.00	.04	—	.07	—	.03	.02	—
Bridgeport	.04	—	.02	.00	—	.14	—	—	.00	—	.00	—	—	.04	—
Providence	.07	—	.00	.00	—	.02	—	.00	.00	—	.27	—	.00	.00	—
Hartford	.00	—	.00^a	.00	—	.00	—	—	.00	—	.00	—	.00^a	.00	—
New Haven	.09	—	.02	.00	—	.04^a	—	—	.00	.05^a	—	—	.06^a	.00^a	—
Middle Atlantic															
Washington, D. C.	.15	—	.24	.00^a	.14	.05	.00	.00	.00	.14	1.11	—	.18	—	.03^a
Newark	.11	—	.10	.53	.09	.13	.93^a	.23	.39	.11	.19	—	.16	.48	.02^a
Philadelphia	.26	.00	.03	.01	.06	.32	.00	.03	.00	.15	.68	—	.15	1.06^a	.13^a
Pittsburgh	.55	—	.22	.00	—	.54	—	.24	—	—	1.29	—	.37	.00^a	.00^a
Baltimore	.52	—	.02	.00	—	.53	—	.00	.00	—	1.24	—	.10	—	—
Rochester	.00	—	.00	.00	.05	.00	—	.00^a	.00	—	.00	—	.00	.00	—
New York City	.78	.35	.62	.44	—	.69	1.17	.47	.75	.09	1.22	—	.48	.40	.00
Buffalo	.00	—	.00	.00	—	.00	.00^a	.00^a	.05	.05^a	.00	1.82	.13	.00	—
Norfolk	.43	—	.00	—	—	.74	—	—	—	.21^a	.67	—	—	—	.22
Harrisburg	.92	—	.00	—	—	.79	—	—	—	.36^a	.97	—	.00	—	—
South															
Miami	1.54	—	—	—	—	2.06	1.39	—	—	.00	1.63	1.34	—	—	—
Louisville	.00	—	.04	—	—	.00	—	.00^a	—	—	.00	—	—	—	—
New Orleans	.02	.10^a	.00	—	—	.01	.23	—	—	.18	.17	.11	—	—	.22

(continued)

APPENDIX TABLE 4-S3 (continued)

City	Previously Occupied					Newly Built					New Construction				
	S&L	M.C.	C.B.	M.S.	L.I.	S&L	M.C.	C.B.	M.S.	L.I.	S&L	M.C.	C.B.	M.S.	L.I.
Ft. Lauderdale	1.41	–	–	–	–	2.22	–	–	–	–	1.67	–	–	–	–
Memphis	1.36	.46	–	–	.00ᵃ	1.24	.85	–	–	–	1.02	.33	–	–	.00ᵃ
Tampa	.86	–	.25	–	–	.93	–	–	–	.02	1.46	–	–	–	.00
Houston	.77	.35ᵃ	1.00	–	.15	.95	–	–	–	.07	.74	.32	.20ᵃ	–	.03
Atlanta	1.40	.99	1.64	–	.35	1.29	1.00	1.11ᵃ	–	.44	1.66	1.00ᵃ	–	–	.42
Dallas	.75	–	.01	–	.12	.82	–	.00	–	.08	.72	–	.00	–	.08
Ft. Worth	1.12	.81ᵃ	–	–	.34	1.12	.92	–	–	.17	.96	–	–	–	.16
North Central															
Detroit	.51	.96	.38	–	.19	.69	1.00	.22	–	.18	.48	–	.40	–	.05
Milwaukee	.81	.34	.09	–	.00	1.00ᵃ	–	.28ᵃ	–	–	.77	.06	.15	–	.05
Minneapolis	.60	.30	.03	.00	.13	.88	.04	.00	.00	.00	1.04	.34	.06	–	.00
Cincinnati	.30	–	.61	–	.00ᵃ	.18	–	.40	–	.00ᵃ	.30	–	.61	–	–
Chicago	1.43	.62	.62	–	.00	1.40	.62	.75	–	.00	1.98	1.03	.90	–	.04
Cleveland	.58	.12	.00	–	.09	.52	.22	.00	–	.11	1.45	–	.45	–	.03
Kansas City	.93	1.00	.77	–	.25	1.01	.96	–	–	.00	1.08	1.00ᵃ	.81	–	.00ᵃ
St. Louis	1.04	–	.04	–	.03	.85	–	.07	–	.00	1.10	–	.08	–	.00ᵃ
Indianapolis	1.18	–	.00	–	.04	1.03	–	–	–	.38	1.56	–	.00	–	.16
West															
Seattle	1.24	.58	.43	.54	.07	1.14	.80	.51	.52	.00	1.98	.89	.82	1.27	.48
Denver	1.20	1.00	.18	–	.65	1.10	.97	.33	–	.73	2.35	1.00ᵃ	.66	–	.64
San Francisco	1.22	.22	.31	–	.28	1.06	.23	.33	–	.22	2.20	.79	.73	–	.00

(continued)

APPENDIX TABLE 4-S3 (concluded)

City	Previously Occupied					Newly Built					New Construction				
	S&L	M.C.	C.B.	M.S.	L.I.	S&L	M.C.	C.B.	M.S.	L.I.	S&L	M.C.	C.B.	M.S.	L.I.
San Jose	1.17	.23	.45	—	.14	1.18	.29	.29	—	.18	1.84	.83[a]	.81[a]	—	.00
Portland, O.	.98	.00	.22	—	.00	.39	—	—	—	—	1.54	—	—	—	.17
Los Angeles	1.02	.36	.53	—	.14	.62	.24	.25[a]	—	.18	2.69	1.00	.89	—	.21
San Diego	1.88	—	1.00	—	.03[a]	1.98	—	—	—	.17	2.96	—	1.33[a]	—	.22
Honolulu	1.13	—	1.00[a]	—	—	1.07	—	—	—	—	1.11	—	.80[a]	—	—

[a]6–10 observations. All other cells represent 11 or more observations. Less than 6 left out.

APPENDIX TABLE 4-S4. *Average Loan/Value Ratio, Selected Cities, by Loan Purpose and Lender Type Category (per cent)*

City	Previously Occupied					Newly Built					New Construction				
	S&L	M.C.	C.B.	M.S.	L.I.	S&L	M.C.	C.B.	M.S.	L.I.	S&L	M.C.	C.B.	M.S.	L.I.
Northeast															
Boston	72.1	—	61.4	68.1	—	69.8	—	61.6	66.9	—	70.8	—	60.8	65.4	—
Bridgeport	70.9	—	63.6	69.3	—	74.5	—	—	69.2	—	67.2	—	—	63.1	—
Providence	68.6	—	63.7	68.7	—	69.4	—	61.9	65.5	—	66.5	—	59.4	64.5	—
Hartford	78.3	—	61.5[a]	64.5	—	79.4	—	—	67.5	—	70.5	—	61.9[a]	63.5	—
New Haven	78.4	—	57.2	65.5	—	80.8[a]	—	—	58.4	74.3[a]	—	—	59.1[a]	61.4[a]	—
Middle Atlantic															
Washington, D. C.	70.3	—	61.9	66.4[a]	70.7	77.0	69.2	65.0	67.2	64.5	73.5	—	62.8	—	67.4
Newark	72.4	—	59.8	66.2	67.0	67.7	64.6[a]	62.3	66.9	65.4	56.0	—	57.1	58.8	63.5[a]
Philadelphia	72.9	68.5	62.2	62.9	64.9	71.3	66.5	64.2	66.6	70.6	72.8	—	56.3	71.4[a]	65.6
Pittsburgh	73.8	—	62.4	60.4	—	72.5	—	59.1	—	—	75.0	—	61.2	68.9[a]	60.9[a]
Baltimore	74.3	—	59.8	64.4	—	75.3	—	63.1	67.6	—	69.0	—	56.6	—	—
Rochester	72.6	—	67.1	67.2	—	76.4	—	54.4[a]	71.2	—	72.0	—	62.3	70.5	—
New York City	73.5	68.7	65.7	67.7	69.0	75.4	78.6	64.7	75.1	66.6	71.5	—	59.3	69.8	62.8
Buffalo	70.8	—	62.6	65.6	—	70.1	78.6[a]	58.1[a]	63.5	65.6[a]	67.1	77.2	67.1	61.9	—
Norfolk	64.0	—	67.8	—	—	70.1	—	—	—	72.0[a]	65.8	—	—	—	58.6
Harrisburg	76.1	—	65.0	—	—	81.2	—	—	—	74.2[a]	73.2	—	60.3	—	—
South															
Miami	74.5	—	—	—	—	78.5	69.4	—	—	70.6	74.1	70.4	—	—	—
Louisville	71.5	—	60.6	—	—	76.7	—	66.3[a]	—	—	80.9	—	—	—	—
New Orleans	72.1	65.0[a]	52.8	—	—	77.4	65.5	—	—	65.7	71.7	63.6	—	—	66.8

(continued)

APPENDIX TABLE 4-S4 (continued)

City	Previously Occupied					Newly Built					New Construction				
	S&L	M.C.	C.B.	M.S.	L.I.	S&L	M.C.	C.B.	M.S.	L.I.	S&L	M.C.	C.B.	M.S.	L.I.
Ft. Lauderdale	77.3	–	–	–	–	74.8	–	–	–	–	75.9	–	–	–	–
Memphis	78.9	70.9	–	–	55.3[a]	84.0	69.1	–	–	–	79.3	68.7	–	–	68.3[a]
Tampa	70.1	–	83.4	–	–	73.6	–	–	–	67.3	72.4	–	–	–	69.0
Houston	74.7	67.8[a]	56.9	–	67.9	78.7	68.8	64.1[a]	–	67.7	77.0	68.6	64.0[a]	–	68.3
Atlanta	71.7	66.9	67.9	–	67.1	75.3	–	66.7	–	69.4	72.9	73.2[a]	–	–	69.6
Dallas	74.0	–	59.4	–	65.3	79.1	–	–	–	72.5	76.4	–	52.6	–	70.5
Ft. Worth	76.2	67.8[a]	–	–	70.0	79.4	74.2	–	–	72.0	75.8	–	–	–	69.0
North Central															
Detroit	73.7	71.1	60.6	–	66.5	78.1[a]	74.9	57.0	–	62.8	72.1	–	56.1	–	59.9
Milwaukee	76.6	65.2	58.5	–	68.4	78.4	–	54.3[a]	–	–	74.6	60.5	62.3	–	67.2
Minneapolis	72.2	66.8	63.2	67.0	67.2	73.5	69.3	63.1	67.3	69.0	74.5	67.3	60.8	–	68.8
Cincinnati	71.4	–	54.6	–	74.1[a]	70.5	–	58.6	–	70.9[a]	74.4	–	49.5	–	–
Chicago	74.6	65.9	57.2	–	67.5	74.4	60.5	53.0	–	66.2	75.4	64.7	56.5	–	70.4
Cleveland	74.1	63.4	59.3	–	67.3	70.3	63.1	55.2	–	63.8	69.1	–	61.8	–	55.9
Kansas City	78.6	66.3	61.5	–	63.3	81.5	66.1	–	–	58.5	74.4	73.0[a]	67.3	–	68.5[a]
St. Louis	75.5	–	58.6	–	66.4	75.2	–	57.1	–	65.5	67.5	–	53.7	–	63.8[a]
Indianapolis	71.8	–	64.6	–	65.6	79.5	–	–	–	64.2	75.0	–	64.2	–	64.8
West															
Seattle	72.4	69.5	63.1	69.0	67.3	78.6	69.3	55.2	68.5	64.4	70.9	67.2	59.1	66.0	67.9
Denver	77.6	72.4	65.7	–	68.4	81.2	67.3	62.6	–	70.9	75.2	62.5[a]	59.2	–	67.9
San Francisco	78.1	64.5	63.3	–	65.8	80.9	67.0	59.0	–	65.7	77.5	62.1	66.7	–	65.9

(continued)

APPENDIX TABLE 4-S4 (concluded)

City	Previously Occupied					Newly Built					New Construction				
	S&L	M.C.	C.B.	M.S.	L.I.	S&L	M.C.	C.B.	M.S.	L.I.	S&L	M.C.	C.B.	M.S.	L.I.
San Jose	77.9	67.9	64.1	—	71.2	78.5	66.0	59.4	—	70.5	74.7	65.4[a]	62.0[a]	—	69.4
Portland, O.	72.8	68.9	61.5	—	70.6	81.7	—	—	—	—	75.5	—	—	—	66.1
Los Angeles	78.6	67.3	52.5	—	67.7	79.5	68.6	49.0[a]	—	69.6	77.9	59.9	57.9	—	66.0
San Diego	77.6	—	57.7	—	67.2[a]	79.4	—	—	—	67.7	79.3	—	59.1[a]	—	70.4
Honolulu	75.2	—	69.6[a]	—	—	77.8	—	—	—	—	74.5	—	66.1[a]	—	—

[a]6–10 observations. All other cells represent 11 or more observations. Less than 6 left out.

APPENDIX TABLE 4-S5. *Mean Purchase Price, Selected Cities, by Loan Purpose and Lender Type Category (thousands of dollars)*

City	Previously Occupied					Newly Built					New Construction				
	S&L	M.C.	C.B.	M.S.	L.I.	S&L	M.C.	C.B.	M.S.	L.I.	S&L	M.C.	C.B.	M.S.	L.I.
Northeast															
Boston	19.6	—	28.0	23.0	—	23.1	—	29.4	26.1	—	22.2	—	32.7	29.9	—
Bridgeport	17.7	—	24.4	20.4	—	21.3	—	—	22.8	—	22.0	—	—	24.6	—
Providence	14.6	—	15.2	15.0	—	17.2	—	20.1	16.7	—	17.8	—	20.7	16.3	—
Hartford	17.9	—	23.9a	22.1	—	17.6	—	—	24.1	—	20.3	—	25.7a	25.1	—
New Haven	18.7	—	21.9	20.2	—	21.7a	—	—	24.5	31.1a	—	—	29.0a	33.7a	—
Middle Atlantic															
Washington, D. C.	26.6	—	25.6	26.5a	30.8	26.8	35.4	35.6	30.4	28.2	24.6	—	32.2	—	35.9
Newark	22.3	—	31.2	23.2	33.8	26.5	21.3a	37.1	26.1	37.1	35.2	—	35.1	27.7	34.7a
Philadelphia	14.6	17.4	18.8	19.4	25.6	18.6	18.1	21.5	22.7	21.4	21.9	—	23.1	18.6a	30.5
Pittsburgh	15.0	—	17.1	25.1	—	22.8	—	25.2	—	—	22.0	—	26.1	32.8a	30.1a
Baltimore	14.4	—	18.7	19.1	—	18.4	—	28.7	21.4	—	22.8	—	23.9	—	—
Rochester	16.8	—	20.6	16.3	—	22.8	—	28.0a	22.3	—	22.7	—	32.5	22.4	—
New York City	22.6	48.7	30.4	25.1	36.3	24.6	24.8	31.9	25.1	37.7	23.5	—	27.1	26.1	25.0
Buffalo	13.7	—	21.1	17.3	—	19.3	17.9a	22.8a	22.1	21.5a	20.5	17.6	22.4	24.0	—
Norfolk	15.1	—	8.5	—	—	22.7	—	—	—	24.1a	22.6	—	—	—	—
Harrisburg	11.7	—	14.4	—	—	20.1	—	—	—	24.9a	19.1	—	18.7	—	34.7
South															
Miami	19.7	—	—	—	—	21.9	30.9	—	—	20.9	27.4	39.2	—	—	—
Louisville	13.7	—	27.0	—	—	17.1	—	21.1a	—	—	19.1	—	—	—	—
New Orleans	18.4	30.0a	26.7	—	—	23.7	30.3	—	—	35.2	24.5	35.4	—	—	31.7

(continued)

APPENDIX TABLE 4-S5 (continued)

City	Previously Occupied					Newly Built					New Construction				
	S&L	M.C.	C.B.	M.S.	L.I.	S&L	M.C.	C.B.	M.S.	L.I.	S&L	M.C.	C.B.	M.S.	L.I.
Ft. Lauderdale	17.6	–	–	–	–	16.4	–	–	–	–	20.1	–	–	–	–
Memphis	18.0	25.6	–	–	35.4[a]	20.3	25.6	–	–	–	22.9	26.6	–	–	32.3[a]
Tampa	12.6	–	8.8	–	–	18.1	–	–	–	31.1	18.8	–	–	–	30.1
Houston	23.3	30.6[a]	14.5	–	34.1	25.6	–	–	–	34.1	21.5	25.2	–	–	35.4
Atlanta	16.5	31.9	15.7	–	34.7	21.4	32.7	22.0[a]	–	28.9	21.8	28.1[a]	30.4[a]	–	30.4
Dallas	17.4	–	15.4	–	34.1	22.1	–	21.5	–	27.0	26.1	–	22.3	–	30.0
Ft. Worth	11.8	30.6[a]	–	–	25.1	17.9	21.2	–	–	26.5	20.8	–	–	–	29.9
North Central															
Detroit	18.3	21.5	20.9	–	24.2	22.6	22.2	22.9	–	24.8	24.6	–	26.8	–	28.8
Milwaukee	16.5	19.3	24.1	–	24.6	19.4[a]	–	23.2[a]	–	–	21.9	26.5	26.6	–	25.4
Minneapolis	18.2	25.5	25.2	22.4	29.1	24.7	28.0	25.2	23.0	29.5	23.3	31.3	29.2	–	31.2
Cincinnati	16.4	–	25.6	–	24.5[a]	21.2	–	25.0	–	27.5[a]	22.7	–	39.8	–	–
Chicago	21.1	28.8	28.8	–	33.2	23.6	30.5	33.2	–	34.9	25.2	34.0	37.1	–	37.7
Cleveland	19.5	25.4	24.3	–	26.7	24.6	33.8	30.4	–	27.3	27.4	–	36.1	–	33.6
Kansas City	16.2	22.5	14.2	–	24.0	22.6	22.7	–	–	29.5	20.1	20.4[a]	24.8	–	37.2[a]
St. Louis	14.6	–	18.9	–	26.3	22.3	–	23.3	–	28.9	21.3	–	18.9	–	34.7[a]
Indianapolis	11.2	–	24.5	–	29.8	21.1	–	–	–	28.3	20.9	–	29.5	–	30.9
West															
Seattle	17.7	29.3	23.6	23.7	23.6	21.1	24.7	27.6	23.6	30.6	22.0	31.8	29.1	31.4	23.4
Denver	16.1	26.0	23.0	–	27.7	21.0	27.5	28.4	–	29.2	21.7	31.8[a]	30.3	–	29.2
San Francisco	23.3	36.0	31.9	–	35.7	26.6	33.7	30.2	–	33.8	26.4	41.3	30.1	–	35.3

(continued)

APPENDIX TABLE 4-S5 (concluded)

City	Previously Occupied					Newly Built					New Construction				
	S&L	M.C.	C.B.	M.S.	L.I.	S&L	M.C.	C.B.	M.S.	L.I.	S&L	M.C.	C.B.	M.S.	L.I.
San Jose	22.5	35.8	25.7	—	30.5	28.6	34.4	30.8	—	33.6	44.4	45.1[a]	38.3[a]	—	36.5
Portland, O.	13.9	27.7	20.2	—	28.0	20.6	—	—	—	—	18.2	—	—	—	27.6
Los Angeles	22.8	36.4	30.1	—	35.8	25.6	41.3	44.2[a]	—	34.0	30.5	48.3	37.4	—	41.9
San Diego	20.2	—	22.8	—	35.4[a]	21.2	—	—	—	29.3	19.7	—	27.7[a]	—	31.4
Honolulu	27.0	—	39.4[a]	—	—	29.1	—	—	—	—	31.8	—	32.8[a]	—	—

[a]6–10 observations. All other cells represent 11 or more observations. Less than 6 left out.

APPENDIX TABLE 4-S6. *Mean Loan Amount, Selected Cities, by Loan Purpose and Lender Type Category (thousands of dollars)*

City	Previously Occupied					Newly Built					New Construction				
	S&L	M.C.	C.B.	M.S.	L.I.	S&L	M.C.	C.B.	M.S.	L.I.	S&L	M.C.	C.B.	M.S.	L.I.
Northeast															
Boston	13.9	—	17.0	15.5	—	15.9	—	17.7	17.4	—	15.1	—	19.9	19.0	—
Bridgeport	12.5	—	15.2	14.2	—	15.6	—	—	15.6	—	14.9	—	—	15.3	—
Providence	10.0	—	9.6	10.2	—	11.8	—	12.0	11.0	—	11.8	—	12.6	10.6	—
Hartford	13.7	—	14.3[a]	14.2	—	13.9	—	—	16.2	—	14.0	—	15.2[a]	15.8	—
New Haven	14.4	—	12.9	13.1	—	17.3[a]	—	—	14.3	23.2[a]	—	—	16.1[a]	19.9[a]	—
Middle Atlantic															
Washington, D. C.	18.6	—	15.7	17.6[a]	21.4	20.5	24.3	22.5	20.5	17.8	18.0	—	20.2	—	24.1
Newark	15.9	—	18.3	15.2	22.6	17.7	14.0[a]	23.4	17.3	24.3	19.3	—	19.3	16.2	21.3[a]
Philadelphia	10.6	12.0	11.7	12.2	16.4	13.2	12.1	13.8	15.2	15.1	15.8	—	13.1	13.3[a]	20.2
Pittsburgh	11.0	—	10.5	14.9	—	16.6	—	14.6	—	—	16.4	—	15.9	22.4[a]	18.8[a]
Baltimore	10.6	—	11.0	12.2	—	13.8	—	18.2	14.4	—	15.6	—	13.7	—	—
Rochester	12.4	—	13.7	11.1	—	17.4	—	14.2[a]	15.8	—	16.0	—	19.7	15.6	—
New York City	16.4	32.9	19.7	16.9	24.3	18.1	19.3	20.0	18.6	25.5	16.7	—	15.8	18.0	15.5
Buffalo	9.5	—	12.9	11.3	—	13.4	14.1[a]	12.7[a]	14.0	14.0[a]	13.8	13.6	14.6	14.6	—
Norfolk	9.6	—	5.5	—	—	15.9	—	—	—	17.4[a]	14.8	—	—	—	19.9
Harrisburg	8.8	—	9.3	—	—	16.1	—	—	—	18.5[a]	13.9	—	11.1	—	—
South															
Miami	14.6	—	—	—	—	17.1	21.7	—	—	14.7	20.3	27.4	—	—	—
Louisville	10.0	—	16.1	—	—	13.0	—	14.1[a]	—	—	15.4	—	—	—	—
New Orleans	13.2	19.5[a]	14.3	—	—	18.4	19.8	—	—	22.5	17.5	22.7	—	—	21.3

(continued)

APPENDIX TABLE 4-S6 (continued)

City	Previously Occupied					Newly Built					New Construction				
	S&L	M.C.	C.B.	M.S.	L.I.	S&L	M.C.	C.B.	M.S.	L.I.	S&L	M.C.	C.B.	M.S.	L.I.
Ft. Lauderdale	13.6	—	—	—	—	12.2	—	—	—	—	15.1	—	—	—	—
Memphis	14.3	18.1	—	—	18.4[a]	17.0	17.8	—	—	—	18.1	17.9	—	—	21.8[a]
Tampa	9.0	—	6.8	—	—	13.4	—	—	—	20.3	13.5	—	—	—	20.8
Houston	17.5	20.9[a]	9.3	—	23.2	20.1	—	—	—	23.3	16.4	17.5	20.4[a]	—	23.9
Atlanta	11.9	21.1	10.9	—	22.7	16.2	22.6	13.6[a]	—	20.1	15.9	20.6[a]	—	—	21.0
Dallas	12.9	—	8.9	—	21.9	17.3	—	13.9	—	19.4	19.7	—	11.9	—	20.9
Ft. Worth	9.0	21.0[a]	—	—	17.9	14.1	15.8	—	—	19.1	15.8	—	—	—	20.5
North Central															
Detroit	13.6	15.0	12.3	—	15.8	17.4	16.1	12.9	—	15.5	17.5	—	15.0	—	17.1
Milwaukee	12.6	12.8	14.2	—	17.0	15.1[a]	—	13.0[a]	—	—	16.1	16.0	17.0	—	16.8
Minneapolis	13.2	17.3	15.8	15.1	19.3	17.9	19.5	15.9	15.4	20.3	17.2	20.9	17.0	—	21.3
Cincinnati	11.6	—	13.9	—	18.2[a]	14.7	—	14.7	—	19.7[a]	16.9	—	19.5	—	—
Chicago	15.6	18.8	16.2	—	22.2	17.5	18.3	17.3	—	23.1	18.7	21.7	20.7	—	26.1
Cleveland	14.3	16.1	14.3	—	17.4	17.0	21.2	16.7	—	16.9	18.8	—	22.2	—	18.7
Kansas City	12.9	14.8	9.0	—	15.1	18.3	14.9	—	—	17.6	15.0	14.8[a]	16.5	—	25.2[a]
St. Louis	11.0	—	11.2	—	17.5	16.5	—	13.2	—	18.4	14.4	—	10.1	—	22.1[a]
Indianapolis	8.1	—	15.7	—	18.5	16.8	—	—	—	18.3	15.3	—	18.6	—	20.0
West															
Seattle	13.0	20.0	15.0	16.3	15.7	16.5	17.1	15.7	16.3	19.8	15.5	21.1	17.2	20.3	15.9
Denver	12.4	18.4	15.1	—	18.8	17.0	18.4	17.2	—	20.7	16.1	19.7[a]	17.9	—	19.9
San Francisco	18.2	23.0	20.1	—	23.4	21.4	22.2	17.7	—	22.1	20.3	25.0	19.9	—	22.7

(continued)

APPENDIX TABLE 4-S6 (concluded)

City	Previously Occupied					Newly Built					New Construction				
	S&L	M.C.	C.B.	M.S.	L.I.	S&L	M.C.	C.B.	M.S.	L.I.	S&L	M.C.	C.B.	M.S.	L.I.
San Jose	17.5	24.1	16.2	—	21.7	22.2	22.8	18.8	—	23.7	33.1	29.5[a]	25.0[a]	—	25.1
Portland, O.	10.2	19.1	12.5	—	20.0	17.0	—	—	—	—	13.8	—	—	—	18.2
Los Angeles	17.9	23.7	15.7	—	24.0	20.2	27.6	20.6[a]	—	23.5	23.6	28.4	21.9	—	27.5
San Diego	15.8	—	13.3	—	23.6[a]	16.9	—	—	—	20.1	15.5	—	17.1[a]	—	22.2
Honolulu	20.3	—	27.8[a]	—	—	22.3	—	—	—	—	23.2	—	21.8[a]	—	—

[a]6–10 observations. All other cells represent 11 or more observations. Less than 6 left out.

APPENDIX TABLE 4-S7. *Average Maturity, Selected Cities, by Loan Purpose and Lender Type Category (years)*

City	Previously Occupied					Newly Built					New Construction				
	S&L	M.C.	C.B.	M.S.	L.I.	S&L	M.C.	C.B.	M.S.	L.I.	S&L	M.C.	C.B.	M.S.	L.I.
Northeast															
Boston	20.9	—	17.8	22.2	—	22.5	—	20.2	23.4	—	21.9	—	18.6	20.6	—
Bridgeport	22.9	—	20.0	22.9	—	24.9	—	—	24.7	—	23.8	—	—	22.5	—
Providence	19.3	—	17.8	19.4	—	21.8	—	19.0	21.4	—	20.0	—	18.5	19.2	—
Hartford	25.0	—	21.1[a]	23.2	—	26.3	—	—	24.2	—	25.8	—	20.6[a]	24.2	—
New Haven	24.2	—	17.1	22.2	—	26.7[a]	—	—	22.9	25.0[a]	—	—	19.3[a]	21.9[a]	—
Middle Atlantic															
Washington, D. C.	22.3	—	15.4	23.3[a]	25.8	26.2	26.7	25.2	—	25.1	24.5	—	20.5	—	24.5
Newark	22.7	—	19.4	22.7	25.7	25.0	25.0[a]	22.4	23.5	26.5	21.3	—	19.7	21.6	27.3[a]
Philadelphia	20.3	22.5	16.1	21.2	21.9	23.5	22.5	19.1	23.5	26.3	23.4	—	16.3	23.8[a]	23.8
Pittsburgh	19.1	—	14.7	19.4	—	23.1	—	18.5	21.7	—	23.3	—	19.5	23.3[a]	23.6[a]
Baltimore	19.5	—	13.4	18.7	—	24.0	—	16.7	26.3	—	22.7	—	15.0	—	—
Rochester	21.0	—	21.2	21.1	—	26.8	—	20.8[a]	26.3	—	26.7	—	21.3	26.0	—
New York City	23.4	22.7	20.4	24.1	25.7	28.1	29.6	22.0	28.8	27.0	26.6	—	18.3	26.3	26.1
Buffalo	20.3	—	5.0	22.7	—	26.1	30.0[a]	5.0[a]	27.0	26.7[a]	24.3	30.0	5.0	26.1	—
Norfolk	16.3	—	11.1	—	—	22.3	—	—	—	25.8[a]	20.1	—	—	—	—
Harrisburg	18.0	—	16.2	—	—	25.4	—	—	—	27.9[a]	18.6	—	16.3	—	24.0
South															
Miami	20.8	—	—	—	—	23.0	23.8	—	—	30.0	24.2	24.2	—	—	—
Louisville	22.0	—	17.4	—	—	27.0	—	16.9[a]	—	—	27.9	—	—	—	—
New Orleans	21.1	24.4[a]	9.8	—	—	24.1	25.7	—	—	27.3	23.3	23.4	—	—	27.8

(continued)

APPENDIX TABLE 4-S7 (continued)

City	Previously Occupied					Newly Built					New Construction				
	S&L	M.C.	C.B.	M.S.	L.I.	S&L	M.C.	C.B.	M.S.	L.I.	S&L	M.C.	C.B.	M.S.	L.I.
Ft. Lauderdale	22.5	—	—	—	—	23.4	—	—	—	—	24.9	—	—	—	—
Memphis	25.2	25.4	—	—	25.6[a]	29.0	25.4	—	—	—	29.6	25.7	—	—	26.0[a]
Tampa	18.6	—	12.4	—	—	24.1	—	—	—	25.2	24.5	—	—	—	24.4
Houston	20.1	21.7[a]	9.2	—	21.0	22.0	23.8	14.3[a]	—	23.3	21.8	24.1	15.8[a]	—	24.3
Atlanta	17.6	23.4	10.9	—	24.1	24.1	—	17.5	—	24.8	21.1	24.5[a]	—	—	24.4
Dallas	18.7	—	11.6	—	22.1	24.4	—	—	—	25.0	23.2	—	12.8	—	24.3
Ft. Worth	17.5	22.5[a]	—	—	20.5	24.4	23.3	—	—	24.1	24.2	—	—	—	22.9
North Central															
Detroit	22.8	22.6	15.7	—	23.3	24.4	25.1	21.0	—	25.4	25.2	—	18.6	—	25.0
Milwaukee	22.3	19.8	12.7	—	23.5	26.1[a]	—	10.3[a]	—	—	24.1	22.4	17.7	—	24.5
Minneapolis	19.9	21.8	18.1	22.8	24.5	24.6	24.1	19.9	24.2	26.7	24.9	23.6	18.9	—	26.1
Cincinnati	18.0	—	12.5	—	28.3[a]	21.8	—	15.8	—	25.2[a]	22.8	—	11.7	—	—
Chicago	21.5	22.7	17.2	—	24.2	24.4	23.2	18.7	—	25.9	24.3	23.5	18.6	—	25.5
Cleveland	21.6	21.2	16.9	—	23.6	23.3	23.7	17.8	—	26.0	22.2	—	17.6	—	23.2
Kansas City	22.0	21.9	13.7	—	22.9	26.8	23.7	—	—	22.2	23.4	24.4[a]	23.3	—	24.9[a]
St. Louis	19.8	—	14.6	—	22.1	25.6	—	17.8	—	24.2	22.0	—	13.4	—	23.9[a]
Indianapolis	15.0	—	18.8	—	21.1	23.9	—	—	—	24.2	23.1	—	20.2	—	24.4
West															
Seattle	20.1	22.2	17.2	21.3	23.6	23.0	24.8	16.9	23.4	24.1	21.6	24.2	15.8	22.1	23.8
Denver	21.6	23.7	15.5	—	26.8	24.7	23.9	18.3	—	27.5	23.4	25.7[a]	18.8	—	24.8
San Francisco	24.7	23.3	18.2	—	26.2	27.6	25.1	18.4	—	27.0	25.0	24.5	17.9	—	24.7

(continued)

APPENDIX TABLE 4-S7 (concluded)

City	Previously Occupied					Newly Built					New Construction				
	S&L	M.C.	C.B.	M.S.	L.I.	S&L	M.C.	C.B.	M.S.	L.I.	S&L	M.C.	C.B.	M.S.	L.I.
San Jose	25.1	24.6	17.9	—	26.0	26.5	24.7	19.1	—	26.4	25.6	25.6[a]	18.9[a]	—	25.7
Portland, O.	18.9	22.7	15.2	—	24.5	25.8	—	—	—	—	22.7	—	—	—	23.3
Los Angeles	24.7	24.0	15.8	—	25.8	26.9	24.5	18.9[a]	—	27.2	25.7	24.1	17.5	—	26.7
San Diego	25.2	—	16.0	—	24.5[a]	27.5	—	—	—	24.0	25.8	—	18.3[a]	—	25.0
Honolulu	22.3	—	22.9[a]	—	—	27.0	—	—	—	—	25.8	—	22.6[a]	—	—

[a] 6–10 observations. All other cells represent 11 or more observations. Less than 6 left out.

APPENDIX TABLE 4-T1. *Mean Effective Interest Rate, Selected Cities, by Type of Lender and Loan Purpose (per cent)*

City	All Loans	Loan Purpose			Type of Lender				
		New Construction	Newly Built	Previously Occupied	Life Insurance	Mortgage Companies	Savings and Loan	Mutual Savings	Commercial Banks
Northeast									
Boston	5.30	5.29	5.24	5.31	5.22[a]	—	5.47	5.28	5.22
Bridgeport	5.56	5.57	5.58	5.55	5.44[a]	—	5.66	5.51	5.61
Providence	5.61	5.63	5.59	5.61	—	—	5.75	5.52	5.48
Hartford	5.67	5.58	5.66	5.69	5.48[a]	—	5.90	5.55	5.46
New Haven	5.57	5.64	5.54	5.58	5.49	—	6.04	5.50	5.67
Middle Atlantic									
Washington, D. C.	5.78	6.05	5.64	5.74	5.46	5.50	5.82	5.25	5.73
Newark	5.66	5.61	5.64	5.67	5.51	5.82[a]	5.75	5.73	5.46
Philadelphia	5.64	5.84	5.52	5.67	5.41	5.52	5.83	5.41	5.62
Pittsburgh	5.78	5.81	5.64	5.80	5.27	—	5.83	5.38	5.75
Baltimore	5.61	5.87	5.54	5.62	5.27	—	5.83	5.40	5.59
Rochester	5.72	5.67	5.68	5.76	—	—	5.82	5.66	5.57
New York City	5.76	5.87	5.86	5.69	5.53	5.96	5.94	5.73	5.63
Buffalo	5.80	5.82	5.73	5.83	5.63	6.17	5.92	5.68	5.76
Norfolk	5.97	5.84	5.96	6.03	5.55	—	6.03	—	6.00
Harrisburg	6.06	6.05	5.99	6.08	5.70	—	6.16	—	5.98
South									
Miami	6.10	6.08	6.14	6.09	5.72	5.76	6.11	—	—
Louisville	5.89	5.87	5.89	5.89	5.64[a]	—	5.92	—	5.59

(continued)

APPENDIX TABLE 4-T1 (continued)

City	All Loans	Loan Purpose			Type of Lender				
		New Construction	Newly Built	Previously Occupied	Life Insurance	Mortgage Companies	Savings and Loan	Mutual Savings	Commercial Banks
New Orleans	6.01	5.97	5.92	6.06	5.50	5.55	6.09	—	5.74
Ft. Lauderdale	6.13	6.10	6.15	6.11	—	5.81a	6.13	—	—
Memphis	6.03	5.79	6.02	6.08	5.44	5.64	6.10	—	6.23a
Tampa	6.14	6.13	6.07	6.22	5.56	—	6.17	—	6.63
Houston	6.17	6.16	6.14	6.23	5.52	5.66	6.23	—	6.42
Atlanta	6.25	6.25	6.11	6.39	5.57	5.66	6.33	—	6.43
Dallas	6.28	6.06	6.18	6.45	5.45	—	6.35	—	6.38
Ft. Worth	6.23	5.90	6.10	6.56	5.63	5.82	6.56	—	5.79a
North Central									
Detroit	5.76	5.67	5.72	5.82	5.47	5.79	5.80	—	5.71
Milwaukee	5.71	5.58	5.53	5.75	5.30	5.44	5.83	—	5.46
Minneapolis	5.78	5.82	5.67	5.79	5.47	5.56	5.91	5.56	5.59
Cincinnati	5.74	5.67	5.57	5.81	5.46	—	5.90	—	5.42
Chicago	5.85	5.94	5.76	5.85	5.42	5.42	5.97	—	5.49
Cleveland	5.80	5.84	5.69	5.81	5.48	5.50	6.05	—	5.56
Kansas City	5.97	5.96	5.89	6.03	5.42	5.75	6.04	—	5.86
St. Louis	6.02	5.96	5.84	6.09	5.40	—	6.14	—	5.72
Indianapolis	6.00	5.88	5.76	6.11	5.39	—	6.31	—	5.39
West									
Seattle	6.14	6.30	5.93	6.11	5.61	5.77	6.35	5.87	6.06

(continued)

APPENDIX TABLE 4-T1 (concluded)

City	All Loans	Loan Purpose			Type of Lender				
		New Construction	Newly Built	Previously Occupied	Life Insurance	Mortgage Companies	Savings and Loan	Mutual Savings	Commercial Banks
Denver	6.20	6.31	6.10	6.22	5.62	5.76	6.38	—	5.86
San Francisco	6.22	6.36	6.00	6.26	5.62	5.59	6.39	—	5.91
San Jose	6.12	6.05	5.88	6.21	5.54	5.57	6.37	—	5.94
Portland, O.	6.27	6.29	5.92	6.31	5.53	5.60	6.37	—	5.91
Los Angeles	6.41	6.63	6.19	6.41	5.61	5.72	6.45	—	6.04
San Diego	6.56	6.61	6.39	6.57	5.31	5.66[a]	6.68	—	6.12
Honolulu	6.63	6.61	6.63	6.65	5.79[a]	—	6.65	—	6.26

[a]6–10 observations. All other cells represent 11 or more observations. Less than 6 left out.

APPENDIX TABLE 4-T2. Mean Contract Interest Rate, Selected Cities, by Type of Lender and Loan Purpose (per cent)

City	All Loans	Loan Purpose			Type of Lender				
		New Construction	Newly Built	Previously Occupied	Life Insurance	Mortgage Companies	Savings and Loan	Mutual Savings	Commercial Banks
Northeast									
Boston	5.29	5.28	5.23	5.30	5.21[a]	—	5.46	5.26	5.22
Bridgeport	5.56	5.57	5.57	5.55	5.44[a]	—	5.65	5.51	5.60
Providence	5.60	5.61	5.59	5.61	—	—	5.73	5.52	5.48
Hartford	5.67	5.58	5.66	5.69	5.48[a]	—	5.90	5.55	5.46
New Haven	5.57	5.64	5.54	5.58	5.48	—	6.03	5.50	5.67
Middle Atlantic									
Washington, D. C.	5.73	5.89	5.63	5.72	5.44	5.50	5.76	5.25	5.69
Newark	5.62	5.56	5.61	5.62	5.50	5.69[a]	5.73	5.64	5.43
Philadelphia	5.61	5.76	5.50	5.64	5.39	5.52	5.77	5.41	5.61
Pittsburgh	5.68	5.65	5.56	5.72	5.27	—	5.71	5.38	5.69
Baltimore	5.56	5.71	5.51	5.57	5.25	—	5.72	5.40	5.58
Rochester	5.72	5.67	5.68	5.76	—	—	5.82	5.66	5.57
New York City	5.65	5.74	5.74	5.59	5.53	5.79	5.80	5.65	5.53
Buffalo	5.79	5.80	5.72	5.83	5.63	6.00	5.92	5.67	5.74
Norfolk	5.88	5.76	5.84	5.95	5.51	—	5.91	—	6.00
Harrisburg	5.96	5.94	5.92	5.98	5.64	—	5.99	—	5.98
South									
Miami	5.82	5.82	5.82	5.82	5.71	5.53	5.83	—	—
Louisville	5.88	5.86	5.89	5.88	5.64[a]	—	5.92	—	5.56

(continued)

APPENDIX TABLE 4-T2 (continued)

City	Loan Purpose				Type of Lender				
	All Loans	New Construction	Newly Built	Previously Occupied	Life Insurance	Mortgage Companies	Savings and Loan	Mutual Savings	Commercial Banks
New Orleans	6.00	5.95	5.91	6.06	5.47	5.53	6.08	–	5.74
Ft. Lauderdale	5.83	5.84	5.80	5.88	–	5.53[a]	5.83	–	–
Memphis	5.84	5.69	5.84	5.87	5.44	5.54	5.90	–	6.00[a]
Tampa	5.97	5.92	5.94	6.06	5.55	–	5.99	–	6.54
Houston	6.04	6.05	6.00	6.09	5.50	5.61	6.08	–	6.22
Atlanta	6.01	5.98	5.91	6.12	5.50	5.50	6.07	–	6.05
Dallas	6.16	5.96	6.06	6.31	5.43	–	6.21	–	6.38
Ft. Worth	6.08	5.81	5.97	6.37	5.60	5.67	6.36	–	5.79[a]
North Central									
Detroit	5.67	5.60	5.62	5.73	5.45	5.63	5.71	–	5.63
Milwaukee	5.60	5.50	5.44	5.64	5.29	5.40	5.70	–	5.43
Minneapolis	5.70	5.70	5.61	5.72	5.46	5.53	5.79	5.56	5.59
Cincinnati	5.66	5.57	5.51	5.73	5.46	–	5.84	–	5.28
Chicago	5.62	5.67	5.56	5.62	5.42	5.29	5.71	–	5.35
Cleveland	5.74	5.70	5.64	5.76	5.47	5.48	5.94	–	5.55
Kansas City	5.82	5.81	5.75	5.87	5.40	5.59	5.88	–	5.69
St. Louis	5.88	5.84	5.73	5.93	5.40	–	5.96	–	5.71
Indianapolis	5.82	5.72	5.65	5.91	5.37	–	6.05	–	5.39
West									
Seattle	5.93	6.01	5.78	5.94	5.58	5.65	6.08	5.74	5.93

(continued)

APPENDIX TABLE 4-T2 (concluded)

City	All Loans	Loan Purpose			Type of Lender				
		New Construction	Newly Built	Previously Occupied	Life Insurance	Mortgage Companies	Savings and Loan	Mutual Savings	Commercial Banks
Denver	6.02	6.01	5.94	6.05	5.52	5.60	6.15	—	5.81
San Francisco	6.06	6.09	5.88	6.09	5.59	5.55	6.19	—	5.83
San Jose	5.97	5.85	5.78	6.06	5.52	5.52	6.17	—	5.85
Portland, O.	6.09	6.06	5.86	6.13	5.52	5.60	6.15	—	5.85
Los Angeles	6.24	6.26	6.11	6.25	5.58	5.66	6.28	—	5.91
San Diego	6.24	6.20	6.13	6.27	5.28	5.50[a]	6.33	—	5.91
Honolulu	6.45	6.43	6.46	6.46	5.79[a]	—	6.46	—	6.11

[a]6–10 observations. All other cells represent 11 or more observations. Less than 6 left out.

APPENDIX TABLE 4-T3. *Mean Fees and Charges, Selected Cities, by Type of Lender and Loan Purpose (per cent)*

City	Loan Purpose				Type of Lender				
	All Loans	New Construction	Newly Built	Previously Occupied	Life Insurance	Mortgage Companies	Savings and Loan	Mutual Savings	Commercial Banks
Northeast									
Boston	.06	.03	.04	.08	.03[a]	—	.06	.08	.02
Bridgeport	.03	.05	.09	.01	.05[a]	—	.09	.00	.09
Providence	.04	.14	.01	.03	—	—	.09	.00	.00
Hartford	.00	.00	.00	.00	.05[a]	—	.00	.00	.00
New Haven	.01	.03	.01	.02	.06	—	.06	.00	.03
Middle Atlantic									
Washington, D.C.	.34	1.04	.05	.15	.12	.00	.38	—	.17
Newark	.23	.27	.19	.25	.09	.85[a]	.12	.51	.12
Philadelphia	.15	.50	.10	.15	.12	.00	.30	.01	.04
Pittsburgh	.54	.97	.46	.43	.00	—	.68	.00	.25
Baltimore	.28	.94	.23	.23	.15	—	.61	.00	.03
Rochester	.00	.00	.00	.00	—	—	.00	.00	.00
New York City	.68	.84	.79	.59	.06	1.14	.87	.52	.59
Buffalo	.04	.14	.03	.00	.03	1.18	.00	.02	.03
Norfolk	.49	.47	.66	.38	.21	—	.58	—	.00
Harrisburg	.52	.56	.48	.51	.39	—	.92	—	.00
South									
Miami	1.64	1.62	1.93	1.54	.01	1.38	1.66	—	—
Louisville	.01	.06	.00	.00	.00[a]	—	.00	—	.14

(continued)

APPENDIX TABLE 4-T3 (continued)

City	All Loans	Loan Purpose			Type of Lender				
		New Construction	Newly Built	Previously Occupied	Life Insurance	Mortgage Companies	Savings and Loan	Mutual Savings	Commercial Banks
New Orleans	.08	.17	.06	.02	.18	.14	.07	—	.00
Ft. Lauderdale	1.87	1.67	2.20	1.40	—	1.76[a]	1.87	—	—
Memphis	.48	.68	1.16	1.27	.00	.69	1.28	—	.56[a]
Tampa	.98	1.30	.85	.80	.02	—	1.08	—	.33
Houston	.79	.64	.90	.73	.07	.30	.85	—	.67
Atlanta	1.34	1.55	1.19	1.36	.42	1.00	1.42	—	1.49
Dallas	.68	.61	.72	.69	.09	—	.77	—	.00
Ft. Worth	.80	.57	.80	.95	.20	.89	1.09	—	.00[a]
North Central									
Detroit	.51	.42	.64	.51	.14	.99	.52	—	.37
Milwaukee	.59	.45	.49	.64	.02	.18	.81	—	.11
Minneapolis	.47	.77	.37	.39	.04	.20	.73	.00	.03
Cincinnati	.35	.44	.27	.36	.00	—	.28	—	.54
Chicago	1.35	1.70	1.18	1.27	.02	.83	1.54	—	.67
Cleveland	.33	.80	.28	.30	.09	.14	.61	—	.03
Kansas City	.92	.93	.95	.89	.10	.98	.98	—	.80
St. Louis	.77	.68	.70	.80	.02	—	1.00	—	.05
Indianapolis	.88	.96	.64	.87	.15	—	1.28	—	.00
West									
Seattle	1.18	1.65	.89	.90	.20	.76	1.55	.72	.57

(continued)

APPENDIX TABLE 4-T3 (concluded)

City	Loan Purpose				Type of Lender				
	All Loans	New Construction	Newly Built	Previously Occupied	Life Insurance	Mortgage Companies	Savings and Loan	Mutual Savings	Commercial Banks
Denver	1.05	1.80	.96	.94	.67	.98	1.31	—	.25
San Francisco	1.01	1.63	.76	1.01	.22	.27	1.26	—	.37
San Jose	.88	1.20	.70	.91	.14	.32	1.22	—	.47
Portland, O.	.99	1.39	.36	.84	.07	.00	1.13	—	.25
Los Angeles	1.04	2.39	.57	.99	.17	.41	1.08	—	.59
San Diego	1.98	2.57	1.66	1.79	.15	1.00[a]	2.16	—	1.08
Honolulu	1.10	1.09	1.07	1.12	.00[a]	—	1.11	—	.89

[a]6–10 observations. All other cells represent 11 or more observations. Less than 6 left out.

APPENDIX TABLE 4-T4. *Average Loan/Value Ratio, Selected Cities, by Type of Lender and Loan Purpose (per cent)*

City	All Loans	Loan Purpose			Type of Lender				
		New Construction	Newly Built	Previously Occupied	Life Insurance	Mortgage Companies	Savings and Loan	Mutual Savings	Commercial Banks
Northeast									
Boston	67.2	64.9	66.5	67.7	67.7[a]	—	71.6	67.7	61.4
Bridgeport	69.7	64.6	72.0	69.3	67.9[a]	—	72.3	69.0	60.5
Providence	66.8	64.7	67.6	67.0	—	—	68.5	67.4	63.1
Hartford	69.6	64.3	72.1	69.1	65.5[a]	—	78.1	65.4	60.8
New Haven	64.5	61.8	62.7	65.9	72.4	—	78.9	62.8	57.8
Middle Atlantic									
Washington, D. C.	72.4	72.9	74.8	69.5	66.7	69.2	73.5	—	62.8
Newark	66.0	58.1	66.5	66.4	65.8	63.9[a]	70.1	65.8	59.9
Philadelphia	68.1	68.2	67.7	68.3	67.6	67.0	72.6	64.1	62.2
Pittsburgh	70.2	71.0	69.8	70.1	63.3	—	73.8	61.3	61.8
Baltimore	69.0	66.3	70.5	68.4	62.2	—	74.0	65.7	60.0
Rochester	70.2	70.5	71.2	69.7	—	—	72.7	69.0	64.5
New York City	69.5	67.1	74.7	67.7	67.1	78.3	73.6	69.9	64.8
Buffalo	66.9	66.3	65.9	67.8	66.3	77.7	69.6	64.2	63.2
Norfolk	66.2	63.2	69.5	64.6	63.4	—	66.6	—	65.3
Harrisburg	70.9	68.2	74.8	71.3	73.6	—	75.9	—	63.4
South									
Miami	75.0	74.0	77.8	74.5	70.5	70.7	75.1	—	—
Louisville	73.6	79.1	76.1	70.4	66.1[a]	—	74.7	—	63.3

(continued)

APPENDIX TABLE 4-T4 (continued)

City	Loan Purpose				Type of Lender				
	All Loans	New Construction	Newly Built	Previously Occupied	Life Insurance	Mortgage Companies	Savings and Loan	Mutual Savings	Commercial Banks
New Orleans	71.1	70.2	74.3	70.7	66.5	64.4	72.6	—	53.2
Ft. Lauderdale	75.5	75.8	74.7	77.1	63.5	67.6[a]	75.6	—	—
Memphis	79.1	73.7	81.3	77.7	62.3	69.3	81.4	—	56.7[a]
Tampa	71.9	71.8	73.0	71.0	67.9	—	72.0	—	79.4
Houston	76.1	75.4	78.0	73.4	68.0	68.8	77.2	—	59.4
Atlanta	72.6	72.6	74.1	71.2	69.1	68.6	73.3	—	67.1
Dallas	74.9	74.6	78.1	72.9	70.3	—	76.0	—	59.3
Ft. Worth	74.7	72.3	76.5	74.3	70.6	72.0	77.3	—	62.7[a]
North Central									
Detroit	70.8	68.1	72.0	71.7	62.6	73.7	73.7	—	58.7
Milwaukee	71.6	69.0	69.6	72.4	68.1	63.1	76.3	—	59.2
Minneapolis	69.7	71.5	69.7	69.1	68.4	67.9	72.9	67.2	62.9
Cincinnati	66.6	63.0	65.1	67.7	72.6	—	71.5	—	55.3
Chicago	71.4	72.2	69.1	71.6	68.4	64.4	74.7	—	56.3
Cleveland	66.4	64.3	64.0	67.1	63.8	63.5	73.2	—	58.9
Kansas City	76.2	72.6	78.0	76.0	62.9	67.2	79.2	—	62.2
St. Louis	71.4	63.5	72.2	71.7	65.8	—	75.1	—	58.0
Indianapolis	70.4	70.8	71.0	70.0	65.1	—	73.3	—	63.9
West									
Seattle	70.4	69.0	73.0	70.1	66.5	68.9	72.8	68.2	60.9

(continued)

APPENDIX TABLE 4-T4 (concluded)

City	All Loans	Loan Purpose			Type of Lender				
		New Construction	Newly Built	Previously Occupied	Life Insurance	Mortgage Companies	Savings and Loan	Mutual Savings	Commercial Banks
Denver	74.6	71.4	76.4	74.4	69.0	68.8	78.3	—	64.5
San Francisco	74.9	73.2	75.2	75.0	65.8	65.1	78.5	—	63.4
San Jose	73.9	70.5	73.4	74.5	70.6	67.1	77.7	—	63.3
Portland, O.	73.0	74.2	77.8	71.6	68.8	67.8	74.5	—	59.2
Los Angeles	77.7	75.5	78.1	77.9	68.2	66.7	78.6	—	53.3
San Diego	76.7	77.3	77.1	76.4	68.6	67.9[a]	78.2	—	58.4
Honolulu	76.3	74.0	77.8	75.1	62.7[a]	—	75.6	—	68.6

[a]6–10 observations. All other cells represent 11 or more observations. Less than 6 left out.

APPENDIX TABLE 4-T5. *Mean Purchase Price, Selected Cities, by Type of Lender and Loan Purpose (thousands of dollars)*

City	Loan Purpose				Type of Lender				
	All Loans	New Construction	Newly Built	Previously Occupied	Life Insurance	Mortgage Companies	Savings and Loan	Mutual Savings	Commercial Banks
Northeast									
Boston	24.5	29.7	26.4	23.4	44.5[a]	—	20.4	24.2	28.9
Bridgeport	20.9	22.6	22.1	20.2	25.2[a]	—	20.1	21.0	24.3
Providence	15.9	17.8	17.4	14.9	—	—	15.9	15.6	16.2
Hartford	21.7	24.3	21.7	20.9	32.1[a]	—	17.9	23.3	25.3
New Haven	22.7	30.0	24.7	20.6	28.7	—	20.1	22.4	23.9
Middle Atlantic									
Washington, D. C.	26.7	25.2	27.8	26.6	30.2	35.4	26.1	30.1	29.3
Newark	26.9	32.4	29.3	25.7	35.9	29.3[a]	24.3	23.9	32.1
Philadelphia	18.1	23.0	20.4	16.8	25.1	18.0	15.7	20.4	19.9
Pittsburgh	18.9	23.7	23.4	16.3	30.0	—	17.8	26.3	20.0
Baltimore	18.7	23.4	20.7	17.0	25.9	—	16.7	20.1	21.8
Rochester	20.0	23.3	23.1	17.2	—	—	19.5	19.5	24.3
New York City	26.8	25.1	25.9	27.7	34.8	25.4	23.5	25.2	30.1
Buffalo	18.8	21.7	21.1	16.1	22.5	17.7	16.7	20.3	21.6
Norfolk	19.5	27.3	22.5	14.5	31.3	—	18.8	—	11.1
Harrisburg	15.6	19.6	20.7	13.0	25.8	—	14.4	—	15.6
South									
Miami	22.6	27.8	22.2	19.9	22.9	36.6	22.3	—	—
Louisville	16.8	21.0	17.4	15.2	21.7[a]	—	15.7	—	27.9

(continued)

APPENDIX TABLE 4-T5 (continued)

City	All Loans	Loan Purpose			Type of Lender				
		New Construction	Newly Built	Previously Occupied	Life Insurance	Mortgage Companies	Savings and Loan	Mutual Savings	Commercial Banks
New Orleans	22.8	26.1	26.6	19.4	33.7	33.1	21.1	—	28.0
Ft. Lauderdale	18.2	20.3	16.5	17.7	—	30.6a	18.0	—	—
Memphis	20.5	25.0	21.2	18.6	31.4	25.8	19.4	—	12.1a
Tampa	17.3	20.0	19.3	12.7	30.0	—	16.5	—	10.9
Houston	24.7	23.3	26.1	23.7	34.6	27.9	24.0	—	20.5
Atlanta	20.9	22.6	23.1	17.6	30.1	32.1	19.6	—	17.7
Dallas	21.1	26.4	22.6	17.8	29.5	—	20.6	—	18.0
Ft. Worth	19.6	25.1	20.9	15.0	27.4	24.8	15.6	—	19.0a
North Central									
Detroit	21.4	25.4	23.0	19.0	25.8	22.0	20.4	—	23.2
Milwaukee	19.6	24.0	21.6	18.3	24.3	23.6	17.4	—	24.6
Minneapolis	22.5	25.4	26.0	20.9	29.9	27.9	20.0	22.7	25.7
Cincinnati	20.9	30.7	23.2	18.6	26.4	—	17.7	—	27.5
Chicago	24.3	27.8	26.2	22.6	35.3	31.7	22.3	—	30.4
Cleveland	23.5	32.2	27.4	21.9	28.2	27.5	20.7	—	25.9
Kansas City	20.0	22.5	23.3	16.8	29.2	22.3	19.1	—	20.2
St. Louis	18.0	22.8	22.8	16.0	28.3	—	16.8	—	19.6
Indianapolis	19.5	24.6	24.8	15.6	30.0	—	14.8	—	27.2
West									
Seattle	22.9	24.5	23.3	21.2	26.0	27.9	20.3	25.6	25.9

(continued)

APPENDIX TABLE 4-T5 (concluded)

		Loan Purpose			Type of Lender				
City	All Loans	New Construction	Newly Built	Previously Occupied	Life Insurance	Mortgage Companies	Savings and Loan	Mutual Savings	Commercial Banks
Denver	20.5	24.5	23.3	18.4	28.7	27.3	18.1	—	24.7
San Francisco	26.6	29.3	29.1	25.7	34.9	35.7	24.0	—	31.5
San Jose	27.8	42.0	31.0	24.7	32.9	36.6	25.3	—	27.7
Portland, O.	17.6	20.0	22.9	15.5	28.4	34.5	15.9	—	24.1
Los Angeles	24.3	32.2	26.9	23.4	36.2	37.9	23.5	—	32.8
San Diego	21.3	21.5	23.0	20.8	31.7	31.3[a]	20.2	—	25.5
Honolulu	29.2	31.9	29.2	27.2	32.7[a]	—	29.0	—	35.5

[a] 6–10 observations. All other cells represent 11 or more observations. Less than 6 left out.

APPENDIX TABLE 4-T6. *Mean Loan Amount, Selected Cities, by Type of Lender and Loan Purpose (thousands of dollars)*

City	Loan Purpose				Type of Lender				
	All Loans	New Construction	Newly Built	Previously Occupied	Life Insurance	Mortgage Companies	Savings and Loan	Mutual Savings	Commercial Banks
Northeast									
Boston	16.2	18.8	17.3	15.5	30.4[a]	—	14.3	16.2	17.5
Bridgeport	14.5	14.5	15.7	13.9	16.6[a]	—	14.4	14.5	14.6
Providence	10.5	11.5	11.6	9.9	—	—	10.8	10.4	10.1
Hartford	14.8	15.3	15.4	14.1	21.3[a]	—	13.8	15.1	14.9
New Haven	14.5	17.7	15.8	13.5	20.9	—	15.7	13.9	13.8
Middle Atlantic									
Washington, D. C.	19.2	18.3	20.6	18.5	19.8	24.3	19.1	20.0	18.2
Newark	17.4	18.4	19.3	16.6	23.6	17.5[a]	16.7	15.5	19.0
Philadelphia	12.2	15.6	13.8	11.3	16.9	12.1	11.3	13.1	12.3
Pittsburgh	13.1	16.6	16.3	11.2	19.3	—	13.0	16.1	12.1
Baltimore	12.7	15.4	14.4	11.4	15.8	—	12.3	13.1	13.0
Rochester	14.0	16.1	16.2	12.1	—	—	14.1	13.5	15.2
New York City	18.3	16.6	18.9	18.4	23.2	19.7	17.1	17.5	19.2
Buffalo	12.4	14.2	13.8	10.7	14.9	13.8	11.4	12.9	13.3
Norfolk	12.8	16.8	15.6	9.3	19.3	—	12.6	—	6.7
Harrisburg	10.9	13.3	15.6	9.1	18.9	—	10.8	—	9.8
South									
Miami	16.9	20.5	17.1	14.7	16.0	25.9	16.7	—	—
Louisville	12.3	16.4	13.2	10.7	14.6[a]	—	11.8	—	17.6

(continued)

276   *Essays on Interest Rates*

APPENDIX TABLE 4-T6 (continued)

City	Loan Purpose				Type of Lender				
	All Loans	New Construction	Newly Built	Previously Occupied	Life Insurance	Mortgage Companies	Savings and Loan	Mutual Savings	Commercial Banks
New Orleans	16.1	18.2	19.5	13.6	22.1	21.4	15.3	–	15.3
Ft. Lauderdale	13.6	15.2	12.2	13.6	–	19.2ª	13.5	–	–
Memphis	16.1	18.2	17.1	14.4	19.0	17.9	15.9	–	6.2ª
Tampa	12.4	14.2	14.1	9.0	20.1	–	12.0	–	7.7
Houston	18.8	17.4	20.2	17.6	23.5	19.3	18.5	–	13.4
Atlanta	15.2	16.4	17.1	12.6	20.7	22.0	14.5	–	11.9
Dallas	15.8	19.5	17.5	13.0	20.5	–	15.7	–	10.5
Ft. Worth	14.6	18.0	15.9	11.1	19.4	17.9	12.1	–	12.4ª
North Central									
Detroit	15.0	17.0	16.3	13.6	16.0	15.8	15.0	–	13.4
Milwaukee	13.8	16.4	14.7	13.0	16.3	14.9	13.2	–	14.7
Minneapolis	15.5	17.8	18.0	14.3	20.3	19.0	14.6	15.3	16.0
Cincinnati	13.5	18.2	15.0	12.2	19.2	–	12.5	–	15.0
Chicago	16.9	19.6	17.6	15.8	23.9	20.2	16.5	–	16.8
Cleveland	15.3	20.5	17.1	14.5	17.5	17.4	15.0	–	15.2
Kansas City	15.2	16.2	17.9	12.8	18.5	14.9	15.2	–	12.6
St. Louis	12.7	14.5	16.2	11.3	18.5	–	12.5	–	11.4
Indianapolis	13.4	16.9	17.5	10.6	19.0	–	10.9	–	17.3
West									
Seattle	16.0	16.7	16.9	14.9	17.2	19.0	14.8	17.3	15.9

(continued)

APPENDIX TABLE 4-T6 (concluded)

		Loan Purpose			Type of Lender				
City	All Loans	New Construction	Newly Built	Previously Occupied	Life Insurance	Mortgage Companies	Savings and Loan	Mutual Savings	Commercial Banks
Denver	15.0	17.1	17.4	13.5	19.8	18.5	14.1	—	15.7
San Francisco	19.5	20.9	21.4	19.0	22.8	22.9	18.8	—	19.9
San Jose	20.3	29.9	22.6	18.3	23.2	24.5	19.6	—	17.5
Portland, O.	12.9	14.7	17.5	11.1	19.7	23.1	12.0	—	14.2
Los Angeles	18.7	23.9	20.7	18.1	24.5	24.4	18.4	—	17.4
San Diego	16.3	16.3	17.6	15.9	21.8	20.3[a]	15.9	—	15.1
Honolulu	21.7	23.1	22.4	20.4	20.2[a]	—	21.6	—	24.6

[a] 6–10 observations. All other cells represent 11 or more observations. Less than 6 left out.

APPENDIX TABLE 4-T7. *Average Maturity, Selected Cities, by Type of Lender and Loan Purpose (years)*

City	Loan Purpose				Type of Lender				
	All Loans	New Construction	Newly Built	Previously Occupied	Life Insurance	Mortgage Companies	Savings and Loan	Mutual Savings	Commercial Banks
Northeast									
Boston	21.4	20.3	22.7	21.2	28.6[a]	—	21.3	22.2	18.3
Bridgeport	23.4	22.9	24.7	22.8	24.3[a]	—	24.0	23.2	20.5
Providence	19.5	19.5	21.4	18.9	—	—	20.1	19.7	18.0
Hartford	24.3	24.3	25.0	23.8	28.0[a]	—	25.6	23.7	20.7
New Haven	22.4	21.7	23.6	21.8	25.8	—	25.2	22.4	17.7
Middle Atlantic									
Washington, D. C.	24.1	24.3	26.1	21.9	25.2	26.7	24.3	—	18.8
Newark	22.6	21.6	24.8	21.8	26.3	25.0[a]	23.5	22.7	19.7
Philadelphia	21.0	21.8	22.9	20.1	24.3	22.5	21.0	21.9	16.8
Pittsburgh	19.6	22.4	22.3	18.1	22.9	—	20.6	20.1	16.2
Baltimore	20.1	21.0	22.4	18.6	24.6	—	21.3	19.9	14.4
Rochester	23.4	26.0	26.0	21.1	—	—	23.6	23.7	21.2
New York City	23.9	23.8	27.9	22.0	26.2	29.4	25.8	25.5	20.2
Buffalo	22.3	23.7	26.1	19.4	27.3	30.0	22.5	25.0	5.0
Norfolk	19.1	21.5	22.2	15.8	24.9	—	19.0	—	12.4
Harrisburg	18.4	18.6	24.5	17.3	28.6	—	18.9	—	16.2
South									
Miami	22.3	24.2	23.4	20.8	29.6	24.0	22.2	—	—
Louisville	24.0	26.8	26.5	21.6	26.1[a]	—	24.6	—	17.4

(continued)

APPENDIX TABLE 4-T7 (continued)

City	Loan Purpose				Type of Lender				
	All Loans	New Construction	Newly Built	Previously Occupied	Life Insurance	Mortgage Companies	Savings and Loan	Mutual Savings	Commercial Banks
New Orleans	22.2	23.6	24.7	20.5	27.0	24.2	22.2	–	10.1
Ft. Lauderdale	23.8	24.9	23.4	22.5	–	23.0[a]	23.8	–	–
Memphis	26.8	27.4	28.4	24.8	26.5	25.4	27.3	–	6.3[a]
Tampa	22.3	24.4	24.2	18.4	25.0	–	22.4	–	13.2
Houston	22.5	21.9	24.3	19.8	23.1	23.3	22.6	–	11.6
Atlanta	20.4	21.4	22.4	17.8	24.6	23.7	20.1	–	11.8
Dallas	21.2	22.9	24.1	18.5	24.2	–	21.3	–	13.0
Ft. Worth	21.7	23.3	24.2	18.2	22.9	23.3	21.2	–	13.7[a]
North Central									
Detroit	23.0	24.0	24.7	21.9	24.9	24.3	23.6	–	17.2
Milwaukee	20.8	22.5	20.5	20.3	23.7	21.4	22.6	–	13.7
Minneapolis	21.1	24.0	23.8	19.7	25.8	23.2	21.5	23.1	18.4
Cincinnati	17.6	17.7	19.2	17.0	26.6	–	19.0	–	13.5
Chicago	21.9	23.9	23.3	21.0	25.1	23.2	22.5	–	17.7
Cleveland	20.0	20.4	21.6	19.6	24.4	21.8	22.0	–	17.1
Kansas City	23.4	23.6	26.0	21.4	23.1	23.2	23.9	–	17.4
St. Louis	20.3	20.1	24.5	18.9	23.0	–	21.4	–	15.0
Indianapolis	19.2	22.7	23.3	16.4	22.8	–	18.1	–	19.5
West									
Seattle	21.5	21.6	23.5	20.3	23.8	23.9	21.3	21.8	16.7

(continued)

APPENDIX TABLE 4-T7 (concluded)

| City | All Loans | Loan Purpose | | | Type of Lender | | | | |
		New Construction	Newly Built	Previously Occupied	Life Insurance	Mortgage Companies	Savings and Loan	Mutual Savings	Commercial Banks
Denver	21.8	23.1	24.0	20.5	26.4	24.0	22.7	—	16.3
San Francisco	24.4	23.7	26.5	23.9	26.4	23.9	25.1	—	18.1
San Jose	24.6	24.6	25.9	24.1	26.2	24.8	25.4	—	18.2
Portland, O.	20.6	22.5	24.8	18.9	24.2	23.2	20.8	—	15.0
Los Angeles	24.9	25.3	26.8	24.6	26.6	24.1	25.0	—	16.4
San Diego	25.2	25.4	26.8	24.8	24.5	24.2[a]	25.7	—	16.9
Honolulu	24.4	25.6	27.0	22.3	21.7[a]	—	24.4	—	22.8

[a] 6–10 observations. All other cells represent 11 or more observations. Less than 6 left out.

5

The Ex Ante Quality of Direct

Placements, 1951-61   *Avery B. Cohan*

INTRODUCTION

The ideal measure of the ex ante quality of any debt instrument is, as Macaulay pointed out nearly thirty years ago, the probability that interest and principal will be paid in full and on time.[1] This measure is "ideal" for two primary reasons: *first,* probabilities would take ac-

NOTE: An earlier version of this manuscript was approved for publication by the Board of Directors in October 1968.

This study is a companion study to *Yields on Corporate Debt Directly Placed* published by the National Bureau in November 1967.

I am obliged to the Life Insurance Association of America, which provided most of the necessary financial support for this study—as it did for the study of yields; to the Graduate School of Business Administration of the University of North Carolina (and its Dean, Maurice W. Lee), which provided research assistance and computer time; and to the Workshop in Finance of the Graduate School of Business Administration of the University of North Carolina (and especially to three of its most vocal members: DeWitt C. Dearborn, Henry Latané, and Robert Litzenberger). I am obliged also for the help and counsel of: Lawrence Fisher, Harold Fraine, Milton Friedman, Sidney Homer, Robert Hendrickson, William Hale, Lawrence Jones, Richard McEnally, Robert Parks, Stanley Trustman, and Henry Wallich.

But my greatest obligation is, perhaps, to the Bureau's Review Committee consisting of Jack Guttentag, F. Thomas Juster, Phillip Cagan, and Geoffrey Moore, all of whom, and especially Dr. Moore, devoted much time and energy to the various preliminary versions of the manuscript.

Joan Tron edited the manuscript with great patience, skill, and understanding. H. Irving Forman drew the charts.

[1] Frederick R. Macaulay, *Some Theoretical Problems Suggested by the Movements of Interest Rates, Bond Yields and Stock Prices in the United States since 1856,* New York, NBER, 1938, p. 60.

count of expected economic conditions—as underlying ratios (e.g., times charges earned, debt-equity ratios, and so forth) either separately or combined in some way, cannot; and economic conditions are probably more important than the intrinsic chararteristics of an issue in determining whether that issue will fault during its life and, if so, to what degree. *Second,* probabilities are continuous and cardinal, not discrete and ordinal as are, for example, agency ratings.

There is also a third reason, albeit of a somewhat different order: if lenders, in the process of assessing a new issue, thought of ex ante quality as a probability, and proceeded to articulate the probability, as defined above, appropriate to that issue, they would be led directly to the yield they should require on that issue.[2]

Presumably, when Macaulay used the term "probability" he meant objective (not subjective) probability—as with a fair coin tossed under ideal conditions. But a debt instrument is not a coin, and although objective probabilities for debt instruments must in fact exist, no attempt has been made to unearth them.[3] This study, using a sample of direct placements, attempts to derive the *subjective* probabilities present in the minds of lenders when the direct placements in question were bought.[4] This study is admittedly exploratory, and the results are valid only to the degree that the following proposition is valid: the subjective probability can be derived from the ratio of the return on a government bond to the return on a direct placement of the same maturity— provided that the ratio is adjusted for "extraneous influences" (e.g., differential call deferment) and provided also that various assumptions about the characteristics of the relevant portions of the market for long-term corporate capital are satisfied.

Before discussing the "extraneous influences" and the assumptions, it will be worthwhile to speculate on how the subjective probabilities might be formulated and used by lenders. The subjective probability, which is the object of study here, is the product of two subsidiary proba-

---

[2] If, for example, the probability that all payments on a proposed new ten-year issue would be made on time were estimated to be .895, and the prevailing yield on ten-year riskless securities were 5.00 per cent, the required return on the new issue would be approximately 1.0617 (see below, p. 285 ff.).

[3] Some progress might be made in this direction by using the data, covering the period 1900–43, amassed by the National Bureau's Bond Project.

[4] Direct placements are long-term loans made directly to business by life insurance companies and pension and mutual funds. For a detailed definition, see Avery B. Cohan, *Yields on Corporate Debt Directly Placed,* New York, NBER, 1967, pp. 8–11.

bilities, namely, (1) the probability that a proposed new issue with specific characteristics will be paid off in full and on time provided given economic conditions prevail during its life, and (2) the probability that such economic conditions will in fact prevail. Table 5-1 illustrates (albeit in a highly simplified situation) the process of using the two subsidiary probabilities to reach the probability implicit, as above, in the relationship between the return on a government bond and the return on a direct placement of the same maturity. For the purposes

TABLE 5-1. *Illustration of Calculation on Hypothetical Issue, of Probability of Repayment in Full and on Time*

State of Nature[a]	P_1	P_2	$P_1 \times P_2$
1. Continuous growth, no recessions	.25	.95	.2375
2. Steady upward trend, periodic minor recessions	.65	.80	.5200
3. Steady upward trend, periodic minor recessions, one severe depression	.10	.50	.0500
Total	1.00		.8075

NOTE: P_1 = the probability of each state of nature; P_2 = the probability for repayment in full and on time, for a given state of nature.
[a]See text explanation.

of the illustration three possible economic climates ("states of nature") are postulated to prevail during the life of the debt instrument in question: (1) continuous growth in real GNP at full employment, no recessions; (2) steady upward trend in real GNP, periodic minor recessions with moderate (6–7 per cent) unemployment; and (3) steady upward trend in real GNP, periodic minor recessions, as above, one severe depression lasting 12–18 months with peak unemployment of 12–14 per cent.

These three "states of nature" are, of course, assumed to be mutually exclusive and no other "states of nature" are assumed to be possible. The sum of the probabilities under P_1 in Table 5-1 is thus 1.00. These probabilities simply quantify the hypothetical lender's expectations about the economic atmosphere that will prevail during the life of the debt instrument. The probabilities under P_2 in Table

5-1 are the probabilities, subjectively formulated by the hypothetical lender, that all payments of interest and principal will be made in full and on time, given the corresponding state of nature. These probabilities are thus conditional. They do not add to 1.00.[5]

Where do the probabilities under P_2 (in column 2) come from and what do they really mean? In order to answer these questions we assume a ten-year issue, interest and principal payable annually, and a highly knowledgeable, sophisticated, and systematic lender! The lender, after formulating the probabilities in column 1 (P_1), examines the proposed issue and asks himself what the probability is that such an issue would meet its first payment, at some assumed rate of interest and schedule of amortization, given the first "state of nature." He reflects on the history of issues of this general type and decides that the probability is high, .995. He then asks himself what probability should be attached to the second payment, given that the first has been made in full and on time. He decides that it also is .995. And so forth for each of the succeeding eight years (the successive probabilities need not be the same: they can either rise or decline or take on any movement whatever).[6] Then, in order to ascertain the probability that all payments will be made in full and on time, he multiplies all ten conditional probabilities together. If he has chosen probabilities that are all equal he need only raise .995 to the tenth power. In Table 5-1 the product of the ten probabilities is equal to $(.995)^{10}$ or .950. The latter figure is then the probability that all payments will be made in full and on time given the first state of nature. The lender then repeats the process for each of the other two states of nature, does the necessary arithmetic, and obtains the final probability, .8075, given at the bottom of column 3 of Table 5-1. This is the probability we

---

[5] The analogy is with a game under the rules of which the player draws first from an urn containing 25 red balls, 65 green balls, and 10 white balls. The probability that the player will draw a red, green, or white ball is 1.00. If he draws a red ball he then draws from an urn containing 95 $10 bills and 5 pieces of paper bearing the legend: go back to start. If he draws a green ball he then draws from an urn containing 80 $10 bills and 20 pieces of paper bearing the above legend. If he draws a white ball he draws from an urn containing 50 $10 bills and 50 pieces of paper. The conditional probabilities that he will draw a $10 bill on his second draw are thus, respectively, .95, .80, and .50. The probability, at the start of the game, that he will draw a $10 bill is therefore .8075.

[6] The subjective probabilities fixed, at any given time on any given issue, separately by a number of lenders would presumably fluctuate normally about their mean.

are here trying to derive, i.e., the subjective probability that all payments will be made in full and on time—whatever the state of nature.

A few comments on the foregoing "description" of the "lending process" are perhaps in order:

(1) The description sounds artificial: few lenders, if any, would go through the kind of deliberate process described above and few, if any, would so much as think in terms of probabilities. Yet all the probabilities illustrated in Table 5-1 are implicit in every yield every lender sets—given the rate on riskless securities of the same maturity as the proposed issue.[7]

(2) The final probability, .8075 in the illustration, can be used explicitly to fix the return (i.e., $1 +$ yield) on the proposed issue, given the return prevailing on riskless securities of the same maturity as the proposed new issue. The lender knows, if he is sensible, that on the average he cannot expect to earn more than the return on comparable riskless securities—if he lends in a competitive market.[8] He therefore uses the rate on comparable riskless securities as his discount rate. He then sets up the following present value equation:

$$1 = \frac{rP_1}{1+g} + \frac{r(P_1P_2)}{(1+g)^2} + \cdots + \frac{(1+r)(P_1P_2 \ldots P_{10})}{(1+g)^{10}},$$

where r is the coupon on the proposed new issue; g is the prevailing rate on governments of the same maturity; and P_1, P_2, $\ldots$, P_{10} are the annual probabilities described above, .979 in the illustration.[9]

The foregoing equation simply means that the present value of the future payments on the proposed new issue cannot exceed the present value of the future payments on a government security of the same maturity.

The lender can now proceed in either of two ways: he can solve for r iteratively or he can solve, in general terms, for P and then solve for r. The latter course is simpler. Solving for P gives:

$$P = \frac{1+g}{1+r}$$

if all the conditional P's $(P_1, P_2, \ldots, P_{10})$ are the same, $P = P_1 = P_2 = \ldots P_{10}$. If the $P_1, P_2, \ldots, P_{10}$ differ among themselves, P is

[7] Regardless of the proposed amortization schedule of the proposed new issue—provided only that the two *maturities* are the same.

[8] This matter is discussed further below.

[9] Actually, in the illustration, $P^{10} = .8075$ and $\sqrt[10]{.8075} = .979$.

simply the nth root of their product or, in the above illustration, .979.[10]

Now that the lender knows that $P = (1 + g)/(1 + r)$, he can obtain r readily. Substituting the simple probability obtained in the illustration above ($\sqrt[10]{.8075} = .979$), and assuming that ten-year governments are selling to return 1.04, r (the required yield on the proposed issue) is 6.23 per cent approximately.[11] Again, few lenders, if any, go through this process explicitly but each and every one of them, with no exceptions, and whether they know it or not, go through it implicitly. Even if a lender does nothing but look at an issue casually and then fix a yield on it, he is making implicit assumptions about the probabilities described above.[12]

The proposed new issue would not be identical to governments in certain "extraneous" ways. The lender might want protection against call and if he did he would have to reduce his required yield accordingly. In addition, he would want to be compensated for that part of the cost of running his investment department that he would not incur if he bought only governments. Also, if he happened to be poorly diversified and therefore risk averse, or if he were risk averse for any other reason, he might seek additional yield on that account. But in any case, working from the underlying probabilities and the return on governments of the same maturity as the proposed new issue, he could determine an appropriate yield on the new issue and adjust, according to his disposition, for call, risk preference, and so forth.[13]

The raw materials of this study are the returns, i.e., the $(1 + r)$'s and the $(1 + g)$'s. In effect we are trying to reverse the process described above: instead of deriving the return (or the yield) from the subjective probabilities, as above, we attempt here to derive the subjective probabilities from the returns. However, the observed returns, as the foregoing illustration makes clear, reflect the effect of various

[10] $(.979)^{10} = .8075$.

[11] $1.04/.979 = 1.0623$.

[12] The process is, of course, a trial-and-error process: in order to assign the initial P's, the lender would have to assume a coupon rate and amortization schedule. He would proceed to obtain a required yield and if this yield and the yield assumed were materially different, he would assume a yield somewhere between the yield initially assumed and the tentative required yield and go through the process again. He would proceed by this process of successive approximation until the two yields were the same.

[13] Whether the lender would in fact be able to obtain an extra risk aversion premium is perhaps doubtful. This fact may explain, in part, why small insurance companies during the period in question were, in effect, unable to bid successfully for direct placements.

extraneous influences. And the derivation process itself is obviously based on a number of assumptions. And unless the ratio $(1 + g)/(1 + r)$ can be adjusted for extraneous influences and/or if the assumptions are not reasonably accurate, it (the ratio) will not be a pure risk ratio—i.e., it will not be the probability we are seeking.

(3) The following illustration may serve to make the meaning of the P's and the P^n's somewhat clearer. In order to keep the necessary computations within reasonable bounds, we assume a sample of 10,000 three-year bonds, all in the same risk class, sold at the same time at par with a coupon of 6 per cent, and that three-year governments are selling to yield 4 per cent. We assume further that we have adjusted the yield on the risky bonds for extraneous influences and, of course, that the various necessary assumptions are satisfied. We invest $1 in each bond.

First, we obtain the average probability by dividing $(1 + g)$ by $(1 + r)$ and find that it is approximately .9811. Second, we set up the following equation, assuming that $P_1 = P_2 = P_3$:[14]

$$10,000 = \frac{600(.98113)}{1.04} + \frac{600(.98113)^2}{(1.04)^2} = \frac{10,600(.98113)^3}{(1.04)^3}$$

$$= \frac{588.68}{1.04} + \frac{577.57}{1.0816} + \frac{10,011.28}{1.124864}$$

$$= 566.04 + 534.00 + 8,899.99$$

$$= 10,000 \ (10,000.03)$$

How should this result be interpreted? On its face, the result means that of the 10,000 bonds 189 will not make either the first payment or any subsequent payment. Of the 9811 remaining alive at the end of the first period, 185 will not make the second or third payments. And of the 9,626 remaining alive at the end of the second period, 181 will not make the final payment. But obviously, we need not interpret the probabilities in this rigid way: we could assume merely that the interest payments on all bonds in the first period would total $588.68 (.98113 × $600) and that, in the second period, they would total $577.57 [(.98113)^2 × 600] and that interest and principal in the final period would total $10,011.28 [(.98113)^3 × $10,600]. But this is merely one particular example of the most general case, namely, that the cash inflows on the risky bond, discounted at the rate on riskless securities of the same maturity, must be equal to one times the

[14] To repeat: this assumption is not necessary—provided only that $P_1 \times P_2 \times P_3 = P^3$ or, in this case, .9445.

number of dollars invested—in this case $10,000. And the ratio $(1 + g) / (1 + r)$ simply measures the extent to which the promised cash flows are expected to be reduced in order that the above equality will hold. In other words, the actual cash flows can assume any pattern or shape whatsoever: some of the 10,000 bonds may default and be subsequently "worked out," some may be a total loss, some may merely be late in paying interest or principal, and so forth, provided only that $(1 + r) P = (1 + g)$. We could say, as above, that 10,000 $-P(10,000)$ tells us how many bonds will be a total loss, i.e., will make no payments at all, namely, 189. But we could also say that P tells us how much of the original expected cash inflow, $11,800 appropriately discounted, is not really expected to be received, namely, $1,800, so that the actual present value of the group of 10,000 bonds would really be expected to be $10,000—or the present value of $10,000 invested in riskless securities of the same maturity.

(4) The final compound probabilities (the figure .8075 at the bottom of Table 5-1) are fairly sensitive to the values of the subsidiary probabilities. If, for example, the probability of state of nature number 1 had been fixed at zero and the probability of state of nature number 2 correspondingly raised to .90, the other probabilities remaining the same, the final compound probability would have been reduced to about .77. If the probabilities of state of nature numbers 2 and 3 had been fixed, respectively, at .80 and .20, the final probability would have been about .74.

The next section of the paper summarizes findings. The section thereafter examines, in some detail, the extraneous influences and the assumptions. We then derive and adjust the average and compound probabilities. The final section evaluates the results.

SUMMARY

This study does, essentially, four things: (1) It attempts to assess the effect of the extraneous influences on the yield differential between corporates and governments; (2) It suggests a new measure of the quality of new corporate debt issues, namely, the *probability* that all payments of interest and principal will be made in full and on time; (3) It computes this measure quarterly for a large sample of the direct placements bought by life insurance companies during the period 1951–61, separately for industrials, utilities, and finance company issues; (4) It adjusts the results for what appear, in fact, to be the two most important extraneous influences, namely, the effect on yields on direct placement of (a) risk-aversion on the part of the life insurance companies and (b) differential call deferment as between direct placements and governments.

The findings will be of primary interest to policy makers, students of the business cycle, and regulatory agencies. They will perhaps also be of interest to investors and to those scholars and practitioners who are interested in developing better measures of the quality of both new and outstanding credit instruments.

The conclusions are: (1) Of the various extraneous influences, only two are likely to affect the probabilities in a significant way for the present purpose, namely, differences in call provisions when yields are generally high and expected to fall, and risk aversion on the part of lenders.

(2) Because the life insurance companies are risk averse, yield differentials (and hence the probabilities) are sensitive to fluctuations in the volume of lower-grade financing. In 1955–57, for example, when the volume of lower-grade financing was very heavy, the life insurance companies required yields on direct placements that were substantially higher than necessary to compensate for the risk of default alone. When the effect on the probabilities of the volume of lower-grade financing was removed (by use of regression techniques), they (the probabilities) rose by as much as 14 percentage points (see Charts 5-4, 5-5, and 5-6).

(3) Long-term governments have, generally, much longer call deferment than direct placements. For this reason yields on direct placements are higher, relative to yields on governments, than they would be on the basis of risk alone. These differences range roughly from 5 to 40 basis points and affect the compound probabilities by as much as 10–12 percentage points (see Charts 5-12, 5-13, and 5-14).

(4) The quality of direct placements may have deteriorated slightly during the period under study. The average probability, as defined above, for the direct placements bought in 1951–53 was .807 for industrials, .809 for utilities, and .816 for finance company issues. In 1959–61, these probabilities had declined, respectively, to .763, .781, and .778 (see Table 5-13).

(5) For the period as a whole, average compound probabilities were .783 for industrials, .795 for utilities, and .811 for finance

company issues (see Table 5-13). For the period 1900–43, the "realized compound probabilities" implicit in the Hickman-Fraine results (for issues comparable, in composition, to the direct placement sample) were .754 for industrials and .721 for utilities.

ASSUMPTIONS AND EXTRANEOUS INFLUENCES

As indicated above, the term "quality ex ante" is here taken to mean the estimate, explicit or implicit, made by the lender at time of issue, of the probability that the promise made by the borrower will be kept in full. This estimate, although usually based on "objective" data (i.e., on the historical record), must be subjective because, in its nature, it cannot be anything else: it is a subjective evaluation of the historical record in the context of the circumstances surrounding the purchase of the new debt instrument. And it is perfectly possible for two identical issues, bought at different times, to have different probabilities attached to them by lenders.

Ideally then, we are seeking, for each new issue (and for new issues on the average), period by period, an estimate of the subjective probability of repayment in full and on time, i.e., the probability that the realized yield on any bond (or group of bonds) will be equal to the promised yield on that bond (or group of bonds). And, of course, if we could obtain a time series of such probabilities, we would be able to observe whether the probabilities were increasing (higher quality) or decreasing (lower quality).[15]

Unhappily, probabilities in the above sense, even if explicitly formulated, are not part of the public record: they appear only via their

---

[15] We should, of course, be very careful about the inferences we draw from the behavior of the probabilities—after all, from the lenders viewpoint, the expected yield on the worst bonds, taken as a group, should be equal to the rate on riskless bonds. We could say only that as quality, in the above sense, declined, defaults per dollar of bonds bought would probably increase. But the fact that quality, in this sense, had declined would not necessarily mean that the insurance companies were or would be "worse off." In fact, it doubtless means the reverse, provided yields had been properly determined on lower quality issues: if yields had been appropriately determined on lower quality issues the insurance companies would be able, in effect, to invest their enormous flows of cash to yield the current rate on riskless securities. If they tried to invest these cash flows directly in riskless securities, they would, doubtless, drive yields on those securities down to a point below, probably well below, the prevailing yield on such securities.

effect on yields. Now, assuming that bonds can be grouped into homogeneous risk classes, the expected value of $1 worth of bonds in any risk class should be equal to the expected value of $1 worth of bonds in every other risk class and to the value of $1 of riskless bonds. This, in turn, means that the yield differential between a direct placement and a government bond of the same maturity should be a measure or an index, in some sense, of the probability we seek, provided (1) that governments are considered by investors to be riskless; (2) that the direct placement market is a fully competitive market from the point of view of the issuer, i.e., that no issuer need pay more for money than the yield on governments of the same maturity (and relevant nonquality characteristics) plus an appropriate risk premium; (3) that the buyers of direct placements are able to move funds freely from one type of security to another—mortgages, direct placements, other corporates, governments—in order to take advantage of whatever yield differentials may appear; (4) that the direct placement and government bonds being compared have the same nonquality characteristics; (5) that the yields being compared are net yields, i.e., that the yield on the direct placement is net of any cost of origination; and (6) that the buyers of direct placements are risk neutral.

Of these six provisos, the last is perhaps the most important. If lenders are in fact risk averse, they will tend to require, on lower-grade securities, yields higher than necessary to compensate for the pure risk of default alone. And if they do, the yield differentials on which this study is based will be distorted.

But under study here are only those corporate issues (direct placements) bought directly by large financial institutions rather than by "the public." Large financial institutions ought not to have risk preferences. What, after all, is risk preference? If an investor holds a large, diversified bond portfolio, there ought to be no real difference to him between a riskless bond and a very risky one, provided the degree of risk of the risky bond has been properly assessed and the yield on it is such that its expected value is the same as that on the riskless bond.[16] In other words, the large investor who has sufficient cash coming in, in each period, to meet his obligations (as the life companies do) and who is able to hold, relative to total assets, small

---

[16] Except to the extent that substantial defaults may be misinterpreted by management to mean that a portfolio manager has not been doing his job properly.

amounts of a large number of issues is really taking no risk what-ever—provided he has properly assessed the probabilities. For such an investor, the investment problem consists essentially in assessing probabilities, calculating appropriate yields on new issues, forecast-ing the future course of interest rates and "arbitraging" the market. But, to repeat, if such investors are in fact risk averse, i.e., if they prefer bonds with a lower expected variance of return to bonds with a higher expected variance of return, they will require yields higher than necessary to compensate for pure risk alone. And hence, the yield differential between direct placements and governments will be higher than would otherwise be the case.

So far as the other assumptions, above, are concerned, we assume:

(1) *That governments are free of the risk of fault.* This assumption seems reasonable enough.

(2) *That the direct placement market is a competitive market.* It follows that no borrower has to pay more for money than the rate on a comparable government security plus an appropriate risk premium. This assumption does not seem unreasonable, given the fact that the direct placement market is made up of over sixty life insurance companies, plus a number of pension and mutual funds.

(3) *That the large financial institutions are able to switch the various assets in their portfolios so as to equate yields on all types of assets at the margin.* In other words, if expected yields on direct placements were to rise above the yield on governments (or vice versa), the insurance companies should be free to sell mortgages or governments or anything else in order to buy direct placements (or in the converse case, to sell direct placements in order to buy govern-ments). This assumption is dubious because no satisfactory secondary markets exist in either direct placements or mortgages.

On the other hand, during the period under study here, the insur-ance companies held a large volume of governments: $13,459 million at the beginning of 1951 and $6,134 million at the end of 1961.[17] If, during the period, expected yields on direct placements had been above yields on governments for very long, the life insurance com-panies could have sold more governments than they actually did sell, in order to buy direct placements. Further, if expected yields on direct placements had been below the yield on governments for very long, holdings of direct placements would not have increased continuously

---

[17] The great bulk of these securities were held by the sixty largest life companies, i.e., by the principal purchasers of direct placements.

during the period, as in fact they did. In other words, if expected yields on direct placements had long been below the yield on governments, cash flow would not have been reinvested in direct placements. And, in such case, the volume of direct placements held by the insurance companies would have declined in at least some periods. In fact, however, the reverse occurred.

(4) *That the direct placement and government bonds being compared have the same nonquality characteristics.* The two most important nonquality characteristics, apart from maturity, are marketability and call protection. In general, direct placements are not marketable but usually can be called by the borrower after some specified period of time. Government securities, on the other hand, are highly marketable and generally cannot be called at all—they are generally protected against call through their lives (there are occasional exceptions: some long-term governments can be called five to ten years prior to maturity but not before then).

The difference in call protection means that, other things being equal, yields on governments should be lower than yields on direct placements. But the amount by which they will be lower will vary depending on expectations as to the future course of interest rates. When rates are expected to rise, the difference on this score will be zero or negligible. When rates are expected to go down, the difference may be as much as 40 basis points.

In addition, other things being equal, yields on governments should be lower because of their greater marketability—although it seems likely that the insurance companies attach little if any importance to marketability and, in order to obtain it, would be willing to sacrifice little if any yield on the direct placements they buy. But, perhaps, some part of the yield differential between direct placements and governments is due to differences in marketability between the two types of securities.

No adjustment has been made here for differences in marketability between governments and direct placements. An adjustment has, however, been made for differential call deferment on the basis of data which has recently become available. This adjustment is admittedly rough.[18]

(5) *That the yields being compared are net yields.* In general,

---

[18] Gordon Pye, "The Value of Call Deferment on a Bond: Some Empirical Results," *Journal of Finance,* December 1967, p. 632. Pye's results became available after all the basic calculations here had been done.

when an insurance company buys government securities, it has no transactions cost and, hence, the yield offered on the government is the net yield the insurance company actually receives. But the yields used here on direct placements, are not net yields in the above sense: every insurance company that is active in the direct placement market maintains a securities department at an annual cost which is not negligible in absolute terms, but which probably does not exceed one-tenth of one per cent of funds invested each year. Thus, if net yield were calculated taking these "transaction costs" into account, it would be lower than the nominal yield by perhaps 8 to 10 basis points.[19] In other words, the yields on direct placements used in this study are somewhat higher than they would have been if they could have been put on a "net" basis.

For this reason also, then, yields on governments are somewhat understated relative to yields on direct placements, and the measures derived below are biased somewhat downward. No attempt has been made to adjust for this bias.

In sum, then, the first three assumptions seem reasonable and ought not to bias the results one way or the other. The biases introduced by the fact that direct placements are not readily marketable and by the differential "transactions cost" of direct placements are probably slight and no attempt has been made to adjust for them. Adjustments have been made, however, for "risk aversion" and for differential call deferment.

Obtaining Probabilities

As indicated above, $P = (1 + g)/(1 + r)$, where r is the coupon on a risky security with specified maturity,[20] g is the yield on a government bond of the same maturity, and P is the subjective average probability we seek.

[19] The estimate comes from trade sources. The yield on a new acquisition of \$1 with maturity of 15 years and a nominal yield of 4 per cent, would be reduced to about 3.92 per cent if the cost of acquisition were one-tenth of one per cent, thus:

$$1.001 = \frac{.04}{(1+g)} + \cdots + \frac{1.04}{(1+g)} \ 15; g \div .0392.$$

[20] Virtually all the direct placements in the present sample were sold at par. For those few that were not, yield rather than coupon was used.

Ideally, in order to obtain the *P*'s we should take the following steps: (1) Monthly series should be constructed for yields on governments for every maturity from five to forty years. These yields should be free of extraneous (e.g., coupon) influences. (2) The yield on each direct placement should be adjusted to make it comparable with the yield on a riskless security of the same maturity, in terms of call provisions and the other extraneous influences.[21] (3) Each of the riskless yields, so obtained, should be divided by the yield on each direct placement bought in the same month and of the same maturity, e.g., the yield in January 1951 on riskless securities of maturity of ten years should be divided by the yield on each direct placement bought in the same month of maturity of ten years, and so forth, for each other maturity and each other month. The output of this process would be a "probability," in the above sense, for each direct placement bought in each month. (4) Each probability, so obtained, should then be raised to the nth power, where n is maturity. The resulting number would be the probability that the final payment would be made on time, given that all prior payments had been made on time. (5) Each such probability should then be weighted by the size of the issue and averaged by period (quarterly). The resulting weighted average probabilities would constitute an estimate of the over-all quality of the "aggregate direct placement" bought by the life insurance companies in each period.

In essence, the procedure which has been used is as follows: (1) Using the monthly series by maturity on long-term governments constructed by the Morgan Guaranty Trust, we have obtained simple probabilities, as above, for each direct placement.[22] (2) Each such simple probability has been weighted by the size of the issue to which it pertains, and weighted average simple probabilities have been obtained quarterly—for industrials, utilities, and finance companies, separately. These weighted average simple "probabilities" are given in Tables 5-2, 5-3, and 5-4 and are shown in Charts 5-1, 5-2, and 5-3 for industrials, utilities, and finance companies, respectively.[23]

---

[21] None of the direct placements under study here is convertible.

[22] The Morgan Guaranty series, in effect, reads yield by maturity off a curve, fitted by hand to issues of comparable coupon. For a description of the sample of direct placements, see Cohan, *op. cit.*, pp. 11–17.

[23] The usual market rating is simply an absolute yield *differential*, stated in basis points or percentage points, between a base series and the series being measured. The measure used here is the *ratio* of the two returns, i.e., the ratio of the expected return on a government to promised return on a risky security.

TABLE 5-2. *Industrial Direct Placements, Weighted Average Simple Probabilities, Quarterly, 1951–61*

	Quarter			
Year	1	2	3	4
1951	.990	.990	.988	.989
1952	.988	.988	.990	.988
1953	.985	.990	.985	.983
1954	.988	.984	.988	.989
1955	.988	.990	.990	.982
1956	.986	.987	.988	.985
1957	.982	.982	.982	.981
1958	.980	.983	.980	.988
1959	.984	.987	.987	.984
1960	.986	.986	.980	.984
1961	.983	.984	.984	.988

NOTE: Average, 1951–61 = .9858.

TABLE 5-3. *Public Utility Direct Placements, Weighted Average Simple Probabilities, Quarterly, 1951–61*

	Quarter			
Year	1	2	3	4
1951	.988	.990	.990	.990
1952	.991	.988	.989	.994
1953	.986	.993	.987	.989
1954	.986	.993	.992	.992
1955	.988	.989	.994	.987
1956	.988	.990	.987	.983
1957	.983	.985	.985	.985
1958	.989	.983	.987	.988
1959	.991	.992	.988	.984
1960	.987	.987	.988	.988
1961	.990	.987	.991	.993

NOTE: Average, 1951–61 = .9885.

TABLE 5-4. *Finance Company Direct Placements, Weighted Average Simple Probabilities, Quarterly, 1951–61*

Year	Quarter			
	1	2	3	4
1951	.970	.988	.977	.984
1952	.977	.990	.987	.987
1953	.986	.983	.980	.981
1954	.987	.989	.993	.985
1955	.993	.989	.993	.990
1956	.986	.986	–	.982
1957	.985	.979	.983	.980
1958	.978	.979	.983	.982
1959	.985	.988	.987	.988
1960	.987	.987	.978	.982
1961	.980	.979	.989	.983

NOTE: Average, 1951–61 = .9843.

CHART 5–1. Industrial Direct Placements, Weighted Average Simple Probabilities, Quarterly, 1951–61

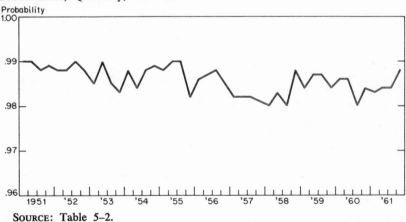

SOURCE: Table 5–2.

(3) Next, each individual simple probability was raised to the power equal to the maturity of the issue in order to obtain the probability that the realized yield on the issue would be equal to the promised yield. (4) Each such compound probability was then weighted by the size of the issue to which it pertained, and a weighted average compound probability was obtained quarterly for industrials, utility, and

CHART 5–2. Public Utility Direct Placements, Weighted Average Simple Probabilities, Quarterly, 1951–61

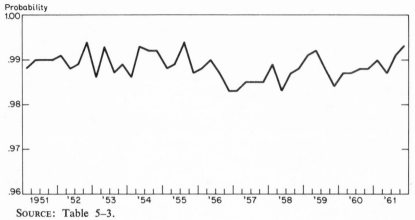

SOURCE: Table 5–3.

CHART 5–3. Finance Company Direct Placements, Weighted Average Simple Probabilities, Quarterly, 1951–61

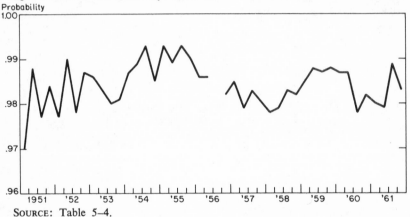

SOURCE: Table 5–4.

finance company issues, separately. These compound probabilities are given in Table 5-5 and set forth in Charts 5-4, 5-5, and 5-6.

What the P's Show

The industrial and utility P series (Charts 5-1, 5-2, and 5-3) behave in much the same way. Each fluctuates more or less randomly around what is virtually a horizontal line from 1951 to mid-1956. Each then

TABLE 5-5. *Weighted Probabilities to Maturity, All Series, 1951–61*

Year and Quarter	Industrials	Utilities	Finance Companies
1951			
1	.809	.742	.784
2	.826	.767	.850
3	.844	.790	.830
4	.756	.743	.785
1952			
1	.792	.799	.788
2	.750	.801	.822
3	.799	.747	.766
4	.800	.867	.882
1953			
1	.776	.759	.808
2	.832	.825	.773
3	.799	.752	.772
4	.764	.765	.758
1954			
1	.753	.769	.817
2	.793	.818	.845
3	.795	.844	.865
4	.808	.826	.817
1955			
1	.802	.762	.897
2	.814	.787	.910
3	.845	.863	.892
4	.784	.795	.845
1956			
1	.740	.770	.821
2	.761	.798	.801
3	.811	.720	–
4	.734	.730	.799
1957			
1	.710	.673	.805
2	.680	.660	.760
3	.687	.686	.768
4	.663	.670	.695

(continued)

TABLE 5-5 (concluded)

Year and Quarter	Industrials	Utilities	Finance Companies
1958			
1	.690	.777	.800
2	.719	.711	.775
3	.729	.757	.736
4	.785	.719	.787
1959			
1	.773	.784	.755
2	.773	.848	.803
3	.776	.775	.831
4	.760	.626	.778
1960			
1	.782	.751	.792
2	.769	.731	.809
3	.683	.751	.713
4	.726	.702	.782
1961			
1	.770	.758	.776
2	.732	.751	.740
3	.752	.796	.804
4	.807	.816	.725
Average			
1951–61	.7671	.7632	.7991
1951–53	.7956	.7798	.8015
1959–61	.7586	.7574	.7757

moves persistently downward until 1957–58. Each then recovers and again begins to fluctuate randomly around a virtually horizontal line. The finance company P series fluctuates randomly around an upward trend from 1951 to the end of 1955. It then moves persistently downward until the first quarter of 1958; it then recovers and fluctuates erratically until the end of the period. The three compounded series show much the same pattern as their simple counterparts—although, in all three series, compounding has accentuated the persistent downward movement in the middle of the period.

The persistent downward movement over a three-year period in all six series could, of course, be taken to mean that the quality of the

CHART 5–4. Industrials, Weighted Average Probabilities to Maturity, Quarterly, 1951–61

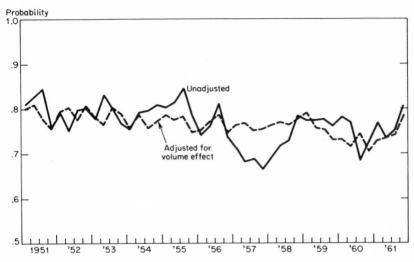

SOURCE: Tables 5–5 and 5–11.

CHART 5–5. Utilities, Weighted Average Probabilities to Maturity, Quarterly, 1951–61

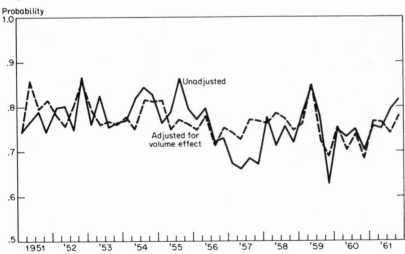

SOURCE: Tables 5–5 and 5–11.

CHART 5–6. Finance Companies, Weighted Average Probabilities to Maturity, Quarterly, 1951–61

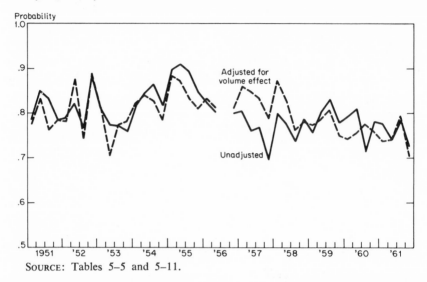

SOURCE: Tables 5–5 and 5–11.

direct placements bought from 1955 to 1958 declined steadily during that period or that, for other reasons (e.g., risk aversion), yields on direct placements rose, relative to yields on governments, as the volume of lower-grade securities purchased increased.

In an attempt to decide which of these two possibilities was more likely to be correct, probability ratios were constructed, separately for industrial, utility, and finance company issues, for an issue of fixed characteristics.

The procedure was as follows: Quarterly yield series had been constructed, for another purpose, for an industrial, a utility, and a finance company issue, each of fixed characteristics. Each of these series is analogous to a cost of living index based on a rigidly fixed basket of commodities.[24] Each quarterly return $(1 + \text{yield})$ for each of these series was then divided into the return during the same quarter on a comparable government. The resulting "probability ratios" are given in Table 5-6 and in Charts 5-7, 5-8, and 5-9. Inasmuch as each of the three series is, to repeat, based on a set of fixed characteristics, i.e., is of constant intrinsic quality, we would have expected the proba-

---

[24] The method by which these series were constructed is discussed in detail in *Yields on Corporate Debt Directly Placed*, New York, NBER, 1967, pp. 72–73.

TABLE 5-6. *Direct Placements, Return on Long-Term Governments Divided by Computed Return on Direct Placement of Fixed Characteristics, Quarterly, 1951–61*

Year and Quarter	Industrials	Utilities	Finance Companies
1951			
1	.987	.988	.985
2	.994	.990	.984
3	.984	.988	.985
4	.988	.982	.983
1952			
1	.986	.992	.983
2	.983	.991	.983
3	.985	.986	.983
4	.987	.984	.982
1953			
1	.985	.987	.983
2	.986	.987	.980
3	.987	.988	.980
4	.983	.989	.981
1954			
1	.983	.789	.982
2	.984	.988	.983
3	.984	.986	.983
4	.984	.988	.983
1955			
1	.989	.990	.987
2	.987	.989	.987
3	.987	.991	.987
4	.985	.990	.986
1956			
1	.985	.988	.987
2	.984	.987	.985
3	.983	.986	.984
4	.982	.985	.982

(continued)

TABLE 5-6 (concluded)

Year and Quarter	Industrials	Utilities	Finance Companies
1957			
1	.982	.982	.981
2	.983	.984	.981
3	.981	.983	.979
4	.979	.983	.977
1958			
1	.978	.986	.983
2	.981	.984	.982
3	.986	.987	.983
4	.985	.988	.983
1959			
1	.983	.988	.984
2	.986	.988	.986
3	.984	.987	.983
4	.985	.984	.982
1960			
1	.989	.985	.983
2	.983	.986	.983
3	.979	.985	.911
4	.982	.984	.982
1961			
1	.984	.986	.982
2	.984	.985	.981
3	.983	.988	.981
4	.984	.990	.982

bility ratios to fluctuate randomly around a horizontal line if no extraneous influence, such as risk aversion, had been present. But in fact the three fixed characteristics series behave in much the same way as the weighted average probability ratios derived from actual issues: the ratio starts to fall in 1955 and continues downward for three years in the case of industrials, one and a half years in the case of utilities, and nearly two years in the case of finance companies.

This must mean that, during this period, yields on an industrial issue, a utility issue, and a finance company issue, each of fixed char-

CHART 5–7. Industrials, Yield on Long-Term Governments Divided by Computed Yield on Fixed Characteristic Direct Placements, Quarterly, 1951–61

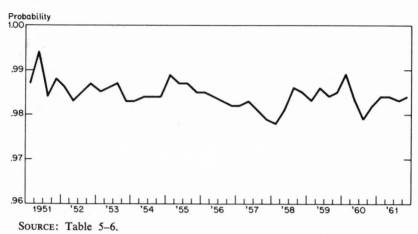

SOURCE: Table 5–6.

CHART 5–8. Public Utilities, Yield on Long-Term Governments Divided by Computed Yield on Fixed Characteristic Direct Placements, Quarterly, 1951–61

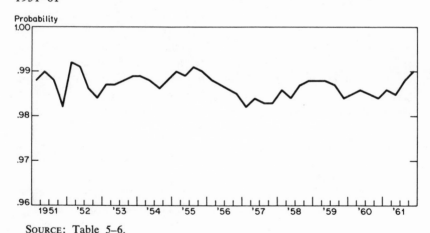

SOURCE: Table 5–6.

acteristics, rose relative to yields on governments. And this in turn would appear to mean that lenders, during the period, regarded an issue of fixed characteristics as being of progressively decreasing quality. But the period in question was fairly prosperous and, during such a period,

CHART 5–9. Finance Companies' Issues, Yield on Long-Term Governments Divided by Computed Yield on Fixed Characteristic Direct Placements, Quarterly, 1951–61

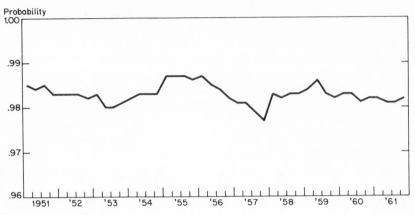

SOURCE: Table 5–6.

we would expect lenders to regard an issue of fixed characteristics as being of progressively improving quality rather than the reverse. This fact suggested the possibility that influences in addition to quality were affecting the behavior of the probability ratios—perhaps, as suggested above, the volume of lower-grade issues coming to market during the years 1955–57. Although the insurance companies themselves may not be risk averse, the National Association of Life Insurance Commissioners requires progressively higher loss reserves against "lower-grade" securities. This means, among other things, that in years in which the life insurance companies buy large amounts of lower-grade securities, their earnings and surplus are less than they otherwise would have been. This in turn, at least in the short term, may affect the ability of the insurance companies, both stock and mutual, to pay dividends, reduce premiums, and so forth.[25]

In other words, if insurance companies were risk-neutral, they would make a reasonably rapid adjustment to an increase in the demand for long-term money (regardless of quality) by selling governments and buying direct placements. The adjustment would not be instantaneous and, therefore, the probability ratio would fluctuate

[25] For a comprehensive discussion of this matter, see H. G. Fraine, *Valuation of Securities Holdings of Life Insurance Companies,* Homewood, Illinois, 1962, Chapter 1 and Appendix A.

randomly over time, unless lenders believed they were buying direct placements of progressively higher or lower quality. But if the insurance companies were risk averse, because of the restrictions imposed on them by NALIC or for other reasons, they would tend to require relatively higher yields, other things being equal, as volume rose.[26] They would, that is, require compensation for the expected value of the penalties they would incur or for the additional risk implicit in the purchase of additional securities with a higher-than-average variance of return. In order to throw some additional light on this hypothesis, probability ratios were constructed for Aaa and Baa publicly held outstandings. These ratios are set forth in Table 5-7 and Chart 5-10. The probability ratio for Aaa's despite a very slight downward trend in 1956–57 is for all practical purposes fluctuating randomly around a horizontal line. The probability ratio for Baa's, however, behaves in much the same way as the probability ratios for the three classes of direct placements, i.e., it moves sharply downward in the middle of the period.

If the foregoing hypothesis is correct, we should find a significant relationship between the volume of direct placement financing and the compounded probabilities, when allowance is made for changes in the various quality variables.

CHART 5–10. Return on Long-Term Governments Divided by Return on Moody's Aaa's or Baa's (Outstanding), Quarterly, 1951–61

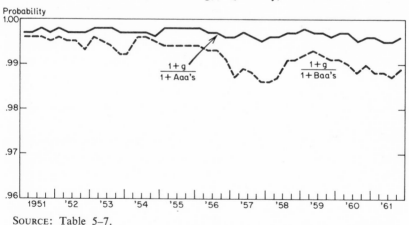

SOURCE: Table 5–7.

[26] Relative to governments, i.e., the ratio of the return on governments to the return on direct placements would decline.

TABLE 5-7. *Return on Long-Term Governments Divided by Return on Moody's Aaa's and Baa's (Outstanding), Quarterly, 1951–61*

Year and Quarter	$\dfrac{1 + g}{1 + \text{Aaa}}$	$\dfrac{1 + g}{1 + \text{Baa}}$
1951		
1	.997	.996
2	.997	.996
3	.998	.996
4	.997	.995
1952		
1	.998	.996
2	.997	.995
3	.997	.995
4	.997	.993
1953		
1	.998	.996
2	.998	.995
3	.998	.994
4	.997	.992
1954		
1	.997	.992
2	.997	.996
3	.997	.996
4	.996	.995
1955		
1	.998	.994
2	.998	.994
3	.998	.994
4	.998	.994
1956		
1	.998	.994
2	.997	.993
3	.997	.993
4	.996	.991

(continued)

TABLE 5-7 (concluded)

Year and Quarter	$\dfrac{1 + g}{1 + \text{Aaa}}$	$\dfrac{1 + g}{1 + \text{Baa}}$
1957		
1	.996	.987
2	.997	.989
3	.996	.988
4	.995	.986
1958		
1	.996	.986
2	.996	.987
3	.997	.991
4	.997	.991
1959		
1	.998	.992
2	.997	.993
3	.997	.992
4	.996	.991
1960		
1	.997	.991
2	.997	.990
3	.995	.988
4	.996	.990
1961		
1	.996	.988
2	.995	.988
3	.995	.987
4	.996	.989
Average, 1951–61	.9968	.9920

NOTE: Return = 1 + yield.

The Time Series Regressions

For the purpose of testing the foregoing hypothesis, three series were available.

(1) *Deliveries.* This series, based on data collected by the SEC, gives the dollar volume of (presumably) all direct placements delivered

by borrowers to lenders. The date of delivery bears no necessary relationship to commitment date—the date on which the amount of the loan and its terms were agreed to by the borrower and the lender—but follows it by varying lengths of time depending on expectations as to the future course of interest rates. If interest rates are expected to rise, borrowers will try to anticipate their needs as far ahead as possible and, hence, the lag between commitment and delivery date will increase. The lag will tend to shorten when interest rates are expected to decline.

But yields on direct placements (and hence the probability ratios) should be sensitive not to deliveries—which, as indicated above, may take place long after yield has been fixed—but rather to commitments, which measure, albeit inversely, the supply of funds available at any given moment of time.

(2) *New Commitments.* Data are available monthly, since September 1952, on new commitments made by a large sample of life insurance companies to corporate borrowers.[27] This series measures the dollar volume of new commitments, to be delivered then or at some subsequent time, made during the month in question by the life insurance companies to corporate borrowers.[28]

(3) *Total Outstanding Commitments.* To arrive at total outstanding commitments at the end of any given period, measure the dollar volume of funds previously committed but not yet delivered to (corporate) borrowers, i.e., the dollar volume of funds newly committed, but not delivered, during the period just ended plus commitments made in all periods prior thereto, but not yet delivered. Total commitments will increase from one period to the next if new commitments exceed deliveries and will fall if deliveries exceed new commitments.[29] Because a substantial percentage of direct placements

---

[27] This does not include business and commercial mortgages.

[28] "A forward investment commitment is a binding agreement on the part of a lending institution to make available a given amount of funds, upon given credit terms, at specified dates or over an agreed-on period of time varying from just over a month to two or three years. The agreement gives the interest rate, maturity, redemption privileges, and so forth and sets forth a schedule of disbursement or 'take-down' of funds. . . ." The "data include some commitments to bond houses to purchase a given amount of a *public* issue. Normally, however, public issues of corporate securities do not give rise to a forward commitment partly because, to appear in the data, the commitment must have a life of over one month." James J. O'Leary, "Forward Investment Commitments of Life Insurance Companies," in *The Quality and Economic Significance of Anticipations Data,* New York, NBER, 1960, pp. 325–326.

[29] $TC_1 - TC_0 = NC_1 - D_1 - K_1$, where $TC_1 =$ total commitments at the end

is below investment grade, this series is, in effect, an index of the volume of lower-grade securities the life insurance companies will take into their portfolios during the ensuing six to twelve months.[30] It is drawn from the same sample as the series on new commitments and it also is available only since September 1952.

The three series described above are given in index number form in Table 5-8 and Chart 5-11.[31] Chart 5-11 makes clear that new commitments, which had been fluctuating more or less randomly (except perhaps for the third quarter of 1954), began a sharp sustained rise in the second quarter of 1955. They "peaked" in the second quarter of 1956 and then fell steadily until the fourth quarter of 1957. This rise in new commitments was reflected, with a lag, in the volume of total commitments which itself peaked in the first quarter of 1957. Total commitments fell off much more slowly than new commitments and did not reach bottom until the fourth quarter of 1959.

Regressions were run on the volume of deliveries and the various quality variables. One regression was run for industrials and one for utilities over the period 1951–61, with the quarterly compounded probabilities as the dependent variable and the quarterly volume of deliveries and quarterly averages of the ten quality variables as the explanatory variables. The volume of deliveries was lagged one quarter in an attempt to make it comparable with the probability ratios, which were, of course, based on commitment date.

of period 1; $TC_0 =$ total commitments at the end of period 0; $NC_1 =$ new commitments made during period 1; $D_1 =$ deliveries made during period 1; and $K_1 =$ cancellations, during period 1, of commitments previously made.

There is an analogy here, of course, between shipments (deliveries), new orders (new commitments), and unfilled orders (total outstanding commitments). Pressure on prices will be greatest when both unfilled orders and new orders are both high and rising. The correlation between the deliveries series and the total commitments series is $-.059$ or, for all practical purposes, zero. The fact that this correlation is low does not mean, of course, that it could not have been improved by establishing "appropriate" lag or lead relationships between them. But given the results presented below, experimentation along these lines did not seem worthwhile.

[30] See T. R. Atkinson, *Trends in Corporate Bond Quality*, New York, NBER, 1967, pp. 29–30.

[31] The coverage of the two commitments series changed somewhat during the period. In 1952, for example, 58 companies representing 66.6 per cent of the assets of all U.S. life insurance companies reported commitments. In 1961, 64 companies representing 65.2 per cent of the assets of all U.S. life insurance companies did so. No attempt has been made to adjust the commitment figures for these small differences.

TABLE 5-8. *Deliveries, Total Commitments, and New Commitments of Direct Placements to Corporate Borrowers, Quarterly, 1951–61 (1953 quarterly average = 100)*

Year and Quarter	Deliveries	Total Commitments[a]	New Commitments[b]
1951			
1	140.8	NA	NA
2	92.1	NA	NA
3	126.3	NA	NA
4	102.6	NA	NA
1952			
1	125.0	NA	NA
2	105.3	NA	NA
3	148.7	123.0	NA
4	119.7	96.3	84.5
1953			
1	94.7	105.9	119.6
2	110.5	102.2	119.7
3	97.4	100.0	78.8
4	97.4	91.9	81.9
1954			
1	94.7	101.5	115.1
2	131.6	99.3	91.7
3	119.7	108.9	153.9
4	118.4	87.4	82.3
1955			
1	88.2	85.9	79.2
2	125.0	95.6	120.8
3	105.3	97.0	119.7
4	114.5	92.6	102.8
1956			
1	152.6	99.3	118.6
2	126.3	117.8	177.7
3	119.7	135.6	173.1
4	115.8	140.7	127.9

(continued)

TABLE 5-8 (concluded)

Year and Quarter	Deliveries	Total Commitments[a]	New Commitments[b]
1957			
1	117.1	147.4	97.4
2	115.8	145.9	95.0
3	128.9	134.1	66.4
4	125.0	119.3	78.6
1958			
1	113.2	118.5	77.1
2	103.9	114.8	94.8
3	100.0	123.7	122.3
4	106.6	102.2	88.4
1959			
1	125.0	103.7	92.2
2	118.4	96.3	96.5
3	102.6	80.0	74.9
4	134.2	72.6	74.5
1960			
1	111.8	91.9	138.9
2	90.9	89.6	99.3
3	123.7	88.9	95.4
4	123.7	85.2	104.2
1961			
1	135.5	89.6	114.8
2	159.2	100.0	159.0
3	163.2	85.2	86.9
4	151.3	74.1	102.8

[a]Total commitments outstanding at end of quarter.
[b]New commitments made during quarter.
NA = not available.

The quality variables included were those which when calculated quarterly had shown significance in the cross-section analysis of yields, as follows:[32] $X_2 =$ the mean of the log of the total capital of each borrower; $X_3 =$ the mean of the log of the average term of each issue;

[32] These variables, except X_{16} and X_{17}, are numbered as they are numbered in the Bureau's study of yields on direct placements (Cohan, *op. cit.*). They are discussed in detail and defined in Chapter 2 of that study.

CHART 5–11. Deliveries, New Commitments, and Total Commitments of Direct Placements, Quarterly, 1951–61

Index (1953 average = 100)

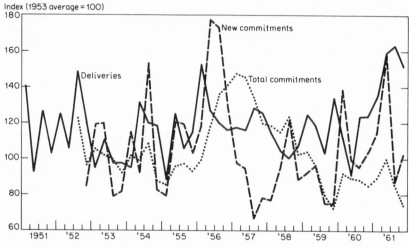

SOURCE: Table 5–8.

$X_4 =$ the mean of the log of times proforma interest was earned, for each borrower; $X_5 =$ the mean of the lien position of each issue; $X_6 =$ the mean of the industrial classification of each issuer; $X_8 =$ the mean of the log of the size of each issue; $X_{12} =$ the mean of the log of the average earnings of each borrower, before interest and taxes; $X_{13} =$ the mean of the log of the maturity of each issue; $X_{15} =$ the mean of the log of the ratio of total long-term debt to total capital of each borrower; $X_{16} =$ the standard deviation of X_8 above; $X_{17} =$ the standard deviation of X_{13}, above.[33]

The last two variables were included in order to try to detect any variation in the dependent variable due solely to an unusually large issue or an unusually long maturity. The individual probabilities, as explained above, were raised to the power represented by the maturity of the issue in question and then weighted by the amount of that issue. This procedure meant that the weighted average probability for any given quarter could be materially affected by a large issue with a long maturity—if the sample in that quarter happened to be small.

[33] The values used for the above variables (X_2 through X_{17}) are given in Tables B-6 through B-13 of the study of yields on direct placements. X_5 and X_6 were coded.

The results given by the foregoing regressions were not really satisfactory and the volume of deliveries showed no significance in either of them. The R for industrials was .699 and only two variables showed significance: X_4 and X_{15}. The results for utilities were even less satisfactory than those for industrials: R was .511 and no variable was significant when all were run simultaneously—although average term (X_3) and coverage (X_4) were on the border of being so.

Very high R's had not really been expected primarily because the dependent variable, a subjective probability, was subject to substantial errors of measurement. On the other hand, the delivery data did not really respond to the hypothesis primarily because, as indicated above, delivery can and often does occur with a substantial lag after commitment date. And this lag itself will tend to vary over time depending on expectations on the future course of interest rates. This variability of the lag between commitment and delivery meant that a simple adjustment, such as lagging the deliveries series some fixed interval, would probably not be satisfactory.

A second set of regressions was then run with the "total commitments" series substituted for the deliveries series. This series was lagged two quarters, e.g., the volume of commitments at the end of the third quarter of 1953 was presumed to exert its effect on yields during the first quarter of 1954, and so forth.[34] A two-quarter lag produced a somewhat better fit than a one-quarter lag or no lag at all. This can be rationalized, readily enough, on the grounds that it simply takes time for lenders to decide whether an increase in loan applications is merely random and temporary or is likely to be sustained.[35]

---

[34] These regressions were run for the period 1953–61 instead of for the period 1951–61 because, as indicated above, the commitments series begins in 1952.

When the regressions were run with no lag, R was .810 for industrials and .765 for utilities. The coefficient on the volume of financing was $-.0976$ $(t = -4.11)$ for industrials and $-.0861$ $(t = -3.04)$ for utilities.

[35] The outstanding commitments series began in September of 1952 and, for this reason, six observations of the original forty-four (four in 1951 and two in 1952) had to be eliminated. Two additional observations on the dependent variable had to be eliminated because of the two-quarter lag.

This left thirty-six observations on the dependent variable, i.e., the thirty-six weighted average P^n's, beginning in the first quarter of 1953. These thirty-six were regressed, step-wise and separately for industrials and utilities, on the eleven quarterly averages listed above.

This process separated the significant from the nonsignificant independent variables and provided estimates of the coefficients for those that had shown

TABLE 5-9. *Industrial Direct Placements, Regression of Compound Probabilities on Total Outstanding Commitments and Various Quality Variables, Significant Coefficients and Standard Errors*

Variables		b_i	σ_{bi}	t
X_1	Volume of financing	−.1261	.0216	−5.84
X_2	Total capital	+.0414	.0189	+2.19
X_4	Times charges earned	+.1239	.0299	+4.14
X_8	Size of issue	−.0349	.0265	−1.32
X_{15}	Dollars of long-term debt per dollar of total capital	+.1433	.0584	+2.45
X_{16}	Standard deviation of size of issue	−.0605	.0292	−2.07

NOTE: $R = .854$; $R^2 = .730$; $F = 13.04$; $P_F = .01$; standard error of estimate = .0257; degrees of freedom = 29.

The substitution of the commitment series for the deliveries series improved the results markedly. Table 5-9 summarizes results for industrials and Table 5-10, for utilities. The R for industrials has risen to .854 (from .699) and five variables, including the volume of commitments, now show significance at .025 (one tail) or better. The volume of commitments shows itself to be by far the strongest variable.

TABLE 5-10. *Public Utility Direct Placements, Regression of Compound Probabilities on Total Outstanding Commitments and Various Quality Variables, Significant Coefficients and Standard Errors*

Variables		b_i	σ_{bi}	t
X_1	Volume of financing	−.1256	.0258	−4.87
X_3	Average term	+.0735	.0366	+2.01
X_4	Times charges earned	+.1447	.0503	+2.88
X_5	Type of Security	−.0738	.0375	−1.97
X_8	Size of issue	−.0244	.0156	−1.56
X_{16}	Standard deviation of size of issue	+.0746	.0244	+3.06
X_{17}	Standard deviation of maturity	+.2010	.0679	+2.96

NOTE: $R = .805$; $R^2 = .648$; $F = 7.36$; $P_F < .01$; standard error of estimate = .0366; degrees of freedom = 28.

significance (see Tables 5-9 and 5-10). No regressions could be run on the finance company P^m's because satisfactory averages of the independent variables could not be constructed.

Similar results were obtained for utilities: R rose from .511 to .805 and six variables showed significance at .025 or better. One variable, X_8, showed significance at approximately .05. Again, as for industrials, the volume of commitments showed itself to be the strongest variable.

Computed Probabilities

In order to eliminate the effect on the P^n's of fluctuations in the volume of total commitments, P^n's were computed, for both industrials and utilities, with the volume of financing held constant at its mean value for the period. The quality variables that had shown significance were, of course, allowed to vary. The computed P^n's are given in Table 5-11 and in Charts 5-4 and 5-5 where they are plotted against the actual P^n's. These computed P^n's respond to the question: In the subjective view of lenders, was the quality of new direct placements, on the average, improving or worsening after allowance was made for the effect of the volume of financing? An answer to this question is provided by Charts 5-4 and 5-5. In both series, the "sag" in the middle has totally disappeared. Both series now show a slight downward trend until 1959, then a drop followed by a recovery beginning in the last quarter of 1960. In the computed series, of course, only the quality variables are allowed to vary and therefore the movement of the two series reflects variation in them alone (plus, of course, a random component).[36]

[36] The adjusted series in Chart 5-6 for finance company issues was obtained by using the regression coefficient on volume of financing for industrials. This regression coefficient was virtually identical to the regression coefficient on volume of financing for utilities (see Tables 5-9 and 5-10). It seemed reasonable, therefore, to suppose that, had time series regressions been run for finance company issues, the regression coefficient on volume of financing would not have differed materially from the other two. In any case, the adjustment affects the finance company series in much the same way as it affects the other two series: The systematic downward movement between 1955 and 1957 has disappeared. The series now shows a slight upward trend from 1951–57, and a downward trend thereafter.

The computed probabilities are, in effect, weighted indexes of characteristics adjusted for the volume of lower-grade financing, the weights given to the characteristics being held constant through the period. The procedure assumes, of course, that expectations about future business conditions did not change systematically in one direction or the other during the period. Experiments with adjusting the *actual* P^n's for the effect of the volume of financing suggest that the foregoing assumption is reasonable.

TABLE 5-11. *Direct Placements, Weighted Average Compound Probabilities, Quarterly*

Year and Quarter	Industrials	Utilities	Finance Companies
1951			
1	.800	.743	.775
2	.809	.858	.833
3	.775	.793	.761
4	.755	.815	.784
1952			
1	.795	.778	.781
2	.803	.755	.875
3	.775	.802	.742
4	.807	.859	.889
1953			
1	.777	.788	.809
2	.762	.757	.703
3	.802	.767	.775
4	.787	.758	.781
1954			
1	.757	.778	.821
2	.788	.749	.840
3	.757	.816	.825
4	.773	.811	.782
1955			
1	.787	.813	.882
2	.775	.748	.871
3	.783	.772	.830
4	.747	.761	.808
1956			
1	.752	.747	.833
2	.772	.780	.812
3	.787	.712	—
4	.745	.753	.810

Adjustment for Differential Call Deferment

The probabilities assigned by lenders to new direct placements were really somewhat higher than those given in Tables 5-2, 5-3, 5-4,

TABLE 5-11 (concluded)

Year and Quarter	Industrials	Utilities	Finance Companies
1957			
1	.764	.741	.859
2	.767	.726	.847
3	.751	.772	.832
4	.754	.767	.786
1958			
1	.763	.762	.873
2	.770	.786	.826
3	.753	.773	.760
4	.777	.746	.780
1959			
1	.791	.761	.773
2	.756	.849	.786
3	.753	.721	.808
4	.729	.687	.747
1960			
1	.731	.755	.741
2	.715	.701	.755
3	.745	.741	.775
4	.703	.682	.759
1961			
1	.730	.768	.736
2	.732	.765	.740
3	.742	.740	.794
4	.785	.780	.703
Average			
1951–1961	.7655	.7667	.7977
1951–53	.7872	.7894	.7923
1959–61	.7427	.7458	.7597

NOTE: Probabilities were computed on the assumption that total outstanding commitments remained unchanged during the period.

5-5, and 5-11 above, because the probabilities given in those tables do not take account of differential call deferment between governments and direct placements. As indicated above, governments are generally protected from call throughout their lives. The direct placements under study here were protected only for varying relatively small portions of their lives. Table 5-12 indicates that industrial direct placements had an average maturity, during the period, of about 16 years. In the first part of the period (1951–55) they were protected against call, on the average, for 4.9 years and in the last part of the period (1956–61) for 7.5 years. But the sixteen-year governments with which they are compared were, in effect, protected against call through virtually

TABLE 5-12. *Direct Placements, Calculation of Adjustment for Differential Call Deferment Between Direct Placements and Long-Term Governments*

	1951–55	1956–61
Industrials and Finance		
Average maturity (years)	16.1	16.4
Average period of noncallability (years)	4.9	7.5
Difference	11.2	8.9
Adjustment[a] (basis points)	5-14	20[b]
Utilities		
Average maturity (years)	25.2	24.7
Average period of noncallability (years)	1.4	5.2
Difference	23.8	19.5
Adjustment (basis points)	11-23	41[b]

SOURCE: Avery Cohan, *Yields on Corporate Debt Directly Placed*, New York, NBER, 1967, Tables B-8 and B-12.

[a]See pp. 319-320.

[b]For eight quarters only. See pp. 319-320.

their whole lives. Some attempt must be made therefore to adjust for this difference—especially because, instinct suggests, its impact on the compounded probabilities may be large.

The question we are asking here, therefore, is: If direct placements had been protected against call for their whole lives, instead of for some shorter period, what would the effect have been on the probabilities, simple and compound, given above.

Protection against call is desired by lenders, especially when interest rates are high, to prevent refunding should interest rates decline. Most lenders are willing to pay a price, in terms of lower yield, in order to obtain such protection. Presumably, the longer the period of call deferment the higher the price they are disposed to pay, that is, the larger the amount of yield they are willing to sacrifice. Presumably also, if direct placements had been protected against call for their whole lives, the yields on them would have been lower and the probabilities derived above, higher. We adjust the simple probabilities first.

In his recent article, Pye has suggested that, holding quality constant, "for a typical long-term bond with typical call features a discount of about four basis points is produced by a five-year deferment (of call) . . . when the one year interest rate is in the lower range ($2\frac{3}{4}$–4 per cent) of those observed form 1959 through 1965. . . . When the interest rate is in the upper range . . . (4–5$\frac{1}{4}$ per cent), a discount of about thirteen basis points is produced."[37] Pye also suggests that when interest rates are in the lower range, "discounts may be in the area of forty basis points" for a thirty-year bond. When interest rates are in the higher range, the discount for such a bond might be as much as seventy basis points. Pye made his estimates by comparing high-grade corporates with varying deferments—maturity and quality rating held constant. These estimates purport to represent the price of pure call deferment and we should be able to use them, therefore, to obtain rough estimates of that part of the yield differential, between direct placements and governments, that is due to differential call deferment.[38]

During the period under study the rate on one-year governments was above $3\frac{3}{8}$ per cent during the last three quarters of 1957, the last three quarters of 1959, and the first two quarters of 1960, or for eight quarters in all.

Using this fact, the figures given in Table 5-12, and Pye's Table III,[39] we can make rough adjustments in basis points for those quarters during which the one-year government rate was above $3\frac{3}{8}$ per cent and those quarters during which it was at or below $3\frac{3}{8}$ per cent, separately for industrials, utilities, and finance company issues. In making the adjustment, we have assumed that the difference between maturity and period of noncallability for both periods (see Table 5-12) was 10 years for industrials and 20 years for utilities. This assumption has been made in order to avoid the hazards of interpolating between Pye's estimates, which are for successive five-year periods in the relevant range.

The adjustments are given in Table 5-12.[40] They were obtained for

[37] Gordon Pye, *op. cit.*
[38] We assume, in what follows, that governments are noncallable.
[39] *Op. cit.,* p. 630.
[40] There are two adjustments under the column 1951–55. One is for those quarters during which the one-year rate was in the neighborhood of $2\frac{1}{8}$ per

industrials and finance company issues, by first obtaining the discount for noncallability for fifteen-year bonds from Pye's Table III for each period—namely, 8 to 18, and 29 basis points, respectively. These figures represent estimates of the prices, in basis points, lenders were disposed to pay for fifteen years of protection against call when one-year interest rates were 2⅛ per cent (8 basis points), 3⅜ per cent (18 basis points), and 4⅝ per cent (29 basis points). But industrials during the period had 5 to 7 years of call protection worth, depending on the level of the one-year rate, respectively, about 3, 4, and 9 basis points. The latter figures were therefore substracted from the former to obtain the adjustments for industrials for differential call of about ten years, namely, 5, 14, and 20 basis points, for the three levels of the one-year rate. Finally, the adjustment in basis points was used to adjust the probabilities both simple and compound. The adjustment for utilities was obtained by analogous procedure.

How do the adjustments given in Table 5-12 affect the simple probabilities given in Tables 5-2, 5-3, and 5-4? The individual probabilities are affected by one-tenth or one-fifth of one per cent or, for practical purposes, not at all, and the three averages by about one-tenth of one per cent, as shown in the table below.

	Unadjusted	Adjusted
Industrials	.9858	.9868
Utilities	.9885	.9904
Finance companies	.9841	.9855

The Compound Probabilities

The quarterly compound probabilities adjusted for the volume effect (Table 5-11) were adjusted as follows for differential call deferment: first, weighted average maturities were obtained for each quarter, separately for industrials, utilities, and the issues of finance companies; second, the maturities so obtained were used to reduce the compound probabilities (adjusted for the effect of the volume of financing) to simple form. For example, the compound probability given in Table

cent and the other when it was in the neighborhood of 3⅜ per cent. There is only one adjustment under the column 1956–61, because the one-year rate did not rise above 4⅝ per cent in any quarter during the period 1956–61.

5-11 for industrials for the first quarter of 1951 was .800. The weighted average maturity of all industrial direct placements in the first quarter of 1951 was 21 years.[41] The twenty-first root of .800 was then extracted and found to be approximately .9894. To this simple probability was added .001 to adjust for call. The resulting figure, .9904, was then raised to the twenty-first power, yielding a compound probability of about .817. The figures given in columns 2, 4, and 6 of Table 5-13 are the result of this process, i.e., they have been adjusted both for the effect of the volume of financing and for differential call deferment. Charts 5-12, 5-13, and 5-14 compare the compound probabilities adjusted for both effects with those adjusted for the effect of the volume of financing alone.

The compound probabilities adjusted for call and the volume of financing are all perceptibly higher than those adjusted for the volume of financing alone. The average probabilities over the 44 quarters are as follows:

	Adjusted for Volume Only	Adjusted for Both Volume and Call
Industrials	.7655	.7831
Utilities	.7667	.7954
Finance Companies	.7977	.8111

The probabilities continue to show some slight deterioration from the beginning of the period. The average compound probability for the direct placements bought in 1951–53 was .807 for industrials, .809 for utilities, and .803 for finance company issues. For 1959–61, these probabilities were, respectively, .763, .781, and .778, or a deterioration of 5.5 per cent for industrials, 3.5 per cent for utilities, and 3.1 per cent for finance company issues. Atkinson's findings (especially his chart describing the average rating class for the Bureau's sample of direct placements) conforms, in general, to the findings here. Atkinson qualifies his findings as follows: ". . . apart from the fact that the two beginning years (1951–52) were relatively high in quality and the last two years of low quality, it could be said that there was no change based on this measure. . . ."[42]

---

[41] Weights were the dollar amount of each issue.
[42] Atkinson, *op. cit.*, pp. 30–31.

TABLE 5-13. *Direct Placements, Weighted Average Simple Probabilities Adjusted for Differential Call Deferment and Weighted Average Compound Probabilities Adjusted for Differential Call Deferment and for the Volume of Financing, Quarterly, 1951–61*

Year and Quarter	Industrial		Utilities		Finance Companies	
	P (1)	P^a (2)	P (3)	P^n (4)	P (5)	P^n (6)
1951						
1	.989	.809	.988	.762	.964	.778
2	.989	.817	.994	.879	.987	.839
3	.982	.781	.990	.812	.966	.764
4	.989	.765	.993	.838	.984	.790
1952						
1	.988	.803	.990	.798	.976	.785
2	.991	.813	.984	.768	.993	.884
3	.989	.784	.992	.823	.985	.750
4	.989	.815	.994	.880	.987	.893
1953						
1	.985	.784	.988	.804	.986	.815
2	.986	.769	.990	.778	.977	.708
3	.985	.808	.987	.783	.981	.780
4	.985	.793	.988	.777	.984	.787
1954						
1	.988	.766	.987	.793	.987	.827
2	.983	.794	.990	.770	.988	.846
3	.986	.764	.990	.833	.990	.833
4	.986	.780	.991	.831	.983	.788
1955						
1	.987	.794	.991	.831	.992	.889
2	.987	.783	.988	.766	.985	.875
3	.986	.790	.990	.792	.988	.836
4	.978	.752	.985	.775	.987	.815
1956						
1	.986	.768	.986	.779	.987	.845
2	.988	.789	.989	.815	.987	.825
3	.986	.801	.986	.749	–	–
4	.985	.760	.984	.781	.983	.820

(continued)

Table 5-13 (concluded)

Year and Quarter	Industrial		Utilities		Finance Companies	
	P (1)	P^n (2)	P (3)	P^n (4)	P (5)	P^n (6)
1957						
1	.986	.779	.987	.813	.989	.871
2	.987	.800	.988	.810	.987	.870
3	.986	.782	.990	.854	.988	.858
4	.988	.790	.990	.852	.987	.815
1958						
1	.985	.770	.988	.780	.986	.877
2	.986	.777	.988	.802	.984	.831
3	.982	.765	.988	.807	.985	.774
4	.988	.793	.989	.788	.981	.790
1959						
1	.986	.804	.990	.804	.986	.788
2	.986	.771	.992	.884	.982	.796
3	.985	.783	.984	.785	.985	.831
4	.982	.755	.987	.759	.985	.776
1960						
1	.983	.758	.987	.825	.984	.769
2	.982	.743	.985	.773	.983	.780
3	.985	.760	.988	.778	.983	.787
4	.982	.717	.986	.722	.979	.769
1961						
1	.979	.741	.990	.811	.977	.746
2	.984	.746	.988	.800	.979	.751
3	.984	.756	.988	.778	.988	.810
4	.987	.799	.991	.825	.983	.717
Average						
1951–61	.9856	.7798	.9886	.8018	.9839[a]	.8088[a]
1951–53	.9872	.7951	.9899	.8087	.9808	.7978
1959–61	.9838	.7611	.9880	.7962	.9827	.7767

NOTE: 1951–53 – Utilities computations based on N = 17 and N = 19. 1951–61 – Utilities average rounds the same for N = 17 or N = 19.

[a]Based on 43 quarters.

CHART 5–12. Industrials, Weighted Average Probabilities to Maturity, Adjusted for Volume Effect and for Effect of Both Volume and Differential Call Deferment, Quarterly, 1951–61

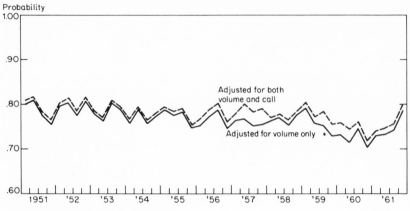

SOURCE: Tables 5–11 and 5–13.

CHART 5–13. Public Utilities, Weighted Average Probabilities to Maturity, Adjusted for Volume Effect and for Effect of Both Volume and Differential Call Deferment, Quarterly, 1951–61

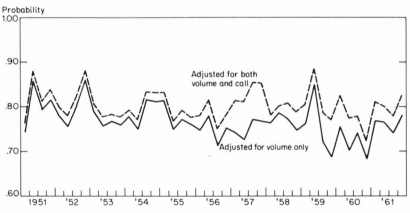

SOURCE: Tables 5–11 and 5–13.

EVALUATION OF RESULTS

Subject to certain qualifications, assumed to be minor, the results presented above purport to represent the subjective probability assigned by lenders to the composite (aggregate) new direct placement

CHART 5–14. Finance Companies, Weighted Average Probabilities to Maturity, Adjusted for Volume Effect and for Effect of Both Volume and Differential Call Deferment, Quarterly, 1951–61

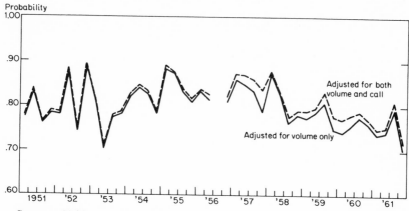

SOURCE: Tables 5–11 and 5–13.

bought by them in each of the 44 quarters from January 1, 1951, to December 31, 1961, i.e., the subjective probability that all payments of interest and principal would be made in full and on time.

In principle, the results should be evaluated by trying, a priori, to decide (a) whether all significant extraneous influences have been removed and (b) whether the assumptions on which the model rests are reasonably accurate. If these two prerequisites were satisfied, we would be able to conclude that the results must, in fact, represent a reasonably accurate image of the subjective views of lenders of the quality of the issues they bought during the period, at the time they bought those issues.

But, unhappily, we cannot be sure, a priori, that the prerequisites are in fact satisfied and therefore a second test has been applied: Are the probabilities, both simple and compound, reasonably close to recent realized experience? We would expect "recent realized experience" to be virtually decisive in estimating current probabilities. We discuss the simple probabilities first.

Simple Probabilities

Hickman's data, as adjusted by Fraine, make it possible to estimate ex post simple "probabilities" for various classes of issues extinguished during the period of 1900–43, i.e., the respective probabilities that lenders would have assigned to each issue in each risk class had they had perfect foresight.[43] These probabilities are given, separately for industrials and utilities, by agency rating in Table 5-14. These probabilities were obtained by dividing the realized yield by the promised

TABLE 5-14. *Estimated Simple Probabilities for Industrials and Utilities by Agency Rating, 1900–43*

Agency Rating	P^a (1)	Percentage^b (2)	Column 1 x Column 2 (3)
		INDUSTRIALS	
Aaa	1.000	–	–
Aa	1.000	.042	.0420
A	.994	.076	.0755
Baa	.991	.376	.3726
Ba	.975	.505	.4924
B and below	.980	–	–
Total		1.000	.9825
		UTILITIES	
Aaa	.999	.008	.0080
Aa	1.000	.030	.0300
A	.999	.272	.2717
Baa	.992	.222	.2202
Ba	.976	.468	.4568
B and below	.954	–	–
Total		1.000	.9867

^{a}Computed from data given in H.G. Fraine, *Valuation of Securities Holdings of Life Insurance Companies*, Homewood, Illinois, 1962, Table 2-8.

^{b}From Avery Cohan, *Yields on Corporate Debt Directly Placed*, New York, NBER, 1967, Table C-3.

yield for each agency rating.[44] Each such probability, as explained above, is the average probability that any single payment will be made in full and on time and is comparable to the simple probabilities presented in Tables 5-2, 5-3, and 5-4, above.

[43] Perfect foresight with respect to each risk class but not, of course, with respect to each issue in each class.

[44] These yields are weighted average yields. See Hickman, *Corporate Bond Quality, op. cit.,* pp. 54ff.

What is the rationale of this procedure, i.e., of obtaining an ex post probability by dividing the actual realized yield by the promised yield? The procedure simply assumes that the yield actually realized should have been used as the discount rate at issue. If it had been, the present value equation would have been:

$$1 = \frac{rP}{(1 + g')} + \cdots + \frac{(1 + r)P^n}{(1 + g')^n},$$

where r is the promised yield on the direct placement and g' is the realized yield on it. Solving this equation for P gives:

$$P = \frac{(1 + g')}{(1 + r)},$$

or the realized yield divided by the promised yield. Table 5-14 shows that the realized probabilities decline more or less systematically as quality declines.

We know from the National Bureau's study of direct placements that about 72 per cent of utility direct placements would probably have been rated Baa or below by the agencies.[45] Moreover, about 50 per cent of industrials and about 48 per cent of utilities would have probably been rated Ba or below. If we take weighted averages of the probabilities in the first column of Table 5-14, using as weights the percentages given in Table C-3 of the National Bureau's yield study, we obtain a weighted average of .9825 for industrials and of .9867 for utilities.[46] The details of the calculation are given in column 3 of Table 5-14. Tables 5-1, 5-2, and 5-3 tell us that the average simple probability for 1951–61 for industrials was .9858, for utilities, .9885, and for finance companies, .9841. In other words, during the period 1951–61, lenders assigned to new direct placements simple probabilities that were slightly higher than prewar experience suggested should have been assigned to them. Given the favorable experience since World War II, this is, of course, what we would have expected a priori.[47]

---

[45] Cohan, *op. cit.,* pp. 158–161.

[46] In other words, the realized probabilities by quality class, out of the Hickman sample, are weighted by the percentage of each quality class in the direct placement sample. The procedure answers the question: If, during the period 1951–61 lenders had assigned, to each new direct placement, the probability indicated by experience to be "appropriate" to it, given its quality, what would the average probability over all direct placements bought in the years 1951–61 have been?

[47] See Atkinson, *op cit.,* pp. 42ff.

Compound Probabilities

How do the compound probabilities compare with the compound probabilities implicit in the Hickman-Fraine results? In order to answer this question, weighted average maturities were computed, separately for industrials and utilities, for the Hickman sample.[48]

These averages were 16 years for industrials and 24 years for utilities. When the simple realized probabilities, given above, derived from the Hickman results are raised to the appropriate power, the results are approximately: industrials, .754, and utilities, .721; as compared with .783 for industrials, .795 for utilities, and .811 for finance company issues for the period 1951–61.[49]

The Hickman-Fraine data bear, of course, on the period 1900 – 43. What about the period since then? Atkinson has shown that between 1943 and 1965, default rates were very low—about one-tenth of one per cent on the average for the 22 years.[50] This is very much less than the default rate experienced in any of the four decades between 1900 – 39.[51] This highly favorable experience, of course, implies much higher probabilities than lenders fixed during the period, 1951–61. But in interpreting the behavior of lenders in this regard, we should bear in mind that they have doubtless weighed heavily the fact that borrowers have experienced little, if any, real adversity since World War II, i.e., borrowers have not had to weather a serious recession. In addition, of course, the data included in this study do not go beyond 1961. If data for subsequent years were available they probably would show that, with quality held constant, the probabilities have trended further upward since 1961.

In sum, we have now found that both the simple and the compound ex ante probabilities for the period 1951–61 are perceptibly higher than the realized probabilities implicit in the Hickman-Fraine results covering the years 1900–43, for approximately comparable issues. This undoubtedly reflects the highly favorable experience of lenders since World War II.

---

[48] Hickman, *Statistical Measures, op. cit.,* Table 94.

[49] The figures used for 1951–1961 are from Table 5-13, i.e., they are adjusted for the effect of both volume and differential call deferment.

[50] That is, of the amount in good standing at the beginning of each year. Atkinson, *op. cit.,* p. 43.

[51] Atkinson gives the following rates: 1900 – 09 — 0.9 per cent; 1910 – 19 — 2.0 per cent; 1920 – 29 — 1.0 per cent; 1930 – 39 — 3.2 per cent.

But now, do the results presented above represent also a reasonably accurate image of the objective probabilities—as distinct from what lenders, ex ante, thought the objective probabilities were? This is equivalent to asking whether the subjective probabilities are likely to turn out to be good predictors of the eventual outcome.

The short answer to this question is, of course, that the subjective probabilities do not purport to be predictors: in assigning probabilities to issues being bought currently, lenders can obviously be wrong, one way or the other, about the probabilities they assign to the various "states of nature."[52] And if they are wrong, realized results will be different from expected results.

Nevertheless, we may learn something about the relationship between the subjective and the objective probabilities by comparing the subjective ex ante probabilities implicit in the Hickman-Fraine data with the estimated "realized probabilities" given above. In other words, the comparison is between the ex ante probabilities and the realized probabilities both derived from the Hickman-Fraine data. This comparison is a precarious undertaking, at best, primarily because Hickman calculated market ratings by using yields on the best corporate bonds (which, in fact, are not riskless) rather than yields on governments.[53] Moreover, the great bulk of the bonds in his sample were callable in less than one year. The procedure here is based on the assumption that these two effects are approximately offsetting. Thus, if the return on the best corporates were 1.04 and the promised return on a callable risky security were 1.06, Hickman's market rating would be the difference between the two, multiplied by 100. A corresponding probability would be .9811 ($1.04/1.06 = .9811$). Now, if each of the two returns is reduced by 25 basis points, in order to reduce the numerator to approximately the level of a government and in order to adjust the denominator for differential call deferment, the result is the same to the fourth decimal place ($1.0375/1.0575 = .9811$). In calculating the Hickman-Fraine ex ante probabilities, the midpoints of their class intervals have been used.[54]

For each of their market-rating classes the following steps were taken: first, a comparable riskless return was obtained by subtracting the midpoint of the market rating from the promised return, e.g., for

[52] It seems highly likely that lenders would be able to assign probabilities, with a high degree of accuracy, to the risk of default given the state of nature.

[53] Hickman, *Corporate Bond Quality, op. cit.,* p. 282.

[54] See Fraine, *op. cit.,* Table 2-9, pp. 50–51.

market-rating class 1, industrials, $1.0330 - .0025 = 1.0305$.[55] An estimated ex ante probability was then obtained by dividing this figure by the promised return, $1.0305/1.0330 = .998$ (see Table 5-15).

Unhappily, we cannot obtain the corresponding compound ex ante probabilities for the Hickman sample because data on maturity by market rating are not available. But the results suggest that the differences between the ex ante simple probabilities and the eventual out-

TABLE 5-15. *Hickman–Fraine Sample of Corporate Bonds, Estimated Ex Ante and Realized Probabilities, 1900–43*

Market Rating (basis points) (1)	Ex Ante Probability P (2)	Realized Probability P (3)
	INDUSTRIALS	
Under 50 (25)[a]	.998	1.000
50–100 (75)	.993	.999
100–150 (125)	.988	.995
150–200 (175)	.983	.989
200–250 (225)	.979	.991
250 and over (275)	.974	.987
	UTILITIES	
Under 50 (25)[a]	.998	.999
50–100 (50)	.993	.997
100–150 (125)	.988	.995
150–200 (175)	.983	.989
200–250 (225)	.970	.992
250 and over (275)	.975	.981

[a]Midpoint of class interval.

come for the Hickman sample were substantial—especially in the lower grades.[56]

[55] Subtracting the midpoint produces an estimated yield on a best bond of the same maturity. See Hickman, *Corporate Bond Quality, op. cit.,* pp. 282–283.

[56] For example, for industrials, if we assume that the issues in the poorest class had an average maturity of 10 years, the compound ex ante and "realized" probabilities would be respectively $(.974)^{10}$ and $(.987)^{10}$ or .768 and .877. This would mean that although 23.2 per cent of the issues in that class were expected to default, only 12.3 per cent actually did so. At fifteen years the corresponding figures would be .673 (ex ante) and .821 (realized).

Fraine does, however, give weighted average promised and realized yields over all utilities and all industrials separately. And we are able, with his figures, to compute a weighted average market rating. This is done in Tables 5-16 and 5-17. With these three figures, namely, weighted average promised and realized yields and weighted average

TABLE 5-16. *Hickman–Fraine Sample of Corporate Bonds, Derivation of Mean Market Rating for Utilities, 1900–43*

Market Rating (basis points) (1)	Dollar Amount (billions) (2)	Column 1 x Column 2 (3)
25	5.7	142.5
75	7.6	570.0
125	4.8	600.0
175	2.9	507.5
225	1.1	247.5
275	0.8	220.0
Total	22.9	2287.5

NOTE: $\frac{2287.5}{22.9}$ = 100 basis points, mean market rating.

SOURCE: Column 1–Table 5-15, column 1; column 2–H.G. Fraine, *Valuation of Securities Holdings of Life Insurance Companies,* Homewood, Illinois, 1962, Table 2-9.

TABLE 5-17. *Hickman–Fraine Sample of Corporate Bonds, Derivation of Mean Market Rating for Industrials, 1900–43*

Market Rating (basis points) (1)	Dollar Amount (billions) (2)	Column 1 x Column 2 (3)
25	1.2	30.0
75	3.1	232.5
125	3.0	375.0
175	2.7	472.5
225	1.4	315.0
275	1.1	302.5
Total	12.5	1727.5

NOTE: $\frac{1727.5}{12.5}$ = 138 basis points, mean market rating.

SOURCE: Same as Table 5-16.

market ratings (and using the weighted average maturities computed above for the Hickman-Fraine sample), we are able to compute ex ante and realized compound probabilities for all utilities separately and for all industrials separately. These are given in Table 5-18. In interpreting these figures we should bear in mind that lower grade bonds obviously did much less well than high grade bonds. We may guess that for bonds graded Baa and below the ex ante probabilities were 10–15 per cent below "realized" probabilities. Perhaps this will also turn out to be the case for the direct placements bought during the years 1951–61.

TABLE 5-18. *Hickman–Fraine Sample of Corporate Bonds, Comparison of Estimated Simple and Compound Ex Ante Probabilities With "Realized" Simple and Compound Probabilities, 1900–43*

Probabilities	Industrials	Utilities
Simple		
Ex ante	.990	.990
Realized	.991	.991
Compound		
Ex ante	.787	.811
Realized	.826	.851
Realized as percentage		
of ex ante		
Simple	100.10	100.10
Compound	104.96	104.93

SOURCE: Same as Table 5-16.

In summary:

(1) The simple subjective probabilities found here, covering the period 1951–61, are somewhat higher than the simple "realized probablities" implicit in the Hickman-Fraine results for the period 1900–43. This is true for the simple probabilities both unadjusted and adjusted for differential call deferment.

(2) When the simple probabilities, adjusted for differential call deferment are compounded, they (the compound probabilities) are found to be considerably higher than the compound "realized probabilities" implicit in the Hickman-Fraine results.

(3) Both (1) and (2) are what one would expect given the favor-

able climate and experience that have characterized the period since 1943.

(4) When the Hickman-Fraine "realized" simple probabilities are compared with rough estimates of the ex ante simple probabilities implicit in their data, the latter are found to be smaller than the former— and the difference increases as quality worsens. This result may mean that lenders anticipated economic conditions substantially worse than those that in fact occurred.[57] But it may mean that during the period 1900 – 43 lenders were strongly risk averse and therefore insisted on extra risk premium, especially on lower grade issues. In trying to decide whether and to what extent this factor has influenced the results for direct placements for the period 1951–61, we should bear in mind that during the period 1900 – 43 the buyers of corporate bonds were, to a large extent, a multitude of individual investors who were, for the most part, unable to diversify. The buyers of direct placements, on the other hand, are sixty or more large financial institutions who, for the most part, understand diversification and practice it.[58]

(5) Compound ex ante probabilities could not be computed, by market rating, for the Hickman-Fraine sample because data on maturity by market rating were not available. Compound probabilities were computed, however, for all industrials together and all utilities together. They were found to be about 5 per cent below the "realized" probabilities implicit in the Hickman-Fraine results.

CONCLUSION

As indicated at the outset, this study has been exploratory. It has attempted to ascertain whether the subjective probabilities present (if only subconsciously) in the mind of lenders when they fix yields on new issues can be derived from the observed ratios between ex ante returns on government bonds, presumed riskless, and ex ante returns on direct placements of the same maturity. Two major adjustments of the observed ratios have been made, one for the effect of the volume of financing and the other for the effect of differential call deferment.

[57] In assessing this possibility we should bear in mind that $27,151 million of the bonds in Hickman's sample were extinguished before 1931. This was just slightly less than the volume of bonds still outstanding on January 1, 1931— $28,555 million.

[58] They are presumed here to be "risk averse" only because of the penalties imposed by the NALIC on purchases of low grade securities. See above, p. 304.

On the whole, the results seem reasonable. Perhaps, therefore, the conclusion is warranted that the techniques used merit further consideration—especially for the purpose of assessing the ex ante quality of new issues—and especially if more refined adjustments could be made for call deferments and if an adjustment could be included for differential transactions costs.

6

The Cyclical Behavior
of the Term Structure
# of Interest Rates
Reuben A. Kessel

EXPLANATIONS OF THE TERM STRUCTURE
OF INTEREST RATES

It is the thesis of this investigation that the term structure of interest rates can be explained better by a combination of the expectations and liquidity preference hypotheses than by either hypothesis alone. Alternatively, these two hypotheses can be viewed as complementary ex-

NOTE: This essay was first published as Chapters 1 and 4 of NBER Occasional Paper 91, 1965.

The members of the staff reading committee for this manuscript were Gary Becker, Jacob Mincer, and Hyman Minsky. All were very helpful.

Earlier versions of this paper were presented at the money workshop of the University of Chicago, faculty seminars at the Universities of Pennsylvania and California at Los Angeles, and the Econometrica Society meetings in Pittsburgh in 1962. I have greatly benefited from the comments of colleagues at both the National Bureau and the University of Chicago.

David Meiselman, Paul Cootner, and John M. Culbertson provided invaluable criticism in their roles as discussants at the Econometrica Society meetings in 1962.

I wish to thank Messrs. Melvin G. de Chazeau, George B. Roberts, and Paul A. Samuelson of the National Bureau Board of Directors' reading committee.

Joan Tron edited the manuscript, and H. Irving Forman drew the charts. I am grateful to Judy Tompkins for hand computing and data collection, and to Richard Kilgore for machine computing.

A grant of electronic computer time to the National Bureau of Economic Research by the International Business Machines Corporation was utilized for computing the regressions in this study.

planations of the same phenomenon—the term structure of interest rates. The evidence to be examined in support of this view falls into two classes. One is the findings of previous investigators; the works of Macaulay, Culbertson, Meiselman, Walker, and Hickman contain evidence relevant for evaluating the substantive merits of this thesis. The other class consists of evidence gathered as part of the present investigation.

What Is the Expectations Hypothesis

The expectations hypothesis has been enunciated by Fisher, Keynes, Hicks, Lutz, and others.[1] It has had widespread appeal for theoretical economists primarily as a result of its consistency with the way similar phenomena in other markets, particularly futures markets, are explained. In contrast, this hypothesis has been widely rejected by empirically minded economists and practical men of affairs. It was rejected by economists because investigators have been unable to produce evidence of a relationship between the term structure of interest rates and expectations of future short-term rates. (Others have found it difficult to accept the view that long- and short-term securities are perfect substitutes for one another in the market.) Meiselman contends that previous investigators have not devised operational implications of the expectations hypothesis. Moreover, he contends, they have examined propositions which were mistakenly attributed to the expectations hypothesis, and when these propositions were found to be false, they rejected the expectations hypothesis.[2]

Briefly, the expectations hypothesis asserts that a long-term rate constitutes an average (a weighted average in the case of coupon-bearing securities) of expected future short-term rates. It says that forward rates (or marginal rates of interest) constitute unbiased estimates of future spot rates.[3] It is based on the assumption that short-

[1] See Friedrich A. Lutz, "The Structure of Interest Rates," in the American Economic Association, *Readings in the Theory of Income Distribution,* Philadelphia, 1946, p. 499; and Joseph W. Conard, *An Introduction to the Theory of Interest,* University of California, 1959, Part III.

[2] David Meiselman, *The Term Structure of Interest Rates,* Englewood Cliffs, New Jersey, 1962, pp. 10 and 12.

[3] A spot rate is a rate on funds for immediate delivery; it is today's rate for money to be delivered today for a specified period of time. In contrast, a forward rate is today's rate for money to be delivered in the future for a specified period of time. This time period could be anything, a day, a year, or a decade.

and long-term securities, default risks aside, can be usefully viewed as identical in all respects except maturity. It implies that the expected value of the returns derived from holding long- and short-term securities for identical time periods are the same.

The word *future* should be emphasized in discussing the expectations hypothesis, since it concerns the effects of expectations about future short-term rates upon the current term structure of interest rates. To illustrate with a simplified example: assume that two-year securities yield 3 per cent and one-year securities 2 per cent. The forward rate on one-year money one year hence, or the marginal cost of extending a one-year term to maturity for an additional year, is 4 per cent; this is arithmetic, not the expectations hypothesis. The expectations hypothesis, as interpreted by Lutz and Meiselman, but not by Hicks, states that the forward rates are unbiased estimates of future short-term rates. For the preceding example, it implies that the market expects the rate on one-year securities one year hence to be 4 per cent. Four per cent is not only the forward rate—it is the expected one-year rate one year hence; i.e., it is what the market thinks the one-year rate will be one year hence.

Conversely, assume a 2 per cent rate on two-year maturities and a 3 per cent rate on one-year maturities. Then the yield on one-year securities one year hence which will equalize the net yield from holding two one-year securities successively with that of holding one two-year security is 1 per cent. This must follow if one accepts the view that securities are alike in all respects except term to maturity.[4]

Existing Evidence

Macaulay

Macaulay was among the first to produce empirical evidence that related long-term rates to expectations of future short-term rates. Before the founding of the Federal Reserve System, there existed a pronounced and well-known seasonal in the call money rate. The widespread knowledge of the existence of this seasonal implied that time money rates, which are loans from one to six months that are otherwise similar to call money loans, should turn up before the seasonal rise in

[4] These calculations ignore compounding of interest and intermediate payments in the form of coupons.

call money rates. Macaulay found that time money rates did in fact anticipate the seasonal rise in call money rates and concluded that this constituted ". . . evidence of definite and relatively successful forecasting."[5] Macaulay was unable to uncover additional evidence of successful forecasting. He warned against concluding that forecasting was not attempted. Macaulay's contention was that evidence of successful forecasting is rare because successful forecasting is also rare.[6]

Hickman

W. Braddock Hickman, in a preliminary, unpublished, but nevertheless widely cited and read, NBER manuscript prepared in 1942, reports the results of his tests of the expectations hypothesis.[7] Like Macaulay, he sought evidence of successful forecasting; unlike Macaulay, he failed to find it. He compared observed or actual yield curves with those predicted one year or more ahead by the term structure of interest rates, as interpreted by the Lutz-Meiselman variant of the expectations hypothesis. For such a comparison, expected yield curves must be determined at one point and actual yield curves at a later point of time. If the expectations hypothesis is valid, Hickman reasoned, then expected yield curves will be correlated with observed yield curves.

Hickman found that simply assuming that this year's yield curve will be the same as next year's gave what he regarded as better predictions of subsequently observed yield curves than the expectations hypothesis. This was one of the early uses of an inertia hypothesis as a benchmark for evaluating the predictive content of a substantive hypothesis. Hickman did not employ correlation analysis. If he did, as shall be shown, his conclusion that inertia is the better predictor would be more difficult if not impossible to sustain. In addition, he subjected the expectations hypothesis to two additional tests. All of his tests are based on the view that the validity of the expectations hypothesis hinges upon accurate forecasts. Meiselman does not regard this finding

---

[5] Frederick R. Macaulay, *Movements of Interest Rates*, p. 36. The reappearance of a seasonal in the money market in recent years has made it possible to reproduce Macaulay's experiment with a new body of data.

[6] *Ibid.*, p. 33.

[7] W. Braddock Hickman, "The Term Structure of Interest Rates: An Exploratory Analysis," NBER, 1942, mimeographed.

as relevant. "Anticipations may not be realized yet still determine the structure of rates in the manner asserted by the theory."[8]

Culbertson

Culbertson's empirical research is similar to Hickman's; both ran tests based on the assumption that forward rates are accurate predictions of future spot rates. Culbertson examined the yields of short- and long-term governments for identical periods of time. He argued that if the expectations hypothesis is valid, then yields to investors ought to be the same whether short- or long-term securities are held. (His calculations take into account both income streams and capital gains and losses.) He found marked differences in returns for the same holding periods. Since he found it difficult to believe that speculators would operate in the government securities markets and predict as badly as his results suggested, he rejected the expectations hypothesis.[9]

Walker

Walker's test of the expectations hypothesis also was based on the assumption that the market could predict accurately. However, it was more like Macaulay's work in this respect than that of Hickman and Culbertson. Both he and Macaulay revealed the consistency between the implications of accurate expectations and the expectations hypothesis; both observed instances in which the expectations of the market could be presumed to be accurate; and both found the behavior of the market was consistent with the expectations hypothesis.[10]

[8] Meiselman, *op cit.*, p. 12. Hickman also had some doubts about the relevance of his test or any other test. The difficulties in conceiving of a means for testing the expectations hypothesis led Conard to contend erroneously, as Meiselman's work demonstrates, that only by assuming the market predicts accurately is it possible ". . . to build a theory whose predictions can be meaningfully tested." See Conard, *op cit.*, p. 290.

[9] ". . . the explanation of broad movements in the term structure of rates must be sought principally in factors other than behavior governed by interest rate expectations." See John M. Culbertson, "The Term Structure of Interest Rates," *Quarterly Journal of Economics*, November 1957, p. 502.

Meiselman, *op. cit.*, p. 12, regards this and Hickman's work as tests of non-existent implications of the expectations hypothesis.

[10] Charls E. Walker, "Federal Reserve Policy and the Structure of Interest Rates on Government Securities," *Quarterly Journal of Economics*, February 1954, p. 19.

Walker's work deals with governmental interest rate policy during World War II. Around the beginning of that war, the Federal Reserve System and the Treasury embarked upon a policy of stabilizing, through open market operations and the maturity composition of new issues, the existing levels of rates on government securities. At that time, the yield curve was sharply rising; the bill rate was three-eighths of 1 per cent, one-year securities yielded 1 per cent, and long-term securities 2.5 per cent. If the expectations hypothesis is correct, the prestabilization term structure implied that future short-term rates were expected to be higher than existing short-term rates. In contrast, the stabilization policy implied that future short-term rates would be the same as current short-term rates. When the financial community became convinced that the monetary authorities could and would make this policy effective, it also became convinced that existing long-term rates were inconsistent with revised expectations of future short-term rates: long-term rates were too high. Hence, there was a tremendous shift out of short- and into long-term securities by the holders of governmental obligations. Such a shift is implied by the expectations hypothesis, given the prewar term structure and its wartime stabilization.[11] This shift in large part converted the stabilized yield on bills to a nominal rate similar to some other wartime prices.

Walker's results, unlike Macaulay's findings, cannot be interpreted as providing unambiguous support for the expectations hypothesis because they are also consistent with an implication of the liquidity preference hypothesis. Liquidity preference as a theory of the term structure of interest rates implies that the longer the term to maturity of a security, the higher its yield. Yield differentials between long- and short-term securities constitute equalizing differences that reflect differences in risks of capital losses. The establishment of a ceiling on long-term bond yields implies a floor or support price for their capital values. A price support program for long-term bonds implies that much of the

---

[11] If a rising yield curve exists, long-term securities yield more than short-term because the market anticipates offsetting losses on capital account attributable to holding long-term securities. The elimination of these anticipated capital losses implies that the yield of long-term securities is truly greater than that of short-term securities.

Conversely, a declining yield curve implies that future short-term rates will be lower. Hence, the holders of long-term securities trade a lower income on current account for anticipated capital gains. The stabilization of such a yield curve means that these anticipated capital gains cannot be realized, hence, that the yield of short-term securities is truly greater than that of long-term securities.

risk of capital loss is eliminated. Therefore, long maturities become relatively more attractive investment media.

Although Walker's results do not discriminate between expectations and liquidity preference, they do discriminate between expectations and liquidity preference on the one hand and market segmentation on the other. If the holdings of governments by the major institutions of the financial community changed as much as Walker reports they did, this constitutes evidence against the market segmentation hypothesis; if the market segmentation hypothesis is correct, Walker should not have observed a shift in the maturity distribution of governments by the major institutions of the financial community.[12]

The expectations hypothesis has been rejected for its unrealistic assumptions, particularly the assumption that short- and long-term securities of equivalent default risk can be treated as perfect substitutes. Many practitioners in financial markets, committing the fallacy of composition, reason that no one regards bills and long-term bonds as alternatives because they observe that many institutions specialize in a particular maturity spectrum. As long as some ranges of maturities are considered as alternatives by individual participants in this market, and in the aggregate these ranges cover the entire maturity spectrum, the market will act as though bills and bonds are alternatives. Yet every participant in this market may deal in a highly circumscribed maturity spectrum.

Mrs. Robinson has contended that the purchasers of a consol must know the course of future interest rates for ". . . every day from today till Kingdom Come."[13] Hickman and Luckett have enunciated, less colorfully, essentially the same argument.[14]

Presumably the size of the bonus a promising high school or college baseball player receives in exchange for his affiliation with a major

---

[12] This interpretation of Walker's findings as well as the contention that his results are consistent with liquidity preference does not appear in the original paper. Walker regarded his evidence as supporting the Lutz variant of expectations. For another statement of what the market segmentation hypothesis is, see Conard, *op. cit.,* p. 304.

[13] See Joan Robinson, "The Rate of Interest," *Econometrica,* April 1951, p. 102.

[14] Dudley G. Luckett, "Professor Lutz and the Structure of Interest Rates," *Quarterly Journal of Economics,* February 1959, p. 131. Hawtrey also seems to be a member of the school that rejects the expectations hypothesis because of difficulties in predicting short-term rates. He argues that short- and long-term rates are determined in completely segregated and independent markets. See Ralph G. Hawtrey, "A Rejoinder," *The Manchester School,* October 1939, p. 156.

league club is a function of his expected performance as a ball player. This interpretation, which is widely accepted, implies that the market predicts the performance of a ball player over his entire career. In order to properly calculate the size of these bonuses, the market must predict batting averages, fielding performance, and, in the case of pitchers, pitching effectiveness. Emotional stability, which appears to be irrelevant for determining future short-term rates, must also be predicted for ball players, since many become emotionally unstable in the face of severe competition and hence lose some of their economic value.[15]

Meiselman

Meiselman is the first investigator to employ an operational test of the expectations hypothesis that does not depend upon accurate foresight for its validity. If a relationship exists between expectations and the term structure of interest rates, then its existence can be detected despite inaccurate predictions. The understanding by economists of how expectations are formed and revised in the light of new information has improved enormously in recent years. Meiselman, by utilizing this knowledge, was able to make the expectations hypothesis operational even when the market could not anticipate future rates of interest correctly. He showed that expectations, whether or not they are correct, nevertheless affect the term structure of rates. His results constitute striking evidence that the expectations hypothesis has empirical validity.[16]

The expectations hypothesis implies that the term structure of interest rates constitutes at one moment of time a set of predictions of short-term rates at various moments of time in the future. For

[15] The objection to the expectations hypothesis for the lack of "realism" in its assumptions has led to an attempt to find an alternative, more realistic set of assumptions. See Burton G. Malkiel, "Expectations, Bond Prices, and the Term Structure of Interest Rates," *Quarterly Journal of Economics,* May 1962, No. 2, p. 197. The author claims his model is ". . . in closer conformity with the practices of bond investors who had always considered the Lutz theory chimerical." (See p. 218.) Conformity here should not be interpreted as predicting better; there is no test of the predictive powers of the models in the Malkiel paper. Conformity refers to the conformation of the assumptions of Malkiel's model with descriptions of how bond investors behave.

[16] Meiselman, *op. cit.,* Chapter 2.

every instant of time, there exists a term structure or yield curve and a set of implicit forward rates. These forward rates are, if the hypothesis is correct, expected short-term rates. If two term structures separated temporally are compared, the earlier contains predictions of future short-term rates and the later the data, i.e., the realized or actual short-term rates necessary for an evaluation of the accuracy of these predictions. Recent work on expectations suggests that if a realized or actual short-term rate is above its predicted level, then the predictions for other rates, yet to be realized, will be revised upward. Conversely, if the actual rate is below the predicted, then other predicted rates will be revised downward during the time interval between observations.

To illustrate: Assume at T_0, say January 1, 1960, the following relationships between yield and term to maturity are revealed by the market:

Yields as a Function of Term to Maturity at T_0

1-year governments yield	1.0 per cent
2	2.0
3	3.0
4	4.0

The expectations hypothesis, given this data at T_0, implies that the market expects future one-year rates to be higher than the current one-year rate. Since the one-year rate is 1 per cent and the two-year rate 2 per cent, the forward rate on one-year money one year hence must be 3 per cent for the returns on these alternatives to be equal. Analogously, if the current two-year rate is 2 per cent and the three-year rate 3 per cent, then the forward rate on one-year money two years later must be high enough to compensate for the difference between 2 and 3 per cent for two years. Therefore, a one-year rate of 5 per cent is implied for two years hence.

Market Predictions at T_0 of Expected One-Year Rates

Expected one-year rate for T_1, the year beginning 1/1/61, is 3.0 per cent
$$T_2 \qquad\qquad 1/1/62, \quad 5.0$$
$$T_3 \qquad\qquad 1/1/63, \quad 7.0$$

Assume at T_1, a year later, that the following relationships between yield and term to maturity are revealed by the market:

Yields as a Function of Term to Maturity at T_1

1-year governments yield	2.0 per cent
2	3.3
3	4.0

Clearly the one-year rate observed in the market at T_1 (2 per cent) is less than it was expected to be a year ago (3 per cent). The difference between the anticipated one-year rate one year hence at T_0 and the realized one-year rate at T_1 (both rates are for an identical moment of time but are measured one year apart) is defined as the error. If recently acquired knowledge on the formation of expectations is correct, then forecasts of expected one-year rates for T_2 and T_3, i.e., for January 1, 1962, and 1963, will have been revised downward during the year 1960, or between T_0 and T_1.

One can infer from the term structure of interest rates at T_0 and T_1 how much these estimates of future short-term rates have been revised.

Market Predictions at T_0 and T_1

Expected One-Year Rate for One Year, Beginning in	T_0	T_1	Change in Forecast, or Magnitude of Forecast Revision (per cent)
January 1, 1962 (T_2)	5.0	4.6	−0.4
January 1, 1963 (T_3)	7.0	5.4	−1.6

At T_1 the expected one-year rates beginning at T_2 and T_3 are 4.6 and 5.4 per cent, respectively. The difference between 5.0 and 4.6 per cent measures the change in the forecast one-year rate for T_2; the difference between 7.0 and 5.4 measures the change in the forecast one-year rate for T_3. Hence, if the expectations hypothesis is correct, then errors and forecast changes should be positively correlated.[17] Meiselman found that his error terms (i.e., the difference between predicted and actual one-year rates) and his forecast revisions were in fact positively correlated.

The distinction between anticipated and unanticipated interest rate changes is crucial for an understanding of how Meiselman tested the expectations hypothesis. If forward rates a year apart are as depicted by Chart 6-1, then the expectations hypothesis would imply that there has been no change in the rates forecast. Yet the rates for one-,

---

[17] Meiselman defines the error as the spot minus the forward; the revision of the forecast is defined as the later forecast less the earlier.

CHART 6–1. Marginal Rates of Interest With Stable Expectations

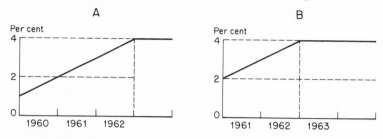

two-, and three-year maturities must have changed during this year; yield curves were not constant. Nevertheless, the expected one-year rates for particular moments of time were unchanged. The observations that are correlated, i.e., the error term and the forecast revision, refer to interest rates for particular dates.[18]

Meiselman correlated errors with contemporaneous revisions in forecasts. For the example used, there are two forecast revisions, −0.4 and −1.6, that are correlated with the error, −1.0. The future spot rates whose estimates were revised will be observed in the market as spot, and not forward, rates one and two years after the spot rate in the error term can be observed. For the data Meiselman employed, the future spot rates whose estimates were revised will be observed in the market as spot rates one through eight years after the spot rate in his error term can be observed. In both the example and Meiselman's work, forward rates pertaining to subsequently observable one-year spot rates for particular moments of calendar time were observed a year apart. The difference between observations which pertain to the same spot are forecast revisions. Since Meiselman observed his forward and spot one-year rates yearly, he observed eight forward rate revisions and one error term every year (with, of course, the exception of the earliest year that his data encompasses). Meiselman produced eight regressions relating forward rate revisions to errors observed simultaneously. He found significant relationships for all eight, with correlation coefficients ranging from a low of .59 to a high of .95. All eight regression lines went through the origin, in the sense that the constant terms of the regressions were insignificantly different from zero.

---

[18] An implication of this distinction is the proposition that stock prices can vary over time with no change in expectations of future earnings, if the market expects earnings to fluctuate. Hence, insofar as investors anticipate cyclical changes in the profitability of enterprises, anticipated cyclical variations in stock prices should exist.

This led to the inference that forward rates are unbiased estimates of future spot rates, which implies, when trends in interest rates are ignored, that yield curves are on the average flat. Short- and long-term rates will tend to be equal. If forward rates are biased upward, then yield curves, again ignoring trends, are on the average positively sloped. Hence, short-term rates will average less than long-term rates, and both, on the average, will rise with term to maturity. Such differentials between different terms to maturity, usually referred to as liquidity premiums, reflect the greater liquidity of short maturities.[19] Meiselman argues that the absence of a constant term in his regressions implies the absence of liquidity premiums. If the constant term is zero, a forward rate that is equal to the subsequently observed actual spot rate, i.e., a zero error term, implies no forecast revision. If forecasts are not revised when the error term is zero, then Meiselman infers that liquidity premiums are absent. To show that this inference is incorrect, consider the following formal statement of the hypothesis Meiselman tests:

$$_{t+m}E_t - {}_{t+m}E_{t-1} = \beta({}_tR_t - {}_tE_{t-1}). \tag{1}$$

Let E represent expected rates, R spot rates, F forward rates, and L liquidity premiums. The pre-subscript represents a year of calendar time. The post-subscript measures the moment a rate is either inferred from the term structure or observed as an actual spot rate. The forward and spot rates Meiselman considered were for one year only. Hence, $_{t+m}E_t$ is the expected one-year spot rate for the year $t + m$ that is inferred from the term structure of interest rates at moment t. The expected one-year spot rate for the year $t + m$ that is inferred from the term structure of interest rates at moment $t - 1$ is $_{t+m}E_{t-1}$. The difference between the post-subscripts t and $t - 1$ is, for Meiselman's study, one year.

One cannot observe expected rates directly; the term structure of interest rates reveals only forward rates. Whether or not $E = F$, or $E + L = F$, must be established by empirical evidence. Suppose liquidity premiums exist and they increase monotonically at a decreasing rate as a function of term to maturity. Then the longer the time

---

[19] The Hicksian view of the term structure of interest rates implies that forward rates are biased and high estimates of future short-term rates. He viewed the "normal" yield curve as being positively sloped. See John R. Hicks, *Value and Capital,* London, 1946, pp. 135–140. Lutz explicitly rejected the view that liquidity premiums exist because he could observe short-term rates above corresponding long-term rates and he regarded this as a contradiction of the liquidity preference hypothesis. See Lutz, *op. cit.,* p. 528.

interval between the moment a one-year forward rate is inferred from a term structure and the moment it becomes a spot rate, the greater the liquidity premium. Similarly, year-to-year changes in forward rates for specific calendar years will increase as they get closer in time to becoming spot rates. The largest increase will occur during the year a forward rate becomes a spot rate.[20]

If the forward rate, F, is equal to the expected rate, E, plus a liquidity premium, L, then substituting in (1) yields

$$(_{t+m}F_t - {}_{t+m}L_t) - (_{t+m}F_{t-1} - {}_{t+m}L_{t-1}) = \beta[{}_tR_t - (_tF_{t-1} - {}_tL_{t-1})].$$

Let $- {}_{t+m}L_t + {}_{t+m}L_{t-1} = \Delta L$. Then the restatement of Meiselman's hypothesis becomes

$$_{t+m}F_t - {}_{t+m}F_{t-1} = \beta(_tR_t - {}_tF_{t-1}) + \beta_tL_{t-1} - \Delta L.$$

Letting $\alpha = \beta_tL_{t-1} - \Delta L$, results in

$$_{t+m}F_t - {}_{t+m}F_{t-1} = \beta(_tR_t - {}_tF_{t-1}) + a. \qquad (2)$$

This is the regression equation Meiselman computed. He found that the observed constant was insignificantly different from zero. Hence, he inferred that α or $\beta_tL_{t-1} - \Delta L$ is also insignificantly different from zero.

A zero constant term is equally consistent with either $\beta_tL_{t-1} = \Delta L = 0$ or $\beta_tL_{t-1} = \Delta L > 0$. Hence, this piece of evidence is inappropriate for establishing the validity of the proposition that forward rates are unbiased estimates of expected spot rates; it is consistent with the existence of liquidity premiums. The proposition that forward rates are unbiased estimates of future spot rates remains untested.

Meiselman's own work, the work of Hickman, the time series of short- and long-term governments for the past forty years, and some new evidence presented here, all support the view that the term structure of interest rates, as interpreted by the expectations hypothesis, embodies biased and high estimates of future short-term rates. Meiselman used Durand's yield curves for high-grade corporates from 1900 through 1954 for his tests. For each of these years, Durand estimated a yield curve. If an average is computed of the yields for each term to maturity, i.e., an average of all fifty-five one-year maturities, two-year maturities, etc., the composite yield curve which results reflects average conditions for all fifty-five years. This curve is in fact positively

---

[20] For the purpose of determining whether or not forward rates are biased or unbiased estimates of spot rates, the liquidity content of spot rates is irrelevant. It is only the difference, if any, between the liquidity content of forward and spot rates that matters.

sloped (see Chart 6-2). Since interest rates, if anything, were trending down during these fifty-five years, forward rates must have been arithmetically high estimates of spot rates.

If liquidity premiums exist, the frequency of high estimates ought to be greater than that of low estimates and the average of the differences between estimated and actual rates ought to be positive. Hence, Meiselman's error terms ought to have a significantly higher frequency of minus than plus signs and their average ought to be negative. Tests of these implications with the Wilcoxon two-sample and signed-rank tests lead to their acceptance.[21]

The foregoing demonstrates that forward one-year rates were on the average greater than actual one-year rates. It suggests that they were also greater than expected one-year rates and that they systematically overstate what the market expects one-year rates to be. This conclusion is based on an analysis of the inputs for Meiselman's independent variable. What about the dependent variable, i.e., the forward-rate changes that are regarded by Meiselman as prediction changes? Since forward rate changes are the difference between observations, separated by a year, of forward rates that pertain to a specific spot rate observable in the future, the first forward rate must be inferred from data further out on a yield curve than the second. Hence, if liquidity preference is operative (if it produces positively sloped yield curves), then the first forward rate ought to be, on the average, greater than the second. Meiselman observed prediction changes separated by one through eight years from the moment of time relevant for the measurement of the error term. The first forward rate is, on the average, larger than the second for all eight regressions. It is hard to rationalize this observation as a chance event; the probability of drawing eight successive negative numbers from a population in which negative and positive numbers are equally represented is less than 1 per cent. On the whole, this evidence is consistent with a positively sloped yield curve that flattens out as term to maturity increases; it is what one would expect to be derived from data summarized by Chart 6-2.

Meiselman's changes in forward rates and error terms constitute a measure of the marginal costs, more precisely the rate of change

[21] See W. Allen Wallis and Harry V. Roberts, *Statistics: A New Approach*, Glencoe, 1956, pp. 596–598. Significance levels of 6 and 2 per cent were produced using one tail of the normal distribution. Of the fifty-four forward one-year rates, thirty-five were high and nineteen were low.

CHART 6–2. Average Yield as a Function of Term to Maturity, Durand Data, 1900–54

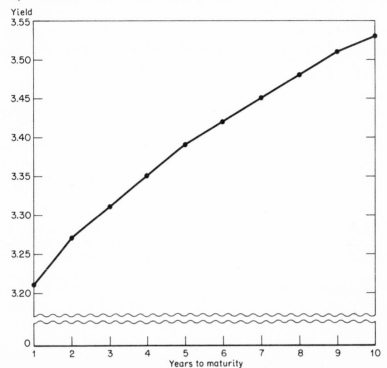

SOURCE: 1900–42, Durand, *Corporate Bonds;* 1943–47, Durand and Winn, *Basic Yields of Bonds;* 1948–51, *The Economic Almanac, 1956,* National Industrial Conference Board.

of yield with respect to term to maturity, of reducing term to maturity by a year. The pecuniary values at the margin, as revealed by the market, of liquidity changes attributable to changes in term to maturity of one year are computed. They behave, roughly speaking, as one would expect; the longer it takes for a forward rate to become a spot rate, the greater the premium of forward over spot. With but two exceptions out of a possible nine cases, liquidity premiums decrease monotonically as term to maturity increases (see Table 6-1).

Hickman's data are consistent with Meiselman's findings. Predicted yield curves for the years 1936 through 1942, with a year between the time predicted and actual yield curves are observed, were all high. Even more interesting, and this is consistent with Meiselman's data,

TABLE 6-1. *Meiselman's Error Term and Forecast Revisions*

	Years Until Second Observation Becomes a One-Year Spot Rate	Per Cent
Mean error term[a]	0	−.143
Mean forward rate revision[b]	1	−.101
	2	−.078
	3	−.065
	4	−.077
	5	−.054
	6	−.040
	7	−.049
	8	−.022

NOTE: These data were obtained through personal communication with Meiselman.

[a]Mean of differences between one-year forward and spot rates.

[b]Mean change in one-year forward rates as term to maturity decreases by one year.

Hickman's results show that the longer the interval between predicted and observed or actual yield curves, the greater the bias in the estimates.[22] This empirical finding is an implication of a positively sloped yield curve when trends in rates are absent.

The data on yields of governments for the nine most recent business cycles, a period of roughly forty years, clearly indicate that the average yields of short-term governments are less than long-term governments. All nine cycles, without exception, conform to this generalization. These data constitute additional evidence that the term structure of rates, as interpreted by the expectations hypothesis, yields biased estimates of future short-term rates. If forward rates are not expected rates, but expected rates plus a liquidity premium, one should expect these time series to show that yields of short-term governments are usually less than long-term governments. Since Meiselman and Hickman worked with Durand's data, which reflect the yields of high-grade corporates, these data on the relative yields of short- and long-term governments for these nine cycles constitute independent evidence of the existence of bias in the predictions of the expectations hypothesis.

Unfortunately, this evidence is not unexceptionable. The fifty-five yearly observations of Durand, which Meiselman used, have a down-

[22] There are twenty-eight predictions, all too high.

ward trend. In 1900, Durand's basic thirty-year rate was 3.30 per cent; in 1954, it was 3.00 per cent. If declining short-term rates are unanticipated, the predicted rates of the expectations hypothesis will exceed actual rates. From 1935 through 1942, the downward trend is still greater; the thirty-year basic rate fell from 3.50 to 2.65. Hence, if the long-term downward trend in rates has been unanticipated by the market, the relationship between the yields of short- and long-term governments may be a consequence of forecasting errors.[23]

Meiselman, like Walker, produced evidence relevant for evaluating the validity of the market segmentation hypothesis; unlike Walker, Meiselman points out the relevance of his work for this hypothesis. ". . . the systematic behavior of the yield curve would appear to contradict the widely held view that the market for debt claims is 'segmented' or 'compartmentalized' by maturity and that rates applicable to specific maturity segments can best be analyzed by rather traditional partial equilibrium supply and demand analysis where transactors act on the basis of preference for specific maturities. . . ."[24] The correlation between forward rate revisions and error terms demonstrates that changes in the yields of one- and two-year securities are related to changes in yields of maturities up to nine and ten years. Consequently, at least for this maturity range, the market is not segmented enough to invalidate this test of the expectations hypothesis.

New Evidence

Confining tests of the expectations hypothesis to circumstances for which expectations can be presumed to be accurate has produced only fragmentary evidence. Expectations can be presumed to be accurate only under very special circumstances. Hence, forward rates can equal expected spot rates and yet differ from realized spot rates. But even this limited approach has not been fully exploited. Clearly, in a world in which spot rates are positive, and this would surely encompass the two most recent decades, one could assume that the market never expects negative spot rates. Therefore, if

---

[23] Hickman found that a simple projection of the previous year's yield curve produced numerically closer predictions than the expectations hypothesis, which is consistent with the foregoing interpretation. His finding is also, of course, consistent with an upward bias in the predictions of the expectations hypothesis.

[24] Meiselman, *op. cit.,* p. 34.

negative forward rates were observed, this would constitute evidence against the expectations hypothesis. Conversely, if negative forward rates were not observed, this would be evidence for the hypothesis.

The behavior of the term structure of bill yields during September 1960 contradicts the expectations hypothesis. In that month the forward rate on one-week money, inferred from the term structure of bill yields with maturities on December 8th and 15th, was often negative.[25]

For nine of the twenty-one trading days in September 1960, negative forward rates for one-week money could be observed. To restate the foregoing, on these nine dates in September 1960 (and this same phenomenon could be observed in September 1959) there existed some bills whose asked prices were higher than the asked prices for bills with one week less to maturity. Since it is unreasonable to argue that the market expected the spot rate for one-week bills on September 8th, or any other week since the end of World War II, to be negative, it follows that forward rates are not expected spot rates.

Critics have rejected the expectations hypothesis because the predictions of future short-term rates implied by the theory differed from subsequently observed actual rates. Meiselman argues that these critics have rejected the hypothesis for the wrong reasons. His position, that expectations need not be correct to determine the term structure of interest rates, is, of course, valid. Yet, given free entry and competition in securities markets, should not one expect to find a relationship between expectations as inferred from the term structure of interest rates and subsequently observed actual rates? It is of course unreasonable to expect expectations or predictions of future short-term rates to be absolutely accurate. New information coming to the market after a prediction is made will lead to prediction revisions and less than perfect forecasts. Yet new information should not lead to biases in the estimates; a mean bias should not be present. Hence, the average difference between predicted and actual rates ought to be insignificantly different from zero. The absence or presence of a mean bias in the relationship constitutes a test of whether or not forward rates are expected rates. Similarly, for very short intervals between the inference of predictions and the observation of actual short-term rates, there should be some observable advantage for the expectations hypothesis

[25] The asked prices reported on the quote sheets of C. J. Devine were the source of price data. Salomon Bros. & Hutzler quote sheets contained data that led to the same conclusion.

over some form of inertia hypothesis as a predictor of future short-rates. If not, why should the market waste its time and energy, which are scarce resources, in trying to predict future short-term rates?[26]

To control for trends in rates, and to measure forward and actual rates uninfluenced by capital gain considerations, the forward and actual yields of Treasury bills were examined from the beginning of 1959 through March 1962. All of the forward rates implicit in the term structure of interest rates during that time for two-, four-, six-, eight-, nine-, and thirteen-week bill rates were computed and compared with actual yields. The time period under investigation began and ended with the 91-day bill rate at the same level, approximately 2.75 per cent, although it rose sharply to 4.50 per cent and fell to 2.25 before it came back to its original level. The results of this investigation are tabulated in Table 6-2.

These results, along with the evidence already cited, strongly support the belief that forward rates are biased and high estimates of future short-term rates. Hence, they are not the predictions of the market. In addition, these findings support the common belief that there exists a preference for short-term over long-term securities in the market. This preference produces a yield differential that constitutes an equalizing difference. The greater pecuniary yield of long-term securities represents compensation for the nonpecuniary advantages associated with holding short-term securities.

These findings also suggest that the futures market for money may be unlike other futures markets. Generally, one finds that forward prices are below corresponding spot prices when spot prices are rising and above them when spot prices are falling. For the futures market for money, however, forward rates in the Treasury bill market are typically above spot rates even when the latter are rising. During an upswing, the extent to which this occurs narrows, and some reversals, i.e., spot rates in excess of forward rates, occur. However, these reversals are surprisingly infrequent.

On theoretical grounds, one should expect liquidity premiums to vary with the level of interest rates. Treasury bills, like other securities, can be viewed as providing two streams of income: one is a pecuniary

[26] Meiselman went too far in dismissing the work of Hickman and Culbertson. The expectations hypothesis, as he and Lutz interpreted it, does imply that there ought to be equality in the yields of short- and long-term rates in the absence of trends. If there is not, either the people operating in this market are doing an unbelievably bad job or this constitutes evidence against the Meiselman version of the expectations hypothesis.

TABLE 6-2. *Distribution of Errors in Predicting Treasury Bill Rates*

	14-Day Rates	28-Day Rates	42-Day Rates	56-Day Rates	63-Day Rates	91-Day Rates
No. of observations	124	143	146	137	113	125
Frequency of high predictions	93	132	135	120	91	119
Average size of errors (per cent)	.199	.567	.599	.444	.455	.669
Average actual rates (per cent)	2.34	2.39	2.54	2.67	2.79	2.91

NOTE: Bills with precisely 182 and 91 days to maturity were used to compute the forward 91-day rate. Ninety-one days after this computation, the spot 91-day rate was observed and compared with the forward rate. Similarly, bills with 126, 112, 84, 63, 56, 42, 28, and 14 days to maturity were used to compute forward rates and to measure spot rates.

Bid and asked prices, obtained from government bond dealers, were averaged to obtain the prices used. The daily quote sheets of Salomon Bros. & Hutzler, C. J. Devine & Co., were the sources of bid and asked prices. These daily price reports quote bid and asked prices of bills for specified days to maturity from the time payment is received.

Forward 91-day rates were computed by subtracting the current 91-day rate from twice the current 182-day rate. This method of computing forward rates increases the difficulties of detecting an upward bias in the estimates of the expectations hypothesis. It understates forward relative to spot rates. Indeed, if the estimates of the expectations hypothesis were unbiased, this computing procedure would show a downward bias. Bill yields are bankers discount yields, and equal discount yields for different maturities are not comparable. For example, a 4 per cent discount yield on a 90-day bill implies a yield on a 360-day basis of 4.04 per cent. In contrast, a 4 per cent discount yield on a 180-day bill implies a yield of 4.08 on a 360-day basis. In general, the longer the term to maturity of a bill, the more its discount yield understates its bond equivalent yield. Hence, the procedure followed produces lower estimates of forward rates than would be produced by a correct computation.

yield measured by interest rates; the other is a nonpecuniary yield as a money substitute. The average difference in 28- and 56-day bill yields can be viewed as an equalizing difference that reflects the greater value of the former as a money substitute. Economics customarily think of a rise in interest rates as implying an increase in the cost of holding money. By parity of reasoning, an increase in interest rates should also imply an increase in the cost of holding money substitutes. Since 28-day bills are better money substitutes than 56-day bills, a rise in interest rates implies that the opportunity costs of holding the former should rise relative to that of holding the latter. For this condition to be satisfied, yields of 56-day bills must rise relative to those of 28-day bills. Such a rise implies an increase in liquidity premiums, i.e., an increase in the spread between forward and actual 28-day rates. This reasoning is consistent with the results obtained for the range of bill maturities studied; the opportunity costs of holding any specified maturity, instead of a longer and hence less liquid maturity, increases as interest rates rise. Conversely, these opportunity costs decrease when rates fall. Within the range of bill maturities observed, and contrary to what is true for the yield curve as a whole, yield curves are steepest when rates are high and flattest when rates are low.

If the spread between 28- and 56-day bills increases with a rise in rates, and if liquidity premiums increase, then the premium of forward over spot money should also increase. This implies that what Meiselman and Hickman erroneously regarded as error terms, the difference between forward and subsequently observed spot rates, should be a positive function of the current level of spot rates. To determine whether or not this inference is correct, the difference between forward and subsequently observed 28-day spot rates was regressed on current 28-day spot rates. This is equivalent to regressing liquidity premiums plus or minus a forecasting error on current 28-day rates. These results are consistent with the hypothesis that liquidity premiums rise with the level of spot rates. The premium of forward over spot 28-day rates increases by one basis point for every increase of about five basis points in the spot rate.

The foregoing conclusion was derived from 137 monthly observations during the three business cycles from October 1949 through February 1961. They are supported by the results obtained from a regression using 138 weekly observations of 91- and 182-day bills from January 1959 through February 1961. For the latter test, the regression coefficient was about twice the former. A rise of about two and a half basis points in the 91-day bill rate is associated with a rise of about one basis point in the premium of forward over spot 91-day rates.[27]

---

[27] For the 91-day bills, the weekly observations cover a period when there were 182- and 91-day bills outstanding simultaneously. The regression coefficient was .43 with a standard error of .05.

For the 28-day bills, observations were obtained once a month. Typically, more than one observation could have been used in any month. The observation

Since both interest rates and business conditions vary with the cycle, the finding that liquidity premiums rise with interest rates raises the question, are liquidity premiums a function of the level of interest rates or of the stage of the business cycle? In order to investigate this question, forward and actual 28-day bill rates were computed monthly from the term structure of 56- and 28-day bills for the three latest complete business cycles. During these three cycles, there was an upward trend in interest rates. Therefore, if liquidity premiums vary with the level of rates, it should be possible to observe that they rise secularly. The regression of the difference between predicted and actual 28-day rates on time for these three cycles does indicate an upward trend. Hence, liquidity premiums are positively related to the level of interest rates.[28]

The existence of liquidity premiums implies that the expectations hypothesis yields biased and high estimates of future short-term rates. It does not reveal in any direct way whether or not the market has any power to correctly anticipate subsequently observed spot rates. If liquidity premiums are held constant, if expected and not forward rates are observed, does a significant relationship exist between these expected rates and subsequently observed spot rates?

Forward rates for specific periods of calendar time and subsequently observed spot rates for the same periods were subjected to correlation analysis. This corrects, in a very crude way, for bias in the estimates of future spot rates attributable to liquidity premiums. Forward rates, which can be regarded as market predictions when adjusted for liquidity premiums, were inferred from the term structure of 182- and 91-day bill rates. (These rates were computed using an average of bid and asked prices adjusted for bankers discount.)

The results of this test indicate that the expectations hypothesis

chosen was the one closest to the middle of the month. The regression coefficient was .22 with a standard error of .03.

The effects of bankers discount were eliminated from these data.

The association of a rise in liquidity premiums with a rise in the level of rates can also be shown by regressing the difference between forward and subsequently observed spot rates upon their sum.

The validity of these tests depends upon the absence of positive correlation between forecasting errors and spot rates. Unfortunately it is difficult to disentangle forecasting errors from liquidity premiums.

[28] Of 137 predictions of the Lutz variant of the expectations hypothesis, 121 were high, five low, and eleven were correct. The effects of bankers discount were eliminated from these data.

definitely does have predictive content. For 138 predictions of 91-day bill rates from the beginning of 1959 through the first quarter of 1962, the expectations hypothesis explained 58 per cent of the observed variation. The question remains whether an inertia hypothesis could do equally well or better. Perhaps the observed correlation could be attributable to serial correlation in the data.

To determine whether or not the results obtained should be imputed to correct expectations, two variants of an "inertia hypothesis" were considered. One "predicted" 91-day bill rates 91 days hence by assuming no change. The other extrapolated into the future the difference between current 91-day rates and those 91 days ago.

The correlations for both variants of the inertia hypothesis tested were the same; each explained 48 per cent of the observed variation. The expectations hypothesis explained approximately 20 per cent more of the observed variation. During most of the period of observation, from about the middle of 1959 through the middle of 1960, there was a sharp rise and fall in rates. For the remainder of the period, interest rates were roughly stable. If the two hypotheses are compared for the period when rates were highly unstable (this reduces the number of observations to fifty), then expectations explain 48 per cent of the observed variations, whereas the variants of inertia each explain 30 per cent. The comparative advantage of the theory was stronger, as one would expect, when interest rates were unstable.

Is the observed difference between these correlation coefficients significant? Could it have occurred as a result of chance? To answer this question, forward and current spot rates were correlated with subsequently observed spot rates and the partial correlation coefficients were computed. The addition of current spot rates increased the fraction of the observed variation explained from 58 to 59 per cent. The partial regression coefficient for expectations was significant and positive (the partial regression coefficient was .86, with a standard error of .14). In contrast, the partial regression coefficient for inertia was negative and also significant (the regression coefficient was —.31, with a standard error of .18).

These results indicate clearly that the expectations hypothesis does have predictive content that cannot be attributed to inertia. However, the negative coefficient for inertia requires explanation. The hypothesis presented here views the forward rate as a function of expected spot rates plus a liquidity premium. But liquidity premiums are a function of the level of spot rates: when current spot rates are high, the premium over spot that is reflected in the forward rate is also high, and vice versa. Hence, the larger the spot rate, the larger the number that ought to be deducted from forward rates to obtain the expected rates of the market. Therefore, the negative coefficient which is observed is consistent with the view that liquidity premiums exist and vary directly with the level of interest rates, more specifically with spot rates.

To restate this argument more formally, using symbols already defined:

1. $_{t+1}F_t = {}_{t+1}E_t + {}_tLP_t.$

2. $_tLP_t = f(_tR_t).$

3. $_{t+1}F_t - f(_tR_t) = {}_{t+1}E_t.$

4. $_{t+1}E_t = {}_{t+1}R_{t+1} + U.$

5. $_{t+1}F_t - f(_tR_t) = {}_{t+1}R_{t+1} + U.$

The data used to evaluate the predictive content of the expectations hypothesis are reproduced in Chart 6-3. The thick line depicts actual 91-day rates. The thin lines indicate forward rates adjusted and unadjusted for liquidity premiums. The point of origin of the thin lines at the thick line represents the moment a forward rate is inferred; the terminal point of the thin line measures the magnitude of the forward rate at the moment when the actual 91-day rate corresponding to this forward rate can be observed. Liquidity premiums were measured using the regression equation obtained by regressing the difference between forward and realized 91-day rates on current spot rates. These results suggest that within the range of maturities encompassed by Treasury bills, expectations do influence the term structure of interest rates, and the market forecasts future spot rates with some degree of accuracy. However, to obtain the expectations of the market, liquidity premiums must be deducted from forward rates.[29]

[29] The fact that forward rates are usually higher than actual spot rates may have led Hickman to abandon the search for a relationship between them. An inertia hypothesis could produce numerically closer predictions to spot rates than the expectations hypothesis, yet the latter could produce stronger correlations. It is the strength of the correlations, if one accepts the view that liquidity premiums exist, that is relevant for evaluating these alternatives. Insofar as liquidity premiums are a constant or linear function of forward rates, they do not influence the correlation of forward with spot rates. For the two sets of seven pairs of observations in Hickman's study, representing one-year forecasts, the correlation coefficient for expectations was .725; for inertia, .721. When both

CHART 6–3. Market Expectations of Future 91-Day Bill Rates

——— Forward rates
------ Forward rates adjusted for liquidity premiums
—— Spot rates

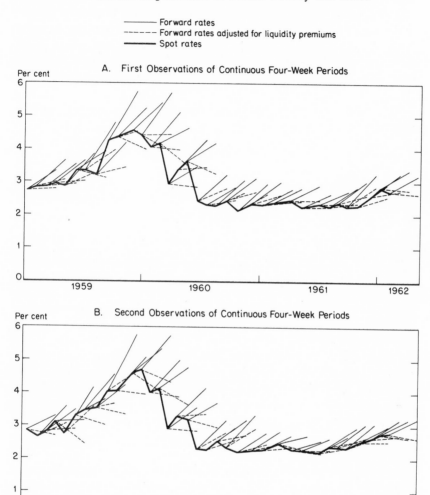

A. First Observations of Continuous Four-Week Periods

B. Second Observations of Continuous Four-Week Periods

(continued)

variables were included in a multiple correlation, neither had a significant partial correlation coefficient. Hence, no basis is provided by correlation analysis for arguing that one or the other variable explained the observed variation. If one plots forward rates and the variant of inertia Hickman employed, there is almost a constant difference between them.

CHART 6-3 (concluded)

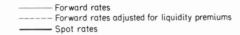

——————— Forward rates
— — — — — Forward rates adjusted for liquidity premiums
——————— Spot rates

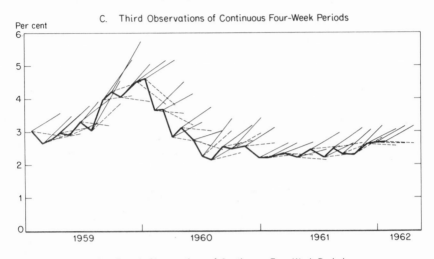

C.   Third Observations of Continuous Four-Week Periods

Per cent

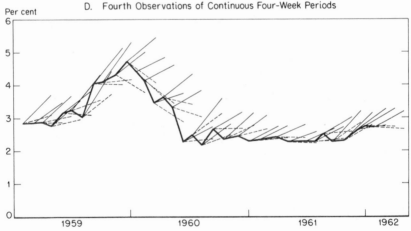

D.   Fourth Observations of Continuous Four-Week Periods

Per cent

Thus far, this analysis does not reveal how stable the liquidity preference function is. Is the relationship between spot rates and liquidity premiums stable enough to permit one to estimate liquidity premiums for one business cycle and use these estimates to uncover successfully the expectations of the market, as distinguished from forward rates, for a second cycle? To answer this question, the regression of the difference between forward and subsequently observed 28-day spot rates upon current 28-day spot rates, for the two cycles from October 1949 through April 1958, was used to estimate liquidity premiums for the following cycle. Then inertia and expectations were compared as a means of forecasting subsequently observed spot rates. Expectations was definitely the better predictor. The standard error of estimate was .50 for inertia against .38 for expectations. The partial regression coefficient for inertia was —.07; for expectations, it was .75. The standard error of the regression coefficient was .19 for inertia and .16 for expectations. Multiple correlation analysis, using forward rates adjusted for liquidity premiums, yields results almost identical with those obtained with unadjusted forward rates.[30]

These results suggested that the data Meiselman employed, which were compiled by Durand, should be reexamined to see if forward rates do predict subsequently observed spot rates. Hence, forward and current spot rates were considered as independent variables and subsequently observed spot rates as the dependent variable in a multiple regression equation. This involves using the same data Meiselman used to compute what he regards as an error term. No evidence of successful forecasting was detected; inertia appeared to be the better independent variable.

To utilize more recent data that are qualitatively more comparable to the data Meiselman utilized, the experiment performed with forward and spot three-month Treasury bills was repeated using monthly forward and spot one-year governments for 1958 through 1961. One- and two-year rates were read off the fixed maturity yield curve published monthly in the Treasury Bulletin.[31] Again, forward and current spot rates were treated as independent variables and subsequently observed spot rates as the dependent variable. The result is consistent with that using three- and six-month bills and reinforces the view that the market has some power to forecast successfully. However, taken by itself it does not constitute quite as convincing evidence of the existence of successful forecasting. This is what one

---

[30] For the three cycles, 1949 to 1961, the simple correlation coefficients indicated that expectations explained 88 per cent of the observed variation whereas inertia, i.e., extrapolating no change, explained 82 per cent.

[31] I am indebted to H. Irving Forman of the National Bureau staff for these measurements.

would expect; it is harder to forecast a year into the future than it is to forecast for three months.

If the rationalization of the statistical findings using three- and six-month bills is correct, then forward rates should have a positive coefficient and current one-year rates a negative one. One should also expect to find that the partial correlation coefficient for expectations would be smaller in the case of one- and two-year Treasury securities than it was for three- and six-month bills.

These anticipations are in general borne out. The sign of the regression coefficient for one-year spot rates is negative. For three- and six-month bills, this regression coefficient is 75 per cent greater than its standard error; for one- and two-year governments, it is a third larger than its standard error. For three- and six-month bills, the regression coefficient for forward rates is positive and six times its standard error; in the case of one- and two-year governments, it is positive but only nine-tenths its standard error.

Possibly the most convincing evidence that the market can forecast, with modest accuracy, one-year spot rates one year into the future was obtained through the following experiment. Liquidity premiums embodied in one-year forward rates for the 1958–61 cycle were estimated from an equation derived from the difference between forward and subsequently observed spot rates regressed on current one-year rates for the 1954–58 cycle. The expected rates of the market for the 1958–61 cycle were then obtained by subtracting the estimated liquidity premiums from forward rates. The mean square errors in the implicit forecasts of the market, i.e., the difference between forward rates less liquidity premiums and subsequently observed spot rates were compared with those generated by assuming next year's one-year spot rates will be identical with current rates. Although neither independent variable appeared in some absolute sense to yield very good forecasts, it is clear that expectations was significantly better as an independent variable than inertia. For thirty-five monthly observations, the mean square error was 2.09 for inertia, .91 for expectations. The elimination of liquidity premiums contributed importantly to this reduction in error. Without such adjustment, the mean square error of the forward rates was 1.91, only slightly less than that for inertia. These results show that if one is predicting one-year rates one year hence, and the current one-year rate is known, adding the two-year rate to one's knowledge constitutes a valuable piece of information.

Time series of forward and spot one-year rates during the period

1958 to 1961 are reproduced as Chart 6-4. These data, as well as the data for forward and spot three-month bills, suggest that the market can detect spot rates that are abnormally high or low. All of the forward rates are biased estimates. However, if one examines the slopes

CHART 6–4. Forward and Spot One-Year Rates on Government Securities

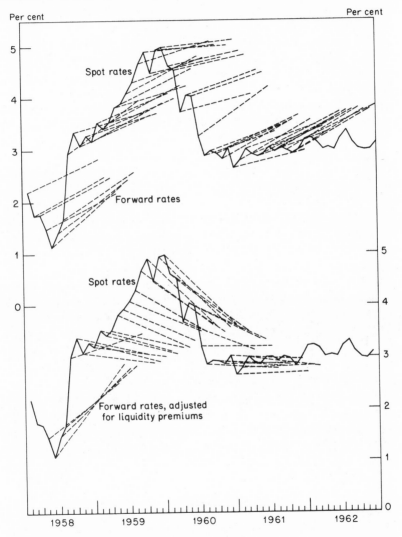

SOURCE: Derived from Treasury yield curves, using one- and two-year rates.

of the lines connecting current spot rates with forward rates for one year into the future, these lines appear flattest when current spot rates are highest. Hence, if the market can abstract from liquidity premiums (which produce the bias) then it appears that the market can forecast. That is, when rates are high, the market expects them to fall, and conversely, as the adjusted forward rates in the lower part of the chart suggest. This is consistent with the view that the market has some notion of what constitutes a normal rate of interest.

What causes the observed difference between the results using Durand's data on corporates and the recent data on one- and two-year governments? The evidence provides the basis for highly speculative answers at best. Durand's data encompass fifty-five years and are yearly observations; the data on governments encompass five years and are monthly observations. Possibly the market cannot distinguish betwen cyclically and secularly high and low rates of interest. If the market could anticipate cyclical changes better than secular changes, there would be an observed difference in forecasting accuracy over one cycle as compared with many cycles. When spot rates are high cyclically, their subsequent change is quite different from that when they are high secularly. If the forecasts of the market are the same in either case, studies of the accuracy of forecasts will lead to different results depending upon the time period under investigation.

Another avenue for explaining secular and cyclical differences is the study of the stability of liquidity premiums over time. Before the 1930's, judging by Durand's data, liquidity premiums were much smaller or possibly nonexistent. There seems to have been a structural change in the economy in this respect since the early 1930's. Possibly this can be attributed to the abolition of interest on demand deposits, or perhaps to a change in attitude toward risk that led to changes in liquidity premiums. In any case, instability of liquidity premiums could account for the observed difference in the secular and cyclical correlations of forward and one-year spot rates.

Still another avenue for explaining these findings is data limitations. Durand did not use a criterion such as least squares for his curve fitting. He fitted only yield curves that do not have maximums or minimums. When his yield curves were not flat throughout, they either increased or decreased monotonically with term to maturity and then flattened out. By definition, Durand could not observe a yield curve with any other shape. He offers no explanation for this self-imposed constraint.

In the postwar period, when short-term rates have been above long-term rates, yield curves have been hump shaped. These curves at first rise with term to maturity, reach a maximum, and then fall and finally flatten out. It is difficult to believe that this was not also true during some of the fifty-five years encompassed by Durand's data. If one examines both the data and the curves fitted, it is clear that humped yield curves could just as correctly have been fitted some of the time. Since this was not done, one- and two-year rates derived from Durand's curves are probably high estimates of true one- and two-year rates, and are high relative to longer maturities.

If one examines the yield curves Durand fitted to data in the 1920's, yield curves for governments and corporates have opposite slopes for three of these years. Indeed, the data on governments presented above show short-term governments yielding, on average, less than long-term governments in the 1920's. Durand's findings on corporates indicate just the opposite.

Another difficulty, ignored by both Hickman and Meiselman, is the fact that Durand's yield curves are drawn for coupon bonds. Hence, the Hicksian formula for internal rates of return or yield to maturity, which implicitly assumes the absence of coupons, is inappropriate for computing forward rates. To compute forward rates correctly, both coupons and yields to maturity, or internal rates of return, must be known.

If one accepts the view that yield curves were, on average, positively sloped during the fifty-five years Durand observed, then coupon rates for bonds with one or two years to maturity must have, on average, exceeded internal rates of return. If coupons exceed internal rates of return, then it can be shown that the Hicksian formula underestimates forward rates. However, the measurement errors which can be attributed to ignoring coupons seem to be small compared to those attributable to uncertainties regarding the shape of Durand's yield curves. Using coupons of 6 per cent, errors in computing forward rates seem to be on the order of two or three basis points.

The figures on bill rates collected provide new data to repeat Meiselman's experiments. The results of tests of the expectations hypothesis using Treasury bills are tabulated in Table 6-3. Treasury bills with terms to maturity of less than six months are the source of price data.

Since these correlations are all unambiguously significant, they provide additional support for Meiselman's view that a relationship between expectations and the term structure of interest rates exists.

TABLE 6-3. *Correlation of Forecast Revisions With Errors as Defined by Meiselman, 1958–61*

Type of Error	Correlation Coefficient	Regression Coefficient
1. Error in forecast of two-week rates with changes in expected two-week rates two weeks hence	.37	.40
2. Error in forecast of two-week rates with changes in expected two-week rates eleven weeks hence	.36	.26
3. Error in forecast of four-week rates with changes in expected four-week rates twelve weeks hence	.21	.27
4. Error in forecast of six-week rates with changes in expected six-week rates eighteen weeks hence	.59	.62
5. Error in forecast of eight-week rates with changes in expected eight-week rates sixteen weeks hence	.85	.59

NOTE: The existence of liquidity premiums implies that the errors as defined by Meiselman are typically larger than the true errors the market committed. The true errors are the differences between forward rates minus liquidity premiums and spot rates; the true forecast revisions are the observed revisions net of liquidity differences.

SOURCE: Line 1: Correlation of changes in predicted two-week bill rates with forecasting errors implied by the expectations hypothesis, i.e., with the difference between predicted and actual two-week rates. The error terms were obtained by comparing predictions implied by four- and two-week bill rates with actual two-week bill rates two weeks later. The prediction changes were obtained from the difference between the predicted two-week rate four weeks hence and then, two weeks later, two weeks into the future. The first prediction was obtained through the use of six- and four-week bills; the second was measured through the use of four- and two-week bills.

Line 2: Correlation of changes in predicted two-week bill rates as inferred from eleven- and nine-week bills and, two weeks later, from nine- and seven-week bills with the difference between predicted and actual two-week rates. The independent variables for this and the test described in line 1 are identical.

Line 3: Correlation of changes in predicted four-week bill rates with the prediction errors implied by the expectations hypothesis. The independent variable is the

(continued)

NOTES TO TABLE 6-3 (concluded)

difference between predictions implied by eight- and four-week bill rates and, four weeks later, actual four-week bill rates. The dependent variable, the prediction change, is the difference between the predicted four-week rate implied by the sixteen- and twelve-week bill rates and, four weeks later, the predicted four-week rate implied by the twelve- and eight-week bill rates.

Line 4: Correlation of changes in predicted six-week bill rates with prediction errors. The independent variable is the difference between predictions implied by twelve- and six-week bill rates and, six weeks later, actual six-week bill rates. The dependent variable, the prediction change, is the difference between the predicted six-week rate implied by the twenty-four- and eighteen-week rates and, six weeks later, the predicted six-week rate implied by the eighteen- and twelve-week bill rates.

Line 5: Correlation of changes in predicted eight-week bill rates with prediction errors. The independent variable is the difference between predictions implied by sixteen- and eight-week bill rates and, eight weeks later, actual eight-week bill rates. The dependent variable, the prediction change, is the difference between the predicted eight-week rate implied by the twenty-four- and sixteen-week rates and, eight weeks later, the predicted eight-week rate implied by the sixteen- and eight-week rates. This may be illustrated by the following sample calculation. On November 28, 1961, the sixteen-week rate was 2.61, and the eight-week rate 2.51. The expectations hypothesis implies that the eight-week rate eight weeks hence, on January 23, 1962, is expected to be 2.71. This is twice the sixteen-week rate less the eight-week rate. The actual eight-week rate on January 23, 1962, eight weeks after November 28, was 2.61. Hence, the error is −.10. The first prediction in the data from which line 5 was derived was inferred from the twenty-four- and sixteen-week rates on November 28, 1961. These were 2.72 and 2.61, respectively. Hence, the predicted rate for March 20, 1962, which is three times the twenty-four week rate less twice the sixteen-week rate, is 2.94. Eight weeks later, on January 23, 1962, the sixteen-week rate was 2.72, and the eight-week rate was 2.61. Hence, the predicted eight-week rate for March 20, 1962, was 2.83, and the prediction change −.11.

His major conclusion—that there is validity in the expectations hypothesis—is sound, despite his failure to isolate unanticipated changes in interest rates and to recognize that forward rates were not expected rates. What about the data Meiselman used? How are the liquidity premiums related to the level of rates for Durand's data? The regression of the difference between forward and subsequently observed spot one-year rates against current one-year rates reveals little variation in the "error" with the level of spot rates. The regression coefficient is .09 with the standard error of .06, and only about 4 per cent of the variation is explained. In contrast, for the same regression using forward and spot one-year governments for the 1958–61 cycle, the regression coefficient is one, with a standard error of .10, and 70 per cent of the variation is explained. Clearly the difference between forward and spot rates for the government data appears to be much more sensitive to variations in spot rates than it is for Durand's data.

The reappearance of a seasonal in the money market in recent years implies that it is possible to repeat Macaulay's experiment with a new body of data. If the expectations hypothesis is correct, seasonal adjustment factors ought to vary systematically with term to maturity. More specifically, just as the time money rates "anticipated" seasonal changes in call money rates, changes in, say, sixty-day seasonal adjustment factors ought to "anticipate" changes in thirty-day factors. Hence, it should be possible to construct a set of seasonal adjustment factors for sixty-day rates if the factors for thirty-day rates are known; knowledge of seasonal adjustment factors for thirty-day bills implies knowledge of these factors for bills of longer maturity.

To test this hypothesis, weekly moving seasonal adjustment factors were computed for twenty-seven- and fifty-five-day bills for 1959, 1960, and 1961, using bid prices unadjusted for bankers discount. If the expectations hypothesis is correct, a set of seasonal adjustment factors for fifty-five-day bills constructed out of twenty-seven-day factors ought to be more strongly correlated with actual fifty-five-day factors than just twenty-seven-day factors alone. For every week, a simple average of twenty-seven-day factors for that week and for four weeks in the future was computed. This should be, according to the expectations hypothesis, a fifty-five-day seasonal. The correlation of this set of theoretical seasonal adjustments with actual fifty-five-day adjustment factors was stronger than the correlation between twenty-seven- and fifty-five-day factors. Converse results ought to hold for a fifty-five-day seasonal adjustment constructed out of twenty-seven-day factors, if the adjustment factors are obtained by averaging the current twenty-seven-day seasonal with that of four weeks in the past. This seasonal, when correlated with the fifty-five-day seasonal directly computed, ought to exhibit less correlation than exists for the relationship between twenty-seven- and fifty-five-day factors. Hence, the rank ordering of correlations alone, quite apart from the question of whether or not there is a significant difference between the correlations, constitutes evidence that the market anticipates seasonal movements in rates. These findings are summarized in Table 6-4.

The Durand data and the data collected for this study provide a means for discriminating between expectations and liquidity preference on the one hand and market segmentation on the other. The

TABLE 6-4. *Coefficients Between Weekly Seasonal Factors in Treasury Bill Rates, 1959–61*

Type of Seasonal Program	Average of 27-Day Seasonals (current and 4-weeks hence) With 55-Day Seasonal	27-Day Seasonal With 55-Day Seasonal	Average of 27-Day Seasonals (current and 4-weeks past) With 55-Day Seasonal
Multiplicative	.844	.811	.520
Additive	.804	.750	.486

market segmentation hypothesis implies that differences in maturity account for differences in substitutability between securities. If maturity differences are held constant, then the substitutability or the cross elasticity of demand ought also to be constant. In contrast, the expectations hypothesis implies that a seven-year security is more like an eight-year security than a one-year security is like a two-year security. The expectations hypothesis implies that the common element in two securities separated by a year in maturity increases monotonically as term to maturity increases.

Similarly, if one accepts the view that liquidity preference varies with the level of rates, then the premium increases as the level of rates increases. Hence, if securities separated by a year in term to maturity are examined, one should expect the common element to increase as term to maturity increases. Because both liquidity preference and expectations have common implications, this test does not discriminate between them. It does, however, produce evidence that must be regarded as discriminating between expectations and liquidity preference on the one hand and market segmentation on the other.

The foregoing tests were performed with two independent sets of data: the Durand data that Meiselman used and yields to maturity, for the latest cycle, read off the yield curve in the *Treasury Bulletin* by a draftsman. The test employed was a simple rank test. The expectations and liquidity preference hypotheses imply that the correlations between securities separated by a year in term to maturity ought to increase monotonically as term to maturity increases. Hence the theory forecasts a set of ranks that can be compared with the observed ranks to see if they are positively correlated.

Consistent results were obtained using these independent sets of data. The ranks predicted by the expectations and liquidity preference hypotheses and the actual ranks were highly correlated. Each set of data consisted of nine pairs of ranks. Using the Olds rank correlation test, and interpreting the implications of the liquidity preference and expectations as implying a one-tail test, both significance levels were under 2 per cent.[32]

The foregoing analysis of the implications of liquidity preference and expectations for the correlation between the yields of securities separated by a constant time span as term to maturity increases also implies that yield curves ought to flatten out with maturity. Given that the weights assigned to marginal rates of interest, in the determination of average or internal rates of return, decrease with maturity, then yield curves must flatten out with maturity. This assumes that the variance in forward rates is independent of term to maturity.

The evidence presented supports the Hicksian theory of the term structure of interest rates; it supports the view that both expectations and liquidity preference determine the term structure of interest rates. These results show that forward rates should be interpreted as expected rates plus a liquidity premium. If forward rates are so interpreted, then the expectations of the market seem to forecast subsequently observed short-maturity spot rates; the relationship between expected and subsequently observed spot rates cannot be rationalized as the workings of chance.

With respect to the market segmentation hypothesis, the evidence is less clear. These findings show that this hypothesis is not of the same magnitude as liquidity preference and expectations in the determination of the term structure of rates. The fact that forward rates embody short-term forecasts of spot rates that have a perceptible degree of accuracy implies that liquidity premiums are stable. Hence, the scope for the impact of market segmentation upon the term structure of rates must be limited. The Meiselman findings on the relationship between what he termed forecast revisions and errors support this view, as do the tests presented here

A proponent of market segmentation may argue that these tests, in particular, the test based on holding absolute maturity differences constant while varying relative maturity differences, are based on incorrect interpretations of market segmentation. Economic literature does not contain a statement of the market segmentation hypothesis that is as rigorous as those available either for liquidity preference or expecta-

[32] The test employed is described in W. Allen Wallis, "Rough-and-Ready Statistical Tests," *Industrial Quality Control*, March, 1952.

tions. Therefore, the possibility of misinterpretation cannot be easily dismissed. The Walker findings which deal with the root of the market segmentation hypothesis are particularly relevant. He showed that institutions have sharply changed the maturity composition of their holdings in response to market forces. This seems to strike at the very foundation of the market segmentation thesis. The only contrary evidence uncovered—this is also subject to the same uncertainties about its relevance—is the existence of negative forward rates in the bill market. Such occurrences seem to be rare, and therefore relatively insignificant, but should not be dismissed entirely. There is always the possibility that more of such evidence exists or that the effects of market segmentation are relatively subtle and the tests employed too crude to detect its existence.[33]

THE APPLICATION OF THE LIQUIDITY PREFERENCE AND EXPECTATIONS HYPOTHESES TO THE CYCLICAL BEHAVIOR OF INTEREST RATES

Applications of the Lutz-Meiselman Model

If both liquidity effects and incorrect expectations are disregarded, one should expect to find that long-term rates are higher than short-term rates when the latter are low and lower than short-term rates when the latter are high; in the absence of trends in interest rates, the average yields of short- and long-term rates should be equal. Insofar as short-term rates are relatively low about cyclical troughs and high about peaks, yield curves ought to be negatively sloped at peaks and positively sloped at troughs. Peaks and troughs in specific cycles of short-term rates should be anticipated by movements in long-term rates. If the market anticipates increases or decreases in short-term rates, long-term rates should move in advance in the same direction. Hence, if peaks and troughs in short-term rates are coincident with the reference cycle, peaks and troughs in long-term rates ought to lead the business cycle, and the longer the maturity, the greater the lead. The reasoning here is the same as that which led Macaulay to expect time money rates to lead call money rates.

[33] There were negative forward rates in the bill market in the 1930's. At that time rates were relatively low and taxes on bank deposits in Illinois were high enough to make it profitable to take a negative yield rather than be subject to taxation on deposits.

Analytically, the 91-day rate can be regarded as a spot or instantaneous rate of interest which reflects money market conditions at specific phases of the cycle. In contrast, the yield on long-term governments represents an average of the current and expected spot rates over the course of three or four reference cycles. Because the term to maturity of long-term governments is longer than the usual reference cycle, the yields of these securities reflect an average of spot rates during both expansions and contractions. Hence, long-term rates vary relatively less than short-term rates. Money market conditions during a specific phase of a cycle are largely "averaged out" (the effects of abnormally low or high spot rates largely cancel) in the determination of the long-term rate. In contrast, money market conditions during specific cycle phases are completely reflected in bill yields. As a result, short-term rates ought to be more variable over the cycle than long-term rates. The expectations hypothesis implies that the shorter the term to maturity of a security, the smaller the number of spot rates that are averaged in order to determine its yield; consequently, the larger its variance over the cycle. Cyclical movements in the short- relative to the long-term rate can be analyzed as if the latter were a permanent or normal rate of interest and the short-term rate contained a large transitory component. This transitory component is largest about peaks and troughs. When positive, at peaks, short-term rates are high relative to long-term rates; when negative, at troughs, short-term rates are relatively low.[34]

[34] This implies that the correlation between a moving average of short- and long-term rates over the cycle would be greater than the correlation between current short- with long-term rates. A moving average would abstract from cyclical effects on short-term rates; it would depict permanent short-term rates and abstract from transitory effects. It also would, of course, reduce the amplitude of the fluctuations in short- relative to long-term rates; in effect, it converts short- to long-term rates.

The view that the long-term rate is an average of short-term rates explains why Hicks found that time series of short- and long-term rates were less strongly correlated than averages of past and present short-term rates (both weighted and unweighted) and long-term rates. Presumably averages reflect expectations of "permanent" short-term rates. Hence, they are more like long-term rates than actual short-term rates which embody a transitory component that is negative at troughs and positive at peaks. See Hicks, *op. cit.*, p. 28. Hawtrey's position is similar to that of Charles C. Abbott, "A Note on the Government Bond Market," *Review of Economic Statistics*, Vol. 17, 1935, p. 9. Both reasoned that the forces that affect short maturity yields are largely independent of the forces that affect long maturity yields because fluctuations in short-term rates are much greater than those in long-term rates.

The market regards current short-term rates as abnormally high when they are above long-term rates, and expects them to fall in the future. At such times, holders of long-term securities expect to win capital gains because the passage of time will eliminate the abnormally high short-term rates from the average of present and future short-term rates that is the long-term rate. The opposite occurs when short-term rates are relatively low; i.e., the holders of long-term securities expect to incur capital losses as low short-term rates are eliminated from the average that is the long-term rate.

This does not, in itself, imply that it is more profitable to hold long- than short-term securities when rates are expected to fall. If the expectations of the market are correct, then the high yields of short- relative to long-term securities would just offset expected capital gains on the latter. The yield differential in this case represents what the market thinks is necessary to equalize the holding period yields of these securities, taking into account both coupons and capital gains. Conversely, when short-term rates are abnormally low, they are expected to rise. The abnormally large yield advantage of long-term securities in this case represents what the market thinks is necessary to offset the expected capital losses attributable to holding them. Whether or not the holding period yields of short-term relative to long-term securities are greater or less over the cycle depends upon which way the market erred in predicting future short-term rates. A fall in short-term rates that is larger than anticipated favors the holders of long-term securities, and vice versa.

These implications of the expectations hypothesis for the cyclical behavior of interest rates are in part incorrect because liquidity preference is not an independent variable in the analysis. Yet they go far towards providing an interpretation of the behavior of yield differentials between long- and short-term governments since 1920. In particular, they further our understanding of the sharp movements in short-term rates that occurred during this time.

In the 1920's there were two periods when short-term rates were above long-term rates (see Chart 6-5). During 1920, and again in 1929, the market anticipated lower future short-term rates. Although the absolute level of short-term rates during 1920 was about seventy-five basis points higher than it was in 1929, the anticipated fall was much greater in 1929. The yield advantage of short-term over long-term securities in 1929 was at least twice as great as it was in 1921. The fall in short-term rates from 1929 to 1931 was about 450 basis

CHART 6–5. Yields of U.S. Government Securities, 1920–63

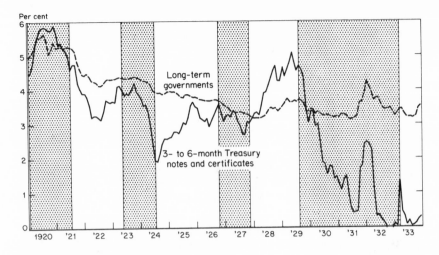

NOTE: Shaded areas represent business cycle contractions; unshaded areas, expansions.

points, whereas the fall from 1920 to 1922 was about 275 basis points. Both downward movements were greater than the other declines in short-term rates during this period.

In more recent years (1957 and 1959), short-term rates were again higher than long-term rates (see Chart 6-6). The absolute level of rates was higher in 1959 but the yield differential between long- and short-term securities was about the same. The subsequent downward movements in short-term rates were of roughly equal magnitude, about 275 basis points, and were the largest declines since the 1920's. In the 1930's, short-term relative to long-term rates were especially low. This was a consequence of abnormally low short-term rates; they were at historical lows.

The implications of a pure expectations model for the cyclical behavior of interest rates are inconsistent with the following observations: (1) short maturities yield less over the cycle than long maturities; yield curves are more often than not positively sloped; (2) short-term rates fail to exceed long-term rates at peaks as much as they fall below long-term rates at troughs; (3) the variance over the cycle in yields of three-month Treasury bills is less than the variance of nine- to twelve-month governments; (4) when short-term

CHART 6–6. Yields of U.S. Government Securities, 1954–61

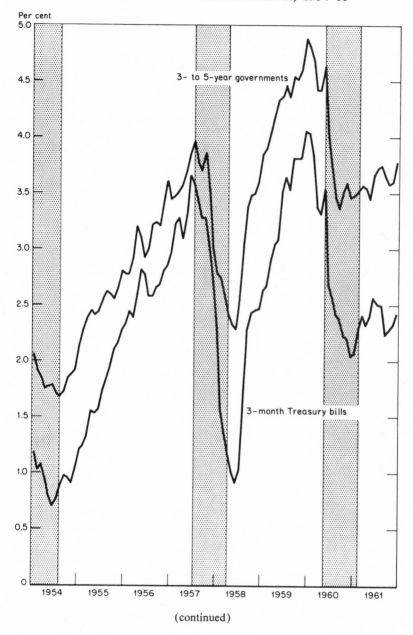

Per cent

3- to 5-year governments

3-month Treasury bills

(continued)

CHART 6–6 (concluded)

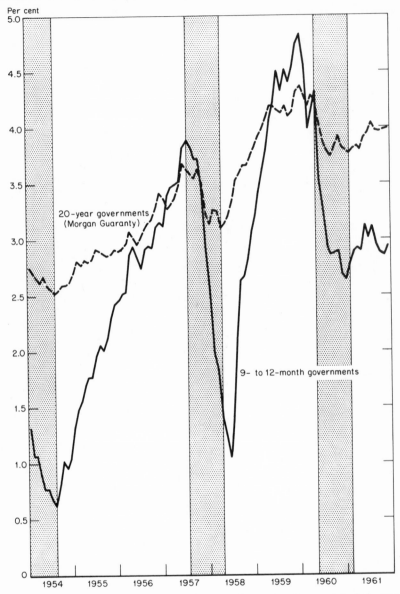

Per cent

NOTE: Shaded areas represent business cycle contractions; unshaded areas, expansions.

rates are above long-term rates, it is not the shortest term to maturity that bears the highest yield, i.e., yield curves at first rise with term to maturity and then fall; (5) long-term rates fail to lead turning points in short-term rates.

Applications of the Hicks Model

Cyclical Behavior of Governments

To explain these observations, liquidity preference must be added to the analysis. This implies that interest rates no longer measure the total return derived from holding securities. Securities also yield a nonpecuniary or liquidity income to their holders. The evidence presented indicates that the nonpecuniary return from securities is inversely related to term to maturity and directly related to the level of pecuniary yields. The shorter the term to maturity, the larger the fraction of the total return from a security that is nonpecuniary, and vice versa. The higher the level of interest rates, the wider the spread between the total return from a security and its pecuniary yield, and vice versa.

If, abstracting from differences in expectations of future short-term rates, the total return attributable to all maturities is the same, i.e., the sum of pecuniary and nonpecuniary returns is equal for all terms to maturity, then the pecuniary yield must be an increasing function of term to maturity. Therefore, if expectations have a random effect on yield curves, the average yield curve will be positively sloped, and short-term rates will, on the average, be lower than long-term rates. The interaction of expectations and liquidity preference to produce a "normal" yield curve is shown in Chart 6-7. The "total return" curve is flat; it depicts a market in which future short-term rates are expected to be the same as the current rates. The liquidity yield is the fraction of total yields for any given maturity that is nonpecuniary. Subtracting the nonpecuniary component from total return leaves the pecuniary yield curve, which is the yield curve observed in the market.[35]

[35] Liquidity return as a percentage of total return was obtained by first fitting a yield curve to average yields as a function of term to maturity for the three latest reference cycles. Then the ratios of yields for particular maturities to twenty-year government bond yields were computed. The difference between the ratio for any given term to maturity and one constitutes the fraction of total yield that is nonpecuniary for that term to maturity.

CHART 6–7. "Normal" or Average Yield Curve

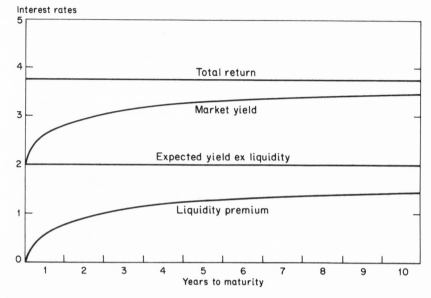

Liquidity preference produces asymmetry in the relationship between short- and long-term rates at cycle peaks and troughs. It accounts for the failure of short-term rates to exceed long-term rates at peaks by as much as they fall below long-term rates at troughs.

At cyclical troughs, both liquidity and expectational forces operate independently to establish short-term rates below long-term rates. Liquidity preference produces a pecuniary yield differential of long-term over short-term securities. At troughs, the market regards the current short-term rate as abnormally low and expects it to be higher in the future. Hence, expectations also push short-term below long-term rates. Both effects operate to widen the spread between these rates (Chart 6-8). The total-return curve slopes positively because the market expects future yields on short maturities, both pecuniary and nonpecuniary, to be higher than current short maturity yields. Subtracting the liquidity component from the total yield curve produces a market yield curve with a long-short differential greater than the differential for the corresponding total yield curve.

At cyclical peaks, in contrast to cyclical troughs, liquidity and expectational forces produce opposite effects on yield curves. Liquidity preference, as always, operates to establish short-term below long-

CHART 6–8. Yield Curve at Cyclical Troughs

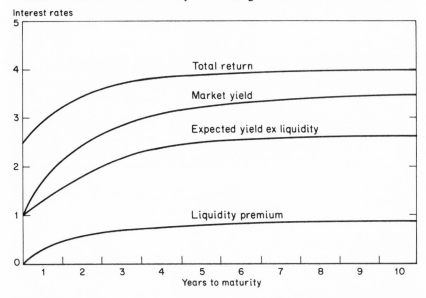

term rates. However, expectations act in the opposite direction. Because the market expects future short-term rates to be lower, the total yield curve declines as a function of term to maturity. Whether or not the resulting market yield curve is rising, falling, or both depends upon the relative strength of these opposing forces. Because these forces work in opposite directions at cyclical peaks but in the same direction at troughs, short-term yields do not exceed long-term yields at peaks as much as they fall below long-term yields at troughs.

The foregoing analysis implies that flat market yield curves should be interpreted as indicating that the market expects future pecuniary yields of short maturities to be lower than current short-term rates. With no change in expectations, the fraction of the total return that is nonpecuniary for a forward rate which pertains to a specific period of calendar time will rise with the passage of time. Hence, its pecuniary yield will fall below current spot rates. A flat market yield curve is shown in Chart 6-9. A falling total-return curve is a necessary condition for its existence.

Charts 6-10 and 6-11 depict yield curves with segments that are negatively sloped (yield curves with such shapes are also referred to as humped). Such curves are produced by expectations of sharply

CHART 6–9. A Flat Yield Curve

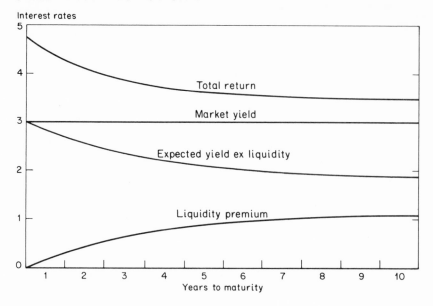

CHART 6–10. Yield Curve at Cyclical Peaks

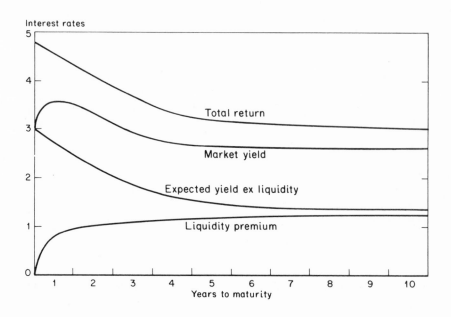

CHART 6–11. Effects of Alternative Expectations of Falling Rates Upon the Shape of Yield Curves

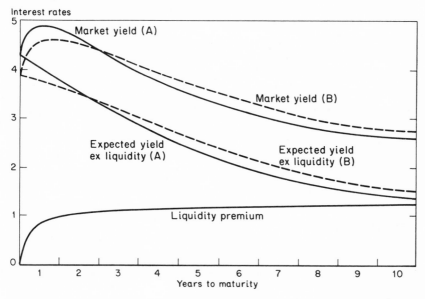

falling interest rates, i.e., interest rates that are falling more sharply than those in Chart 6-8. The more sharply interest rates are expected to fall, the shorter the term to maturity of the peak in yields; the more gradual the expected fall, the further out on the yield curve the peak will be. If the expected fall in short-term rates is very gradual, no negative segment appears. Yield curves with negative segments have been relatively rare, at least since the 1920's; expectations of interest-rate declines are usually not sharp enough to offset the effects of liquidity preference.

Liquidity preference also explains why the shortest term to maturity is not the highest yielding security in the term structure at cyclical peaks. In order for a yield curve to exist that has the shortest term to maturity bearing the highest yield, expectations of extremely sharp declines in short-term rates are required. Such expectations, while a theoretical possibility, did not exist during the two most recent cyclical peaks and possibly have never existed.

The liquidity preference hypothesis implies that nonpecuniary yields are a decreasing function of term to maturity. Hence, the range of pecuniary yields that will be observed in the market will increase with term to maturity. For example, suppose liquidity yields for Treasury bills and nine- to twelve-month governments are at all times 50 and 25 per cent of total returns. Further, assume that total returns, which are of course not directly observable in the market, range from 4 to 8 per cent. Pecuniary yields will then range from 2 to 4 per cent for bills, and from 3 to 6 per cent for nine- to twelve-month governments. Hence, liquidity preference implies that the variance in yields over the cycle increases with term to maturity.

The expectations hypothesis implies just the opposite: that the shorter the term to maturity, the greater the variance. Therefore, the actual variance observed in the market for any specified term to maturity represents a composition of these conflicting forces. The available evidence on variance as a function of term to maturity suggests that liquidity effects dominate expectational effects for governments with maturities equal to or less than nine-to-twelve months. For three- to five-year governments and longer maturities, expectational effects dominate. The absence of time series between these maturity ranges precludes a precise estimate here of the borderline separating the domains of dominance of expectations and liquidity.

During expansions, yield differentials between Treasury bills and nine- to twelve-month governments widen. Insofar as liquidity effects dominate expectational effects, liquidity premiums ought to widen from trough to peak since, according to the liquidity preference hypothesis, they are an increasing function of the absolute level of interest rates. Consequently, if only liquidity effects are at work, the differentials between bills and nine- to twelve-month governments would increase more than the increases observed. Adding expectations to the analysis implies, given the assumption that the market can recognize transitorily high or low levels of spot rates, the addition of an opposing force. Converse implications are implied for contractions. Liquidity operates to narrow, and expectations to widen, the spread between bills and nine- to twelve-month governments. Since liquidity is dominant for this maturity range, the observed spreads decrease during contractions. For evidence on how these differentials have actually behaved, see Charts 6-6 and 6-12.

These findings for governments do not necessarily apply to corporates or to the issues of government agencies unless the nonpecuniary component of total yield is the same. In general, governments appear to be more liquid, ignoring the influence of term to maturity, than

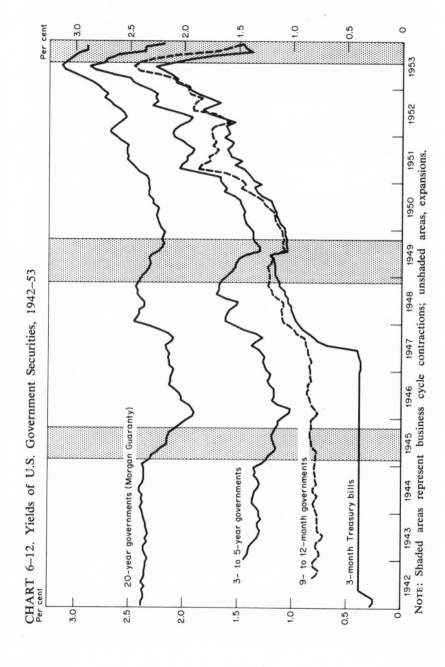

CHART 6–12. Yields of U.S. Government Securities, 1942–53

20-year governments (Morgan Guaranty)

3- to 5-year governments

9- to 12-month governments

3-month Treasury bills

NOTE: Shaded areas represent business cycle contractions; unshaded areas, expansions.

Essays on Interest Rates

either agency issues or corporates.[36] Among short-term securities, governments have a comparative liquidity advantage over agencies or corporates. The bill market has very low transactions costs and bid and asked prices are firm for extremely large transactions. This suggests that when yield curves are humped, the peak in yields will have a longer term to maturity for corporates than for governments.

In the absence of liquidity premiums, and assuming the market can forecast turning points in the specific cycles of interest rates, cyclical peaks in long-term rates would precede those of short-term rates and would be observable first. Similarly, troughs in long-term rates would precede troughs in short-term rates. The rationale that Macaulay used to argue that the seasonal peak in time money rates should precede that in call money rates is relevant here. Insofar as the market can predict turning points in short-term rates, the long-term rate (which is an average of future short-term rates) should reach its peak first in anticipation of the peak in short-term rates.

When liquidity preference is introduced into the analysis, however, the sequence in the timing of peaks and troughs of long- and short-term securities becomes less obvious. If liquidity premiums are a function of spot rates, then an amount is added to long-term rates which increases as short-term rates increase and reaches a peak when the latter reach their peak. The peak in long-term rates must occur later, therefore, than it would have occurred in a world of pure expectations.

How much later this peak will occur can only be partially determined by a priori reasoning. It is clear that the peak in long-term rates should not occur after the peak in short-term rates. Since the maximum amount that will be added to long-term rates because of liquidity preference will occur when short-term rates reach their peak, the peak in long-term rates must either precede or be synchronous with that of short-term rates.

Since the end of World War II, the behavior of time series of govern-

---

[36] The evidence for the proposition that agency issues are less liquid than governments is of two kinds. (1) Agencies have higher transactions costs. The spread between bid and asked prices, as reported in dealer quotation sheets, ranges from two-thirty-seconds for short-term securities to a whole point, the equivalent of ten dollars, for long-term securities. (2) The value of agencies as collateral for bank loans is poorer than it is for governments. Per dollar of borrowing, the market value of collateral in the form of agencies, term to maturity aside, is higher than it is for governments. The Joint Economic Committee *Study of the Dealer Market,* p. 95, reports that the margin requirements for agencies are 5 per cent.

ments with various terms to maturity indicates that all securities, irrespective of maturity, reach their peaks and troughs synchronously. Hence, without going further into the question of whether liquidity premiums add enough to long-term rates to delay their peaks until all peaks are synchronous, irrespective of term to maturity, one cannot say, using this evidence alone, whether the market can or cannot predict turning points in interest rates. In view of the inability of the market to predict turning points of other series, on balance, it seems reasonable to interpret these findings as being consistent with the view that the market cannot predict turning points in specific cycles of interest rates.[37]

Cyclical Behavior of Agency Issues and Corporates

The thesis has been advanced that liquidity premiums are caused primarily by a desire to avoid the risk of capital loss. The evidence indicates that yield differentials, when only liquidity differences exist, increase with the absolute level of rates. The observations of an upward trend in liquidity premiums for the three latest cycles, and regressions of liquidity premiums upon spot rates, show that liquidity premiums increase when interest rates increase. This thesis has implications for the cyclical and secular behavior of other rates of interest. It implies that low-quality bonds ought to yield more, the cycle aside, than high-quality bonds because they are relatively less liquid, i.e., price variance is greater as a result of the greater default risk. Consequently, it should be possible to observe that high-quality bonds yield less than low-quality bonds generally and that the yield differential between high- and low-quality bonds increases from trough to peak, and decreases from peak to trough. By symmetrical reasoning, the spread between government agency issues and governments, ignoring term to maturity, should increase with the absolute level of interest rates.

To test one of these propositions, yield differentials between governments and government agency issues were regressed against their sums. The results of this test are mixed. For nine- to twelve-month

[37] The highest correlation (.98) of seasonally adjusted time series for three-month Treasury bills with nine- to twelve-month governments was obtained by assuming the two series to be synchronous. The correlations with one-, two-, and three-month leads and lags were: .95 for one month, .90 for two, and .83 for three. No difference, to two decimal places, was observed for leads and lags of equal duration.

maturities, the spreads between governments on the one hand, and Federal National Mortgage Association, Federal Land Bank, and Federal Home Loan Bank issues on the other, are consistent with the hypothesis advanced; spreads increase as the absolute level of interest rates increases. The same is true for maturities ten years and over. The best results were obtained by regressing the yield differential between a government bond, the three and one-quarter of 1983, and an index of AA utility yields of bonds with coupons of three and one-eighth to three and three-eighths against their sum. The correlation was positive and 40 per cent of the variation in the spread was explained.[38] However, for three- to five-year governments and FLB and FNMA issues, the slopes of the regression coefficients were negative, one significantly so.

The consequences of changes in the level of interest rates for yield differentials between low- and high-quality bonds over the cycle is somewhat more difficult to detect. During contractions, the level of rates falls and the market usually increases its estimates of the risks of default by the issuers of low-quality securities. Conversely, the level of rates rises during expansions and the market usually decreases its estimates of the risks of default. Hence, liquidity and cyclical forces work in opposite directions upon yield differentials. During the post-World War II period, the revaluation of risks over the cycle has dominated liquidity forces. Hence, the yields of Baa Moody's bonds, for all categories, have fluctuated less than corresponding Aaa bonds.

The behavior of low- and high-quality bond yield differentials over time seems to support the view that the level of rates and these differentials are related. Since 1945, the spread between Moody's AAA and BAA series has increased with the level of interest rates. The regression of the difference on the sum indicates that the difference rises with the level of rates.

Prewar investigations of the relationship between the yield differential of high and low grade bonds and the level of interest rates also conforms to this finding.

---

[38] All of the agency issues exhibited a significant downward trend over time in yield differentials compared with governments. Presumably this reflects the diffusion of knowledge about the investment merits of these securities that has occurred in recent years. The data for the agencies consist of incomplete series, mostly for the last decade, compiled by Charles E. Quincey and Co., and Allen Knowles, the fiscal agent of the Federal Home Loan Banks. The AA utility series is compiled by Salomon Bros. & Hutzler.

Ratios of promised yields (or yield spreads) to the basic rates on high-grade issues deserve more attention than they can be given in this report. According to the classical theory of investment values, the simple yield spread, or algebraic difference between the promised yield and basic rate, would provide the best measure of the risk premium for issues properly priced in the market, since the yield is conceived of as the algebraic sum of the pure rate of interest and the risk premium. It is a matter of record, however, that yield spreads frequently narrow when basic rates fall, and widen when basic rates rise . . . , perhaps because of the efforts of investors to compensate for changes in basic rates.[39]

For any preassigned cyclical downturn in bill rates, yield differentials between low and high grade bonds should decrease most during severe and least during mild contractions. Conversely, during strong upturns, the differential ought to increase more for sharp than for mild recoveries. The data on the behavior of differentials between low and high grade bonds, since the end of World War II, while they support the view that there has been a secular rise in the differential, do not support the view that the differential is at a maximum at peaks and minimum at troughs. In fact, the maximum differential seems to appear midway between the cyclical peak and the trough. This seems to be accounted for by differences between low and high grade bonds in the timing of their specific cycle peaks and troughs. In the postwar period, specific cycle peaks and troughs of high grade bonds consistently preceded those of low grade bonds. Hence, the maximum yield differential between the two could not have been associated with business cycle turning points.[40]

---

[39] W. Braddock Hickman, *Corporate Bond Quality and Investor Experience,* Princeton University Press for NBER, 1958, p. 288. For further discussion, see the following pages.

[40] Part of the increase in the measured yield differential between low and high grade bonds is attributable to differences between the economic, as distinguished from the temporal, term to maturity of these bonds. If calendar term to maturity is the same for both grades, then economic term to maturity, which Macaulay termed duration, must be shorter on the lower grade issues. (See *Movements of Interest Rates,* Chapter II, for a discussion of this point.) The weights assigned to receipts in the near, relative to the distant, future for computing yield to maturity is greater for low than high-quality bonds. Hence, a rise in rates during an expansion, with no change in investor attitudes towards risk, will increase measured yield differentials for the same reason that yields of three- to five-year governments rise relative to twenty-year governments during an expansion. This same point explains why the market believes that if interest rates are expected to fall, securities with equal yields and terms to maturity will have different

                         Essays on Interest Rates

Hickman's investigation of the relationship between low and high grade bond yields over time suggests that the long run rate of return to investors in low grade bonds is greater than it is for high grade bonds. He concludes that "the highest returns were obtained by investors who could afford to take the greatest risks."[41] He found that both the variance and the average rate of return was greatest for investments in low grade bonds. In this respect, his finding is symmetrical with the relationship between long- and short-term government yields, taking into account both capital gains and interest receipts.

relative price rises if their coupons are not the same. The size of the coupons will be inversely related to the rate of change of capital values.

In fact, this phenomenon seems to account for a trivial portion of the cyclical variation in the yield differential between low- and high-quality bonds. To determine the quantitative importance of this effect, a constant risk differential of 1 per cent for all spot and forward rates was assumed for two hypothetical ten-year bonds. At peaks, the higher grade bond was assumed to consist of a six-month spot rate of 5 per cent, with the first forward rate being 4.5 per cent and all succeeding forward rates, 4 per cent. At troughs, the higher grade bond was assumed to consist of a six-month spot rate of 2 per cent, with the first forward rate being 3 per cent and all succeeding forward rates 4 per cent. The yield to maturity of these two postulated securities differed by ninety-eight basis points at troughs, and one hundred and two at peaks.

[41] Hickman, *op. cit.*, p. 138.

7

Expectations at the Short End of the Yield Curve: An Application of Macaulay's Test

Thomas Sargent

The recent interest in the expectations hypothesis and the term structure of interest rates has been marked by an abandonment of the search for accurate forecasting[1] that characterized early empirical work on the term structure. Economists have by and large followed David Meiselman's [15] lead in accepting the proposition that even if expectations prove to be inaccurate, they may still determine the yield structure. Thus, the literature's emphasis has shifted to attempting to explain the process by which expectations are formed.[2]

This paper presents an inspection of the accuracy of the expectations implicit in the yield curve using essentially the same approach followed by Frederick Macaulay [13] in one of the earliest empirical studies of the term structure. Our return to this approach is motivated by several factors. First, existence of accurate forecasting provides a particularly convincing type of evidence confirming the expectations hypothesis. Second, as Kessel [12, p. 7] has noted, the reappearance of a seasonal in money market rates in the 1950's provides a new body of data with which to conduct tests along the lines of Macaulay's. Third, cross-spectral analysis provides a set of tools well suited to performing the required tests.

NOTE: The author thanks Melvin Hinich, Phillip Cagan, Gregory Chow, Stanley Diller, and Jack Guttentag for helpful comments on an earlier draft of this paper.
[1] Kessel [12] is the most notable exception.
[2] For example, see DeLeeuw [4], Malkiel [14], Modigliani and Sutch [17], Wood [21], Van Horne [20], and Bierwag and Grove [1].

MACAULAY'S TEST

The cornerstone of the expectations theory is the proposition that long rates can be thought of as an average of current and anticipated short rates. For bills, which yield no coupons and sell at a discount, the following formula from Hicks [9] is appropriate:

$$R_{nt} = n\sqrt{(1 + R_{1t})(1 + {}_{t+1}r_{1t}) \ldots (1 + {}_{t+n-1}r_{1t})} - 1, \quad (1)$$

where R_{jt} is the yield to maturity on j-period bills at time t and ${}_{t+j}r_{1t}$ is the rate the market expects to prevail on one-period bills in period $t + j$. For interest rates in the usual ranges, the arithmetic average approximation to equation (1),

$$R_{nt} \approx (R_{1t} + {}_{t+1}r_{1t} + \cdots + {}_{t+n-1}r_{1t})/n, \quad (1a)$$

can be used with small error.[3] The formula implies that forecasts of short rates are embedded in long rates, and it was this proposition which Macaulay sought to verify. Macaulay compiled data on call and time rates for the years 1890 through 1913, a period characterized by a pronounced seasonal in money market rates. Since the seasonal was a fairly regular one that speculators could incorporate into their expectations, the longer-maturity time rates should have led call rates at least at the seasonal component of oscillation. This followed when it was noted that on the expectations hypothesis the time rate actually had a forecast of the shorter-maturity call rate impounded within it. Macaulay proceeded to estimate the seasonal component of each series over the period 1890–1913, and he found that the time rate seasonal did appear to lead the call rate seasonal. This he thought constituted "evidence of definite and relatively successful forecasting" [13, p. 36]. However, he could find no evidence of successful forecasting at the nonseasonal frequencies.

The nature of Macaulay's procedure, with its use of a decomposition of time series by frequency and the search for a lead of one series over another at particular frequencies, suggests that the tools of spectral

---

[3] This can be seen by writing equation (1) as

$$1n(1 + R_{nt}) = [1n(1 + R_{1t}) + \ldots + 1n(1 + {}_{t+n-1}r_{1t})]/n,$$

and noting that for small x, $1n(1 + x) \approx x$.

and cross-spectral analysis would be useful in conducting such a study.[4] By examining the estimated spectral density function for each series, it can easily be determined if an important seasonal component of oscillation, the key necessary condition in Macaulay's experiment, exists in the data. Then by inspecting the coherence coefficient, a measure analogous to the R^2 statistic of correlation analysis, the strength of association between series at the relevant frequencies can be studied. Provided that the coherence coefficient is sufficiently large, the phase statistic, which gives an estimate of the average lead of one series over another over a given frequency band, can be inspected for leads at the relevant frequencies.[5]

In order to determine the consistency of results produced by spectral methods with those obtained by Macaulay, spectral and cross-spectral calculations were made for the period 1890–1913 using the monthly data on call and time rates that Macaulay had studied. Forty-eight was the maximal lag used in obtaining the spectral and cross-spectral estimates from the covariograms.[6] The results are reported in Charts 7-1 through 7-5. The estimated spectral densities, which are given in Charts 7-1 and 7-2, display sizable peaks at periodicities of twelve, six, and three months, which correspond to the seasonal component of oscillation and its first and third harmonics. This means that a good deal of the variance in the series is accounted for by oscillations in these frequency bands, and thus it confirms the existence of a seasonal pattern in each series.

The strength of association between the two series at various components of oscillation can be determined by inspecting the coherence diagram, which appears in Chart 7-3. The coherence coefficient provides a measure of the proportion of the variance occurring in one series over a given frequency band which is explained by the variations over the same frequency band in another series. The coherence is bounded by zero and one, like the R^2 statistic to which it is analogous. Chart 7-3 shows that the call and time rates are highly correlated at the seasonal component, the coherence attaining a value greater than .9

---

[4] For previous applications of spectral techniques in studies of the term structure, see Fand [6], Granger and Rees [8], Dobell and Sargent [5], and Sargent [19].

[5] A comprehensive treatment of spectral analysis can be found in [7].

[6] The spectra and cross-spectra were calculated by using the standard covariance-cosine transformation procedures together with a Parzen window. The calculations were performed by using the ALGOL procedure SPECTRUM, which is available on the Carnegie Tech G-21 computer.

CHART 7–1. Spectral Density of Call Rate, 1890–1913

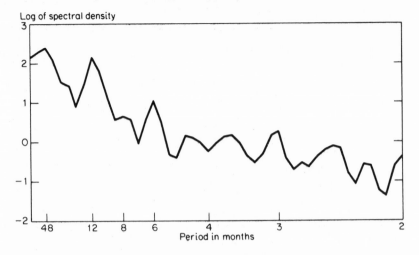

CHART 7–2. Spectral Density of Time Rate, 1890–1913

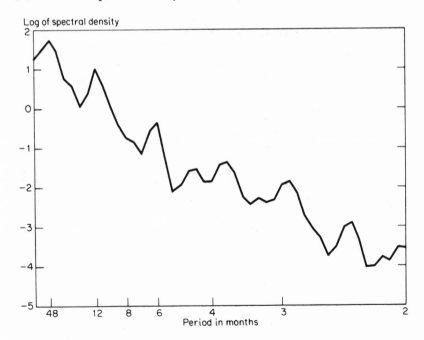

CHART 7-3. Coherence Between Time and Call Rate

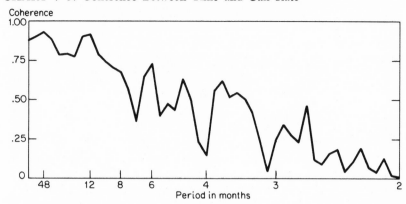

at the twelve-month periodicity. In addition, the coherence function displays peaks in the vicinity of the harmonics of the seasonal.

Chart 7-4 reports the phase of the time rate with respect to the call rate; when it is negative, it indicates that the time rate leads the call rate, while if it is positive, the call rate leads. The graph confirms Macaulay's finding that the time rate leads at the seasonal since the phase statistic is negative at the twelve-month frequency band and its first three harmonics. The results also confirm Macaulay's failure to find evidence of successful forecasting at other low frequency com-

CHART 7-4. Phase of Cross-Spectrum Between Call and Time Rates

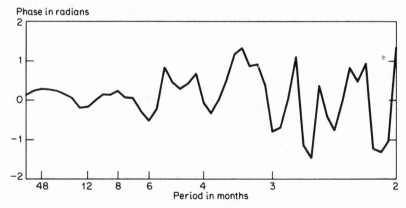

CHART 7–5. Gain of Cross-Spectrum Between Time and Call Rates

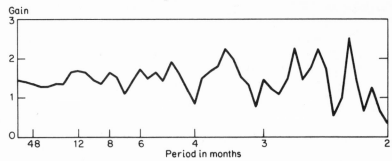

ponents of oscillation, for at none of the nonseasonal frequencies is there a negative phase shift coupled with a large coherence.[7]

The spectral results are thus consistent with Macaulay's findings in every respect. However, we should note certain limitations inherent in following Macaulay's procedure of comparing call and time rates. In particular, a problem arises from the ambiguous nature of the maturity of a call loan. While it is clear that its maturity was less than that of time loans, it undoubtedly varied over time, and probably in a systematic fashion with the level of rates. Given the pronounced seasonality in rate levels, it is not unlikely that the maturity of call loans itself displayed a seasonal component. Since the magnitude of the lead that Macaulay's mechanism produces depends sensitively on the maturity difference between call and time loans, such variations in the maturity of call loans distort the time structure of the relationship between call and time rates. This is a particularly serious problem with the harmonics of the seasonal, since here the variations of the maturity of call loans are likely to be large relative to the period of the oscillation, and this produces quite serious distortions in any results we may obtain.[8]

---

[7] Chart 7-5 reports the gain of the call rate with respect to the time rate over each frequency band. The gain statistic is essentially the regression coefficient $b(w_j)$ at each frequency for the model

$$y_t(w_j) = b(w_j)x_t(w_j),$$

where $y_t(w_j)$ is the call rate at frequency w_j and $x_t(w_j)$ is the time rate at w_j. Notice the rise in the gain that occurs at the seasonal and its first several harmonics. This pattern is consistent with Macaulay's comments about the smaller amplitude of time rates at the seasonal frequency [13, p. 36].

[8] For the period 1866–89, we performed a cross-spectral analysis on call rates and the longer-maturity commercial paper rate series compiled by Macaulay. The

Fortunately, this problem does not arise for the data on U.S. Treasury bill yields in the 1950's, which are the major concern of this study. However, before we turn to these data, we must investigate the implications of Macaulay's hypothesis for the behavior of timing with respect to the maturity difference between two bills.

THE TIME PATTERN UNDER ACCURATE FORECASTING

In this section we consider the implications of the extreme hypothesis that the forward short rates impounded in the yield curve accurately forecast the corresponding future spot rates. In our notation this hypothesis is written

$$_{t+j}r_{1t} = R_{1\,t+j}. \tag{2}$$

In the appendix we explore the consequences of invoking the weaker but still very severe hypothesis that the forward rates are unbiased estimators of future spot rates, that is,

$$_{t+j}r_{1t} = R_{1\,t+j} + {}_{t+j}\epsilon_t, j = 1, \ldots, n \tag{2a}$$

where the $_{t+j}\epsilon_t$'s are independent, identically distributed random variables with mean zero and finite variance, which are distributed independently of $R_{1\,t+j}$. Suffice it to say that our proposition about the timing of the relationship between R_{nt} and R_{1t} holds also when (2a) is assumed.

To simplify the exposition, we use the arithmetic approximation to Hicks' formula,

$$R_{nt} = (R_{1t} + {}_tr_{1t} + \cdots + {}_{t+n-1}r_{1t})/_{+1}n. \tag{3}$$

Substituting (2) into (3), we have

$$R_{nt} = (R_{1t} + R_{1t+1} + \cdots + R_{1t+n-1})/n, \tag{4}$$

which says that on the accurate forecasting hypothesis, long rates are arithmetic averages of current and subsequently observes short rates.

Inspection of (4) makes it clear that movements in R_{nt} will display a lead over movements in R_{1t}. It is our objective to derive the actual length of this lag. Before doing this, it may be helpful to set forth the

spectral densities confirmed that seasonals existed in both series and the coherence coefficient was fairly high at the seasonal frequencies. However, while the commercial paper rate led at the twelve-month frequency, it failed to lead at the important harmonics of the seasonal.

following heuristic argument which leads to the correct conclusion. Let us rewrite expression (4) as

$$R_{nt} = \frac{1}{n} R_{1t} + \frac{1}{n} R_{1t+1} + \cdots + \frac{1}{n} R_{1t+n-1}. \qquad (4a)$$

By how much will R_{nt} lead R_{1t}? We know by how many periods each of the terms on the right hand side of (4a) leads R_{1t}: R_{1t} leads R_{1t} by zero periods, R_{1t+1} leads R_{1t} by one period, and R_{1t+j} leads R_{1t} by j periods. Then, since R_{nt} is simply the average of R_{1t+j}, $j = 0, \ldots,$ $n-1$, the lead of R_{nt} over R_{1t} is simply the average of the leads of R_{1t+j}, $j = 0, \ldots, n-1$, over R_{1t}. Hence, we have

lead of R_{nt} over $R_{1t} = \frac{1}{n}$ (lead of R_{1t} over R_{1t} + lead of R_{1t+1} over

$$R_{1t} + \cdots + \text{lead of } R_{1t+n-1} \text{ over } R_{1t}).$$

or we have

lead of R_{nt} over $R_{1t} = \frac{1}{n} [0 + 1 + \cdots + (n-1)]$ periods. (5)

This is the key result of this section. It holds for both assumptions (2) and (2a). In the remainder of this section, and in the appendix, we shall set out a more rigorous development of this relationship. The continuity of the argument will not be badly interrupted if the reader proceeds to the next section at this point.

In order to derive (5), our strategy is to evaluate the phase of the cross-spectrum between long and short rates implied by equation (2). Let us first rewrite (4) as the linear relationship

$$R_{nt} = \sum_{i=0}^{n-1} h_i R_{1t+i}, \qquad (6)$$

where $h_i = 1/n$ for all i. Next we introduce the Fourier transforms of R_{1t}, R_{nt}, and h_i,

$$A(w) = \sum_t R_{1t} e^{iwt},$$

$$B(w) = \sum_t R_{nt} e^{iwt},$$

$$H(w) = \sum_t h_t e^{iwt}.$$

By the convolution theorem, (6) implies

$$B(w) = H(w) A(w), \qquad (7)$$

where $H(w)$ is the transfer function. The spectral densities of R_{1t} and R_{nt} are given by the mathematical expectations of the squared amplitude of their Fourier transforms. Letting $S_j(w)$ be the spectrum of j-period bills, we have

$$S_1(w) = E\,|A(w)|^2,$$
$$S_n(w) = E\,|B(w)|^2,$$

where E is the expectation operator. The cross-spectrum between R_{1t} and R_{nt}, $S_{1n}(w)$, is given by

$$S_{1n}(w) = E\,\overline{A(w)}\,B(w), \tag{8}$$

where $\overline{A(w)}$ is the complex conjugate of $A(w)$. Substituting (7) into (8) we have

$$S_{1n}(w) = E\,H(w)\,|A(w)|^2$$
$$= H(w)\,S_1(w).$$

Hence, we have arg $S_{1n}(w) = $ arg $H(w)$. Next we will express $H(w)$ as

$$H(w) = |H(w)|\,e^{iG(w)}, \tag{9}$$

where $G(w)$ is the phase of the transfer function. $G(w)$ is the expression we are interested in. From (6) we have

$$H(w) = \sum_{t=0}^{n-1} \frac{1}{n}\,e^{iwt}$$

$$= (1 - e^{inw})/n(1 - e^{iw}).$$

Assuming for convenience that n is odd and defining $m = (n-1)/2$, we can write

$$H(w) = e^{imw} \sum_{k=-m}^{m} e^{iwk}$$

$$= 2e^{imw}\,(\tfrac{1}{2} + \cos w \cdots + \cos mw),$$

which corresponds to expression (9) since the term in parentheses is real. Thus, we have arg $H(w) = G(w) = mw$ or

$$\text{arg } H(w) = \frac{n-1}{2}\,w, \tag{10}$$

which is the phase of the cross-spectrum. This is the expression we are after. The amplitude of the transfer function is given by

$$|H(w)| = 2 \ (\tfrac{1}{2} + \cos w + \cdots + \cos mw)$$
$$= \frac{\sin \ (nw/2)}{\sin \ (w/2)} \ .$$

Since angular frequency w equals $2 \ \pi/p$ where p is the length of the period,

$$|H(w)| = \frac{\sin \ (n \ \pi/p)}{\sin \ (\pi/p)} \ .$$

Clearly $|H(w)| = 0$ for $n = jp$, $j = 1, \ 2, \ \ldots$. That is, the amplitude of the transfer function equals zero for n's that are integer multiples of the periodicity being studied. At these frequencies, relation (10) has no meaning. For, since the coherence is zero here, the phase statistic is uniformly distributed on the interval

$$\left[-\frac{\pi}{2}, \frac{\pi}{2} \right].$$

Relation (10) is a precise statement of Macaulay's proposition that on the hypothesis of accurate forecasting, long rates lead spot short rates. The lead relationship is of a simple "fixed-time" form, the phase diagram increasing linearly in angular frequency w with slope $(n - 1)/2$. Such a phase diagram implies that in time the length of the lead is constant across all frequencies. To determine the length of the fixed-time lag, we simply multiply (10), which gives the phase in radians, by time periods per radian or $1/w$. Then the time lag equals

$$[(n - 1)/2] \cdot w \frac{1}{w} = (n - 1)/2 \text{ periods.}$$

Thus, the long rate leads the short by $(n - 1)/2$ periods across all frequencies. This is the same result given by the heuristic argument advanced at the beginning of this section. This is seen when it is noted that it can be shown by induction that $[0 + 1 + 2 + \ldots + (n - 1)]/n = (n - 1)/2$.

Thus, we have established that the time lead of longs over shorts is an arithmetic average of the indexes that show the number of periods forward to which the forward rates in (3) apply. In the next section, relation (10) is used to study the pattern of leads of long bill rates over shorts in the U.S. Treasury bill market in the 1950's.

MACAULAY'S TEST APPLIED TO U.S. TREASURY BILL RATES

It has been demonstrated that the accurate forecasting version of the expectations hypothesis implies that n-period rates lead one-period rates by $[0 + 1 + \ldots + (n-1)]/n$ periods. As a function of angular frequency w the hypothesized lead could be expressed as

$$\phi_n(w) = b_n w, \tag{11}$$

where $b_n = [0 + 1 + \ldots + (n-1)]/n$ periods; where w is expressed in radians per time period; and where $\Phi_n(w)$ is the phase of the cross-spectrum between R_{nt} and R_{1t}. In this section, our procedure will be to estimate the phase diagram of the cross-spectrum between n-period and one-period bills and then to use it to estimate b_n. It can then be determined how closely the estimated b_n's approximate the values implied by the accurate forecasting hypothesis.

We will use relation (1) to explore the adequacy of the accurate forecasting hypothesis in explaining the term structure of U.S. Treasury bill rates in the 1950's. The data are 417 weekly observations on one-, two-, . . . , thirteen-week bill rates for the period January 1953 through December 1960. With a few exceptions, the yield quotations were made on Tuesdays. The lag between sale and delivery is two working days, and consequently the rates correspond to bills delivered on Thursdays. Since Treasury bills always mature on Thursdays, the quotations are for bills with an integer number of weeks to maturity.[9]

We propose to test the accurate forecasting hypothesis by using the phase of the estimated cross-spectrum between one-week and n-week bills, $n = 2, \ldots, 13$, to estimate the parameter of (11) for $n = 2, \ldots, 13$. For the purposes of empirical implementation, a stochastic term must be added to the right side of equation (11). This term is present for several reasons. First, it incorporates the possibility of an error in the specification of (11). For example, accurate forecasting may be possible, if at all, only with respect to certain frequencies of oscillation, so that it is incorrect to specify that (11) holds across all frequencies. The use of the estimated phase, which is itself a random variable, provides another reason for including a stochastic term in

---

[9] See Roll [18] for a further description of the data used here. Professor Roll generously supplied the data for use in this study. We have used averages of bid and ask yields.

(11). This is the standard errors-in-variables cause for the presence of a stochastic term.[10] Of course, there is no reason to expect the variance of the estimated phase to be constant across frequencies. This will only occur if the true coherence is constant across all frequencies. This suggests that we should incorporate the assumption of heteroscedastic disturbances in our specification of (11). Accordingly, we assume

$$\hat{\phi}_n(w_i) = b_n w_i + u_i, \tag{11a_1}$$

$$\text{var } (u_i) = k \text{ var } \hat{\phi}_n(w_i), \tag{11a_2}$$

where u_i is a random term with mean zero and finite variance and where $\hat{\Phi}_n(w_i)$ denotes the estimated phase of the cross-spectrum between n-week and one-week rates at frequency w_i. Equation $(11a_2)$ states the assumption that the disturbance variance is proportional to the variance of the estimated phase, k being the factor of proportionality.

Where the disturbances are heteroscedastic, least squares is an inefficient estimator. However, an estimator that is equivalent to Aitken's efficient generalized least squares estimator is least squares applied to the following equation:

$$\hat{\phi}_n(w_i)/\sqrt{\text{var } \phi_n(w_i)} = b_n \left[w_i/\sqrt{\text{var } \hat{\phi}_n(w_i)}\right] + u_i/\sqrt{\text{var } \hat{\phi}_n(w_i)}. \tag{12}$$

On our assumptions, the variance of the transformed disturbances $u_i/\sqrt{\text{var } \hat{\phi}_n(w_i)}$ is a constant, which means that the inefficiency due to the heteroscedasticity of the u_i's can be eliminated by applying least squares to the transformed equation (12). In the empirical work below, we use an estimate of the asymptotic variance of each estimated phase statistic to transform the variables as indicated in (12).

Spectral densities were estimated for each of the thirteen bill rate series over the period January 1953 through December 1960. One hundred and four was the maximal lag used in the calculations. A typical spectral density for these series is the spectrum for the three-week bill rate which is reported in Chart 7-6. The graph contains peaks at the seventeen-and-one-third- and thirteen-week periodicities and at several harmonics of these periodicities. Not surprisingly, similar spectral shapes were estimated for the other twelve bill rates. The spectral results thus tend to confirm the existence of the seasonal in

---

[10] It should be noted that the error is in the dependent variable while the independent variable is measured exactly. Errors in the dependent variable induce no bias in the least squares estimator of b_j. See Johnston [11, Chapter 6].

CHART 7–6. Spectrum of Three-Week Bill Rate

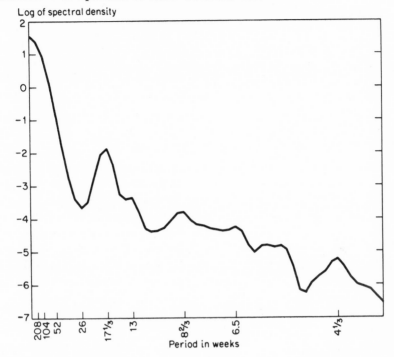

Log of spectral density

Period in weeks

bill rates which Kessel [12] and Conard [3, Chapter 5] found to be present in the 1950's.

Cross-spectra were calculated for each of the longer rates against the one-week bill rate. For periodicities greater than thirteen weeks, the coherence and phase of these cross-spectra are reported in Table 7-1. The estimated phase statistics recorded in this table are the basic data to be used in the regressions described above. The estimated coherence, which is shown in parentheses beneath the estimated phase, is also important for it permits us to estimate an asymptotic variance for the phase statistic at each frequency. The asymptotic variance of phase is approximately given by

$$(r/2s)[1/\text{coh}(w_i) - 1], \tag{13}$$

where r is the maximal lag, s is the number of observations, and $\text{coh}(w_i)$ is the coherence at frequency w_i.[11] By substituting the esti-

[11] See Hinich and Clay [10].

TABLE 7-1. Estimated Phase of Cross-Spectrum Between j-Week and One-Week Bills (measured in radians)

Period in weeks	j Equal to											
	2	3	4	5	6	7	8	9	10	11	12	13
208	.0080 (.9996)	.0115 (.9990)	.0159 (.9975)	.0188 (.9945)	.0193 (.9904)	.0175 (.9853)	.0191 (.9815)	.0165 (.9751)	.0155 (.9706)	.0153 (.9669)	.0153 (.9645)	.0152 (.9633)
104	.0162 (.9995)	.0236 (.9986)	.0337 (.9967)	.0436 (.9930)	.0481 (.9888)	.0480 (.9838)	.0514 (.9786)	.0505 (.9743)	.0508 (.9703)	.0513 (.9672)	.0517 (.9647)	.0522 (.9627)
69.33	.0249 (.9991)	.0372 (.9975)	.0547 (.9936)	.0799 (.9857)	.0935 (.9782)	.1020 (.9691)	.1095 (.9576)	.1157 (.9535)	.1225 (.9469)	.1265 (.9426)	.1303 (.9373)	.1356 (.9323)
52.0	.0310 (.9978)	.0491 (.9947)	.0767 (.9843)	.1234 (.9656)	.1478 (.9495)	.1701 (.9300)	.1870 (.9074)	.2014 (.8987)	.2197 (.8876)	.2319 (.8783)	.2444 (.8666)	.2606 (.8568)
41.6	.0284 (.9951)	.0478 (.9900)	.0879 (.9698)	.1418 (.9358)	.1613 (.9049)	.1790 (.8730)	.1930 (.8444)	.2149 (.8315)	.2367 (.8151)	.2539 (.7956)	.2715 (.7768)	.2869 (.7612)
34.67	.0210 (.9899)	.0367 (.9801)	.0867 (.9425)	.1244 (.8701)	.1034 (.8030)	.0722 (.7412)	.0388 (.6899)	.0770 (.6578)	.0804 (.6188)	.0818 (.5783)	.0923 (.5430)	.0821 (.5187)
29.71	.0242 (.9796)	.0700 (.9555)	.1191 (.8998)	.1278 (.7673)	.0559 (.6542)	-.0506 (.5458)	-.1407 (.4568)	-.1529 (.3687)	-.2375 (.3094)	-.2913 (.2754)	-.3106 (.2339)	-.3776 (.2227)
26.0	.0297 (.9616)	.1106 (.9248)	.1660 (.8608)	.1558 (.6959)	.0603 (.5364)	-.1090 (.3939)	-.2820 (.3004)	-.4756 (.2012)	-.6941 (.1774)	-.8031 (.1707)	-.8928 (.1440)	-1.0164 (.1573)

TABLE 7-1 (concluded)

Period in weeks	j Equal to											
	2	3	4	5	6	7	8	9	10	11	12	13
23.11	.0382 (.9517)	.1064 (.9176)	.1720 (.8678)	.1787 (.7631)	.1263 (.6276)	-.0067 (.5251)	-.1732 (.4739)	-.3740 (.3588)	-.5337 (.3373)	-.6393 (.3300)	-.7260 (.3038)	-.8385 (.3232)
20.8	.0503 (.9746)	.1038 (.9572)	.1798 (.9341)	.2404 (.9021)	.2783 (.8393)	.2430 (.8069)	.1979 (.7716)	.0962 (.6840)	-.0279 (.6311)	-.1169 (.5984)	-.1830 (.5654)	-.2761 (.5417)
18.91	.0496 (.9901)	.1038 (.9815)	.1811 (.9712)	.2622 (.9606)	.3324 (.9392)	.3367 (.9340)	.3433 (.9233)	.3002 (.8927)	.2080 (.8579)	.1396 (.8363)	.0917 (.8205)	.0341 (.7961)
17.33	.0424 (.9919)	.0961 (.9834)	.1689 (.9723)	.2518 (.9605)	.3292 (.9444)	.3456 (.9424)	.3622 (.9333)	.3383 (.9234)	.2559 (.9069)	.1926 (.8971)	.1518 (.8972)	.1082 (.8968)
16.00	.0272 (.9853)	.0671 (.9653)	.1250 (.9332)	.1989 (.9006)	.2706 (.8685)	.2912 (.8555)	.3030 (.8208)	.2743 (.8050)	.1896 (.7855)	.1171 (.7664)	.0722 (.7710)	.0385 (.7918)
14.85	.0127 (.9684)	.0087 (.9081)	.0531 (.7896)	.1189 (.6821)	.1717 (.6022)	.2044 (.5379)	.1658 (.4406)	.0752 (.4070)	-.0490 (.3872)	-.2013 (.3724)	-.2634 (.3918)	-.3071 (.4129)
13.87	.0679 (.9497)	.1027 (.8421)	.2597 (.6648)	.4215 (.5271)	.5702 (.4059)	.7225 (.3129)	.7966 (.1666)	.7344 (.1026)	.4816 (.0572)	-.1080 (.0393)	-.3229 (.0592)	-.3152 (.0650)
13.00	.1370 (.9497)	.2518 (.8592)	.4787 (.7374)	.6933 (.6374)	.9186 (.5290)	1.1205 (.4562)	1.3696 (.3190)	1.4368 (.2475)	1.4853 (.1579)	1.4546 (.0824)	1.2546 (.0677)	1.1312 (.0767)

NOTE: Estimated coherences are in parentheses.

mated coherence into (13), an estimate of the asymptotic variance of
the phase is derived. This is the procedure we have used to estimate
the variances which appear in equation (11a$_2$).

For the frequency bands listed in Table 7-1, least squares estimates
of the parameter b_n *in* (11a) are reported in Table 7-2. For all cross-
spectra, $n = 2, 3, \ldots, 13$, $\hat{b}_n > 0$, so that the phase statistics indicate that the longer rate leads the one-week bill in each instance, as
predicted by the accurate forecasting version of the expectations
hypothesis. In addition, $\hat{b}_n > \hat{b}_{n-1}$ for $n = 3, \ldots, 8$, which is also

TABLE 7-2. *Regression of Phase Statistics on Angular Frequency, All
Frequencies*

n	b_n	R^2_A	DW
2	.1651	.2231	.4814
	(.0203)		
3	.3033	.3550	.7984
	(.0270)		
4	.5192	.5793	.8235
	(.0370)		
5	.7424	.7481	.8653
	(.0500)		
6	.9107	.7689	.8550
	(.0692)		
7	.9435	.7230	.6988
	(.0913)		
8	.9536	.6740	.6794
	(.1130)		
9	.8747	.5854	.7500
	(.1279)		
10	.6583	.3590	.6065
	(.1537)		
11	.4805	.2150	.5677
	(.1720)		
12	.3725	.1382	.5362
	(.1804)		
13	.2457	.0594	.5022
	(.2019)		

NOTE: Estimated standard errors are in parentheses. All frequency bands from
periods of 108 to 13 weeks are included in the regressions. DW is the Durbin-Watson
statistic.

$$\frac{\Phi_n(w)}{\sqrt{\text{var } \Phi_n(w)}} = b_n \frac{w}{\sqrt{\text{var } \Phi_n(w)}}$$

predicted by the accurate forecasting hypothesis. However, this relationship breaks down for $n = 9, \ldots, 13$. In addition, even for $n \leq 8$, the estimated b_n are much smaller than those predicted by the accurate forecasting hypothesis. The estimated b_n are never much more than one-third of the number $(n-1)/2$, which they should equal by hypothesis. Thus, while the time leads are generally in the proper direction, they are much smaller than those predicted by the accurate forecasting hypothesis.

Of course, the foregoing evidence is based on an examination of the phase statistics for all frequency bands with periods greater than or equal to thirteen weeks. We have therefore posed the accurate forecasting test in a harsher form than did Macaulay, who expected evidence of accurate forecasting only at periodicities that occurred with some regularity, primarily the seasonal and business cycle components of oscillation. An examination of the residuals in the regressions summarized in Table 7-2 indicates that expectations tend to be more accurate at the seasonal components of oscillation. In most cases, the residuals at periodicities of fifty-two, seventeen and one-third, and thirteen weeks are positive, indicating that the leads of the long rate over the one-week rates are longer at the seasonal frequencies. To pursue this a bit farther, regression (12) was run only using data for the fifty-two, twenty-six, seventeen and one-third, and thirteen-week periodicities. The results, which are reported in Table 7-3, indicate that for each n, the estimated b_n is larger than the corresponding element in Table 7-2. This indicates that forecasts tended to be more accurate at the seasonal frequencies. However, the magnitude of the increment in accuracy is quite small, so that even these estimates of the b_n's are very much smaller than those predicted by the accurate forecasting hypothesis. This result is in contrast to Macaulay's finding that the quality of forecasts was very much better at the seasonal frequencies than at the other frequencies.

In summary, the accurate forecasting hypothesis generally, though not always, correctly predicts the direction of the lead-lag relationship between bills of different maturities. Yet it rather decisively fails to predict the magnitudes of those leads, under-predicting them by a factor of at least two-thirds. Our comparison of the patterns at the seasonal and nonseasonal frequencies provides support for Kessel's earlier conclusions, although the differences among those frequencies are not as sharp as those discovered by Macaulay in the data on time and call rates.

TABLE 7-3. *Regression of Phase Statistics on Angular Frequency, Selected Frequencies*

n	b_n	R_A^2	DW
2	.1749	.0029	2.0504
	(.0423)		
3	.3353	−.6023	2.3572
	(.0543)		
4	.5542	.09811	2.1232
	(.0938)		
5	.7984	.5875	1.8217
	(.1342)		
6	1.0146	.6854	1.6702
	(.1823)		
7	1.0707	.6339	1.6602
	(.2398)		
8	1.1082	.6074	1.6564
	(.2818)		
9	1.0491	.5485	1.7499
	(.3006)		
10	.8352	.3277	1.9281
	(.3479)		
11	.6497	.2250	2.0987
	(.3575)		
12	.5360	.1631	2.1362
	(.3527)		
13	.4197	.0702	2.1792
	(.3935)		

NOTE: Estimated standard errors are in parentheses. Only fifty-two, twenty-six, seventeen-and-one-third, and thirteen-week frequencies are included in the regressions. DW is the Durbin-Watson statistic.

$$\frac{\hat{\Phi}_n(w)}{\sqrt{\text{var}\,\hat{\Phi}_n(w)}} = b_n \frac{w}{\sqrt{\text{var}\,\hat{\Phi}_n(w)}}$$

CONCLUSIONS

This paper has attempted to illustrate how the tools of spectral and cross-spectral analysis might be used to implement tests of the expectations theory of the term structure along the lines suggested by Macaulay. Like Macaulay's original work and a subsequent study by

Kessel, we have detected some elements of accuracy in the forecasts impounded in the yield curve for Treasury bill rates in the 1950's. But the empirical results of the last section cast rather serious doubt on the utility of the very restrictive version of the expectations hypothesis used in this study. As Kessel found, the qualitative implications of the hypothesis are generally borne out: longer bill rates do lead one-week bill rates, and the lead tends to increase with term to maturity. Yet the data suggest that the lengths of the lags are much shorter than predicted.

Perhaps these somewhat negative results are not surprising in view of the severely strict nature of the requirement that we have imposed on the yield curve in our statement of Macaulay's accurate forecasting hypothesis. Thus, consider the following quite general equation that we might posit to be governing the one-period spot rate,

$$R_{1t} = d_t + \sum_{k=0}^{\infty} c_k\, u_{t-k},$$

where d_t can be thought of as "deterministic" and where u_t is a random variable characterized by

$$E(u_t) = 0$$
$$E(u_t u_s) = \begin{cases} \sigma^2, t = s \\ \sigma, t \neq s. \end{cases}$$

We can appropriately assume that investors can predict the deterministic component d_t perfectly but that predictions of the component $\Sigma c_k u_{t-k}$ are subject to error. For such an R process, the minimum mean squared error forecast of R_{t+j} is given by

$$\hat{R}_{1t+j} = d_{t+j} + \sum_{k=0}^{\infty} c_{k+j} u_{t-k}.$$

The difference between R_{1t+j} and $\hat{R}_{1t+j}$ is given by

$$R_{1t+j} - \hat{R}_{1t+j} = \sum_{k=0}^{j-1} c_k\, u_{t+j-k}$$

rather than zero as posited throughout this paper. Our procedure in this paper, which is admittedly very extreme, amounts to assuming that the variance of the u's is so small that the above expression can be neglected. Since making that assumption seems to be a questionable way of characterizing the evolution of the spot rate, it is not altogether surprising that the implications of the extreme version of Macaulay's hypothesis are not all borne out by the data.

APPENDIX

In the second part of this paper, we suggested that it might be more realistic to replace equation (2) with the assumption that forecasts are unbiased, that is,

$$_{t+j}r_{1t} = R_{1t+j} + {}_{t+j}E_t, \tag{2a}$$

where the $_{t+j}E_t$'s are independent, identically distributed stochastic terms with mean zero and

$$E({}_{t+j}E_t \, {}_{s+i}E_s) = \begin{cases} \sigma_i^2 \text{ if } i = j \text{ and } t = s, \\ 0 \text{ if } i \neq j \text{ or } t \neq s. \end{cases}$$

We also specify that the $_{t+j}E_t$'s are distributed independently of R_{1t+j}'s. Then corresponding to (4) we have

$$R_{nt} = (R_{1t} + R_{1t+1} + \cdots + R_{1t+n-1})/n + ({}_{t+1}E_t + {}_{t+2}E_{1t} + \cdots + {}_{t+n-1}E_{1t})/n.$$

We define

$$U_t = ({}_{t+1}E_t + {}_{t+2}E_{1t} + \cdots + {}_{t+n-1}E_{1t})/n.$$

Then we have

$$R_{nt} = \sum_{i=0}^{n-1} h_i R_{1t+i} + U_t,$$

where $h_i = 1/n$ for all i and where U_t is distributed independently of the R_{1t}'s. We will show that relation (10) continues to hold when (2) is replaced by (2a).

Defining $V(w)$ as the Fourier transform of U_t,

$$V(w) = \sum_t U_t e^{iwt},$$

and defining $A(w)$, $B(w)$, and $H(w)$ as in the text, we have

$$B(w) = H(w) A(w) + V(w).$$

The cross-spectrum between R_{1t} and R_{nt} is then given by

$$S_{1n}(w) = E \, \overline{A(w)} \, B(w),$$

where $\overline{A(w)}$ is the complex conjugate of $A(w)$. Then we have

$$S_{1n}(w) = E \, \overline{A(w)} \, [H(w) \, A(w) + V(w)]$$
$$= E \, H(w) \, |A(w)^2| + E \, \overline{A(w)} \, V(w)$$
$$= E \, H(w) \, |A(w)|^2,$$

since $E \overline{A(w)} \ V(w) = 0$ because R_{1t} and U_t are distributed independently. Hence,

$$S_{1n}(w) = H(w) \ S_1(w),$$

which is the same relation given in the text. It follows that

$$\arg S_{1n} (w) = \frac{n-1}{2} \ w,$$

as shown in the text.

REFERENCES

1. Bierwag, G. O., and Grove, M. A., "A Model of the Term Structure of Interest Rates," *Review of Economics and Statistics,* February 1967.
2. Cagan, P., "Changes in the Cyclical Behavior of Interest Rates," *Review of Economics and Statistics,* August 1966.
3. Conard, J. W., *The Behavior of Interest Rates,* New York, NBER, 1966.
4. DeLeeuw, F., "A Model of Financial Behavior," in Duesenberry, *et. al.,* (eds.), *Brookings Quarterly Econometric Model of the United States,* Chicago, 1965.
5. Dobell, A. R., and Sargent, T. J., "The Term Structure in Canada," *Canadian Journal of Economics,* February, 1969.
6. Fand, D., "A Time Series Analysis of the 'Bills Only' Theory of Interest Rates," *Review of Economics and Statistics,* November 1966.
7. Granger, C. W. J., and Hatanaka, M., *Spectral Analysis of Economic Time Series,* Princeton, 1964.
8. Granger, C. W. J., and Rees, H. J. B., "Spectral Analysis of the Term Structure of Interest Rates," *Review of Economic Studies,* January 1968.
9. Hicks, J. R., *Value and Capital,* London, 1939.
10. Hinich, M. J., and Clay, C. S., "The Application of the Discrete Fourier Transform in the Estimation of Power Spectra, Coherence, and Bispectra of Geophysical Data," *Reviews of Geophysics,* 1968.
11. Johnston, J., *Econometric Methods,* New York, 1963.
12. Kessel, R., *The Cyclical Behavior of the Term Structure of Interest Rates,* New York, NBER, 1965.
13. Macaulay, F., *The Movements of Interest Rates, Bond Yields, and Stock Prices in the United States Since 1856,* New York, NBER, 1938.
14. Malkiel, B. G., *The Term Structure of Interest Rates,* Princeton, 1966.
15. Meiselman, D., *The Term Structure of Interest Rates,* Englewood Cliffs, 1962.

16. Meltzer, A., and von der Linde, G., *A Study of the Dealer Market for Federal Government Securities,* Joint Economic Committee, Washington, D.C., 1960.

17. Modigliani, F., and Sutch, R., "Innovations in Interest Rate Policy," *American Economic Review Papers and Proceedings,* May 1966.

18. Roll, R., "The Efficient Market Model Applied to U.S. Treasury Bill Rates," unpublished Ph.D. dissertation, University of Chicago, 1967.

19. Sargent, T., "Interest Rates in the Nineteen-Fifties," *Review of Economics and Statistics,* May 1968.

20. Van Horne, J., "Interest Rate Expectations, the Shape of the Yield Curve, and Monetary Policy," *Review of Economics and Statistics,* May 1966.

21. Wood, J., "The Expectations Hypothesis, the Yield Curve, and Monetary Policy," *Quarterly Journal of Economics,* August 1964.

8

The Expectations Component of
The Term Structure   *Stanley Diller*

THE TERM STRUCTURE

The term structure of interest rates—the variation in rates in relation to the term to maturity—involves one aspect of the general subject of yield differentials on financial assets.

The markets for short- and long-term securities are distinguished by the supposedly greater substitutability of short-term securities for money, the different economic roles associated with short- and long-term borrowing, the preponderance of short-term securities in Federal Reserve activities, and other factors as well.

Some writers are inclined to emphasize the differences between the short- and long-term markets largely on the basis of the differences among the lenders at various segments of the maturity spectrum, as well as differences in the purpose to which the loans are put. The markets are sometimes described as largely independent segments in which yields are determined by supply and demand conditions peculiar to each segment. Yet, while some lending institutions may reveal preponderant interests in certain maturity segments because of the timing of their liabilities, some part of their portfolios is typically permitted to seek the most favorable yield-risk combinations regardless of maturity. Many institutions, such as trust funds, are relatively free of maturity constraints and can serve as the medium through which the markets interact. Moreover, corporations often vary the maturity of their bor-

NOTE: This paper is based on a paper published in *Economic Forecasts and Expectations: Analysis of Forecasting Behavior and Performance,* Jacob Mincer, ed., New York, NBER, 1969.

rowings in response to market conditions. Recent writers have tended, therefore, to minimize institutional constraints and to emphasize instead the fluidity among markets not only by maturity or quality or type of financial assets but between financial and real assets as well.

This paper starts with a brief description of the expectations hypothesis, which relates the term structure at some time to the expectations at that time of the future interest rates. After describing an earlier test of this hypothesis the paper introduces a model that fits this earlier work into a more general context of autoregressive models and expectations. Particular behavioral models are derived from a general autoregressive model, and the relationship among them is explained. The forecasts implicit, by hypothesis, in the term structure are decomposed into a part attributable to autoregressive (or extrapolative) forecasting and a part not so attributable. The components are related to variables that might be reasonably used to forecast interest rates in an effort to explain the sources of the implied forecasts. Finally, the accuracy of the forecasts is measured and associated with the two components of the forecast.

THE EXPECTATIONS THEORY

Hicks was one of the first to consider the relationship between short- and long-term rates. His proposition is that under certain restrictive assumptions the long-term rate is the geometric mean of the short-term rates spanning the same term to maturity. The well-known formula for the price or present value of a bond is given by equation (1).

$$PV = \frac{C_1}{1+R} + \frac{C_2}{(1+R)_2} + \cdots + \frac{C_n + P}{(1+R)^n}, \qquad (1)$$

where PV is the present value of the current market price of security, C_i is the coupon payments, P is the principal, and R is the market yield. Alternatively, a long-term bond is equivalent to the automatic reinvestment in a consecutive series of short-term bonds at rates current at the time of reinvestment. The formula in this case is:

$$PV' = \frac{C_1}{1+r_1} + \frac{C_2}{(1+r_1)(1+r_2)} + \frac{C_3}{(1+r_1)(1+r_2)(1+r_3)}$$

$$+ \cdots + \frac{C_n + P}{(1+r_1) \ldots (1+r_n)}, \qquad (1a)$$

where r_i is the one-period rate for the ith period. The r_i are called forward rates. In the event there are no coupon payments (i.e., all C are 0), equating the two present value formulas is equivalent to equating the last terms of each:[1]

$$(1 + R)^n = (1 + r_1)(1 + r_2) \ldots (1 + r_n).$$

From the formulas of two maturities (n and $n - 1$) we can derive

$$r_n = \frac{(1 + R_n)^n}{(1 + R_{n-i})^{n-i}} - 1,$$

where R_n is the internal rate of return on a bond with n periods to maturity. In these formulas, the forward rates, r_i, are the short-period rates pertaining to a future period and are determined by the differential between currently observed long rates of appropriate maturity.[2]

The substances of Hicks' hypothesis is that a forward rate is in fact the short-period rate that is expected to prevail in that period and that the long rates of different maturities adjust in order to be consistent with these expected rates. In addition, he hypothesized that changes in the spot rate, i.e., r_1 or R_1, stimulate expectations of subsequent changes in r_i and, hence, in R_i. In this way variations in short-term rates, R_1, produce, via the expectation mechanism, variation in long-term rates R_i ($i > 1$). This hypothesis, often amended (as it was by Hicks) to include the effect of differences in liquidity between long- and short-term securities, has become known as the expectations hypothesis.

The expectations hypothesis is sometimes rejected on the grounds of its alleged implausibility: investors, it is sometimes said, do not attempt to forecast short-term rates far into the future. Properly viewed, however, the expectations hypothesis does not imply implausibile behavior.

The forward rates, which this study equates with forecasts, are not the numbers to which investors directly respond; nor is it correct to

[1] Neil Wallace has estimated the effects of ignoring these restrictions in computing the internal rate of return, R. He concluded that these effects are small. See "The Term Structure of Interest Rates and the Maturity Composition of the Federal Debt," unpublished Ph.D. dissertation, University of Chicago, 1964, pp. 10–12.

[2] While the example is based on adjacent (i.e., a one-period difference in term to maturity) long rates, which together imply a one-period forward rate, the long rates can be spaced arbitrarily to imply forward rates whose maturity equals the difference in maturities between the long rates.

regard them as consciously pinpointed forecasts made by the public looking well into the future, though some individuals may form precise forecasts. Deducing the forward rates from the combinations of long rates and evaluating them as forecasts is an analytical device justified by the hypothesis and the arithmetic of interest rates; the efficacy of this method is independent of judgments of the plausibility of some hypothetical forecasting mechanisms.

Without actually specifying forecasts of rates ad infinitum, investors can react to yield differentials and adjust the maturity of their holdings in accordance with their expectations of rates. Regardless of the certainty of their convictions, investors are continually required to decide on combinations of yield and maturity on the basis of limited information, vague expectations, and publicized market attitudes. Deciding between the purchase of a long- and short-term security does not require a point forecast of a one-year rate twenty years out even though the aggregate of such decisions leads to a yield structure that corresponds with one that point forecasts could produce. In a period of high rates, for example, an investor may well decide to purchase a long-term bond—whether for the capital gain expected when rates ultimately fall or merely to receive a high yield for a long period. Summed over many investors, this thinking would depress long-term yields and produce apparent forecasts of declining rates. The investors who purchase the long-term bond implicitly forecast, at a minimum, that short-term rates will not rise or stay high. Among this group are those who think a decline in rates is imminent and others who think rates will fall only after an inflation subsides, perhaps ten years out. The weight of these opinions will mold the yield curve. While few if any investors will distinguish their 14-year forecast from their 15-year forecast, the availability of the two maturities forces a choice, and the resulting yields will reflect the frequency distribution of investors of various horizons. If by accident the yields become out of line, a sufficient number of investors, indifferent between the two maturities, will set them right. This arbitrage along the yield curve is facilitated by the investors' ability to borrow for the purpose of buying or short-selling securities, as well as by the ability of issuers to vary their maturities to correct imbalances among yields.

Investigations of implied market forecasts—whether interest rates, stock or commodity prices, foreign exchange rates, or personal incomes, profits, and any other economic variables—pertain to the weight of market forces, which are themselves the aggregate of individual and group decisions, rather than personal motivation or institutional anomalies. While these market forces are personified for expositional convenience, and motivations are established for hypothetical decision makers, the efficacy of the analysis is predicated on its ability to predict behavior and not on the plausibility of its expositional devices.

To test the expectations hypothesis it is necessary to treat the forward rates inferred from the term structure of long rates as forecasts. A well-known test by Meiselman[3] is based on an evaluation of the consequences of using the forward rates in a model that has on other occasions successfully described changes in forecasts. Meiselman reasoned that if forward rates are forecasts they would be reviewed as new information came to light. Thus, he supposed that errors in forecasting would lead to revisions of forecasts. He used the error-learning model, which describes the effect of the currently observed error of a prior forecast on the current revision of prior forecasts of some future period,

$$_{t+n}r_t - {}_{t+n}r_{t-1} = a + B(R_t - {}_{t}r_{t-1}) + u, \qquad (2)$$

where $_{t+n}r_t$ is the forecast made in t of the rate expected in period $t + n$; R_t is the spot rate in period t; and u is a random term.

Meiselman used Durand's *Basic Yields*[4] on corporate securities to compute the forward rates for the test. These data permit the computation of ten consecutive one-period forward rates for each observation period, which in turn permit eight regressions of equation (2), i.e., $n = 1, 8$. He found that while each of the eight regression coefficients were significantly different from zero, their magnitude and statistical significance declined as the span of forecast, n, increased. Meiselman regarded these results to be consistent with the hypothesis that the forward rates are forecasts. He argued that the coefficients should fall with increasing span of forecasts since forecasts of increasing span became increasingly remote from the current error, and revisions of this rate were therefore less dependent on the current error.

EXTRAPOLATIVE FORECASTING

Meiselman's error-learning model describes a specific technique of forecasting. Mincer has shown that it is actually a rearrangement of

[3] David Meiselman, *The Term Structure of Interest Rates,* Englewood Cliffs, 1962, Chapter II.

[4] David Durand, *Basic Yields of Corporate Bonds, 1900–1942,* New York, NBER, 1943. The complete set of data is listed in the National Industrial Conference Board's *Economic Almanac 1967–1968,* p. 416.

terms of an autoregressive model,[5] which allows us to view the forecast as dependent on prior values of the forecast and the actual variable. In this way we can interpret some characteristics of the expectations implied in Meiselman's results. Mincer relates the forecasts of a given span to the forecast or actual values of each prior period. For example, a one-period forecast is related to the current actual value and each of the prior actual values; a two-span forecast to the one-span forecast of the prior period, then to the current actual value, and finally to all prior actual values—as in the following equation:

$$_{t+n}F_t = A + B_1(_{t+n-1}F_t) + B_2(_{t+n-2}F_t) + \cdots + B_n A_t \\ + B_{n+1}A_{t-1} + \cdots + _{t+n}E_t , \quad (3)$$

where $_{t+n}F_t$ is the forecast made in t referring to $t + n$, A_{t-i} is the actual value of the series i periods in the past, and E is the random term. This model extrapolates a weighted average of current and past values, substituting extrapolated for actual values between t and $t + n - 1$ for forecasts of $t + n$. In addition to the extrapolative, or autoregressive, component there is an autonomous component, E, of the forecast. Equations (4) and (5) describe the forecasts made in t and $t - 1$, respectively, referring to $t + 1$.

$$_{t+1}F_t = A + B_1 A_t + B_2 A_{t-1} + \cdots + B_{n+1}A_{t-n} + _{t+1}E_t , \quad (4)$$

$$_{t+1}F_{t-1} = A + B_1 \,_t F_{t-1} + B_2 A_{t-1} + \cdots + B_{n+1}A_{t-n} + _{t+1}E_{t-1}. \quad (5)$$

In (5), since A_t is unknown at the time of forecast, $t - 1$, the extrapolated value, $_t F_{t-1}$, is substituted. Subtracting (5) from (4) yields:

$$_{t+1}F_t - _{t+1}F_{t-1} = B_1(A_t - _t F_{t-1}) + (_{t+1}E_t - _{t+1}E_{t-1}), \quad (6)$$

where the last term on the right is a random term. Equation (6) is identical to Meiselman's error-learning model.

By extending this formula to later maturities we can derive the B's from the coefficients in Meiselman's regressions. For the target $t + 2$ the equations are,

$$_{t+2}F_t = A + B_1(_{t+1}F_t) + B_2 A_t + B_3 A_{t-1} + \cdots + _{t+2}E_t. \quad (7)$$

$$_{t+2}F_{t-1} = A + B_1(_{t+1}F_{t-1}) + B_2(_t F_{t-1}) + B_3 A_{t-1} + \cdots + _{t+2}E_{t-1}. \quad (8)$$

Subtracting (8) from (7) yields:

$$(_{t+2}F_t - _{t+2}F_{t-1}) = B_1(_{t+1}F_t - _{t+1}F_{t-1}) + B_2(A_t - _t F_{t-1}) \\ + (_{t+2}E_t - _{t+2}E_{t-1}). \quad (9)$$

[5] See Jacob Mincer, "Models of Adoptive Forecasting," in *Economic Forecasts and Expectations, op. cit.*

The difference equation for $t + 3$ is

$$
({}_{t+3}F_t - {}_{t+3}F_{t-1}) = B_1({}_{t+2}F_t - {}_{t+2}F_{t-1}) + B_2({}_{t+1}F_t - {}_{t+1}F_{t-1}) \\
+ B_3(A_t - {}_tF_{t-1}) + ({}_{t+3}E_t - {}_{t+3}E_{t-1}). \quad (10)
$$

It is clear that the revision variables on the right of (9) and (10) are themselves functions of the current error of forecast. Substituting (6) into (9) yields:

$$
({}_{t+2}F_t - {}_{t+2}F_{t-1}) = B_1[B_1(A_t - {}_tF_{t-1})] + B_2(A_t - {}_tF_{t-1}) \\
+ ({}_{t+2}E_t - {}_{t+2}E_{t-1}) \\
= (B_1{}^2 + B_2)(A_t - {}_tF_{t-1}) + ({}_{t+2}E_t - {}_{t+2}E_{t-1}). \quad (11)
$$

Substituting (6) and (9) into (10) yields:

$$
({}_{t+3}F_t - {}_{t+3}F_{t-1}) = B_1B_1[B_1(A_t - {}_tF_{t-1})] + B_2(A_t - {}_tF_{t-1}) \\
+ B_3(A_t - {}_tF_{t-1}) + ({}_{t+3}E_t - {}_{t+3}E_{t-1}) \\
= (B_1{}^3 + B_1B_2 + B_3)(A_t - {}_tF_{t-1}) \\
+ ({}_{t+3}E_t - {}_{t+3}E_{t-1}). \quad (12)
$$

The weights, B_i, that appear in (6), (11), and (12) are identical to those in the extrapolative forecasting equation, (3). Therefore, each of the eight regression coefficients, M_i, that Meiselman estimated with the error-learning model (2) ($n = 1, 8$) are estimates of the corresponding combinations of B_i in the difference equations above. The M_i, estimated by simple regression (2), provide convenient estimates of the B_i, obtainable alternatively from multiple regression (3). The relationship between the two sets of weights is

$$
\begin{aligned}
M_1 &= B_1 \\
M_2 &= B_1{}^2 + B_2 \\
M_3 &= B_1{}^3 + 2B_1B_2 + B_3
\end{aligned} \quad (13)
$$

and generally,

$$
M_i = \sum_{j=1}^{i} M_{i-j} B_j, \text{ where } M_0 = 1.
$$

It is enough to estimate either set of weights to obtain estimates of the other.

The study estimated both the M_i and B_i directly, the former by duplicating Meiselman's procedure and the latter by a method described below. In addition, using (13), it derived either set from the other and compared the direct and indirect estimates of both sets of weights. Since the sets are empirically estimated stochastic variables, their relationships do not correspond exactly with their algebraically derived relationships. The estimates and statistical tests of their equivalence are shown for illustrative purposes only.

To compare the direct and indirect estimates of either set of weights, a procedure is required to directly estimate the B_i. It is, of course, possible to directly estimate (3) for each value of n, the span of forecast. Alternatively, since the B_i, in principle, are identical for each n, it is convenient to pool the data into one regression involving all spans of forecast, each value of the dependent variable associated with the appropriate prior forecasts and actual values. Table 8-1 lists the direct estimates of M_i and B_i together with the indirect estimates of each from the other, as well as estimates of the significance of the differences between the two sets of estimates.

Columns 1 and 2 are reestimations of Meiselman's reported results with the error-learning model (equation 2). Column 3 combines the directly estimated B_i of equation (3) in accordance with equation (13). While the standard error for the direct estimates are reported, it is very difficult to estimate the standard errors of the indirect estimates of M_i since they involve extensive algebraic manipulation of a stochastic series. While inclusion of an estimate of this error would increase the standard error of the differences between the two estimates of M_i, this effect could be offset by a positive covariance between the two estimates of M_i.[6] Since there is no easy way to evaluate the relative strengths of these opposing influences on the standard error of the differences, it is difficult to estimate the direction of the bias of the results reported in column 4. These considerations aside, the two sets of estimates of M_i are fairly close.

The two estimates of B_i are similar, although the problem just alluded to prevents a conclusive evaluation of the significance of the differences in the two sets of estimates. In both sets, B_1 is large and there is a sharp decline to B_2 followed by a gradual decline. Sampling fluctuation in the direct estimates and the sensitivity of the indirect estimates to sampling fluctuation in the estimated M_i prevent a smooth pattern in the B_i, but the one just described is a reasonable approximation.

---

[6] The well-known formula for the standard error of the difference between two estimates, A and B, is $S_A + S_B - 2C_{A,B}$, where S signifies standard error and C is covariance. A positive covariance lowers the standard error of the difference.

TABLE 8-1. *Direct and Indirect Estimates of the Error-Learning Coefficients, M_i, and the Forecasting Weights, B_i, and Estimates of the Significance of the Differences Between the Direct and Indirect Estimates, Annual Data, 1901–54*

Span of Forecast	Direct Estimate of M_i (1)	Standard Error of Direct Estimate (2)	Indirect Estimate of M_i (3)	t Value of Difference (4)	Direct Estimate of B_i (5)	Standard Error of Direct Estimate (6)	Indirect Estimate of B_i (7)	t Value of Difference (8)
1	.7029	.0312	.7457	1.3718	.7457	.0199	.7029	2.1507
2	.5256	.0419	.6109	2.0286	.0548	.0248	.0318	0.9274
3	.4034	.0466	.5312	2.7446	.0347	.0240	.0114	0.9708
4	.3263	.0486	.3641	0.7798	-.0914	.0192	.0180	-5.6979
5	.2769	.0459	.2864	0.2048	.0522	.0243	.0165	1.4691
6	.2348	.0414	.2546	0.4758	.0051	.0258	.0042	0.0349
7	.2367	.0389	.2477	0.2751	.0412	.0258	.0401	0.0426
8	.2089	.0401	.2209	0.3167	-.0168	.0260	-.0116	-0.2000

NOTE: All estimates are based on the Durand data. Col. 1 duplicates Meiselman's estimates of equation (2); col. 2 lists the standard error of these estimates; col. 3 estimates M_i from B_i in col. 5 using equation (13); col. 4 approximates the significance of difference between cols. 1 and 3 using col. 2 as the estimate of the standard error of difference; col. 5 estimates the coefficients of equation (3) using pooled data for all spans of interest; col. 6 lists standard errors of these estimates; col. 7 estimates B_i from M_i in col. 1 using equation (13); col. 8 approximates the significance of the difference between cols. 5 and 7 using col. 6 as the estimate of the standard error of difference.

THE RETURN-TO-NORMALITY HYPOTHESIS

Since the forecasting equation (3) is formulated as a general autoregressive model, its weights, B_i, tell us a lot about how expectations are formed. We can compare various hypotheses with the empirical estimates. One widely used model hypothesizes a return-to-normality mechanism, whereby forecasts of a series move in the direction of the normal value of the series.[7] This hypothesis is one explanation for the often observed inverse relationship between the slope of a yield curve and the level of rates. Typically, yield curves incline at low levels of rates and decline at high levels.[8] According to the return-to-normality hypothesis, when short-term rates are high they are expected to decline; hence, long-term rates decrease with increasing maturity, and the yield curve declines. The reverse holds for low levels of short-term rates.

Algebraically the return-to-normality hypothesis amounts to the following:

$$_{t+2}F_t - {}_{t+1}F_t = K(A_t - {}_nA_t), K < 0, \qquad (14)$$

where $(_{t+2}F_t - {}_{t+1}F_t)$ is the change expected at t of the target value, in this case, the one-period spot rate, from $t + 1$ to $t + 2$; A_t is the target, or spot, rate at t; $_nA_t$ is the normal rate at t; and K is negative to reflect the inverse relationship between the expected change and the deviation of the spot from the normal rate.

Assuming for the moment that the normal rate does not change, the following regression form gives estimates of K in (14),

$$_{t+n}r_t - {}_{t+n-1}r_t = a + KA_t + V, n = 1,8. \qquad (15)$$

---

[7] The phrase "move in the direction of" distinguishes the forecasts or expected values from the normal value, which generally connotes a long-term tendency rather than a particular point. It should, therefore, vary less than a forecast and, correspondingly, incorporate a greater span of the past variation of the series, to which it should attach more uniformly distributed weights in place of the decaying weights of a point forecast.

[8] This observation is true except at the very short end of the curves, which almost always inclines. This short-period incline combined with an over-all declining yield curve results in the familiar humped yield curve typical of periods of high interest rates. See Reuben Kessel, *The Cyclical Variation of the Term Structure of Interest Rates*, New York, NBER, 1964, p. 25; reprinted as Chapter 6 of this book.

TABLE 8-2. *Statistics Computed From the Regression of the Expected Change of Future Spot Rates on the Level of the Current One-Period Spot Rate, Durand Data, Annual Observations, 1900–54*

Span of Forecast	K (1)	t Value of K (2)	Constant Term (3)	t Value of Constant Term (4)	R^2 (adj) (5)
$_{t+1}r_t - R_t$	−.1627	−7.2109	.6437	7.8584	.4904
$_{t+2}r_t - {}_{t+1}r_t$	−.1264	−11.8510	.4909	12.6817	.7246
$_{t+3}r_t - {}_{t+2}r_t$	−.0997	−17.0387	.3878	18.2505	.8452
$_{t+4}r_t - {}_{t+3}r_t$	−.0741	−12.7946	.2948	14.0311	.7543
$_{t+5}r_t - {}_{t+4}r_t$	−.0737	−8.2939	.3071	9.5246	.5612
$_{t+6}r_t - {}_{t+5}r_t$	−.0475	−7.8774	.1964	8.9637	.5353
$_{t+7}r_t - {}_{t+6}r_t$	−.0332	−6.1131	.1382	7.0177	.4070
$_{t+8}r_t - {}_{t+7}r_t$	−.0361	−8.0801	.1511	9.3173	.5481
$_{t+9}r_t - {}_{t+8}r_t$	−.0250	−4.1018	.0981	4.4308	.2299

NOTE: The regressions were of the form $_{t+n}r_t - {}_{t+n-1}r_t = Q + k_n R_t + V_n$.

where V is a random term.[9] The results of estimating (15) are listed in Table 8-2. These estimates of K are in each case significantly negative, confirming the widely recognized relationship described above. The use of A_t in place of $(A_t - {}_n A_t)$ in (15) implies the following relation:

$$a = a' + K_n A_t,$$

where a is the constant term in (15) and a' is the constant term in the event $(A_t - {}_n A_t)$ is used in place of A_t. On the hypothesis that $a' = 0$, an estimate of the constant normal rate is obtained from the ratio a/K,

[9] Other writers have used the level of rates to estimate the normality effect or else have assigned some arbitrary value or small group of values to the normal value. See, for example, James Van Horne, "Interest Rate Risk and the Term Structure of Interest Rates," *Journal of Political Economy*, 1965, p. 349. Van Horne adds a variable he calls "deviation of actual from accustomed level" to Meiselman's formulation of the error-learning model and he divides his sample period into two subperiods. "For each . . . [sub] period . . . an arithmetic average of the beginning forward rate levels is calculated. This average may be thought to represent the accustomed level for the [sub] period. The deviation is simply the difference of the actual forward rate level from the accustomed level. . . ."

that is, the constant term divided by the regression coefficient. For each n, the estimate is approximately 4 per cent. This number is an estimate of the normal rate.

Just as the decline in the error-learning model coefficients, M_i, was equivalent to a particular pattern of weights in the extrapolative equation (3), so the negative K in (14), interpreted here as indicating an expected return to normality, also implies a particular pattern of weights in (3).[10]

To derive this pattern, define $_nA_t$ of (14) as

$$_nA_t = B_2 A_{t-1} + B_3 A_{t-2} + \cdots + B_n A_{t-n-1}. \tag{16}$$

Substituting (16) into (14) yields

$$_{t+2}F_t - {}_{t+1}F_t = KA_t - K \left(\sum_{i=1}^{n-1} B_{i+1} A_{t-i} \right), \tag{17}$$

where $_{t+1}F_t$ and $_{t+2}F_t$ were defined in equations (4) and (7) above, respectively, the first in terms of the A_{t-1} and the second in terms of $_{t+1}F_t$ and the A_{t-i}. Substituting (4) into (7) yields

$$_{t+2}F_t = (B_1{}^2 + B_2)A_t + (B_1 B_2 + B_3)A_{t-1}$$
$$+ \sum_{i=3}^{n} (B_1 B_i + B_{i+1})A_{t-i-1}. \tag{18}$$

Subtracting (4) from (18) gives

$$_{t+2}F_t - {}_{t+1}F_t = [(B_1{}^2 + B_2) - B_1]A_t$$
$$+ \sum_{i=2}^{n} [(B_1 B_i + B_{i+1}) - B_i]A_{t-i-1}. \tag{19}$$

From (13) it is clear that the expression $[(B_1{}^2 + B_2) - B_1]$ in (19), equal to K in (17), is actually $M_2 - M_1$. In general, the proportion, K, of the deviation of the current rate from the normal rate, which is expected to be offset between $t + n - 1$ and $t + n$, is exactly equal to $M_N - M_{N-1}$. The more rapid the decline in M_i the sooner are future rates expected to overtake the normal rate. The difference in the M_i listed in column 1 of Table 8-1 show the rate of movement toward normality for the particular data used. According to these estimates

---

[10] Mincer, *op. cit.*, designates the pattern that produces a declining M_i and and a negative K as convex. He distinguishes this pattern, which is consistent with many different combinations of weights, from concave and exponential patterns.

approximately half the difference between current and normal rates is expected to be removed over the eight year period.

The rate of movement declines with span of forecast. Other convex patterns of B_i would imply different rates of movement toward normality. In the case of exponential weights, where $M_i = M_{i+1}$, there would be no movement toward normality, and in the case of a concave pattern of B_i, where $M_i < M_{i+1}$, expected rates would move away from normality.[11]

Another implication of the convex pattern of B_i, where $M_i > M_{i+1}$ (and actually an alternate exposition of the relations described above), is that as the span of forecast, n, increases, the weight attached to A_t declines, and the remaining weights both rise and approach equality. In other words, the longer the span of forecast, the lower the weight given to current experience and the greater the weight given to the past. In effect, the longest term forecast approaches the normal rate.

THE RELATIONSHIP AMONG EXTRAPOLATIVE MODELS

The principal conclusion of the above analysis is that three widely used forecasting models, the extrapolative, the error-learning, and the return-to-normality models, are actually three variants of a general extrapolative formula. There are, in principle, as many models as there are combinations of weights from an autoregression, although the word "model" is ordinarily used only when the particular combination of weights is consistent with a plausible behavioral hypothesis. There is a difference, however, between the specification of the model and the parameters that are estimated for it. While the error-learning model is a particular form of the extrapolative model, its application to a given set of data need not result in declining revision coefficients (as the span of forecast increases) and therefore in a particular pattern of implied extrapolative weights. Similarly, while the return-to-normality hypothesis is consistent with the extrapolative model, there is no logical necessity that K be negative. The model is a transformation of the extrapolative models, while the hypothesis that K is negative is subject to empirical test. A negative K is implied by error-learning coefficients that decline with forecast span.

---

[11] See Mincer, *op. cit.*

AUTONOMOUS FORECASTING

There is more to forecasts, of course, than is implied in the extrapolative procedure. Variation in contemporaneous variables may also influence forecasts. Merely correlating these variables with the forecasts, however, would not reveal the extent of this influence. To the extent these contemporaneously correlated variables are themselves autoregressive, they impart an autoregressive component to the forecasts. For this reason part of the observed autoregressiveness of the forecasts may arise from the influence on them of variables that are themselves autoregressive. Whether there exists an autoregressive component of the forecasts independent of that which is imposed by the autoregressive component of functionally related variables is virtually impossible to determine.

It is possible, however, by partitioning the forecasts into autoregressive and random components, to divide the total relation between the forecasts and the other variable into the parts due to either component. One way to effect this partition is to regress the forward rates on the current and past spot rates and interpret the residuals of the regression as estimates of the random component of the forecasts.[12] An observed relationship between these residuals and other current economic variables would indicate that part of the forecast was based on current developments in the market, not entirely of the past.

The regression form used to distinguish the two components of the forecast is

$$ _{t+n}F_t = a + b_1 A_t + b_2 A_{t-1} + \cdots + b_i A_{t-7} + _{t+n}E_t, \qquad (20) $$

where $_{t+n}F_t$ is the forecast made at t referring to $t + n$, A_{t-i} is the spot lagged i periods, and $_{t+n}E_t$ is the residual term (the estimate of the random component of the forecasts). The lag terms are arbi-

---

[12] Another way is to compute a moving average of the current and past spot rate using the weights described above. In principle, a third way is to specify a model that predicts the autonomous (with respect to time, not to other variables) component and leaves a residual estimate of the autoregressive component. In the absence of a definitive method, it is most practical to exhaust one component and let the stated existence of the other component depend on rejecting the null hypothesis of its absence. The likelihood that forecasters utilized nonextrapolative information, given the rejection of the null hypothesis that they did not, is strengthened by the knowledge that part of the stated autoregressive component likely includes the autoregressive effects of contemporaneously related variables.

trarily limited to seven to conserve data. The computed value from the regression, $_{t+n}F_t{}^*$, is the estimate of the extrapolative component of the forecasts and the residual term, $_{t+n}E_t$, of the random or non-extrapolative component.

Equation (20) was fit for spans of one, two, three, and four quarters to Treasury bill yields.[13] The coefficients of determination are listed in column 2 of Table 8-3 and show a close relationship. In spite of

TABLE 8-3. *Partitioned Relationship Between the Index of Industrial Production and the Forward Rates, Treasury Data, Quarterly Observations, 1949–64*

Span of Forecast	$R^2_{F,I}$ (1)	R^2_{F,F^*} (2)	$R^2_{F,F^*,I}$ (3)	*t* Value of b_{F^*} (4)	R^2_{F,I,F^*} (5)	*t* Value of b_I (6)	$R^2_{F,F^*,I}$ (7)
1	.7159	.9543	.8866	21.8365	.0078	.6909	.9667
2	.7806	.9314	.8075	15.9938	.1049	2.6743	.9564
3	.8107	.9177	.7343	12.9808	.1947	3.8404	.9480
4	.8176	.8814	.4705	7.3615	.2394	4.3817	.9003

NOTE: R^2 is the coefficient of determination, I is the index of industrial production, F is the forward rate, and F^* is the extrapolative component.

this strong measure of autoregressiveness the question remains whether there is any relationship between the residuals and other variables that may influence forecasting of interest rates. For present purposes we use the FRB's index of industrial production as a proxy for such other influences.

Column 1 of Table 8-3 lists the coefficients of determination between the forward rates and the production index. Equation (21) measures the effect on the forecast of the extrapolative component (computed from equation 20), $_{t+n}F_t$, the concurrent production index, I, and the random component.

$$_{t+n}F_t = a + b_1(_{t+n}F_t{}^*) + b_2I + u_n. \qquad (21)$$

Columns 3 through 7 list the relevant statistics for these regressions.

Most of the correlation between the forward rates and the index of industrial production is captured by the extrapolative component

[13] The data are read from the yield curve for the middle month of each quarter. The yield curves appear in the *Treasury Bulletin*. The sample period used is 1946–64.

of the forecasts. That is, R^2_{F,F^*} includes most of $R^2_{F,I}$. But there is a net relation between F and I that is independent of F^*. Column 5 of Table 8-3 indicates that the correlation between I and the autonomous component of the forecasts increases with the span of forecast and, except for the first span, is statistically significant. Alternatively, when the relation between the forecasts and current and past spot rates is adjusted for the influence of I, the coefficients of determination (column 3) are smaller than the simple coefficients, listed in column 2. This result highlights the difficulty noted earlier of interpreting the estimated amount of autoregressiveness; the autoregressiveness of I contributes to that of F.

The forecasts of interest rates appear to rely progressively more on autonomous variables, like I, as the span of forecast increases. Consequently, the ability to explain the forecasts does not decline with increasing span of forecast as rapidly as the declining R^2s of equation (20) suggest.

The index of industrial production is merely one of many possible indicators likely to affect the forecasts of interest rates. The observed relationship does not imply that investors actually consulted this particular indicator. The determination of which indicators were actually consulted is a statistical question only insofar as alternate hypotheses are tested. The Dow Jones index of industrial stock prices (denoted by S), for example, yields somewhat stronger results than the index of industrial production. The results of this experiment are shown in Table 8-4. As in the case of the earlier experiment the relation between F and S grows with increasing span. Without the contribution of S the extrapolative component of F deteriorates much more rapidly than when its

TABLE 8-4. *The Partitioned Relationship Between the Dow Jones Index of Industrial Stock Prices and the Forward Rates, Treasury Data, Quarterly Observations, 1949–64*

Span of Forecast	$R^2_{F,S}$ (1)	R^2_{F,F^*} (2)	$R^2_{F,F^*,S}$ (3)	t Value of b_{F^*} (4)	R^2_{F,S,F^*} (5)	t Value of b_S (6)	$R^2_{F,F^*,S}$ (7)
1	.7861	.9543	.8532	18.8278	.0327	1.4359	.9675
2	.8595	.9314	.7215	12.5709	.1704	3.5399	.9596
3	.8892	.9177	.5921	9.4116	.2770	4.8339	.9533
4	.8889	.8814	.2356	4.3359	.3309	5.4918	.9123

NOTE: The form of this table is identical to that of Table 8-3 except for the substitution of industrial stock prices, S, for industrial production, I.

contribution is not isolated (column 3 compared with column 2). But the strengthening relationship shown in column 1 as span of forecast increases is due not only to the effect of S on F^* but also to its autonomous effect, which grows to 33 per cent of the forecast by the fourth span. There is little question but that a more elaborate attempt to specify a model of interest rate forecasting would succeed in reducing further the putative effect of extrapolative forecasting, which in the preceding results appears dominant.

THE ACCURACY OF THE FORECASTS

To measure the accuracy of the forecasts, it is useful to separate the bias from the random error of the forecasts.[14] The distinction is particularly important in the case of the forward rates since they may contain a nonforecasting component that on the average makes the forward rate, when viewed entirely as a forecast, too high. Many writers[15] think that long-term rates are on the average higher than short-term rates because holders require a premium to compensate for the lower liquidity of long-term bonds. If so, and if this nonforecasting component were not isolated, the forward rates, which include the premia, would appear to be less accurate forecasts than they are. However, only the mean of the premia would contribute to the measured bias; any variation in the premia, as a result of variation in their determinants, would accentuate the computed error of forecast.

It is useful to compare the mean square error of the forecasts with a set of benchmark forecasts as well. A convenient benchmark forecast is found by autoregressing the target value A_t on its own past values, which is the general form of the various naive models that are often used in this connection. In the general form,

$$A_t = \sum_{i=1}^{n} b_i A_{t-i} + E. \qquad (22)$$

The so-called "no change" and "same change" models can be derived by setting b_1 and $b_i = 0$ for $i > 1$ in the former case and $b_1 = 2$, $b_2 = -1$, and $b_i = 0$ for $i > 2$ in the latter case. Since in accordance

---

[14] See Mincer and Zarnowitz, "The Evaluation of Economic Forecasts," *Economic Forecasts and Expectations: Analysis of Forecasting Behavior and Performance,* Jacob Mincer (ed.), New York, NBER, 1969.

[15] For example, see Reuben Kessel's article, Chapter 6 of this book.

with (22) the degree of fit of the regression is the measure of accuracy, the benchmark forecasts are the most stringent to use, since they are specifically chosen to maximize the fit.

The total mean square error and the random error[16] of the forecasts, as a ratio to the benchmark, are given in Table 8-5. The ratios in column 1 include the bias and are therefore higher than the corresponding ratios in column 2. While for each span the total mean square error is higher for the forecasts than for the benchmark, the former approach the latter as the forecast span increases. The relative improvement of the forecasts as the span increases is indicated in colunm 2 as well. These numbers are lower than the corresponding numbers in column 1 because the bias term is removed. The relative improvement with span lowers the random error of the forecasts below that of the benchmark by the fourth span.

The improved relative accuracy of the forecasts as span increases

TABLE 8-5. *Ratios of Mean Square Errors and of Their Random Component of Forecasts Relative to Benchmark Forecasts, Treasury Data, Quarterly Observations, 1949–64*

Span of Forecasts	Ratio of Mean Square Errors (1)	Ratio of Random Errors (2)
1	1.1481	1.0854
2	1.4078	1.0701
3	1.2716	1.0341
4	1.0607	0.9607

NOTE: Column 1 gives the ratio of $E(A-F)$ for the forecasts relative to the same term for the autoregressive benchmark. A number greater than 1.0 implies the forecasts have a higher total error than the benchmark forecasts have.

Column 2 gives the ratio of $(1 - r_{AF}^2) \, S_A^2$ for the two sets of forecasts. This term measures the random error, as distinct from the bias. The symbol r_{AF}^2 refers to the coefficient of determination in the regression of the target values, A, on the forecasts, F; S_A^2 is the variance of A. Since the autoregressive benchmark is computed to exclude a bias, the denominators of the ratios in columns 1 and 2 are identical; for the benchmark the total and random errors are the same.

[16] The random error is the component of the mean square error whose expected value is zero; that is, it excludes any bias. A formula for the random error is

$$\text{random error} = (1 - r_{AF}^2) \, S_A^2$$

where r_{AF}^2 is the coefficient of determination in the regression of F on A, and S_A^2 is the variance of A. See Jacob Mincer, *op. cit.*

reveals the increasing importance of the autonomous component of the forecasts with increasing span. Since the gross correlation between A and F is a measure of the accuracy of the forecasts, the decomposition of this correlation into partials for the extrapolative and autonomous components of the forecasts helps show the sources of the forecasts' accuracy and the changes in these sources with increasing span of forecast. The partial correlations for equation (23), shown in Table 8-6, reveal the increasing importance of the autonomous component with increasing span of forecast.

$$A_{t+n} = b_1({}_{t+n}F^*_t) + b_2({}_{t+n}E_t) + {}_{t+n}U_t. \tag{23}$$

TABLE 8-6. *Selected Statistics From the Regression of Target Spot Rates on the Extrapolative and Autonomous Components of the Forecasts, Treasury Data, Quarterly Observations, 1949–64*

Span of Forecast	Partial Correlation Coefficient Squared of ${}_{t+n}F^*_t$ (1)	t-Value of $b_{t+n}F^*_t$ (2)	Partial Correlation Coefficient Squared of ${}_{t+n}E_t$ (3)	t-Value of $b_{t+n}E_t$ (4)	R^2 (multiple) (5)
1	.7898	13.7063	.0862	2.1715	.7856
2	.3165	4.8115	.0972	2.3195	.3378
3	.4555	6.4676	.0511	1.6410	.4499
4	.4143	5.9483	.1377	2.8256	.4431

NOTE: The general form of the regression is given in equation (23). The forecast components were related to a four-term moving average of the quarterly spot rates to make the forecasts and the targets comparable.

SUMMARY AND CONCLUSIONS

The evidence revealed in this study is consistent with the hypothesis that expectations influence the term structure of rates. While the importance of extrapolation in business forecasting is well known, statistical verification of this fact tends to exaggerate the importance of extrapolation. Even where the market or the individual utilizes knowledge of contemporaneous relationships, the autoregressiveness of these related variables redounds on the forecasts themselves. In spite of this exaggeration the data reveal some amount of nonextrapolative forecasting, which contributes to the accuracy of the forecasts.

It is convenient to summarize the extrapolative component of the forecasts, regardless of its source, with an equation that describes each forecast as a linear combination of past forecasts and observed values (that is, targets of earlier forecasts). The convenience stems from the inferences that can be drawn from the pattern of weights in the linear combination. The most obvious inferences concern the relative importance that attaches to earlier forecasts and observed values in determining current forecasts. This study found, for example, that the weight given to the last previous forecast (or observed value, in the case of the one-span forecast) is relatively high but that subsequent weights are much lower, although the rate of decline is small after the decline from the first to the second. Further inferences stem from the parameters of other extrapolative behavioral models that are implied by the weights in the linear combination. So, for example, the error-learning coefficients—the proportions of past errors that are used to correct forecasts of later periods—fall off with increasing span of forecast. This decline does not imply (but is consistent with) a decline in the extrapolative component of longer span forecasts and less still a lower forecasting content of more distant forward rates. On the contrary, the decline in the learning coefficients is implied by the widely observed inverse relationship that exists between the direction of expected change and the difference between the current level and its long-run expectation. By algebraically relating the three models (extrapolative, error-learning, and return-to-normality), the study was able to estimate their parameters. While the three models imply different motivations for the forecasts, they are mutually consistent and statistically indistinguishable.

Apart from analyzing the extrapolative component, the study estimated its importance as the span of forecast changes. It found that the autonomous (or nonextrapolative) component both explained a larger fraction of the variation of longer-span forecasts and accounted for a larger fraction of their accuracy. The second finding, concerning accuracy, is important because it excludes the inference that the falling-off of the extrapolative component signifies a falling-off of the forecasting component of the forward rates. It is consistent also with the idea that autonomous forecasting is more useful for longer-term forecasts—or the obverse, that extrapolative forecasting becomes less useful with increasing span of forecast.

The expectational mechanism described in this report, even if it were the only factor governing yield differentials of varying terms to maturity, does not ensure that as of any given time the yield curve depicts the market's forecasts. A sudden increase in the supply of a particular maturity or a decision by one or more large financial institutions to alter the maturity of their portfolio would alter the shape of the yield curve. But if the market's forecasts have not changed, relative bargains among certain maturities would emerge, and the demand for these maturities would reinstate the original yield curve. Investors may differ in their preference for different maturities for reasons such as liquidity or hedging liabilities and will respond with different degrees of alacrity to the temporary departure of the yield curve from the one reflecting current expectations. Transaction costs may discourage or delay total reinstatement.

This study did not investigate the influence of liquidity preference. Short-term securities are generally thought to be more liquid because of their broader markets, lower transaction costs, greater collateral value, and less volatile price fluctuation. Not all investors, however, value these qualities, and some prefer long-term bonds because they stabilize income, obviate reinvestment, require less management, etc. Most writers think the former group predominates in the market and thus that, apart from the influence of expectations, short-term securities yield less because of their (on balance) greater desirability. The resulting yield curve would incline unless the expectation of a decline in rates dominated the liquidity effect. According to the liquidity hypothesis, there is a spectrum of degrees of liquidity, inversely related to term-to-maturity. A change in the structure of available maturities, as a result, for example, of a major government refinancing, would alter the aggregate liquidity of financial assets. If, for example, the debt were lengthened and as a result over-all liquidity fell, the ensuing demand for liquidity would lower the yields (bid up the prices) on shorter-term securities and alter the term structure that is consistent with a given pattern of expectations. This hypothesis, which includes the effect of changes in the supply of money, is supplementary rather than competitive with the expectations hypothesis. A more exhaustive theory would include the effects of changes in the yield differentials of debt and equity, changes in expected inflation, and many other phenomena as well. These ideas have in common the proposition that the market for securities and indeed for all assets may be usefully viewed as a unit in which different investment concerns—yield, liquidity, risk, taxes, etc.—are synthesized into an over-all price structure.

INDEX